TAKING SIDES

Clashing Views on Controversial

Social Issues

THIRTEENTH EXPANDED EDITION

TAKING SIDES

Clashing Views on Controversial

Social Issues

THIRTEENTH EXPANDED EDITION

Selected, Edited, and with Introductions by

Kurt Finsterbusch
University of Maryland

McGraw-Hill/Dushkin
A Division of The McGraw-Hill Companies

To my wife, Meredith Ramsay, who richly shares with me a life of the mind and much, much more.

Photo Acknowledgment
Cover image: James Gritz/Getty Images

Cover Art Acknowledgment
Charles Vitelli

Library of Congress Cataloging-in-Publication Data
Main entry under title:
Taking sides: clashing views on controversial social issues/selected, edited, and with introductions
by Kurt Finsterbusch.—13th expanded ed.
Includes bibliographical references and index.
1. Social behavior. 2. Social problems. I. Finsterbusch, Kurt, *comp.*
                                                                  302

0-07-319090-X
95-83865

Printed on Recycled Paper

Preface

The English word *fanatic* is derived from the Latin *fanum,* meaning temple. It refers to the kind of madmen often seen in the precincts of temples in ancient times, the kind presumed to be possessed by deities or demons. The term first came into English usage during the seventeenth century, when it was used to describe religious zealots. Soon after, its meaning was broadened to include a political and social context. We have come to associate the term *fanatic* with a person who acts as if his or her views were inspired, a person utterly incapable of appreciating opposing points of view. The nineteenth-century English novelist George Eliot put it precisely: "I call a man fanatical when . . . he . . . becomes unjust and unsympathetic to men who are out of his own track." A fanatic may hear but is unable to listen. Confronted with those who disagree, a fanatic immediately vilifies opponents.

Most of us would avoid the company of fanatics, but who among us is not tempted to caricature opponents instead of listening to them? Who does not put certain topics off limits for discussion? Who does not grasp at euphemisms to avoid facing inconvenient facts? Who has not, in George Eliot's language, sometimes been "unjust and unsympathetic" to those on a different track? Who is not, at least in certain very sensitive areas, a *little* fanatical? The counterweight to fanaticism is open discussion. The difficult issues that trouble us as a society have at least two sides, and we lose as a society if we hear only one side. At the individual level, the answer to fanaticism is listening. And that is the underlying purpose of this book: to encourage its readers to listen to opposing points of view.

This book contains 40 selections presented in a pro and con format. A total of 20 different controversial social issues are debated. The sociologists, political scientists, economists, and social critics whose views are debated here make their cases vigorously. In order to effectively read each selection, analyze the points raised, and debate the basic assumptions and values of each position, or, in other words, in order to think critically about what you are reading, you will first have to give each side a sympathetic hearing. John Stuart Mill, the nineteenth-century British philosopher, noted that the majority is not doing the minority a favor by listening to its views; it is doing *itself* a favor. By listening to contrasting points of view, we strengthen our own. In some cases we change our viewpoints completely. But in most cases, we either incorporate some elements of the opposing view—thus making our own richer—or else learn how to answer the objections to our viewpoints. Either way, we gain from the experience.

Organization of the book   Each issue has an issue *introduction,* which sets the stage for the debate as it is argued in the YES and NO selections. Each issue concludes with a *postscript* that makes some final observations and points the way to other questions related to the issue. In reading the issue and forming your own opinions you should not feel confined to adopt one or the other of the positions presented. There are positions in between the given views or totally outside them, and the *suggestions for further reading* that appear in each issue postscript should help you find resources to continue your study of the subject. At the back of the book is a listing of all the *contributors to this volume*, which will give you information on the social scientists whose views are debated here. Also, on the *On the Internet* page that accompanies each part opener, you will find Internet site addresses (URLs) that are relevant to the issues in that part.

Changes to this edition   This new edition has been significantly updated. There are two completely new issues: *Does the Media Have a Liberal Bias?* (Issue 2) and *Should Same-Sex Marriages Be Legally Recognized?* (Issue 6). In addition, for the issues on moral decline (Issue 1), affirmative action (Issue 10), capitalist economy (Issue 12), welfare (Issue 13), public education (Issue 14), doctor-assisted suicide (Issue 15), white collar crime (Issue 16), and the environment (Issue 19), one or both of the selections were replaced to bring a fresh perspective to the debates. In all, there are 15 new selections. Today the world is changing rapidly in many ways so that new issues arise, old ones fade, and some old issues become recast by events.

A word to the instructor   An *Instructor's Manual With Test Questions* (multiplechoice and essay) is available through the publisher for the instructor using *Taking Sides* in the classroom. A general guidebook, *Using Taking Sides in the Classroom*, which discusses methods and techniques for integrating the pro-con approach into any classroom setting, is also available. An online version of *Using Taking Sides in the Classroom* and a correspondence service for *Taking Sides* adopters can be found at http://www.dushkin.com/usingts/.

Taking Sides: Clashing Views on Controversial Social Issues is only one title in the Taking Sides series. If you are interested in seeing the table of contents for any of the other titles, please visit the Taking Sides Web site at http://www.dushkin.com/takingsides/.

Acknowledgments   I wish to acknowledge the encouragement and support given to this project by Larry Loeppke, former and present list managers for the Taking Sides series, and Nichole Altman, developmental editor.

I want to thank my wife, Meredith Ramsay, for her example and support. I also want to thank George McKenna for many years as a close colleague and coeditor through many early editions of this book.

Kurt Finsterbusch
University of Maryland

Contents In Brief

Contents

dramatically in the last several decades, with very adverse effects on children. Family historian Stephanie Coontz argues that current discussion of family decline includes a false idealization of the traditional family of the past and misleading interpretations of current data on families. She finds that the trends are both positive and negative.

Christopher Jencks, professor of social policy at the Kennedy School at Harvard University, presents data on how large the income inequality is in the United States and describes the consequences of this inequality. Christopher C. DeMuth, president of the American Enterprise Institute for Public Policy Research, argues that the "recent increase in income inequality . . . is a very small tick in the massive and unprecedented leveling of material circumstances that has been proceeding now for almost three centuries and in this century has accelerated dramatically."

Author Charles Murray describes destructive behavior among the underclass. Murray asserts that this type of behavior will result in serious trouble for society even though, according to statistics, the number of crimes committed has decreased. Psychology professor Barry Schwartz states that the underclass is not the major threat to American ideals. He counters that "the theory and practice of free-market economics have done more to undermine traditional moral values than any other social force."

Curtis Crawford, editor of the website www.DebatingRacialPreferences .org, explores all possible options for bettering the situation of disadvantaged minorities in a truly just manner. He argues that the right of everyone, including white males, to nondiscrimination clearly is superior to the right of minorities to affirmative action. Ann Rosegrant Alvarez, professor of social work at Wayne State University, argues that affirmative action policies are increasing equality in the labor market, and they are still necessary because inequality of opportunity still exists.

Political sociologist G. William Domhoff argues that the "owners and top-level managers in large income-producing properties are far and away the dominant power figures in the United States" and that they have inordinate influence in the federal government. Jeffrey M. Berry, a professor of political science, contends that public interest pressure groups that have entered the political arena since the end of the 1960s have effectively challenged the political power of big business.

Robert Kuttner, professor of economics and co-editor of *The American Prospect,* argues that the market has vices as well as virtues. Government must intervene "to promote development, to temper the market's distributive extremes, to counteract its unfortunate tendency to boom-and-bust, to remedy its myopic failure to invest to little in public goods, and to invest too much in processes that harmed the human and natural environment." John Stossel, a TV news reporter and producer of one-hour news specials, argues that regulations have done immense damage and do not protect us as well as market forces.

The editors of the *Economist* present the facts on the declining welfare rolls and the dramatic increase in employment for welfare mothers, and they argue that many of these changes are due to the changes in the welfare laws and not simply a strong economy. Sharon Hayes, professor of sociology at the University of Virginia, got to know many welfare mothers and learned what happened to them since the welfare reform. Her article points out that while quite a few mothers have left welfare since the reform, many cannot hold on to a job and are now worse off than before.

Clint Bolick, vice president of the Institute for Justice, presents the argument for school choice that competition leads to improvements and makes the case that minorities especially need school choice to improve their educational performance. Matthew Yglesias critiques the research that has been interpreted as demonstrating the benefits of school voucher programs. An honest examination of the data finds little educational benefit from school choice so the potential for stripping public schools of needed resources makes vouchers a poor gamble.

Richard T. Hull, professor of philosophy at the State University of New York at Buffalo, asserts that physician-assisted suicide for suffering, terminally ill patients is an act of compassion in providing a desperately sought service. The practice should be regulated to prevent abuse and to stop a too hasty decision by the patient. To totally outlaw it, however, is cruel. Margaret Somerville, Gale Professor of Law and professor in the Faculty of Medicine at McGill University, argues that this is a form of euthanasia, which violates the sanctity of human life, and it is likely to have severe unintended negative consequences on the practice of medicine and the public attitude toward life.

David A. Anderson estimates the total annual cost of crime including law enforcement and security services. The costs exceed one trillion, with fraud (mostly white collar crime) causing about one-fifth of the total. His calculations of the full costs of the loss of life and injury comes to about half of the total costs. It is right, therefore, to view personal and violent crime as the big crime problem. Professor of philosophy Jeffrey Reiman argues that the dangers posed by negligent corporations and white-collar criminals are a greater menace to society than are the activities of typical street criminals.

Ethan A. Nadelmann, director of the Lindesmith Center, a drug policy research institute, argues that history shows that drug prohibition is costly and futile. Examining the drug policies in other countries, he finds that decriminalization plus sane and humane drug policies and treatment programs can greatly reduce the harms from drugs. Eric A. Voth, chairman of the International Drug Strategy Institute, contends that drugs are very harmful and that our drug policies have succeeded in substantially reducing drug use.

Robert H. Bork, senior fellow at the American Enterprise Institute, recognizes that the values of security and civil rights must be balanced while we war against terrorism, but he is concerned that some commentators would hamstring security forces in order to protect nonessential civil rights. For example, to not use ethnic profiling of Muslim or Arab persons would reduce the effectiveness of security forces, while holding suspected terrorists without filing charges or allowing them council would increase their effectiveness. Barbara Dority, president of Humanists of Washington, describes some specific provisions of the Patriot Act to show how dangerous they could be to the rights of all dissidents. She argues that provisions of the act could easily be abused.

PART 6   THE FUTURE: POPULATION/ENVIRONMENT/ SOCIETY   325

Lester R. Brown, founder of the Worldwatch Institute and now president of the Earth Policy Institute, reviews the stress humans have inflicted on the environment in depleting its natural capital and adversely affecting its ecosystems. The result may soon be economic hardship unless we change our course soon. Bjorn Lomborg, a statistician at the University of Aarhus, Denmark, presents evidence that population growth is slowing down, natural resources are not running out, species are disappearing very slowly, the environment is improving in some ways, and assertions about environmental decline are exaggerated.

Murray Weidenbaum, chairman of the Weidenbaum Center at Washington University in St. Louis, argues that economic globalization benefits all countries that participate in world markets. Globalization produces more jobs than it eliminates, he contends, both for the world and for the United States. Herman E. Daly, professor at the School of Public Affairs at the University of Maryland, does not object to international trade and relations, but he does object to globalization that erases national boundaries and hurts workers and the environment.

Professor of management and public policy James Q. Wilson summarizes the research on the impacts of divorce, which shows that divorce has significant and long-term negative impacts on children. Developmental psychologist E. Mavis Hetherington and writer John Kelly present the results from over 30 years of research, which show that "The vast majority of young people from these families are reasonably well adjusted and are coping reasonably well in relationships with their families, friends, and intimate partners."

Dean of Harvard's John F. Kennedy School of Government, Joseph S. Nye, argues that American unilateralism is increasing worldwide anti-American sentiment and reducing what we can achieve abroad. America needs allies and needs to attract, not repel, them. For example, our war on Islamic terrorists requires much help from Islamic moderates. Journalist and TV pundit Charles Krauthammer argues that the United States is the world's single superpower that should use its power to extend "the peace by advancing democracy and preserving the peace by acting as balancer of last resort." He is adamant that the United States should pursue its interests with little heed to world opinion. It should act unilaterally when necessary.

Introduction

Debating Social Issues

Kurt Finsterbusch

What Is Sociology?

"I have become a problem to myself," St. Augustine said. Put into a social and secular framework, St. Augustine's concern marks the starting point of sociology. We have become a problem to ourselves, and it is sociology that seeks to understand the problem and, perhaps, to find some solutions. The subject matter of sociology, then, is ourselves—people interacting with one another in groups and organizations.

Although the subject matter of sociology is very familiar, it is often useful to look at it in an unfamiliar light, one that involves a variety of theories and perceptual frameworks. In fact, to properly understand social phenomena, it *should* be looked at from several different points of view. In practice, however, this may lead to more friction than light, especially when each view proponent says, "I am right and you are wrong," rather than, "My view adds considerably to what your view has shown."

Sociology, as a science of society, was developed in the nineteenth century. Auguste Comte (1798–1857), the French mathematician and philosopher who is considered to be the father of sociology, had a vision of a well-run society based on social science knowledge. Sociologists (Comte coined the term) would discover the laws of social life and then determine how society should be structured and run. Society would not become perfect, because some problems are intractable, but he believed that a society guided by scientists and other experts was the best possible society.

Unfortunately, Comte's vision was extremely naive. For most matters of state there is no one best way of structuring or doing things that sociologists can discover and recommend. Instead, sociologists debate more social issues than they resolve.

The purpose of sociology is to throw light on social issues and their relationship to the complex, confusing, and dynamic social world around us. It seeks to describe how society is organized and how individuals fit into it. But neither the organization of society nor the fit of individuals is perfect. Social disorganization is a fact of life—at least in modern, complex societies such as the one we live in. Here, perfect harmony continues to elude us, and "social problems" are endemic. The very institutions, laws, and policies that produce benefits also produce what sociologists call "unintended effects"— unintended and undesirable. The changes that please one sector of the society may displease another, or the changes that seem so indisputably healthy at first turn out to have a dark underside to them. The examples are endless. Modern urban life gives people privacy and freedom from snooping neighbors that the small town never afforded; yet that very privacy seems to breed an uneasy sense of anonymity and loneliness. Take another example: Hierarchy is necessary for organizations to function efficiently, but hierarchy leads to the creation of a ruling elite. Flatten out the hierarchy and you may achieve social equality—but at the price of confusion, incompetence, and low productivity.

This is not to say that all efforts to effect social change are ultimately futile and that the only sound view is the tragic one that concludes "nothing works." We can be realistic without falling into despair. In many respects, the human condition has improved over the centuries and has improved as a result of conscious social policies. But improvements are purchased at a price—not only amonetary price but one involving human discomfort and discontent. The job of policymakers is to balance the anticipated benefits against the probable costs.

It can never hurt policymakers to know more about the society in which they work or the social issues they confront. That, broadly speaking, is the purpose of sociology. It is what this book is about. This volume examines issues that are central to the study of sociology.

Culture and Values

A common value system is the major mechanism for integrating a society, but modern societies contain so many different groups with differing ideas and values that integration must be built as much on tolerance of differences as on common values. Furthermore, technology and social conditions change, so values must adjust to new situations, often weakening old values. Some people (often called conservatives) will defend the old values. Others (often called liberals) will make concessions to allow for change. For example, the protection of human life is a sacred value to most people, but some would compromise that value when the life involved is a 90-year-old comatose man on life-support machines who had signed a document indicating that he did not want to be kept alive under those conditions. The conservative would counter that once we make the value of human life relative, we become dangerously open to greater evils—that perhaps society will come to think it acceptable to terminate all sick, elderly people undergoing expensive treatments. This is only one example of how values are hotly debated today.

Three debates on values are presented in Part 1. In Issue 1, David Whitman challenges the common perception that morals have declined in America, while Robert H. Bork argues for the decliningmorality thesis. Issue 2 examines a major institution that can be seen as responsible for instilling values and culture in people—the media. This issue focuses in particular on whether the news reporters and anchormen report and comment on the news with professional objectivity and relatively bias free. William McGowan argues that the objectivity of most reporters is sacrificed to political correctness, which supports the liberal social agenda. In contrast, Robert W. McChesney and John Bellamy Foster argue that even though newsmen may lean to the left on average, they largely use official sources for their reports, and the net result supports the status quo.

The final culture/values debate, Issue 3, concerns the cultural impact of immigration. Patrick Buchanan argues that current levels of immigration are too high and that immigrant cultures are too different from American culture to be assimilated. Thus, immigration is threatening America's cultural unity. Ben Wattenberg counters that the cultural impacts of immigration will be minor because annual immigration amounts to only a third of a percent of the United States population. Furthermore, he maintains that immigration contributes to America's power and influence.

Sex Roles, Gender, and the Family

An area that has experienced tremendous value change in the last several decades is sex roles and the family. Women in large numbers have rejected major aspects of their traditional gender roles and family roles while remaining strongly committed to much of the mother role and to many feminine characteristics. Men have changed much less but their situation has changed considerably. Issue 4 considers whether current sex roles are more stressful for women or for men. Jeff Grabmeier contends that women suffer more stress than men because current practices still favor men and that women are not able to cope as well as men with current sex role expectations. Susan Faludi argues the opposite. Men's sex roles are incongruent with the current conditions and men do not know how to deal with the situation. Issue 5 focuses on the causes of communication problems between men and women. It has recently been advanced that such problems are largely the result of radically different conversation styles between the genders. Philip Yancey champions this view, contending that men's concerns about maintaining status and women's concerns about maintaining connections and closeness affects their interpretations of what they hear and say to each other. Mary Crawford asserts that this view has become popularized and exaggerated by the media and that the basis of the thesis is demeaning to women. Issue 6 debates whether same-sex marriages should be legal. The Lambda Legal Defense Fund, a gay rights advocacy group, presents the major arguments for same-sex marriage, and Sam Schulman argues that the traditional definition of marriage should be retained. Issue 7, which has been much debated by feminists and their critics, asks, Is the decline of the traditional family a national crisis? David Popenoe is deeply concerned about the decline of the traditional family, while Stephanie Coontz thinks that such concern amounts to little more than nostalgia for a bygone era.

Stratification and Inequality

Issue 8 centers around a sociological debate about whether or not increasing economic inequality is a serious problem. Christopher Jencks asserts that it is, while Christopher C. DeMuth argues that consumption patterns indicate that inequality has actually decreased in recent decades. Many commentators on American life decry the pathologies of the underclass as the shame of America.

Charles Murray is a leading proponent of this view and his article is republished in Issue 9. Barry Schwartz critiques Murray's view and argues that the current advanced stage of capitalism is largely responsible for eroding American ideals and producing the underclass.

Today one of the most controversial issues regarding inequalities is affirmative action. Is justice promoted or undermined by such policies? Curtis Crawford and Ann Rosegrant Alvarez take opposing sides on this question in Issue 10.

Political Economy and Institutions

Sociologists study not only the poor, the workers, and the victims of discrimination but also those at the top of society—those who occupy what the late sociologist C. Wright Mills used to call "the command posts." The question is whether the "pluralist" model or the "power elite" model is the one that best fits the facts in America. Does a single power elite rule the United States, or do many groups contend for power and influence so that the political process is accessible to all? In Issue 11, G. William Domhoff argues that the business elite have a dominating influence in government decisions and that no other group has nearly as much power. Jeffrey M. Berry counters that liberal citizen groups have successfully opened the policy-making process and made it more participatory. Currently, grassroots groups of all kinds have some power and influence. The question is, how much?

The United States is a capitalist welfare state, and the role of the state in capitalism (more precisely, the market) and in welfare is examined in the next two issues. Issue 12 considers whether or not the government should step in and attempt to correct for the failures of the market through regulations, policies, and programs. Robert Kuttner argues that an active government is needed to protect consumers, workers, and the environment; to bring about greater equality; and to guide economic and social change. John Stossel argue that even well-intended state interventions in the market usually only make matters worse and that governments cannot serve the public good as effectively as competitive markets can. One way in which the government intervenes in the economy is by providing welfare to people who cannot provide for their own needs in the labor market. Issue 13 debates the wisdom of the Work Opportunity Reconciliation Act of 1996, which ended Aid to Families of Dependent Children (which was what most people equated with welfare). The editors of the *Economist* call this act "America's great achievement" because it greatly reduced welfare rolls and dramatically increased the employment of welfare mothers. Sharon Hayes states that the reality is more depressing. The old welfare system helped women who were on welfare to prepare for and obtain good jobs while the new law practically forces women on welfare to take bad jobs at poverty-level wages. The situation of some ex-welfare families has become unmanaged and very stressful.

Education is one of the biggest jobs of government as well as the key to individual prosperity and the success of the economy. For decades the American system of education has been severely criticized. Such an important institution is destined to be closely scrutinized, and for decades the American system of education has been severely criticized and many reforms have been attempted. The main debate on how to improve public schools concerns school choice as presented in Issue 14. Clint Bolick argues that competition improves performance in sports and business so it should do the same in education, and the data support this theory. Also parents should be allowed to send their children to the school of their choice. Matthew Iglesias challenges the data that are used to support school choice and argues that school choice programs could draw resources away from the very schools that need it most.

The final issue in this section—doctor-assisted suicide—is truly one of life and death. The actions of Dr. Jack Kevorkian, who has assisted in over 100 patient suicides, have brought this issue into the public light. In Issue 15, Richard T. Hull refutes the arguments against physician-assisted suicide, and therefore, believes that it is right to do the compassionate and merciful thing in the case of suffering terminally ill patients who request the means for a gentle suicide. On the other hand, Margaret Somerville argues that the sanctity of life forbids its intentional termination under any circumstances.

Crime and Social Control

Crime is interesting to sociologists because crimes are those activities that society makes illegal and will use force to stop. Why are some acts made illegal and others (even those that may be more harmful) not made illegal? Surveys indicate that concern about crime is extremely high in America. Is the fear of crime, however, rightly placed? Americans fear mainly street crime, but Jeffrey Reiman argues in Issue 16 that corporate crime—also known as "white-collar crime"—causes far more death, harm, and financial loss to Americans than street crime. In contrast, David A. Anderson calculates the full costs of crime, both direct and indirect, and concludes that the costs of murder and theft far exceed the cost of white collar crime. These contradictory findings result from differing definitions of white collar crime. A prominent aspect of the crime picture is the illegal drug trade. It has such bad consequences that some people are seriously talking about legalizing drugs in order to kill the illegal drug business. Ethan A. Nadelmann argues this view in Issue 17, while Eric A. Voth argues that legalization would greatly harm society. Drug use would mushroom and damage many lives, whereas the current war on drugs has considerably reduced drug use. Finally, Issue 18 deals with terrorism, perhaps the major problem in America today. We must defend against and prevent it. To do so effectively requires the expansion of police powers, so we passed the Patriot Act. But did the Patriot Act go too far and trample America's liberties? Barbara Dority examines several provisions of the act and observes how extremely unjust their enforcement has been. On the other hand, Robert H. Bork believes that the complaints of people like Dority have tied the hands of the law in the past and that the grave danger we face today requires the strengthening, not weakening, of the act.

The Future: Population/Environment/Society

Many social commentators speculate on "the fate of the earth." The environmentalists have their own vision of apocalypse. They see the possibility that the human race could degrade the environment to the point that population growth and increasing economic production could overshoot the carrying capacity of the globe. The resulting collapse could lead to the extinction of much of the human race and the end of free societies. Other analysts believe that these fears are groundless. In Issue 19, Jester R. Brown shows how human actions are degrading the environment in ways that adversely affect humans. In contrast, Bjorn Lomborg argues that the environment is improving in many ways and that environmental problems are manageable or will have mild adverse effects.

The last issue in this book assesses the benefits and costs of globalization. Murray Weidenbaum argues that economic globalization has been a demonstration of the basic economic theory that global markets and relatively free trade economically benefit all nations that participate. Even workers in the United States have benefited in spite of their complaints. Herman E. Daly counters that globalization, which dissolves national boundaries, hurts both workers and the environment.

The Social Construction of Reality

An important idea in sociology is that people construct social reality in the course of interaction by attaching social meanings to the reality they are experiencing and then responding to those meanings. Two people can walk down a city street and derive very different meanings from what they see around them. Both, for example, may see homeless people—but they may see them in different contexts. One fits them into a picture of once-vibrant cities dragged into decay and ruin because of permissive policies that have encouraged pathological types to harass citizens; the other observer fits them into a picture of an America that can no longer hide the wretchedness of its poor. Both feel that they are seeing something deplorable, but their views of what makes it deplorable are radically opposed. Their differing views of what they have seen will lead to very different prescriptions for what should be done about the problem.

The social construction of reality is an important idea for this book because each author is socially constructing reality and working hard to persuade you to see his or her point of view; that is, to see the definition of the situation and the set of meanings he or she has assigned to the situation. In doing this, each author presents a carefully selected set of facts, arguments, and values. The arguments contain assumptions or theories, some of which are spelled out and some of which are unspoken. The critical reader has to judge the evidence for the facts, the logic and soundness of the arguments, the importance of the values, and whether or not omitted facts, theories, and values invalidate the thesis. This book facilitates this critical thinking process by placing authors in opposition. This puts the reader in the position of critically evaluating two constructions of reality for each issue instead of one.

Conclusion

Writing in the 1950s, a period that was in some ways like our own, the sociologist C. Wright Mills said that Americans know a lot about their "troubles" but they cannot make the connections between seemingly personal concerns and the concerns of others in the world. If they could only learn to make those connections, they could turn their concerns into *issues*. An issue transcends the realm of the personal. According to Mills, "An issue is a public matter: some value cherished by publics is felt to be threatened. Often there is a debate about what the value really is and what it is that really threatens it."

It is not primarily personal troubles but social issues that I have tried to present in this book. The variety of topics in it can be taken as an invitation to discover what Mills called "the sociological imagination." This imagination, said Mills, "is the capacity to shift from one perspective to another—from the political to the psychological; from examination of a single family to comparative assessment of the national budgets of the world. . . . It is the capacity to range from the most impersonal and remote transformations to the most intimate features of the human self—and to see the relations between the two." This book, with a range of issues well suited to the sociological imagination, is intended to enlarge that capacity.

On the Internet . . .

Internet Philosophical Resources on Moral Relativism

This Web site for *Ethics Updates* offers discussion questions, a bibliographical guide, and a list of Internet resources concerning moral relativism.

http://ethics.acusd.edu/relativism.html

The National Institute on Media and the Family

The National Institute on Media and the Family Web site is a national resource for teachers, parents, community leaders, and others who are interested in the influence of electronic media on early childhood education, child development, academic perfor-mance, culture, and violence.

http://www.mediaandthefamily.com

The International Center for Migration, Ethnicity, and Citizenship

The International Center for Migration, Ethnicity, and Citizenship is engaged in scholarly research and public policy analysis bearing on international migration, refugees, and the incorporation of newcomers in host countries.

http://www.newschool.edu/icmec/

National Immigrant Forum

The National Immigrant Forum is a pro-immigrant organization that examines the effects of immigration on U.S. society. Click on the links for discussion of underground economies, immigrant economies, race and ethnic relations, and other topics.

http://www.immigrationforum.org

The National Network for Immigrant and Refugee Rights (NNIRR)

The National Network for Immigrant and Refugee Rights (NNIRR) serves as a forum to share information and analysis, to educate communities and the general public, and to develop and coordinate plans of action on important immigrant and refugee issues.

http://www.nnirr.org

PART 1

Culture and Values

*S*ociologists recognize that a fairly strong consensus on the basic values of a society contributes greatly to the smooth functioning of that society. The functioning of modern, complex urban societies, however, often depends on the tolerance of cultural differences and equal rights and protections for all cultural groups. In fact, such societies can be enriched by the contributions of different cultures. But at some point the cultural differences may result in a pulling apart that exceeds the pulling together. One cultural problem is the perceived moral decline, which may involve a conflict between old and new values. Another cultural problem in America is whether the media has a bias that is significantly removed from the epicenter of American culture. The final problem is whether current immigrants to the United States bring appropriate values and skills.

- Is American in Moral Decline?

- Does the Media Have a Liberal Bias?

- Is Third World Immigration a Threat to America's Way of Life?

ISSUE 1

Is America in Moral Decline?

YES: Robert H. Bork, from *Slouching Towards Gomorrah: Modern Liberalism and American Decline* (Regan Books, 1996)

NO: David Whitman, from *The Optimism Gap: The I'm OK— They're Not Syndrome and the Myth of American Decline* (Walker & Company, 1998)

ISSUE SUMMARY

YES: Robert H. Bork, famous for being nominated for the Supreme Court but not confirmed by the Senate, argues that modern liberalism is responsible for the decline in morals.

NO: Writer David Whitman empirically tests the moral decline thesis and finds that, according to the indicators that he employs, it is a myth.

Morality is the glue that holds society together. It enables people to deal with each other in relative tranquility and generally to their mutual benefit. Morality influences us both from the outside and from the inside. The morality of others affects us from outside as social pressure. Our conscience is morality affecting us from inside, even though others, especially parents, influence the formation of our conscience. Because parents, churches, schools, and peers teach us their beliefs and values (their morals) and the rules of society, most of us grow up wanting to do what is right. We also want to do things that are pleasurable. In a well-functioning society the right and the pleasurable are not too far apart, and most people lead morally respectable lives. On the other hand, no one lives up to moral standards perfectly. In fact, deviance from some moral standards is common, and when it becomes very common the standard changes. Some people interpret this as moral decline, while others interpret it as simply a change in moral standards or even as progress. Take, for example, the new morality that wives should be equal to rather than subservient to their husbands.

The degree of commitment to various moral precepts varies from person to person. Some people even act as moral guardians and take responsibility for encouraging others to live up to the moral standards. One of their major tactics is to cry out against the decline of morals. There are a number of such voices speaking out in public today. In fact, many politicians seem to try to outdo each other in speaking out against crime, teenage pregnancy, divorce, violence in the media, latchkey children, irresponsible parenting, etc.

Cries of moral decline have been ringing out for centuries. In earlier times the cries were against sin, debauchery, and godlessness. Today the cries are often against various aspects of individualism. Parents are condemned for sacrificing their children for their own needs, including their careers. Divorced people are condemned for discarding spouses instead of working hard to save their marriages. Children of elderly parents are condemned for putting their parents into nursing homes to avoid the inconvenience of caring for them. The general public is condemned for investing so little time in others and their communities while pursuing their own interests. These criticisms against individualism may have some validity. On the other hand, individualism has some more positive aspects, including enterprise and inventiveness, which contribute to economic growth; individual responsibility; advocacy of human rights; reduced clannishness and reduced prejudice toward other groups; and an emphasis on self-development, which includes successful relations with others.

The morality debate is important because moral decline not only increases human suffering but also weakens society and hinders the performance of its institutions. The following selections require some deep reflection on the moral underpinnings of American society as well as other societies, and they invite the reader to strengthen those underpinnings.

Many have decried the high levels of crime, violence, divorce, and opportunism, but few argue the thesis of the moral decline of America as thoroughly and as passionately as Robert H. Bork, the author of the following selection. But is he reading the facts correctly? According to David Whitman in the second selection, the common viewpoint that a serious moral decline is in progress is a myth. He argues that numerous morality indicators do not show the decline that the decline thesis expects. Therefore, even in the face of the statistics on crime and divorce, Whitman concludes that there has not been a deterioration of moral conduct.

3

Robert H. Bork

 **YES**

Modern Liberalism and American Decline

This is an [article] about American decline. Since American culture is a variant of the cultures of all Western industrialized democracies, it may even, inadvertently, be . . . about Western decline. In the United States, at least, that decline and the mounting resistance to it have produced what we now call a culture war. It is impossible to say what the outcome will be, but for the moment our trajectory continues downward. This is not to deny that much in our culture remains healthy, that many families are intact and continue to raise children with strong moral values. American culture is complex and resilient. But it is also not to be denied that there are aspects of almost every branch of our culture that are worse than ever before and that the rot is spreading.

"Culture," as used here, refers to all human behavior and institutions, including popular entertainment, art, religion, education, scholarship, economic activity, science, technology, law, and morality. Of that list, only science, technology, and the economy may be said to be healthy today, and it is problematical how long that will last. Improbable as it may seem, science and technology themselves are increasingly under attack, and it seems highly unlikely that a vigorous economy can be sustained in an enfeebled, hedonistic culture, particularly when that culture distorts incentives by increasingly rejecting personal achievement as the criterion for the distribution of rewards.

With each new evidence of deterioration, we lament for a moment, and then become accustomed to it. We hear one day of the latest rap song calling for killing policemen or the sexual mutilation of women; the next, of coercive left-wing political indoctrination at a prestigious university; then of the latest homicide figures for New York City, Los Angeles, or the District of Columbia; of the collapse of the criminal justice system, which displays an inability to punish adequately and, often enough, an inability even to convict the clearly guilty; of the rising rate of illegitimate births; the uninhibited display of sexuality and the popularization of violence in our entertainment; worsening racial tensions; the angry activists of feminism, homosexuality, environmentalism, animal rights—the list could be extended almost indefinitely.

So unrelenting is the assault on our sensibilities that many of us grow numb, finding resignation to be the rational, adaptive response to an environment that is increasingly polluted and apparently beyond our control. That is what Senator Daniel Patrick Moynihan calls "defining deviancy down." Moynihan cites the "Durkheim constant." Emile Durkheim, a founder of sociology, posited that there is a limit to the amount of deviant behavior any community can "afford to recognize." As behavior worsens, the community adjusts its standards so that conduct once thought reprehensible is no longer deemed so. As behavior improves, the deviancy boundary moves up to encompass conduct previously thought normal. Thus, a community of saints and a community of felons would display very different behavior but about the same amount of recognized deviancy.

But the Durkheim constant is now behaving in a very odd way. While defining deviancy down with respect to crime, illegitimacy, drug use, and the like, our cultural elites are growing intensely moralistic and disapproving about what had always been thought normal behavior, thus accomplishing what columnist Charles Krauthammer terms "defining deviancy up." It is at least an apparent paradox that we are accomplishing both forms of redefining, both down and up, simultaneously. One would suppose that as once normal behavior became viewed as deviant, that would mean that there was less really bad conduct in the society. But that is hardly our case. Instead, we have redefined what we mean by such things as child abuse, rape, and racial or sexual discrimination so that behavior until recently thought quite normal, unremarkable, even benign, is now identified as blameworthy or even criminal. Middle-class life is portrayed as oppressive and shot through with pathologies. "As part of the vast social project of moral leveling," Krauthammer wrote, "it is not enough for the deviant to be normalized. The normal must be found to be deviant." This situation is thoroughly perverse. Underclass values become increasingly acceptable to the middle class, especially their young, and middle-class values become increasingly contemptible to the cultural elites.

That is why there is currently a widespread sense that the distinctive virtues of American life, indeed the distinctive features of Western civilization, are in peril in ways not previously seen. . . . This time we face, and seem to be succumbing to, an attack mounted by a force not only within Western civilization but one that is perhaps its legitimate child.

The enemy within is modern liberalism, a corrosive agent carrying a very different mood and agenda than that of classical or traditional liberalism. . . . Modernity, the child of the Enlightenment, failed when it became apparent that the good society cannot be achieved by unaided reason. The response of liberalism was not to turn to religion, which modernity had seemingly made irrelevant, but to abandon reason. Hence, there have appeared philosophies claiming that words can carry no definite meaning or that there is no reality other than one that is "socially constructed." A reality so constructed, it is thought, can be decisively altered by social or cultural edict, which is a prescription for coercion. . . .

The defining characteristics of modern liberalism are radical egalitarianism (the equality of outcomes rather than of opportunities) and radical individualism (the drastic reduction of limits to personal gratification). . . .

Men were kept from rootless hedonism, which is the end stage of unconfined individualism, by religion, morality, and law. These are commonly cited. To them I would add the necessity for hard work, usually physical work, and the fear of want. These constraints were progressively undermined by rising affluence. . . .

The mistake the Enlightenment founders of liberalism made about human nature has brought us to this—an increasing number of alienated, restless individuals, individuals without strong ties to others, except in the pursuit of ever more degraded distractions and sensations. And liberalism has no corrective within itself; all it can do is endorse more liberty and demand more rights. Persons capable of high achievement in one field or another may find meaning in work, may find community among colleagues, and may not particularly mind social and moral separation otherwise. Such people are unlikely to need the more sordid distractions that popular culture now offers. But very large segments of the population do not fall into that category. For them, the drives of liberalism are catastrophic.

The consequences of liberalism, liberty, and the pursuit of happiness pushed too far are now apparent. Irving Kristol writes of the clear signs of rot and decadence germinating within American society—a rot and decadence that was no longer the consequence of liberalism but was the actual agenda of contemporary liberalism. . . . [S]ector after sector of American life has been ruthlessly corrupted by the liberal ethos. It is an ethos that aims simultaneously at political and social collectivism on the one hand, and moral anarchy on the other." I would add only that current liberalism's rot and decadence is merely what liberalism has been moving towards for better than two centuries.

We can now see the tendency of the Enlightenment, the Declaration of Independence, and *On Liberty*. Each insisted on the expanding liberty of the individual and each assumed that order was not a serious problem and could be left, pretty much, to take care of itself. And, for a time, order did seem to take care of itself. But that was because the institutions—family, church, school, neighborhood, inherited morality—remained strong. The constant underestimation of their value and the continual pressure for more individual autonomy necessarily weakened the restraints on individuals. The ideal slowly became the autonomous individual who stood in an adversarial relationship to any institution or group that attempted to set limits to acceptable thought and behavior.

That process continues today, and hence we have an increasingly disorderly society. The street predator of the underclass may be the natural outcome of the mistake the founders of liberalism made. They would have done better had they remembered original sin. Or had they taken Edmund Burke seriously. Mill wrote: "Liberty consists in doing what one desires." That might have been said by a man who was both a libertine and an anarchist; Mill was neither, but his rhetoric encouraged those who would be either or both. Burke had it right earlier: "The only liberty I mean is a liberty connected with order; that not only exists along with order and virtue, but which cannot exist at all without them." "The effect of liberty to individuals is, that they may do what they please: We ought to see what it will please them to do, before we risque congratulations, which may soon be turned into complaints." Burke, unlike the Mill of *On Liberty*, had a true understanding of the nature of men, and balanced liberty with restraint and order, which are, in truth, essential to the preservation of liberty.

The classical liberalism of the nineteenth century is widely and correctly admired, but we can now see that it was inevitably a transitional phase. The tendencies inherent in individualism were kept within bounds by the health of institutions other than the state, a common moral culture, and the strength of religion. Liberalism drained the power from the institutions. We no longer have a common moral culture and our religion, while pervasive, seems increasingly unable to affect actual behavior.

Modern liberalism is one branch of the rupture that occurred in liberalism in the last century. The other branch is today called conservatism. American conservatism, neo or otherwise, in fact represents the older classical liberal tradition. Conservatism of the American variety is simply liberalism that accepts the constraints that a clear view of reality, including a recognition of the nature of human beings, places upon the main thrusts of liberalism—liberty and equality. The difference, it has been said, is that between a hard-headed and a sentimental liberalism. Sentimental liberalism, with its sweet view of human nature, naturally evolves into the disaster of modern liberalism.

"During the past 30 years," William Bennett writes, "we have witnessed a profound shift in public attitudes." He cites polls showing that "we Americans now place less value on what we owe others as a matter of moral obligation; less value on sacrifice as a moral good, on social conformity, respectability, and observing the rules; less value on correctness and restraint in matters of physical pleasure and sexuality—and correlatively greater value on things like self-expression, individualism, self-realization, and personal choice." Though I think the shift in public attitudes merely accelerated in the past thirty years, having been silently eroding our culture for much longer, it is clear that our current set of values is inhospitable to the self-discipline required for such institutions as marriage and education and hospitable to no-fault divorce and self-esteem training.

Our modern, virtually unqualified, enthusiasm for liberty forgets that liberty can only be "the space between the walls," the walls of morality and law based upon morality. It is sensible to argue about how far apart the walls should be set, but it is cultural suicide to demand all space and no walls. . . .

The Collapse of Popular Culture

The distance and direction popular culture has travelled in less than one lifetime is shown by the contrast between best-selling records. A performer of the 1930s hit "The Way You Look Tonight" sang these words to romantic music:

Oh, but you're lovely, /With your smile so warm, /And your cheek so soft, /There is nothing for me but to love you, /Just the way you look tonight.

In our time, Snoop Doggy Dogg's song "Horny" proclaims to "music" without melody:

> *I called you up for some sexual healing. /I'm callin' again so let me come get it. /Bring the lotion so I can rub you. /Assume the position so I can f . . . you.*

Then there is Nine Inch Nails' song, "Big Man with a Gun." Even the expurgated version published by the *Washington Post* gives some idea of how rapidly popular culture is sinking into barbarism:

> *I am a big man (yes I am). And I have a big gun. Got me a big old [expletive] and I, I like to have fun. Held against your forehead, I'll make you suck it. Maybe I'll put a hole in your head. . . . I can reduce it if you want. I can devour. I'm hard as [expletive] steel and I've got the power. . . . Shoot, shoot, shoot, shoot, shoot. I'm going to come all over you. . . . me and my [expletive] gun, me and my [expletive] gun.*

The obscenity of thought and word is staggering, but also notable is the deliberate rejection of any attempt to achieve artistic distinction or even mediocrity. The music is generally little more than noise with a beat, the singing is an unmelodic chant, the lyrics often range from the perverse to the mercifully unintelligible. It is difficult to convey just how debased rap is. . . .

What America increasingly produces and distributes is now propaganda for every perversion and obscenity imaginable. If many of us accept the assumptions on which that is based, and apparently many do, then we are well on our way to an obscene culture. The upshot is that American popular culture is in a free fall, with the bottom not yet in sight. This is what the liberal view of human nature has brought us to. The idea that men are naturally rational, moral creatures without the need for strong external restraints has been exploded by experience. There is an eager and growing market for depravity, and profitable industries devoted to supplying it. Much of such resistance as there is comes from people living on the moral capital accumulated by prior generations. That capital may be expected to dwindle further—cultures do not unravel everywhere all at once. Unless there is vigorous counterattack, which must, I think, resort to legal as well as moral sanctions, the prospects are for a chaotic and unhappy society, followed, perhaps, by an authoritarian and unhappy society. . . .

The Rise of Crime, Illegitimacy, and Welfare

The United States has surely never before experienced the social chaos and the accompanying personal tragedies that have become routine today: high rates of crime and low rates of punishment, high rates of illegitimate births subsidized by welfare, and high rates of family dissolution through no-fault divorce. These pathologies are recent, and it is now widely accepted that they are related to one another.

The proximate cause of these pathologies is the infatuation of modern liberalism with the individual's right to self-gratification along with the kind of egalitarianism, largely based on guilt, that inhibits judgment and reform. These pathologies were easy to fall into and will be vary difficult to climb out of. There is, in fact, no agreement about how to cure them. It may be, in fact, that a democratic nation will be unable to take the measures necessary, once we know what those measures are.

If radical individualism and egalitarianism are the causes, we should expect to see their various effects produced at about the same time as one another. And that is what we do see. During the same years that popular culture was becoming ever more sordid, the pathologies of divorce, illegitimacy, and crime exploded. The story is well documented and may be quickly summarized. The more difficult question, particularly about illegitimacy and welfare, is how to escape what we have done.

Rates of illegitimate births and the commission of serious crimes began rising together and did so at the same time in both the United States and England. National illegitimacy statistics were first gathered in the United States in 1920. Illegitimate births then constituted 3 percent of all births. The proportion slowly went up to just over 5 percent in 1960, and then shot up to 11 percent in 1970, above 18 percent in 1980, and 30 percent by 1991. These are figures for the entire population. Black illegitimacy started from a higher base than white and skyrocketed sooner, reaching 68 percent in 1991. White illegitimacy had reached a little over 2 percent by 1960 and then shot up to 6 percent in 1970, 11 percent in 1980, and just under 22 percent in 1991. Combined black and white illegitimacy in 1992 was 32 percent. These are national averages; illegitimacy is much higher in lower-income communities and neighborhoods.

Crime displays the same pattern. National records about violent crime in the United States were first kept in 1960. The number of violent crimes in that year was just under 1,900 per 100,000 people; the number doubled within ten years, and more than tripled to almost 6,000 by 1980. After a brief decline, the crime rate began rising again and had reached almost 5,700 by 1992. It is thus apparent that crime and illegitimacy trends began rising at almost the same time and then rose together. . . .

Rising crime, illegitimacy, and student rebellion had a common cause. While the middle-class student radicals turned to dreams of revolution and the destruction of institutions, some of the lower classes turned to crime and sexual license, and probably for the same reasons. That fact bodes ill because it suggests a long-developing weakening of cultural constraints, constraints it will be very hard to put back in place. . . .

Crime rates in a number of areas have stopped rising and in some places have begun to decline. It is possible that the rate of violent crimes has gone down in the nation as a whole. This appears to be partially due to better policing, slightly higher rates of incarceration, and a decline in the number of young males, who are almost entirely responsible for violent crime though more and more women are taking up the practice. But, as the Council on Crime report puts it: "Recent drops in serious crime are but the lull before the coming crime storm." That is because the population of young males in the age groups that commit violent crime is about to increase rapidly, producing more violence than we know at present. It is also likely that the coming young felons will commit more serious crimes than today's juvenile offenders do. According to the report, the literature indicates that "each generation of crime-prone boys is several times more dangerous than the one before it, and that over 80 percent of the most serious and frequent offenders escape detection and arrest." . . .

When physical safety becomes a major problem even for the middle classes, we must of necessity become a heavily policed, authoritarian society, a society in which the middle classes live in gated and walled communities and make their places of work hardened targets. After the Oklahoma City bombing, there were serious proposals in Washington to use the Army to provide security. The mayor of Washington, D.C., proposed using the National Guard to supplement the police in that drug-ridden and murder-racked city. Whites tend to dismiss the violence of the inner cities as a black problem. As the killing and the drugs spread to white neighborhoods and suburbs, as they are doing, the response will be far more repressive. Both the fear of crime and the escalating harshness of the response to it will sharply reduce Americans' freedom of movement and peace of mind. Ours will become a most unpleasant society in which to live. Murray poses our alternatives: "Either we reverse the current trends in illegitimacy—especially white illegitimacy—or America must, willy-nilly, become an unrecognizably authoritarian, socially segregated, centralized state." . . .

NO

David Whitman

The Optimism Gap

Much of what everyone "knows" about the state of our nation is wrong. A large majority of Americans now believe that the nation is in decline. The causes of this decline are both familiar and disputed. Conservatives blame family breakdown, crime, and spiritual sloth for our national atrophy. Liberals attribute the decline to the forces of modern-day capitalism, racism, and greed; the poor and the working-class stiffs in the factories can no longer get ahead the way they once did, or so the argument goes. Yet while liberals and conservatives disagree about first causes, they nonetheless agree that the nation, like Rome before the fall, has already been compromised. The American Dream is now endangered. . . .

The Myth of Social Regression

> The trouble with this country is that there are too many people going about saying "the trouble with this country is . . ."
>
> —Sinclair Lewis

. . . Is America, in fact, in a state of decline? . . . To evaluate whether America is declining or advancing, it is necessary to look at whether the nation today is better or worse off in various respects than in the past. Yet the country's political leaders repeatedly duck the compared-to-what question. They are notorious for taking horrifying news stories and transmogrifying them into tales of national atrophy. In 1995, for example, Americans learned of the brutal murder of Deborah Evans and two of her children by three accomplices. One of the accomplices performed a crude C-section on Evans after she died in order to remove a 38-week-old baby whom the alleged murderer claimed for her own. Was the grisly, bizarre murder unusual?

Not according to Newt Gingrich. Here is how the House Speaker analyzed its meaning in a speech to the Republican Governors Association:

> This is not an isolated incident; there's barbarity after barbarity. There's brutality after brutality. And we shake our heads and say "well, what went

wrong?" What's going wrong is the welfare system which subsidized people for doing nothing; a criminal system which tolerated drug dealers; an educational system which allows kids to not learn. . . . And then we end up with the final culmination of a drug-addicted underclass with no sense of humanity, no sense of civilization, and no sense of the rules of life in which human beings respect each other. . . . The child who was killed was endowed by God. And because we aren't willing to say that any more in a public place, and we're not willing to be tough about this any more, and we don't tell four-, five-, and six-year-olds "there are things you can't do, we will not tolerate drug dealing," we then turn around one day and find that we tolerated the decay of our entire civilization. And it's not just violence. In last year's National Assessment of Educational Progress, 74 percent of the fourth-graders could not read at fourth-grade level. . . . A civilization that only has 26 percent of its fourth-graders performing at fourth-grade level is a civilization in danger of simply falling apart.

. . . What is striking about all this is that Gingrich, the former history professor, makes no reference to history. When Gingrich's claims are placed in context, they evaporate. For example, the reading scores for fourth graders that Gingrich decried were all *lower* a quarter century ago when the NAEP tests began for white, black, and Hispanic students. If the current NAEP scores testify to a civilization in danger of falling apart, think of how endangered American society was a quarter century ago. (Gingrich also botched the test results. The test scores showed that about 60 percent of fourth graders were not "proficient" readers, not that 74 percent of them read below grade level. By definition, 50 percent of those tested read above "grade level.")

Similar questions might be posed about Gingrich's claims about the criminal justice system. Does law enforcement really "tolerate" drug dealers? More drug dealers are locked up, serving longer sentences, today than ever before. That does not mean drug dealing has been halted, but it does not suggest a policy of looking the other way. What about the notion that out streets are marked by barbarity after barbarity? Are Americans significantly more likely to murder each other today than a quarter century ago? Not really. The homicide rate was a hair higher in 1995 than in 1970 (8.2 homicides per 100,000 inhabitants in 1995 versus 7.9 homicides per 100,000 inhabitants in 1970). By 1971, and for the remainder of the 1970s in fact, the homicide rate was substantially *higher* than in 1995. . . .

The Good News Surprise

Not all of the news about America is good. Yet most of the country's fundamental economic and social trends have improved over the last quarter century. That fact would surprise millions of Americans who feel as though they are living in Babylon.

Given that the Soviet Union has collapsed, that the threat of nuclear annihilation has almost vanished, and that the nation is now inundated with immigrants who cling to rafts, wade, swim, and run to reach our borders, it may seem an odd time to herald the demise of America. Quite apart from the question of America's standing in the world community, however, many domestic indexes have actually improved. In fact, much of what people presume about key social trends in America is wrong. Here are just a few examples at odds with the conventional wisdom:

Crime

Violent crime in the United States appears to be at its lowest level in a quarter century. There are two ways of tracking trends in crime. The first is to examine the Federal Bureau of Investigation's *Uniform Crime Reports,* which tabulate crimes reported to law enforcement agencies from around the nation. The second source of evidence is the Justice Department's annual national victimization surveys, which are huge polls that randomly sample approximately 100,000 people. The victimization surveys cover crimes not reported to police. (Only about a third of all crimes are reported to law enforcement agencies, and this fraction can change over time.) As a result, the victimization surveys are more representative than conventional crime statistics and are favored by many criminologists.

In 1996, violent crime rates were at their lowest levels since the victimization surveys started in 1973. According to the Justice Department reports, violent crime rates peaked 17 years ago, in 1981, and the rates of aggravated assault and rape are now lower than at any time in the previous 23 years. Meanwhile, property crime, which accounts for the bulk of all crime, had also plummeted to its lowest level since the federal surveys began. In 1996, the rates of household theft and burglary were about half of what they had been in 1973. The drop in property crime is so substantial that New York City now has a lower theft and burglary rate than London, and Los Angeles has fewer burglaries than Sydney, Australia.

Victimization surveys have one important gap: They do not track murders, since homicide victims cannot be interviewed after the fact. However, the FBI's *Uniform Crime Reports* do track homicides and the murder totals are considered accurate, because homicide is a crime that is hard to underreport. In 1996, the homicide rate of 7.4 murders per 100,000 inhabitants was well below the peak of 10.2 murders per 100,000 people in 1980. It was, in fact, virtually identical to the homicide rate in 1969, higher than in the 1950s, but lower than in 1931–34. Most of this well-publicized drop in violent crime has been concentrated in the nation's largest cities. In New York and Boston, fewer people were murdered in 1996 than at any time since the 1960s. In Los Angeles, fewer people were murdered in 1997 than in any year since 1977—even though the city now has 700,000 more residents. . . .

Drugs

Annual government surveys show that illicit drug use among the general population is at levels far below those of a decade or more ago. Overall drug use peaked in 1979, when the nation had 25 million users, almost twice the current number. Since 1992, illicit drug use has essentially stabilized but at lower levels. Cocaine use hit its high in 1985, when 3 percent of adults, or 5.7 million Americans, reported they had used cocaine the previous month.

By 1996, just 0.8 percent of Americans reported use of cocaine in the past month, and the number of current cocaine users had dropped by almost three-fourths since 1985, to 1.75 million. Among high school seniors, marijuana and LSD use has edged upward since 1992. But student use of marijuana remains well below the levels of the late 1970s and early 1980s, as does the use of most hard drugs. In 1981, 21.7 percent of high school seniors reported using an illicit drug other than marijuana during the month previous to when they were surveyed; in 1997, half as many (10.7 percent) did so. High school seniors were also three times more likely to use cocaine in 1985 than they are today. . . .

Scholastic Achievement

Despite much-heralded reports of a nation at educational risk, high school students today do as well as or slightly better than their predecessors of the mid-1970s on both aptitude and achievement tests. As Derek Bok writes in his book *The State of the Nation*, "Contrary to all the alarmist talk, there are even some recent signs of modest improvement" in academic achievement.

The case that student aptitude has fallen rests largely on the fact that Scholastic Aptitude Test (SAT) scores declined between the early 1960s and 1970s and have never fully recovered. However, there are two reasons why those declines don't mean that today's students are performing worse than their parents.

First, only about half of all high school seniors take the SAT each year, and the sample is far from representative. In six states in 1993, more than 70 percent of high school seniors took the SAT, but in ten other states less than 10 percent of seniors did so. Unlike the SAT, the Preliminary Scholastic Aptitude Test (PSAT) is given to representative samples of high school juniors. Both the math and verbal PSAT scores have stayed the same from 1959 to the present. . . .

Race

In the last quarter century, the black middle class has mushroomed. In 1996, black median family income, adjusted for inflation, was at an all-time high, and black poverty and infant mortality rates had edged downward to an alltime low. In 1970, about 1 out of every 17 blacks in the 25- to 34-year-old age group had earned a four-year college degree. By 1994, 1 in 8 had done so.

Orlando Patterson, a left-leaning Harvard sociologist, summarizes the import of these shifts in his 1997 book *The Ordeal of Integration*. "African Americans," he writes, "from a condition of mass illiteracy fifty years ago, are now among the most educated groups of people in the world, with median years of schooling and college completion rates higher than those of most European nations. Although some readers may think this observation is a shocking overstatement, it is not." . . .

As Patterson acknowledges, a minority of blacks in urban ghettos have fared disastrously in the last 25 years. But the big picture is inescapable: Most blacks have prospered, and overt white racism has dramatically declined since the 1960s. Overwhelming majorities of whites today support the principle of equal treatment for the races in schools, jobs, housing, and other public spheres. Interracial friendships and marriages have blossomed as well. In 1970, just 2.6 percent of all new marriages involving an African-American mate were interracial marriages; today, more than 12 percent are interracial unions. Whites' greater openness to interracial marriages is one of the more dramatic attitudinal shifts in the last 25 years. In 1972, only a quarter of whites approved of marriages between blacks and whites. (In 1958, just 4 percent did so.) By 1997, however, over 60 percent of whites approved of interracial marriages. . . .

The Myth of Moral Decline . . .

The Family Values Conundrum

Since 1970, divorce and out-of-wedlock childbearing have skyrocketed in the United States. Many single-parent families manage to flourish, but on average, children raised by single parents are more likely than children raised by both their biological parents to be poor, drop out of school, become pregnant while in their teens, go to juvenile correction facilities, and be unemployed as adults.

. . . [M]any Americans, laypeople and scholars alike, exaggerate the consequences of family breakdown. The crude one-to-one correlation that exists in public discussion—more kids born out of wedlock automatically equals higher crime rates, weaker moral standards, worse schools, sicker children, and so on—has not been borne out in recent years. Crime rates have dropped, scholastic achievement has stabilized or edged upward, and infant mortality has declined, even as the out-of-wedlock birth ratio has risen. Nor is it clear that the ethical standards of Americans have declined.

Here again, when members of the public voice their distress about family breakdown, they are almost always referring to *other* people's families, not their own.

. . . Americans aren't just pleased with their own family life; they are delighted. In a 1997 Mother's Day survey, the Pew Research Center found that 93 percent of mothers with kids under 18 felt their children were a source of happiness all or most of the time; 90 percent said their marriage made them happy all or most of the time; and just 2 percent of moms reported being dissatisfied with the job they were doing rearing their children. In poll after poll, less than 10 percent of Americans say they are worse parents than were their own parents, and compared to the moms and dads of twenty years ago, today's parents are actually much more likely to rate traditional values, such as hard work, religion, patriotism, and having children as being "very important." In their own lives, three out of four adults don't find it difficult to meet their commitments to their families, kids, and employers—even though 90 percent also believe that a "major problem with society" is that people don't live up to their commitments. . . .

The essential paradox is that while Americans believe today's moral breakdown was spawned by the permissiveness of the 1960s, they embrace, on a case-by-case basis, most of the liberties that were part of the 1960s revolution. When Americans are asked, as they were in a 1996 *Wall Street Journal* poll, what kind of impact various social movements have had on today's values, they almost invariably think they are beneficial. Roughly 80 percent of those surveyed by the *Journal* said that the civil rights movement, the environmental movement, and the women's movement all had a positive impact on people's values.

The previous year, the Gallup Organization also quizzed members of the public about whether they thought various changes had been good or bad for society. Hefty majorities of Americans thought the greater openness today toward divorced people was good for society, as was the greater openness about sex and the human body, changes in the role of women, greater cultural and ethnic diversity, the increased willingness to question government authority, and the greater attention paid to equality for racial and ethnic minorities. In only one instance (society's increased acceptance of homosexuality) did most people think social change had harmed society. . . .

By All That's Holy

The problem of "family breakdown" can be thought of as a surrogate Rorschach test. Voters hear of its poignant consequences among divorced friends, or see news stories about latch-key kids and crack babies, and before long, every problem starts looking as though it can ultimately be traced back to family breakdown. One might, for example, infer that organized religion is slipping if out-of-wedlock childbearing and single-parenting are mushrooming. In fact, three in four Americans believe the nation is in spiritual decline. Yet the sway of organized religion is much greater in the United States today than in most Western nations, and the religiosity of Americans is at near record levels.

As Seymour Martin Lipset, a neoconservative intellectual, sums up in his 1996 book *American Exceptionalism,* "The historical evidence indicates that religious affiliation and belief in America are much higher in the twentieth century than in the nineteenth, and have not decreased in the post–World War II era. . . . The standard evidence marshalled to argue that America is experiencing a value crisis is unconvincing." Such counterconventional claims are hard for members of the public to accept, again, because of the optimism gap. Two-thirds of the electorate think that religion is losing its influence on American life. Yet 62 percent say that religion's influence is increasing in their own lives, according to a 1994 *U.S. News & World Report* poll.

Today, a solid majority of Americans belong to churches and synagogues, much as they have since the 1930s, when scientific polling began. In 1997, 68 percent of Americans reported belonging to a church or synagogue, not much below the 73 percent who said they belonged in both 1965 and 1952. Some members of the clergy have asserted that these high levels of church membership conceal a dip in religious commitment and belief. It's true that weekly attendance at religious services was "only" 41 percent in 1997. This was down a bit from its peak in 1958, when 49 percent of Americans said they had attended services the previous week. But attendance in 1997 was very similar to attendance in 1950, when 39 percent of Americans said they had attended a service the previous week. In 1997, the Gallup poll replicated one of its surveys on Americans' religious practices from 1947. The fifty-year update found that the same percentage of Americans pray today (90 percent), believe in God (96 percent), and attend church once a week. About the only difference between the two eras was that Americans were actually more likely to give grace or give thanks aloud in 1997 than in 1947 (63 percent compared to 43 percent).

George Gallup, Jr., summarizes the evidence by observing that "the religious beliefs and practices of Americans today look very much like those of the 1930s and 1940s. The percent of the populace who are active church members today closely matches the figures recorded in the 1930s." Nor is it the case, as Roger Finke and Rodney Stark point out in their influential book *The Churching of America, 1776–1990*, that acceptance of traditional religious doctrine is down. Most Americans still say that religion is central to their own lives: Roughly 60 percent of adults think that religion "can answer all or most of today's problems," and one in three view at least one religious TV show each week. After reviewing church membership records and other historical evidence, Finke and Stark conclude that "to the degree that denominations rejected traditional doctrines and ceased to make serious demands on their followers, they ceased to prosper. The churching of America was accomplished by aggressive churches committed to vivid otherworldliness."

The Ethics "Crisis"

Conceivably, the nation could still be in moral decline even when its citizens claim to be deeply religious. A skeptic might suggest that Americans are simply bigger hypocrites than ever. In 1993, Everett Carll Ladd, the president of the Roper Center for Public Opinion Research, attempted to assess that proposition by examining whether the unethical behavior of Americans had risen in recent decades. In an article titled "The Myth of Moral Decline," Ladd reports his findings: There is no compelling evidence that Americans' moral conduct or ethical standards are slipping, but ever since the introduction of polling in the mid-1930s, most Americans have felt moral standards were in decline. In 1963, for instance, only a third of all adults said they were satisfied "with the honesty and standards of behavior of people in the country today."

Ladd acknowledges there is abundant evidence that large numbers of modern-day Americans err and sin. Yet in tracking trends over time, there is little proof that the moral state of the country's citizenry has deteriorated. Philanthropic giving as a percentage of personal income declined slightly between 1969 and 1972 but has essentially remained steady ever since. However, because Americans' personal incomes have risen substantially since the 1950s, individual citizens are now donating more money to charities than their parents did, even after accounting for inflation. Volunteering seems to have become *more* common. When the Gallup poll first queried people in 1977 about their participation in charitable and social service activities that aid the poor, the sick, and the elderly, a quarter of the populace said they participated. By 1994, that number had doubled to almost half of all adults. . . .

William Bennett may have best summed up the zeitgeist of the day when he observed that "these are times in which conservatives are going to have to face the fact that there is some good news on the landscape. We're going to have to learn to live with it." In some measure, Bennett's curmudgeonly response to good news reflects the fact that conservatives are loath to credit Bill Clinton for progress. But his begrudging acceptance of the good news is also part of an age-old tradition. From era to era, the electorate's mood has swung from boosterish optimism—as during the first two decades after World War II—to the stubborn skepticism popular today. Over a century ago, Charles Dickens deftly captured this skeptical attitude toward politics and public life in his travel journal, *American Notes*. "It is an essential part of every national character to pique itself mightily upon its faults," he observed, "and to deduce tokens of its virtue or its wisdom from their very exaggeration." In America's case, Dickens argued, the "one great blemish in the popular mind . . . and the prolific parent of an innumerable brood of evils, is Universal Distrust. Yet the American citizen plumes himself upon this spirit, even when he is sufficiently dispassionate to perceive the ruin it works; and will often adduce it . . . as an instance of the great sagacity and acuteness of the people."

POSTSCRIPT

Is America in Moral Decline?

Handwringing over weakening morals has long been a favorite pastime. Yet are Americans less moral today than they were a century ago? Consider that slavery has been abolished, civil rights for minorities have been won and generally accepted, tolerant attitudes have greatly increased, and genocide toward Native Americans ceased a long time ago. How could Americans have made so much progress if they have been getting much worse for hundreds of years? Such reflections cast suspicion over themoral decline thesis. On the other hand, this thesis is supported by many trends, such as the increases in crime and divorce (which have recently declined or leveled off). The issue is important because morality is a distinctive trait of the human species and essential to cooperative interactions. If morality declines, coercive restraint must increase to hold harmful behaviors in check, but self-restraint is much less costly than police restraint.

The issue of the trends in morality requires an examination of the blessings and curses of individualism and capitalism. One tenet of individualism is that the rights of the individual generally have priority over the rights of government or of the community. This may provide the freedom for wonderful human achievements but might also protect hateful and even dangerous speech and weaken society in the long run. Capitalism would be another demoralizing factor because it encourages self-interest and the passion for personal gain. Higher education may be another culprit because it relativizes values. In general, the forces behind the demoralization of society as described by Himmelfarb are not likely to be reversed in the medium-term future.

Most of the relevant literature is on aspects of the moral decline. Few works challenge the decline thesis. Examples include Nicholas Lemann's "It's Not as Bad as You Think It Is," *The Washington Monthly* (March 1997) and Gregg Easterbrook's "America the O.K.," *The New Republic* (January 4 & 11, 1999). For an exposition of the moral decline thesis, see Charles Derber's *The Wilding of America: How Greed and Violence Are Eroding Our Nation's Character* (St. Martin's Press, 1996); and Richard Sennett's *The Corrosion of Character* (W. W. Norton, 1998). Richard Stivers attributes the moral decline to a culture of cynicism in *The Culture of Cynicism: American Morality in Decline* (Basil Blackwell, 1994), while Neal Wood attributes it to capitalism in *Tyranny in America: Capitalism and National Decay* (Verso, 2004). Perhaps the solution to whatever decline may exist is moral education, but according to Tianlong Yu in *In the Name of Morality: Character Education and Political Control* (P. Lang, 2004) this may create the potential for some degree of public mind control by the state.

ISSUE 2

Does the News Media Have a Liberal Bias?

YES: Willam McGowan, from *Coloring the News: How Crusading for Diversity Has Corrupted American Journalism* (Encounter Books, 2001)

NO: Robert W. McChesney and John Bellamy Foster, from "The Left-Wing Media?" *Monthly Review* (June 2003)

ISSUE SUMMARY

YES: Journalist Willam McGowan argues that political correctness pertaining to diversity issues has captured media newsrooms and exerts a constraining pressure on reporters.

NO: Robert W. McChesney and John Bellamy Foster argue that news reporting is bent in the direction of the political and commercial requirements of media owners, and heavy reliance on government officials and powerful individuals as primary sources biases news toward the status quo.

"A small group of men, numbering perhaps no more than a dozen 'anchormen,' commentators and executive producers . . . decide what forty to fifty million Americans will learn of the day's events in the nation and the world." The speaker was Spiro Agnew, vice president of the United States during the Nixon administration. The thesis of Agnew's speech, delivered to an audience of midwestern Republicans in 1969, was that the television news media are controlled by a small group of liberals who foist their liberal opinions on viewers under the guise of "news." The upshot of this control, said Agnew, "is that a narrow and distorted picture of America often emerges from the televised news." Many Americans, even many of those who were later shocked by revelations that Agnew took bribes while serving in public office, agreed with Agnew's critique of the "liberal media."

Politicians' complaints about unfair news coverage go back much further than Agnew and the Nixon administration. The third president of the United States, Thomas Jefferson, was an eloquent champion of the press, but after six years as president, he could hardly contain his bitterness. "The man who never looks into a newspaper," he wrote, "is better informed than he who reads them, inasmuch as he who knows nothing is nearer to truth than he whose mind is filled with falsehoods and errors."

The press today is much different than it was in Jefferson's day. Newspapers then were pressed in hand-operated frames in many little printing shops around the country; everything was local and decentralized, and each paper averaged a few hundred subscribers. Today, newspaper chains have taken over most of the once-independent local newspapers. Other newspapers, like the *New York Times* and the *Washington Post,* enjoy nationwide prestige and help set the nation's news agenda. Geographical centralization is even more obvious in the case of television. About 70 percent of the national news on television comes from three networks whose programming originates in New York City.

A second important difference between the media of the eighteenth century and the media today has to do with the ideal of "objectivity." In past eras, newspapers were frankly partisan sheets, full of nasty barbs at the politicians and parties the editors did not like; they made no distinction between "news" and "editorials." The ideal of objective journalism is a relatively recent development. It traces back to the early years of the twentieth century. Disgusted with the sensationalist "yellow journalism" of the time, intellectual leaders urged that newspapers cultivate a core of professionals who would concentrate on accurate reporting and who would leave their opinions to the editorial page. Journalism schools cropped up around the country, helping to promote the ideal of objectivity. Although some journalists now openly scoff at it, the ideal still commands the respect—in theory, if not always in practice—of working reporters.

These two historical developments, news centralization and news professionalism, play off against one another in the current debate over news "bias." The question of bias was irrelevant when the press was a scatter of little independent newspapers. Bias started to become an important question when newspapers became dominated by chains and airwaves by networks, and when a few national press leaders like the *New York Times* and the *Washington Post* began to emerge. Although these "mainstream" news outlets have been challenged in recent years by opinions expressed in a variety of alternative media— such as cable television, talk radio, newsletters, and computer mail—they still remain powerful conveyers of news.

Is media news reporting biased? The media constitutes a major socializing institution, so this is an important question. Defenders of the media usually hold that although journalists, like all human beings, have biases, their professionalism compels them to report news with considerable objectivity. Media critics insist that journalists constantly interject their biases into their news reports. The critics, however, often disagree about whether such bias is liberal or conservative, as is the case with this issue. In the following selections, Willam McGowan argues that the news media tilt to the left, while Robert W. McChesney and John Bellamy Foster contend that the slant of the news media supports a conservative status quo. Though McGowan focuses on social issues, McChesney and Foster focus on political and economic issues where conservative elite influence can more easily be protrayed.

 **YES**

Coloring the News: How Crusading for Diversity Has Corrupted American Journalism

This book represents an effort on my part to pose unwelcome questions . . . , and to raise intelligent dissent about the disturbing conformity that has spread over the journalistic community. For most of the 1990s I have been intrigued by journalism's attempts to deal with the issue of diversity and have followed efforts at major news organizations all around the country. While it has been interesting to see the effects on the internal workings of the newsroom itself, I have also been most curious about the impact that diversity is having on news coverage itself, particularly coverage of what might be called "diversity issues" of immigration, race, gay rights, feminism, and affirmative action. I think it is fair to say that these are the most important social issues facing the country—the core of what the pundits call "the culture wars." Has diversity helped or hindered American journalism's ability to make sense of them, and by extension, American society's ability to come to terms with them? . . .

With the cultural topography of the country shifting beneath our feet, we need a press capable of framing essential questions and providing honest, candid and dependable answers. But the diversity-driven journalism we are getting has not done this, a failure that has consequences for our policy responses and our politics and our national conversation.

Most of those critical of the news industry's diversity effort have been conservatives offended by what they see as reporting skewed against their values. But liberals should also be dismayed. The identity politics that diversity journalism encourages is hardly the "progressive" force that its champions insist it is; for it runs at odds with the goal of assimilation and integration that progressives have historically championed. Liberals might also lament the way diversity journalism has contributed to liberalism's intellectual stagnation, as well as its debilitating self-righteousness, by depriving it of facts and insights that might encourage a re-thinking of dated positions.

Neither a conservative nor a liberal, I consider myself a pragmatist deeply committed to a frank and fair rendering of facts, to an intellectually honest, balanced debate about controversial diversity-related issues, and to the ideal of objectivity, which has come under fire in journalism and in the postmodern,

Adapted with permission from the publisher from *Coloring the News: How Political Correctness Has Corrupted Journalism* by Willam McGowan, Encounter Books, San Francisco, California (© 2003).

multicultural university. Even if you are ideologically predisposed to pro-diversity political positions, I'd like to think that the facts I have marshaled will convince you that the journalism I have scrutinized has a slant to it, and that this slant may not be such a good thing for our country. I believe the public deserves unbiased information to help it through the democratic decisions it needs to make—and that journalism has an obligation to put aside its own political biases in the process of providing that information. Our press needs to rediscover a reverence for "armed neutrality in the face of doctrines," as Giovanni Papini, a disciple of the philosopher William James, once phrased it. To the extent that it has not done this, and to the extent that the diversity crusade plays a role in that failure, there is cause for concern—and a purpose for this book.

~◈~

The coloring of the news is one of those stories that have been happening more or less invisibly for some years. By December 1992, it was not only in the cultural air, but very much on the table at the joint Diversity Summit Meeting of the American Society of Newspaper Editors and the Newspaper Association of America. This get-together had the unmistakable air of a tent revival, full of grim jeremiads, stern calls for repentance and holy roller zeal. Diversity had been fast becoming one of the most contentious issues in American society and in American journalism, responsible for polarizing, if not balkanizing, more than one newsroom around the country. Yet only one side of the issue was present in this crowd. Speaker after speaker got up to declaim in favor of diversity and to warn of editorial sin and financial doom if this cause was not embraced. . . .

On another level, though, the zealotry was entirely understandable. In the preceding few years, the cause of diversity had become a crusade across the length and breadth of the American media, and would be a defining and dominating force in journalism in the decade to come. Almost every day after that 1992 meeting, one could hear echoes from it in newspaper stories and nightly network broadcasts. Diversity was the new religion, and anybody who wanted to be anybody in the news industry had to rally behind it. . . .

~◈~

During the late 1980s I spent a number of years reporting and writing about South Asia, one of the world's most ethnically riven places. I had no ideological predispositions in the matter of ethnic issues or identity politics when I began working there. After a few years as a frontline witness to the tragedy of ethnic violence, however, I left with the understanding that identity politics could be extraordinarily divisive, capable of polarizing a country's political affairs, undermining its economic productivity, weakening its educational institutions, and straining the bonds that hold people together as one nation. The experience also taught me that journalists can play a role in either accelerating the process of ethnic fragmentation or containing it, depending on how committed they are to resisting identity politics and to eschewing the politicization of information.

Given what my South Asian experience revealed to me, it was unsettling to watch the mounting potential for cultural and political fragmentation here in the United States early in the 1990s. Rapidly changing demographics fed by increasingly nonwhite, Third World immigration were combining with a liberal cult of race, ethnicity and gender to mount a broad attack on the sense of a common American identity and the ideal of race-neutrality in public life.

While Americans once automatically saw themselves as a nation of individuals relating to one another through a common culture forged in "the melting pot," the new multicultural vision demanded that America be viewed as a "nation of nations"—a mosaic composed of separate ethnic, racial and gender blocs, each with its own cultural reference points, and each to be judged with respect to the rest of society by its own distinct values and standards. This was a vision that celebrated differences over consensus, and spurned what historian Arthur Schlesinger, in *The Disuniting of America*, referred to as a "transformative identity" based on "the historic promise of America: assimilation and integration." The multicultural vision also supported ethnic, racial and gender grievances against the oppression borne of "white male hegemony," and demanded compensatory preferences to help the aggrieved groups overcome their injury.

This shift from melting pot to mosaic represented a profound change in the ground rules of society, with far-flung implications for the shape of politics and civic culture. In effect it represented a vast national experiment, calling all the old givens into question. Whereas we used to emphasize the melding of individuals into an American whole and tried as much as possible to shun race and ethnicity as factors in the conduct of public life, now we were stressing group identity as a legitimate consideration in making laws and shaping social policy. Whereas colorblindness was once regarded as an uncontested article of liberal faith and the key to the liberal ideal of equality, it was now being disparaged as a defense of the "unleveled playing field." Liberals were once the champions of racial transcendence; now they were fast becoming the biggest exponents of racial determinism—the belief that race, ethnicity, gender and sexual orientation matter above all else.

As antithetical to the core values of traditional liberalism as the new identity politics was, it also defied the sustaining journalistic ethos that traditional liberalism had shaped. For this reason, the press might have been expected to scrutinize closely the premises and assumptions of identity politics, to challenge its attendant cant, and to point out its undesirable consequences where appropriate. Instead, much of mainstream journalism was giving it a pass or, even worse, becoming a vehicle for it. . . .

Stories that might have explored the downside of diversity, its wobbly, unexamined assumptions, or its internal contradictions were either ignored or reported with euphemism and embarrassment, as through a fog of avoidance. Unpalatable facts got an airbrushing, while critical voices remained unsought or unacknowledged. Instead of questioning whether multiculturalism was something we really wanted, and letting the American public decide, the press treated it as an immutable *fait accompli*, ignoring competing perspectives and contradictory information that might have cast another light on the concept. The sins of omission were as bad as those of commission, and brought to mind Orwell's famous observation that propaganda is as much a matter of what is left out, as of what is actually said.

On immigration, for example, journalists have tended to embrace a highly romantic, sentimental and historically distorted script which assumes immigration to be an unqualified blessing and minimizes its costs. As the urban historian Peter Salins puts it, the core questions associated with immigration are: "What are we going to become? Who are we? How do the newcomers fit in—and how do the natives handle it?" But it's clear that if the press asks itself these questions at all, it does so in only the most superficial fashion, gliding over realities that might otherwise curb its enthusiasm.

This is so even when evidence of the downside is obvious, as it was in 1992 in New York's Washington Heights, when the justified use of deadly force on the part of a white undercover patrolman was labeled police racism by the *New York Times* and the three-day riot by illegal immigrant Dominican drug dealers was portrayed as justified community outrage. The media script also tends to work hard at filtering out uncomfortable realities that might legitimize calls for tighter controls on newcomers, such as alien criminality, high rates of dependency on social services, the adverse impact that high rates of immigration have had on wages and the quality of life in areas where newcomers have concentrated. . . .

The antagonism to assimilation runs across a variety of fronts, but is starkest in the coverage of bilingual education and efforts to reform it. "Reporters just can't see this issue beyond their own ideological bent," said Alice Callahan, a left-wing Episcopal priest who works with Latino sweatshop workers in Los Angeles, most of whom supported Proposition 227, a measure against bilingual education, in 1998. "I have been surprised how unwilling they are to entertain a view of this issue different from their own precon- ceived view no matter what the facts are." . . .

With respect to gay and feminist issues, diversity's enhanced sensitivity has purged news coverage of many of the pernicious stereotypes that gov- erned reporting and commentary in the past. But it has also given the cover- age a decidedly partisan edge. Whether the issue be the integration of gays and women into the military, AIDS, abortion, gay marriage or gay adoption, the press has tended to side with gay and feminist interest groups, trimming its news-gathering zeal to filter out realities that might undercut the cause.

The script on gays and feminists also tends to depict any objections to their causes—however well grounded in constitutional, moral or institutional traditions—as outright bigotry, worthy of cartoonish portrayal. Those jour- nalists who voice conservative perspectives—or defend those who do—know they can expect blowback, as much from gay activists in the community as from those within news organizations themselves. After writing a column criticizing gay activists at Harvard in 1997, for instance, conservative *Boston Globe* columnist Jeff Jacoby was attacked by gay newsroom colleagues— including two of his copy editors—as well as the paper's ombudsman, who called Jacoby's work "offensive" and "homophobic." Describing the "chilling effect" such internal criticism has, Jacoby said: "A lot of gay activists think that any point of view different from theirs is not only wrong, but so illegitimate and beneath contempt that it doesn't even deserve to be considered. I know up front that if I want to write about this topic, I have to be prepared to run a gauntlet and to jump a lot of hurdles—not among the readers who I think mostly agree with me, but right here in the newsroom."

In terms of bias, though, no subject bears the mark of the new diversity orthodoxy more than the emotionally divisive issue of affirmative action and the politics of racial preference. For years, most of the national press treated affirmative action with little journalistic rigor and scant regard for contradictory facts. No matter how weighty (or grim) the evidence . . . , most of the journalistic establishment has not been above performing a little cosmetic surgery of its own in order to preserve the correct image.

In recent years there has been more readiness to examine the operational details of preference programs, mainly because of newsworthy efforts on the state and national level to roll back such programs. But the press continues to demonstrate its ideological attachment to affirmative action in the energy it spends discrediting efforts to eliminate preferences, such as California's Proposition 209 in 1996 and Washington State's Initiative 200 in 1998. "There was a reflex in the coverage that started with the assumption that people in [the pro-209 movement] had bad motivations, racial motivations," observed Ronald Brownstein of the *Los Angeles Times*. The ideological slant comes through as well in the hysterical, exaggerated way the short-term consequences of these rollback efforts get reported, as in the much-hyped 1997 "Resegregation of Higher Education" story. Contrary to what so many journalists predicted, steps to end racial preferences in university admissions did not result in "lily-white" campuses. In fact, Asian students, not whites, gained in percentage representation, and those minorities who were displaced from the elite schools actually ended up in places more appropriate to their academic qualifications, where they would graduate at higher rates than before. And by mid-2000, the percentage of minority students throughout the University of California system, the focus of most of the "resegregation of higher education" coverage, was up overall. . . .

Efforts to expand newsroom representation by ethnicity, gender and race have not been accompanied by any corresponding effort to expand or enhance intellectual or ideological diversity or an appreciation for it. Diversity, it turns out, is only skin deep. Surveys done over the course of the last two decades consistently show that journalists on the whole are today more liberal than the average citizen, and that the influx of women and minorities has only accentuated that imbalance since these groups are measurably more liberal than others. At some news organizations, especially those most committed to diversity, having liberal values has practically become a condition of employment. People with more traditional or conservative views have a hard time getting through the door, and if they do get through, they are wary of revealing their views.

The problem is not an active liberal conspiracy. Rather, it is one of an invisible liberal consensus, which is either hostile to, or simply unaware of, the other side of things, thereby making the newsroom susceptible to an unconscious but deeply rooted bias. The answer is not affirmative action for conservatives, but rather a recognition that this bias exists and serves as an invisible criterion affecting the hiring process.

Journalism is a profession that prides itself on its maverick outspokenness and its allergic reaction to preconceived notions. Yet in today's media climate, some notions are considered beyond scrutiny—including the merits of the diversity agenda. "I deplore the fact that the issue is so sensitive that reporters don't want to talk by name," one Washington bureau chief told me, hastening to add, "I don't want to contribute to that, but I would rather not be noted by name either." Indeed, in many ways news organizations have become the same kind of dysfunctional cultures as those found on the multicultural university campuses, where transgressions against the dominant line of thought can result in hostility and ostracism. . . .

The fear of being labeled racist, sexist or homophobic makes many white reporters reluctant to challenge this newsroom advocacy. As a *New York Times* reporter told a writer for *Esquire,* "All someone has to do is make a charge of racism and everyone runs away." And instead of taking hard-line stances against racial and ethnic cheerleading or the prickly hypersensitivity that mistakes rigorous editing for prejudice, many managers respond with solicitude because they don't want open ethnic conflict on their staff or they are worried about jeopardizing their careers. One of my *Los Angeles Times* sources said that "a large responsibility lies with the fifty-year-old, white males who find it easier, as a company, to give in to these groups than to deal with the real problems."

Not to be ignored in assessing the impact of diversity doctrine is the false perception reigning in the profession that this cause is the moral successor to the Civil Rights Movement of the 1960s. Many top editors who cut their teeth as young reporters covering civil rights in the South seem still to be fighting the last war in their effort to reconfigure the newsroom, ignoring today's more complicated ethnic and racial picture.

Among other things, the conflation of civil rights with diversity has extended the shelf life of the outdated paradigm of white oppression and nonwhite victimization, which the media invokes to justify a compensatory system of group preferences. It has also allowed diversity supporters to rationalize and excuse their own excesses and failings. When asked about complaints that the diversity campaign encouraged news organizations to go easy on minority groups, the *New York Time's* Arthur Sulzberger Jr. told *Newsweek's* Ellis Cose, "First you have to get them on the agenda."

Most significantly, though, seeing diversity as the next phase of the Civil Rights Movement has also given the whole media debate about it an overly righteous, moralistic air. This has made it difficult to discuss more subtle issues with the dispassion they require, and has also tended to encourage racial McCarthyism toward critics of the effort by dividing the world between "an enlightened us and unenlightened them," as one *Philadelphia Inquirer* reporter put it. As a result, "the whole debate gets lowered to a grade school level of oversimplification" with little effort expended to see the other side, complained former *Los Angeles Times* reporter Jill Stewart. . . .

In the end, though, the press's diversity crusade has performed its greatest disservice to the country's broader civic culture by oversimplifying complicated issues and by undermining the spirit of public cooperation and trust without which no multiethnic and multiracial society can survive. Instead of making public discourse intellectually more sophisticated, the diversity ethos has helped to dumb it down. Instead of nurturing a sense of common citizenship, the emphasis on diversity has celebrated cultural separatism and supported a race-conscious approach to public life. And instead of enhancing public trust—a critical element in the forging of consensus on the thorny social issues we face—the press's diversity effort has manufactured cynicism through reporting and analysis distorted by double standards, intellectual dishonesty and fashionable cant that favors certain groups over others.

The task of building a workable multiethnic and multiracial society is daunting, but by coloring the news, the diversity crusade has made it even more problematical. As one perceptive reporter at the *San Francisco Chronicle* reflected: "The ultimate goal is a society with as much racial and ethnic fairness and harmony as possible, but we can't get there unless we in the press are ready to talk about it in full."

NO

**Robert W. McChesney
and John Bellamy Foster**

The 'Left-Wing' Media?

If we learn nothing else from the war on Iraq and its subsequent occupation, it is that the U.S. ruling class has learned to make ideological warfare as important to its operations as military and economic warfare. A crucial component of this ideological war has been the campaign against "left-wing media bias," with the objective of reducing or eliminating the prospect that mainstream U.S. journalism might be at all critical toward elite interests or the system set up to serve those interests. In 2001 and 2002, no less than three books purporting to demonstrate the media's leftward tilt rested high atop the bestseller list. Such charges have already influenced media content, pushing journalists to be less critical of right-wing politics. The result has been to reinforce the corporate and rightist bias already built into the media system. . . .

The current attack on media content is presented as an attempt to counter the alleged bias of media elites. In reality, however, it is designed to shrink still further—to the point of oblivion—the space for critical analysis in journalism. In order to understand the form and content of the conservative onslaught on the media it is necessary to have some comprehension of the role played by professional journalism beginning in the early twentieth century.

Prior to 1900, the editorial position of a newspaper invariably reflected the political views of the owner, and the politics were explicit throughout the paper. Partisan journalism became problematic when newspapers became increasingly commercial enterprises and when newspaper markets became predominantly monopolistic. During the Progressive Era—as was chronicled in these pages a year ago—U.S. journalism came under withering attack for being a tool of its capitalist owners to propagate anti-labor propaganda.[1] With profit-making in the driver's seat, partisan journalism became bad for business as it turned off parts of the potential readership and that displeased advertisers. Professional journalism was born from the revolutionary idea that the link between owner and editor could be broken. The news would be determined by trained professionals and the politics of owners and advertisers would be apparent only on the editorial page. Journalists would be given considerable autonomy to control the news using their professional judgment. Among other things, they would be trained to establish their political neutrality.

From *Monthly Review*, vol. 55, no. 2, June 2003, pp. 1–16. Copyright © 2003 by Monthly Review. Reprinted with permission.

Monopoly control over the news in particular markets was not especially important—so the argument went—since, whether or not there were multiple newspapers, trained professionals would provide similar reports, to the extent that they were well trained. There emerged a professional code that, following *The Elements of Journalism*, by Bill Kovack and Tom Rosenstiel, might be reduced in its most ideal form to nine principles:

1. Journalism's first obligation is to the truth.
2. Its first loyalty is to citizens.
3. Its essence is a discipline of verification.
4. Its practitioners must maintain an independence from those they cover.
5. It must serve as an independent monitor of power.
6. It must provide a forum for public criticism and compromise.
7. It must strive to make the significant interesting and relevant.
8. It must keep the news comprehensive and proportional.
9. Its practitioners must be allowed to exercise their personal conscience.

Needless to say, such principles are mere ideals in a society where the media are ultimately controlled by those who hold the purse strings. Under these circumstances, the field for the application of journalism's professional code is narrow, and it has been altered to conform to the political and commercial requirements of the media owners, and the owning class in general. In practice, professional journalism has adopted three biases that have tended to institute an establishment bias: (1) government officials and powerful individuals are regarded as the primary legitimate sources for news; (2) to avoid the controversy associated with providing context, there has to be a news hook or news peg to justify a news story, which further tilts the news toward established institutional actors; and (3) journalists internalize how to "dig here, not there," as Ben Bagdikian put it. In other words, stories about corporate malfeasance are far less likely to be considered newsworthy than stories about government malfeasance.

To be sure, professional journalists puts a premium on fairness and social neutrality, but such principles are notoriously difficult to define since there is always a question of where to put the baseline. This has created a situation where the standards maintained are skewed toward the controlling business elites. The present rightward drift is making this even more of a reality.

The conservative critique is based then on four propositions: (1) the decisive power over the news lies with the journalists—owners and advertisers are irrelevant or relatively powerless; (2) journalists are political liberals; (3) journalists abuse their power to advance liberal politics—thus breaking the professional code; and (4) objective journalism would almost certainly present the world exactly as seen by contemporary U.S. conservatives. For their basic argument to hold the first three propositions must be valid. Moreover, for conservatives to continue to maintain a commitment to professional journalism, the media system would have to meet the standard of "objectivity" expressed by the fourth proposition—this is the unstated assumption underlying their entire argument. But this would spell the end of professional journalism as it is now understood. Indeed, it is our thesis that the conservative critics, while relying on the notion of bias (the violation of the professional code of neutrality) as the basis of their criticism of allegedly left-wing media, are not actually concerned with defending professional journalism at all but with eliminating it—as a no longer necessary concession on the part of those who own and ultimately control the media.

The first proposition is intellectually indefensible and is enough to call the entire conservative critique of the liberal news media into question. No credible scholarly analysis of journalism posits that journalists have the decisive power to determine what is and is not news and how it should be covered. In commercial media, the owners hire and fire and they determine the budgets and the overarching aims of the enterprise. Successful journalists, and certainly those who rise to the top of the profession, tend to internalize the values of those who own and control the enterprise. Sophisticated scholarly analysis examines how these commercial pressures shape what become the professional values that guide journalists. Indeed, the genius of professionalism in journalism is that it allows journalists to adopt the commercial/professional values of the owners, yet, because they are following a professional code, they are largely oblivious to the compromises to authority that they are making. They are taught that there is a legitimate spectrum of opinion, conforming to the range of discussions among those who actually own and control the society. Their professional autonomy, such as it is, does not allow them to go outside that spectrum *in the framing* of stories—no matter how far this removes the resulting journalism from the realities experienced by a majority in the United States and the world.

In the formative period of professionalism, especially in the 1930s, journalists like George Seldes and Haywood Broun, through their union, the Newspaper Guild, strove to establish a professional code which would be progressive and emphasize the need to advance the interests of those outside the power structure. They fought to keep the hands of the owners entirely off the content of the news. We will not keep you in suspense. They lost. The eventually dominant professional code for journalism was small-*c* conservative; its call for reliance upon official sources as the basis of legitimate news, and its definition of official sources as those in power meant it could hardly be otherwise. This episode suggests that a more powerful labor movement and, in particular, more powerful media workers' unions are crucial to protecting the integrity of journalism in a capitalist media system.

The most striking example of the deep flaws built into the professional code comes in the area of coverage of U.S. foreign policy and militarism. The range of legitimate debate in U.S. journalism has been and is the range of debate among the elite. Hence the U.S. right to invade any nation it wishes for any reason is never challenged in the press, because to our elites this is a cardinal right of empire. Likewise, the U.S. equation of capitalism with democracy, or, more specifically, U.S. dominated capitalism with democracy, is also a given among our elites and therefore in professional journalism. For journalists to question these matters on their own reveals them to be partisan and unprofessional, so it is not done. This highlights the severe limitations of professional journalism as a democratic force. With the emergence of global news media, this has presented institutions like CNN with a particular dilemma. If they broadcast their rah-rah U.S. news outside the United States it is dismissed as so much blatant propaganda; if they broadcast critical journalism in the United States it is dismissed as unprofessional. With little sense of irony, during the current Iraq war and occupation, CNN has adopted a two-track approach to its journalism, with the United States and the rest of the world getting very different pictures.

Yet, even with this truncated professional code, the rise of professionalism did grant journalists a degree of autonomy from the immediate dictates of owners. The high-water mark for journalist autonomy was from the 1950s to the 1970s. The great unreported story in journalism of the past quarter century, ironically enough, has been the attack upon journalist autonomy by media owners. Increasingly, the massive conglomerates that have come to rule the U.S. news media have found that the professional "deal" struck in the first half of the twentieth century no longer serves their needs. They have slashed resources for journalism and pushed journalists to do inexpensive and trivial reporting. In particular, expensive and not commercially lucrative investigative and international coverage was reduced if not effectively eliminated. To the extent the conservative critique of the liberal media was based upon a concern about journalists having too much power over determining the news, they have won that battle. Journalists have markedly less autonomy today than two or three decades ago.

In fact, conservatives tacitly acknowledge the transparently ideological basis of the claim that journalists have all the power over the news. The real problem isn't that journalists have all the power over the news, or even most of the power, it is that they have *any* power to be autonomous from owners and advertisers. For conservatives, the influence of owners and advertisers is not a problem since they have both the proper political world-view, and unique rights as owners. The conservative critics thus focus on journalists as a kind of fifth column attacking conservative values from within the media. Newt Gingrich, with typical candor and a lack of PR rhetoric, laid bare the logic behind the conservative critique: what needs to be done is to eliminate journalistic autonomy, and return the politics of journalism to the politics of media owners. This also helps to explain why U.S. rightists tend to be obsessed with pushing public broadcasting to operate by commercial principles; they know that the market will very effectively push the content to more politically acceptable outcomes, without any need for direct censorship.

The second proposition of the conservative critique—that journalists are liberals—has the most evidence to support it. Surveys show that journalists tend to vote Democratic in a greater proportion than the general population. In one famous (though highly criticized as methodologically flawed) survey of how Washington correspondents voted in the 1992 presidential election, something like 90 percent voted for Bill Clinton (the favorite of the larger population that year, and hardly a raging progressive). To some conservative critics, that settles the matter. But, the weakness of the first proposition undermines the importance of how journalists vote, or what their particular political beliefs might be. What if owners and managers have most of the power, both directly and through the internalization of their political and commercial values in the professional code? Surveys show that media owners and editorial executives vote overwhelmingly Republican. An *Editor & Publisher* survey found that in 2000 newspaper publishers favored George W. Bush over Al Gore by a 3 to 1 margin, while newspaper editors and publishers together favored Bush by a 2 to 1 margin. In addition, why should a vote for Al Gore or Bill Clinton be perceived as a reflection of leftist politics? On many or most policies these are moderate to conservative Democrats, very comfortable with the status quo of the U.S. political economy.

Already a problem with the argument is apparent . . . : the terms "liberal" and "left-wing" are used interchangeably. In the conservative argument, the great divide in U.S. politics is between conservatives and the "left," a group that spreads unambiguously from Al Gore and Bill Clinton to Ralph Nader, Nelson Mandela, Noam Chomsky, and Subcommandante Marcos. To listen to the shock troops of the current conservative assault on the journalistic profession, support for Gore or Clinton is virtually indistinguishable from being an anarcho-syndicalist or a Marxist. Bernard Goldberg, author of the recent bestseller *Bias* that purports to demonstrate left-wing media bias, associates, albeit flippantly, political strategists for Clinton with Marx in their contempt for the rich, and adds that, "Everybody to the right of Lenin is a 'right-winger' as far as the media elite are concerned."

To the extent there is any basis whatsoever for such claims, it has to do with the fact that conservatives see any concession to social welfare needs as evidence of creeping socialism. Clinton Democrats and radical leftists become the same because of the conservative measure of what it means to be a leftist. It is based almost exclusively upon what are called social issues, such as a commitment to gay rights, women's rights, abortion rights, civil liberties, and affirmative action. And indeed, on these issues a notable percentage of journalists (like most educated professionals) tend to have positions similar to many of those to their left. For Goldberg "the real menace, as the Left sees it, is that America has always been too willing to step on its most vulnerable—gays, women, blacks. Because the Left controls America's newsrooms, we get a view of America that reflects that sensibility."

But this is absurd. Not only do newsrooms *not* project such sensibilities for the most part, the real divide in U.S. politics is not about issues such as affirmative action and thus between the liberal and conservative sides of elite opinion, but between elite opinion and those outside the elite, especially the left (using the term to refer mainly to those who challenge the system itself). Traditionally, journalists have had some autonomy to carry out news investigations and raise questions—as long as they stayed within the legitimate spectrum of debate established by elite opinion. The actual record of the U.S. news media is to pay very little direct attention to the political left as outside that spectrum, and this applies not only to socialists and radicals but also to what would be called mild social democrats by international standards. What attention the left actually gets tends to be unsympathetic, if not explicitly negative. Foreign journalists write about how U.S. left-wing social critics, who are prominent and respected public figures abroad, are virtually non-persons in the U.S. news media.

The Achilles heel for this conservative critique of journalist liberalism, and therefore entirely absent from their pronouncements, however, is a consideration of journalists' views on issues of the economy and regulation. Here, unlike with social issues, surveys show that journalists hold positions that tend to be more pro-business and conservative than the bulk of the population. It is here, too, that the professional code has adapted to the commercial and political concerns of the owners to generate a stridently pro-capitalist journalism. In the past two decades, labor news has all but been eliminated as a legitimate branch of U.S. journalism. In the 1940s and 1950s there were hundreds and hundreds of full time labor editors and reporters on U.S. daily newspapers; today the total of labor journalists in the mainstream media, including radio and TV, runs in single digits. Business news has vaulted to prominence, to the point where it equals and may well exceed traditional political journalism. And the increased attention to the affairs of business has not generated a well-spring of critical investigative coverage of the political economy; to the contrary, much of the coverage approaches the hagiography of a kept press toward its maximum leader. Today most journalists do not consider the affairs of poor people, immigrants, ethnic minorities, and working people the fodder of journalism, whereas the interests (and happiness) of investors are of supreme importance. . . .

Indeed, any serious look at how questions surrounding class and economic matters are treated would quickly free the journalistic profession from any charges of left-wing bias. Over the past two generations, journalism, especially at the larger and more prominent news media, has evolved from being a blue-collar job to becoming a desirable occupation of the well-educated upper-middle class. Urban legend has it that when the news of the stock market crash came over the ticker to the *Boston Globe* newsroom in 1929, the journalists all arose to give Black Monday a standing ovation. The rich were finally getting their comeuppance! When the news of the stock market crash reached the *Globe* newsroom in 1987, however, journalists were all frantically on the phone to their brokers. As recently as 1971 just over one-half of U.S. newspaper journalists had college degrees; by 2002 nearly 90 percent did. The median salary for a journalist at one of the forty largest circulation newspapers in the United States in 2002 was nearly double the median income for all U.S. workers. Journalists at the dominant media are unlikely to have any idea what it means to go without health insurance, to be unable to locate affordable housing, to have their children in underfunded and dilapidated schools, to have relatives in prison or the front lines of the military, to face the threat of severe poverty. They live in a very different world from most Americans. They may be "liberal" on certain issues, but on the core issues of political economy, they are hardly to the left of the U.S. population. Populist views are anathema to them by training and they tend to be quite comfortable with the corporate status quo. To the extent that their background and values determine the news, it is naive to expect journalists with their establishment-centered professional training to be sympathetic with anything more than a kind of elite centrism, far away from progressive left-wing policies and regulations.

As for the third proposition, that journalists use what limited autonomy they have to advance liberal-of-center politics, the evidence is far from convincing. One of the core points of the professional code is to prevent journalists from pushing their own politics on to the news, and many journalists are proud to note that while they are liberal, their coverage tended to bend the stick the other way, to stave off the charge that they have a liberal bias and are unprofessional. As one news producer stated, "the main bias of journalists is the bias not to look like they favor liberals." "One of the biggest career threats for journalists," a veteran Washington reporter wrote in 2002, "is to be accused of 'liberal bias' for digging up stories that put conservatives in a bad light." It is worth noting that in the current U.S. media environment, few journalists have any such concern about not revealing a pro-conservative bias. Such is done roundly and with little concern about accusations of bias, except from marginalized, ignored, and disgruntled leftists. . . .

As for the final proposition, that truly objective journalism would invariably see the world exactly the way Rush Limbaugh sees it, this points to the ideological nature of the exercise. Despite the attention paid to the news, there has never been an instance of conservatives criticizing journalism for being too soft on a right wing politician or unfair to liberals or the left. It is a one-way street. Conservatives sometimes respond to such criticisms that this is what all media criticism is about—whining that your side is getting treated unfairly. In 1992, Rich Bond, then the chair of the Republican Party, acknowledged that the point of bashing the liberal media was to "work the refs" like a basketball coach does, with the goal that "maybe the ref will cut you a little slack on the next one." Honest scholarship attempts to provide a coherent and intellectually consistent explanation of journalism that can withstand critical interrogation. The conservative critique of the liberal news media is an intellectual failure, riddled with contradictions and inaccuracy.

So why is the conservative critique of the liberal news media such a significant force in U.S. political and media culture? To some extent this is because this critique has tremendous emotional power, fitting into a broader story of the conservative masses battling the establishment liberal media elite. In this world, spun by right-wing pundits like Ann Coulter and Sean Hannity, conservatives do righteous battle against the alliance of

Clinton, Castro, bin Laden, drug users, gays, rappers, feminists, teachers unions and journalists, who hold power over the world. As one conservative activist put it, the battle over media is a "David and Goliath struggle." At its strongest, and most credible, the conservative critique taps into the elitism inherent to professionalism and to liberalism though this right-wing populism turns to mush the moment the issue of class is introduced. To be sure, some conservative media criticism backs away from fire breathing, and attempts to present a more tempered critique, even criticizing the rampant commercialization of journalism.

The main reason for the prominence of the right-wing critique of the liberal news media, however, has little or nothing to do with the intellectual quality of the arguments. It is the result of hardcore political organizing and it takes a lot of financial backers with deep pockets to produce that result. The conservative movement against liberal journalism was launched in earnest in the 1970s. Conservative critics claimed that the liberal media was to blame for losing the Vietnam War. Pro-business foundations were aghast at what they saw as the anti-business sentiment prevalent among Americans, especially middle-class youth, usually a core constituency for support. Mainstream journalism, which in reporting the activities of official sources was also giving people like Ralph Nader sympathetic exposure, was seen as a prime culprit. At that point the political right, supported by their wealthy donors, began to devote enormous resources to criticizing and changing the news media. Around one-half of all the expenditures of the twelve largest conservative foundations have been devoted to the task of moving the news rightward. This has entailed funding the training of conservative and business journalists at universities, creating conservative media to provide a training ground, establishing conservative think tanks to flood journalism with pro-business official sources, and incessantly jawboning any coverage whatsoever that is critical of conservative interests as being reflective of "liberal" bias. The pro-business right understood that changing media was a crucial part of bringing right-wing ideas into prominence and politicians into power. "You get huge leverage for your dollars," a conservative philanthropist noted when he discussed the turn to ideological work. There is a well-organized, well-financed and active hardcore conservative coterie working to push the news media to the right. As a *Washington Post* White House correspondent put it, "the liberal equivalent of this conservative coterie does not exist." . . .

The crucial change in the news media has not been the increased marginalization of the left—that has always been the case—but, rather, the shrinkage of room for critical work in journalism—what was best about the professional system—and the accompanying shift in favorable coverage toward the conservative branch of elite opinion. Looking at the different manner in which the press has portrayed and pursued the political careers of Bill Clinton and George W. Bush reveals the scope of the conservative victory. A Nexus search, for example, reveals that there were 13,641 stories about Clinton avoiding the military draft, and a mere 49 stories about Bush having his powerful father use influence to get him put at the head of the line to get into the National Guard. Bill Clinton's small time Whitewater affair justified a massive seven-year, $70 million open-ended special investigation of his business and personal life that never established any criminal business activity, but eventually did produce the Lewinsky allegations. Rick Kaplan, former head of CNN, acknowledged that he instructed CNN to provide the Lewinsky story massive attention, despite his belief that it was overblown, because he knew he would face withering criticism from the right for a liberal bias if he did not do so. George W. Bush, on the other hand, had a remarkably dubious business career in which he made a fortune flouting security laws, tapping public funds, and using his father's connections to protect his backside, but the news media barely sniffed at the story and it received no special prosecutor. His conviction for driving under the influence of alcohol barely attracted notice. One doubts the head of CNN goes to sleep at night in fear of being accused of being too soft on Bush's business dealings or his past record of inebriation.

The conservative propaganda campaign against the liberal media is hardly the dominant factor in understanding news media behavior. It works in combination with the broader limitations of professional journalism as well as the commercial attack upon journalism. Conservative ideology and commercialized, depoliticized "journalism" have meshed very well, and it is this combination that defines the present moment. Subjected to commercial pressures not seen for nearly a century, if ever, and under attack from conservatives, journalism as we know it is in a perilous state. This may not, however, be a total tragedy, given the fact that such professional journalism has done more to support power than to question it, more to quell democracy than invigorate it. In the wake of the destruction of the old media system it is time to construct a new one. And this time around it should be our media—that of democratic forces—not theirs. In other words, we have to begin the struggle all over again, challenging once again big business domination of the media and the corrosive logic it has produced.

Note

1. See Robert W. McChesney and Ben Scott, "Upton Sinclair and the Contradictions of Capitalist Journalism," *Monthly Review* 54, no. 1 (May 2002): 1–14.

POSTSCRIPT

Does the News Media Have a Liberal Bias?

As the opposing arguments in this issue indicate, we can find critics on both the Left and the Right who agree that the media are biased. What divides such critics is the question of whether the bias is left-wing or right-wing. Defenders of the news media may seize upon this disagreement to bolster their own claim that "bias is in the eye of the beholder." But the case may be that the news media are unfair to both sides. If that were true, however, it would seem to take some of the force out of the argument that the news media have a distinct ideological tilt at all.

Edward Jay Epstein's *News from Nowhere* (Random House, 1973) remains one of the great studies of the factors that influence television news shows. In *Media Events: The Live Broadcasting of History* (Harvard University Press, 1992), Daniel Dayan and Elihu Katz argue that live television coverage of major events helps to create the events and serves an important integrative role for society by deepening most citizens' experience of a common history. A study by S. Robert Lichter et al., *The Media Elite* (Adler & Adler, 1986), tends to support McGowan's contention that the media slant leftward, as does Ann Coulter in *Slander: Liberal Lies about the American Right* (Crown Publishers, 2002), and Bernard Goldberg in *BIAS: A CBS Insider Exposes How the Media Distort the News* (Regency Publishing, 2002), whereas Ben Bagdikian's *The Media Monopoly* 6th edition (Beacon Press, 2000); Mark Hertsgaard's *On Bended Knee: The Press and the Reagan Presidency* (Schocken, 1989); Eric Alterman's *What Liberal Media? The Truth about Bias and the News* (Basic Books, 2003); and Robert Waterman McChesney, *The Problem of the Media: U.S. Communication Politics in the Twenty-First Century* (Monthly Review Press, 2004) lend support to McChesney and Foster's view. A more recent S. Robert Lichter book, coauthored with Linda Lichter and Stanley Rothman, is *Watching America* (Prentice Hall, 1991), which surveys the political and social messages contained in television "entertainment" programs. Several recent memoirs of journalists are very useful for the debate on media bias. See Tom Wicker's *On the Record* (Bedford/St. Martin's, 2002); Ted Koppel's *Off Camera* (Alfred A. Knopf, 2000); and Bill O'Reilly's *The No-Spin Zone* (Broadway Books, 2001). David Halberstam's *The Powers That Be* (Alfred A. Knopf, 1979), a historical study of CBS, the *Washington Post, Time* magazine, and the *Los Angeles Times,* describes some of the political and ideological struggles that have taken place within major media organizations.

Edward Jay Epstein's book, previously cited, uses as an epigraph the following statement by Richard Salant, president of CBS News in the

1970s: "Our reporters do not cover stories from *their* point of view. They are presenting them from *nobody's* point of view." Most probably, Salant had not intended to be facetious or ironic, but the statement so amused Epstein that he parodied it in the title of his book: *News from Nowhere.*

ISSUE 3

Is Third World Immigration a Threat to America's Way of Life?

YES: Patrick Buchanan, from "Shields Up!" *The American Enterprise* (March 2002)

NO: Ben Wattenberg, from "Immigration Is Good," *The American Enterprise* (March 2002)

ISSUE SUMMARY

YES: Political analyst Patrick Buchanan asserts that the large influx of legal and illegal immigrants, especially from Mexico, threatens to undermine the cultural foundations of American unity.

NO: Ben Wattenberg, senior fellow at the American Enterprise Institute, argues that the United States needs a constant flow of immigrants to avoid population decline and also to avoid the diminishment of power and influence.

Before September 11, 2001, many Americans favored the reduction of immigration. After the terrorist attacks on the World Trade Center and the Pentagon by immigrants, some felt even stronger about limiting immigration. But is immigration bad for America, as this sentiment assumes, or does it strengthen America?

Today the number of legal immigrants to America is close to 1 million per year, and illegal ("undocumented") immigrants probably number well over that figure. In terms of numbers, immigration is now comparable to the level it reached during the early years of the twentieth century, when millions of immigrants arrived from southern and eastern Europe. A majority of the new immigrants, however, do not come from Europe but from what has been called the "Third World"—the underdeveloped nations. The largest percentages come from Mexico, the Philippines, Korea, and the islands of the Caribbean, while European immigration has shrunk to about 10 percent. Much of the reason for this shift has to do with changes made in U.S. immigration laws during the 1960s. Decades earlier, in the 1920s, America had narrowed its gate to people from certain regions of the world by imposing quotas designed to preserve the balance of races in America.

But in 1965 a series of amendments to the Immigration Act put all the world's people on an equal footing in terms of immigration. The result, wrote journalist Theodore H. White, was "a stampede, almost an invasion" of Third World immigrants. Indeed, the 1965 amendments made it even easier for Third World immigrants to enter the country because the new law gave preference to those with a family member already living in the United States. Since most of the European immigrants who settled in the early part of the century had died off, and since few Europeans had immigrated in more recent years, a greater percentage of family-reuniting immigration came from the Third World.

Immigrants move to the United States for various reasons: to flee tyranny and terrorism, to escape war, or to join relatives who have already settled. Above all, they immigrate because in their eyes America is an island of affluence in a global sea of poverty; here they will earn many times what they could only hope to earn in their native countries. One hotly debated question is, What will these new immigrants do to the United States—or for it?

Part of the debate has to do with bread-and-butter issues: Will new immigrants take jobs away from American workers? Or will they fill jobs that American workers do not want anyway, which will help stimulate the economy? Behind these economic issues is a more profound cultural question: Will these new immigrants add healthy new strains to America's cultural inheritance, broadening and revitalizing it? Or will they cause the country to break up into separate cultural units, destroying America's unity? Of all the questions relating to immigration, this one seems to be the most sensitive.

In 1992 conservative columnist Patrick Buchanan set off a firestorm of controversy when he raised this question: "If we had to take a million immigrants next year, say Zulus or Englishmen, and put them in Virginia, which group would be easier to assimilate and cause less problems for the people of Virginia?" Although Buchanan later explained that his intention was not to denigrate Zulus or any other racial group but to simply talk about assimilation into Anglo-American culture, his remarks were widely characterized as racist and xenophobic (related to a fear of foreigners). Whether or not that characterization is justified, Buchanan's question goes to the heart of the cultural debate over immigration, which is the tension between unity and diversity.

In the selections that follow, Buchanan contends that immigrants are harming the United States both economically and culturally. He argues that the sheer number of immigrants from other cultures threatens to overwhelm traditional safeguards against cultural disintegration and that this foreign influx is changing America from a nation into a collection of separate nationalities. Ben Wattenberg counters that immigration will benefit the United States, especially by making it a "universal" nation that will be better able to compete in a future that is increasingly global.

 **YES**

Shields Up!

In 1821, a newly independent Mexico invited Americans to settle in its northern province of Texas—on two conditions: Americans must embrace Roman Catholicism, and they must swear allegiance to Mexico. Thousands took up the offer. But, in 1835, after the tyrannical General Santa Anna seized power, the Texans, fed up with loyalty oaths and fake conversions, and outnumbering Mexicans in Texas ten to one, rebelled and kicked the tiny Mexican garrison back across the Rio Grande.

Santa Anna led an army north to recapture his lost province. At a mission called the Alamo, he massacred the first rebels who resisted. Then he executed the 400 Texans who surrendered at Goliad. But at San Jacinto, Santa Anna blundered straight into an ambush. His army was butchered, he was captured. The Texans demanded his execution for the Alamo massacre, but Texas army commander Sam Houston had another idea. He made the dictator an offer: his life for Texas. Santa Anna signed. And on his last day in office, Andrew Jackson recognized the independence of the Lone Star Republic.

Eight years later, the U.S. annexed the Texas republic. An enraged Mexico disputed the American claim to all land north of the Rio Grande, so President James Polk sent troops to the north bank of the river. When Mexican soldiers crossed and fired on a U.S. patrol, Congress declared war. By 1848, soldiers with names like Grant, Lee, and McClellan were in the city of Montezuma. A humiliated Mexico was forced to cede all of Texas, the Southwest, and California. The U.S. gave Mexico $15 million to ease the anguish of amputation.

Mexicans seethed with hatred and resentment, and in 1910 the troubles began anew. After a revolution that was anti-church and anti-American, U.S. sailors were roughed up and arrested in Tampico. In 1914, President Woodrow Wilson ordered the occupation of Vera Cruz by U.S. Marines. As Wilson explained to the British ambassador, "I am going to teach the South Americans to elect good men." When the bandit Pancho Villa led a murderous raid into New Mexico in 1916, Wilson sent General Pershing and 10,000 troops to do the tutoring.

From Patrick Buchanan, "Shields Up!" *The American Enterprise* (March 2002). Adapted from *The Death of the West: How Dying Populations and Immigrant Invasions Imperil Our Country and Civilization* (St. Martin's Press, 2002), pp. 123–133, 139, 141–146. Copyright © 2002 by Patrick J. Buchanan. Reprinted by permission of St. Martin's Press, LLC.

Despite FDR's Good Neighbor Policy, President Cárdenas nationalized U.S. oil companies in 1938—an event honored in Mexico to this day. Pemex was born, a state cartel that would collude with OPEC in 1999 to hike up oil prices to $35 a barrel. American consumers, whose tax dollars had supported a $50 billion bailout of a bankrupt Mexico in 1994, got gouged.

⋯◆⋯

The point of this history? Mexico has an historic grievance against the United States that is felt deeply by her people. This is one factor producing deep differences in attitudes toward America between today's immigrants from places like Mexico and the old immigrants from Ireland, Italy, and Eastern Europe. With fully one-fifth of all people of Mexican ancestry now residing in the United States, and up to 1 million more crossing the border every year, we need to understand these differences.

1. The number of people pouring in from Mexico is larger than any wave from any country ever before. In the 1990s alone, the number of people of Mexican heritage living in the U.S. grew by 50 percent to at least 21 million. The Founding Fathers wanted immigrants to spread out among the population to ensure assimilation, but Mexican Americans are highly concentrated in the Southwest.
2. Mexicans are not only from another culture, but of another race. History has taught that different races are far more difficult to assimilate than different cultures. The 60 million Americans who claim German ancestry are fully assimilated, while millions from Africa and Asia are still not full participants in American society.
3. Millions of Mexicans broke the law to get into the United States, and they break the law every day they remain here. Each year, 1.6 million illegal aliens are apprehended, almost all of them at our bleeding southern border.
4. Unlike the immigrants of old, who bade farewell to their native lands forever, millions of Mexicans have no desire to learn English or become U.S. citizens. America is not their home; they are here to earn money. They remain proud Mexicans. Rather than assimilate, they create their own radio and TV stations, newspapers, films, and magazines. They are becoming a nation within a nation.
5. These waves of Mexican immigrants are also arriving in a different America than did the old immigrants. A belief in racial rights and ethnic entitlements has taken root among America's minorities and liberal elites. Today, ethnic enclaves are encouraged and ethnic chauvinism is rife in the barrios. Anyone quoting Calvin Coolidge's declaration that "America must remain American" today would be charged with a hate crime.

Harvard professor Samuel P. Huntington, author of *The Clash of Civilizations*, calls migration "the central issue of our time." He has warned in the pages of this magazine:

> If 1 million Mexican soldiers crossed the border, Americans would treat it as a major threat to their national security. . . . The invasion of over 1 million Mexican civilians . . . would be a comparable threat to American societal security, and Americans should react against it with vigor.

Mexican immigration is a challenge to our cultural integrity, our national identity, and potentially to our future as a country. Yet, American leaders are far from reacting "with vigor," even though a Zogby poll found that 72 percent of Americans want less immigration, and a Rasmussen poll in July 2000 found that 89 percent support English as America's official language. The people want action. The elites disagree—and do nothing. Despite our braggadocio about being "the world's only remaining super-power," the U.S. lacks the fortitude to defend its borders and to demand, without apology, that immigrants assimilate to its society.

Perhaps our mutual love of the dollar can bridge the cultural chasm, and we shall all live happily in what Ben Wattenberg calls the First Universal Nation. But Uncle Sam is taking a hellish risk in importing a huge diaspora of tens of millions of people from a nation vastly different from our own. It is not a decision we can ever undo. Our children will live with the consequences. "If assimilation fails," Huntington recognizes, "the United States will become a cleft country with all the potentials for internal strife and disunion that entails." Is that a risk worth taking?

A North American Union of Canada, Mexico, and the United States has been proposed by Mexican President Fox, with a complete opening of borders to the goods and peoples of the three countries. *The Wall Street Journal* is enraptured. But Mexico's per capita GDP of $5,000 is only a fraction of America's—the largest income gap on earth between two adjoining countries. Half of all Mexicans live in poverty, and 18 million people exist on less than $2 a day, while the U.S. minimum wage is headed for $50 a day. Throw open the border, and millions could flood into the United States within months. Is America nothing more than an economic system?

◦⟨◉⟩◦

Our old image is of Mexicans as amiable Catholics with traditional values. There are millions of hard-working, family-oriented Americans of Mexican heritage, who have been quick to answer the call to arms in several of America's wars. And, yes, history has shown that any man or woman, from any country on the planet, can be a good American.

But today's demographic sea change, especially in California, where a fourth of the residents are foreign-born and almost a third are Latino, has spawned a new ethnic chauvinism. When the U.S. soccer team played Mexico in Los Angeles a few years ago, the "Star-Spangled Banner" was jeered, an American flag was torn down, and the U.S. team and its few fans were showered with beer bottles and garbage.

In the New Mexico legislature in 2001, a resolution was introduced to rename the state "Nuevo Mexico," the name it carried before it became a part of the American Union. When the bill was defeated, sponsor Representative Miguel Garcia suggested to reporters that "covert racism" may have been the cause.

A spirit of separatism, nationalism, and irredentism has come alive in the barrio. Charles Truxillo, a professor of Chicano Studies at the University of New Mexico, says a new "Aztlan," with Los Angeles as its capital, is inevitable. José Angel Gutierrez, a political science professor at the University of Texas at Arlington and director of the UTA Mexican-American Study Center, told a university crowd: "We have an aging white America. They are not making babies. They are dying. The explosion is in our population. They are shitting in their pants in fear! I love it."

More authoritative voices are sounding the same notes. The Mexican consul general José Pescador Osuna remarked in 1998, "Even though I am saying this part serious, part joking, I think we are practicing La Reconquista in California." California legislator Art Torres called Proposition 187, to cut off welfare to illegal aliens, "the last gasp of white America."

"California is going to be a Mexican State. We are going to control all the institutions. If people don't like it, they should leave," exults Mario Obledo, president of the League of United Latin American Citizens, and recipient of the Medal of Freedom from President Clinton. Former Mexican president Ernesto Zedillo told Mexican-Americans in Dallas: "You are Mexicans, Mexicans who live north of the border."

⋅◈⋅

Why should nationalistic and patriotic Mexicans not dream of a *reconquista*? The Latino student organization known by its Spanish acronym MEChA states, "We declare the independence of our *mestizo* nation. We are a bronze people with a bronze culture. Before the world, before all of North America . . . we are a nation." MEChA demands U.S. "restitution" for "past economic slavery, political exploitation, ethnic and cultural psychological destruction and denial of civil and human rights."

MEChA, which claims 400 campus chapters across the country, is unabashedly racist and anti-American. Its slogan—Por la Raza todo. Fuera de La Raza nada.—translates as "For our race, everything. For those outside our race, nothing." Yet it now exerts real power in many places. The former chair of its UCLA chapter, Antonio Villaraigosa, came within a whisker of being elected mayor of Los Angeles in 2001.

That Villaraigosa could go through an entire campaign for control of America's second-largest city without having to explain his association with a Chicano version of the white-supremacist Aryan Nation proves that America's major media are morally intimidated by any minority that boasts past victimhood credentials, real or imagined.

Meanwhile, the invasion rolls on. America's once-sleepy 2,000-mile border with Mexico is now the scene of daily confrontations. Even the Mexican army shows its contempt for U.S. law. The State Department reported 55 military incursions in the five years before an incident in 2000 when truckloads of Mexican soldiers barreled through a barbed-wire fence, fired shots, and pursued two mounted officers and a U.S. Border Patrol vehicle. U.S. Border Patrol agents believe that some Mexican army units collaborate with their country's drug cartels.

America has become a spillway for an exploding population that Mexico is unable to employ. Mexico's population is growing by 10 million every decade. Mexican senator Adolfo Zinser conceded that Mexico's "economic policy is dependent on unlimited emigration to the United States." The *Yanqui*-baiting academic and "onetime Communist supporter" Jorge Casteñada warned in *The Atlantic Monthly* six years ago that any American effort to cut back immigration "will make social peace in . . . Mexico untenable. . . . Some Americans dislike immigration, but there is very little they can do about it." With Señor Casteñada now President Fox's foreign minister and Senator Zinser his national security adviser, these opinions carry weight.

The Mexican government openly supports illegal entry of its citizens into the United States. An Office for Mexicans Abroad helps Mexicans evade U.S. border guards in the deserts of Arizona and California by providing them with "survival kits" of water, dry meat, granola, Tylenol, antidiarrhea pills, bandages, and condoms. The kits are distributed in Mexico's poorest towns, along with information on where illegal aliens can get free social services in California. Mexico is aiding and abetting an invasion of the United States, and the U.S. responds with intimidated silence and moral paralysis.

With California the preferred destination for this immigration flood, sociologist William Frey has documented an out-migration of African Americans and Anglo Americans from the Golden State in search of cities and towns like the ones in which they grew up. Other Californians are moving into gated communities. A country that cannot control its borders isn't really a country, Ronald Reagan warned some two decades ago.

Concerns about a radical change in America's ethnic composition have been called un-American. But they are as American as Benjamin Franklin, who once asked, "Why should Pennsylvania, founded by the English, become a Colony of Aliens, who will shortly be so numerous as to Germanize us instead of our Anglifying them?" Franklin would never find out if his fears were justified, because German immigration was halted during the Revolutionary War.

Theodore Roosevelt likewise warned that "The one absolutely certain way of bringing this nation to ruin, of preventing all possibility of its continuing to be a nation at all, would be to permit it to become a tangle of squabbling nationalities."

Immigration is a subject worthy of national debate, yet it has been deemed taboo by the forces of political correctness. Like the Mississippi, with its endless flow of life-giving water, immigration has enriched America throughout history. But when the Mississippi floods its banks, the devastation can be enormous. What will become of our country if the levees do not hold?

⋅ィ◉ァ⋅

Harvard economist George Borjas has found no net economic benefit from mass migration from the Third World. In his study, the added costs of schooling, health care, welfare, prisons, plus the added pressure on land, water, and power resources, exceeded the taxes that immigrants pay. The National Bureau of Economic Research put the cost of immigration at $80 billion in 1995. What are the benefits, then, that justify the risk of the balkanization of America?

Today there are 28.4 million foreign-born persons living in the United States. Half are from Latin America and the Caribbean, one fourth from Asia. The rest are from Africa, the Middle East, and Europe. One in every five New Yorkers and Floridians is foreign-born, as is one of every four Californians. As the United States allots most of its immigrant visas to relatives of new arrivals, it is difficult for Europeans to be admitted to the U.S., while entire villages from El Salvador have settled here easily.

- A third of the legal immigrants who come to the United States have not finished high school. Some 22 percent do not even have a ninth-grade education, compared to less than 5 percent of our native-born.
- Of the immigrants who have arrived since 1980, 60 percent still do not earn $20,000 a year.
- Immigrant use of food stamps, Supplemental Security Income, and school lunch programs runs from 50 percent to 100 percent higher than use by the native born.
- By 1991, foreign nationals accounted for 24 percent of all arrests in Los Angeles and 36 percent of all arrests in Miami.
- In 1980, federal and state prisons housed 9,000 criminal aliens. By 1995, this number had soared to 59,000, a figure that does not include aliens who became citizens, or the criminals sent over from Cuba by Fidel Castro in the Mariel boat lift.

Mass emigration from poor Third World countries is good for business, especially businesses that employ large numbers of workers at low wages. But what is good for corporate America is not necessarily good for Middle America. When it comes to open borders, the corporate interest and the national interest do not coincide; they collide. Mass immigration raises more critical issues than jobs or wages—immigration is ultimately about America herself. Is the U.S. government, by deporting scarcely 1 percent of illegal aliens a year, failing in its Constitutional duty to protect the rights of American citizens?

Most of the people who leave their homelands to come to America, whether from Mexico or Mauritania, are good, decent people. They seek the same freedom and opportunities our ancestors sought.

But today's record number of immigrants arriving from cultures that have little in common with our own raises a question: What is a nation? Some define a nation as one people of common ancestry, language, literature, history, heritage, heroes, traditions, customs, mores, and faith who have lived together over time in the same land under the same rulers. Among those who pressed this definition were Secretary of State John Quincy Adams, who laid down these conditions on immigrants: "They must cast off the European skin, never to resume it. They must look forward to their posterity rather than backward to their ancestors." Woodrow Wilson, speaking to newly naturalized Americans in 1915 in Philadelphia, declared: "A man who thinks of himself as belonging to a particular national group in America has yet to become an American."

But Americans no longer agree on values, history, or heroes. What one half of America sees as a glorious past, the other views as shameful and wicked. Columbus, Washington, Jefferson, Jackson, Lincoln, and Lee—all of them heroes of the old America—are under attack. Equality and freedom, those most American of words, today hold different meanings for different Americans.

Nor is a shared belief in democracy sufficient to hold a people together. Half the nation did not even bother to vote in the Presidential election of 2000. Millions cannot name their congressman, senator, or the justices of the Supreme Court. They do not care. We live in the same country, we are governed by the same leaders. But are we one nation and one people?

It is hard to believe that over one million immigrants every year, from every country on earth, a third of them entering illegally, will reforge the bonds of our disuniting nation. John Stuart Mill cautioned that unified public opinion is "necessary to the working of representative government." We are about to find out if he was right.

NO

Ben Wattenberg

Immigration Is Good

Many leading thinkers tell us we are now in a culture clash that will determine the course of history, that today's war is for Western civilization itself. There is a demographic dimension to this "clash of civilizations." While certain of today's demographic signals bode well for America, some look very bad. If we are to assess America's future prospects, we must start by asking, "Who are we?" "Who will we be?" and "How will we relate to the rest of the world?" The answers all involve immigration.

As data from the 2000 census trickled out, one item hit the headline jackpot. By the year 2050, we were told, America would be "majority non-white." The census count showed more Hispanics in America than had been expected, making them "America's largest minority." When blacks, Asians, and Native Americans are added to the Hispanic total, the "non-white" population emerges as a large minority, on the way to becoming a small majority around the middle of this century.

The first thing worth noting is that these rigid racial definitions are absurd. The whole concept of race as a biological category is becoming ever-more dubious in America. Consider:

Under the Clinton administration's census rules, any American who checks both the black and white boxes on the form inquiring about "race" is counted as black, even if his heritage is, say, one eighth black and seven eighths white. In effect, this enshrines the infamous segregationist view that one drop of black blood makes a person black.

Although most Americans of Hispanic heritage declare themselves "white," they are often inferentially counted as non-white, as in the erroneous *New York Times* headline which recently declared: "Census Confirms Whites Now a Minority" in California.

If those of Hispanic descent, hailing originally from about 40 nations, are counted as a minority, why aren't those of Eastern European descent, coming from about 10 nations, also counted as a minority? (In which case the Eastern European "minority" would be larger than the Hispanic minority.)

But within this jumble of numbers there lies a central truth: America is becoming a *universal nation,* with significant representation of nearly all human hues, creeds, ethnicities, and national ancestries. Continued moderate immigration will make us an even more universal nation as time goes on. And this process may well play a serious role in determining the outcome of the contest of civilizations taking place across the globe.

And current immigration rates are moderate, even though America admitted more legal immigrants from 1991 to 2000 than in any previous decade—between 10 and 11 million. The highest previous decade was 1901–1910, when 8.8 million people arrived. In addition, each decade now, several million illegal immigrants enter the U.S., thanks partly to ease of transportation.

Critics like Pat Buchanan say that absorbing all those immigrants will "swamp" the American culture and bring Third World chaos inside our borders. I disagree. Keep in mind: Those 8.8 million immigrants who arrived in the U.S. between 1901 and 1910 increased the total American population by 1 percent per year. (Our numbers grew from 76 million to 92 million during that decade.) In our most recent decade, on the other hand, the 10 million legal immigrants represented annual growth of only 0.36 percent (as the U.S. went from 249 million to 281 million).

Overall, nearly 15 percent of Americans were foreign-born in 1910. In 1999, our foreign-born were about 10 percent of our total. (In 1970, the foreign-born portion of our population was down to about 5 percent. Most of the rebound resulted from a more liberal immigration law enacted in 1965.) Or look at the "foreign stock" data. These figures combine Americans born in foreign lands and their offspring, even if those children have only one foreign-born parent. Today, America's "foreign stock" amounts to 21 percent of the population and heading up. But in 1910, the comparable figure was 34 percent—one third of the entire country—and the heavens did not collapse.

We can take in more immigrants, if we want to. Should we?

⋅⟨◉⟩⋅

Return to the idea that immigrants could swamp American culture. If that is true, we clearly should not increase our intake. But what if, instead of swamping us, immigration helps us become a stronger nation and a *swamper of others* in the global competition of civilizations?

Immigration is now what keeps America growing. According to the U.N., the typical American woman today bears an average of 1.93 children over the course of her childbearing years. That is mildly below the 2.1 "replacement" rate required to keep a population stable over time, absent immigration. The "medium variant" of the most recent Census Bureau projections posits that the U.S. population will grow from 281 million in 2000 to 397 million in 2050 with expected immigration, but only to 328 million should we choose a path of zero immigration. That is a difference of a population growth of 47 million versus 116 million. (The 47 million rise is due mostly to demographic momentum from previous higher birthrates.) If we have zero immigration with today's low birthrates indefinitely, the American population would eventually begin to *shrink*, albeit slowly.

Is more population good for America? When it comes to potential global power and influence, numbers can matter a great deal. Taxpayers, many of them, pay for a fleet of aircraft carriers. And on the economic side it is better to have a customer boom than a customer bust. (It may well be that Japan's stagnant demography is one cause of its decade-long slump.) The environmental case could be debated all day long, but remember that an immigrant does not add to the global population—he merely moves from one spot on the planet to another.

But will the current crop of immigrants acculturate? Immigrants to America always have. Some critics, like Mr. Buchanan, claim that this time, it's different. Mexicans seem to draw his particular ire, probably because they are currently our largest single source of immigration.

Yet only about a fifth (22 percent) of legal immigrants to America currently come from Mexico. Adding illegal immigrants might boost the figure to 30 percent, but the proportion of Mexican immigrants will almost surely shrink over time. Mexican fertility has diminished from 6.5 children per woman 30 years ago to 2.5 children now, and continues to fall. If high immigration continues under such circumstances, Mexico will run out of Mexicans.

California hosts a wide variety of immigrant groups in addition to Mexicans. And the children and grandchildren of Koreans, Chinese, Khmer, Russian Jews, Iranians, and Thai (to name a few) will speak English, not Spanish. Even among Mexican–Americans, many second- and third-generation offspring speak no Spanish at all, often to the dismay of their elders (a familiar American story).

Michael Barone's book *The New Americans* theorizes that Mexican immigrants are following roughly the same course of earlier Italian and Irish immigrants. Noel Ignatiev's book *How the Irish Became White* notes that it took a hundred years until Irish–Americans (who were routinely characterized as drunken "gorillas") reached full income parity with the rest of America.

California recently repealed its bilingual education programs. Nearly half of Latino voters supported the proposition, even though it was demonized by opponents as being anti-Hispanic. Latina mothers reportedly tell their children, with no intent to disparage the Spanish language, that "Spanish is the language of busboys"—stressing that in America you have to speak English to get ahead.

⋅◈⋅

The huge immigration wave at the dawn of the twentieth century undeniably brought tumult to America. Many early social scientists promoted theories of what is now called "scientific racism," which "proved" that persons from Northwest Europe were biologically superior. The new immigrants—Jews, Poles, and Italians—were considered racially apart and far down the totem pole of human character and intelligence. Blacks and Asians were hardly worth measuring. The immigration wave sparked a resurgence of the Ku Klux Klan, peaking in the early 1920s. At that time, the biggest KKK state was not in the South; it was Indiana, where Catholics, Jews, and immigrants, as well as blacks, were targets.

Francis Walker, superintendent of the U.S. Bureau of the Census in the late 1890s, and later president of MIT, wrote in 1896 that "the entrance of such vast masses of peasantry degraded below our utmost conceptions is a matter which no intelligent patriot can look upon without the gravest apprehension and alarm. They are beaten men from beaten races. They have none of the ideas and aptitudes such as belong to those who were descended from the tribes that met under the oak trees of old Germany to make laws and choose chiefs." (Sorry, Francis, but Germany did not have a good twentieth century.)

Fast-forward to the present. By high margins, Americans now tell pollsters it was a very good thing that Poles, Italians, and Jews emigrated to America. Once again, it's the *newcomers* who are viewed with suspicion. This time, it's the Mexicans, Filipinos, and people from the Caribbean who make Americans nervous. But such views change over time. The newer immigrant groups are typically more popular now than they were even a decade ago.

Look at the high rates of intermarriage. Most Americans have long since lost their qualms about marriage between people of different European ethnicities. That is spreading across new boundaries. In 1990, 64 percent of Asian Americans married outside their heritage, as did 37 percent of Hispanics. Black-white intermarriage is much lower, but it climbed from 3 percent in 1980 to 9 percent in 1998. (One reason to do away with the race question on the census is that within a few decades we won't be able to know who's what.)

⁊⦿⁊

Can the West, led by America, prevail in a world full of sometimes unfriendly neighbors? Substantial numbers of people are necessary (though not sufficient) for a country, or a civilization, to be globally influential. Will America and its Western allies have enough people to keep their ideas and principles alive?

On the surface, it doesn't look good. In 1986, I wrote a book called *The Birth Dearth*. My thesis was that birth rates in developed parts of the world—Europe, North America, Australia, and Japan, nations where liberal Western values are rooted—had sunk so low that there was danger ahead. At that time, women in those modern countries were bearing a lifetime average of 1.83 children, the lowest rate ever absent war, famine, economic depression, or epidemic illness. It was, in fact, 15 percent below the long-term population replacement level.

Those trendlines have now plummeted even further. Today, the fertility rate in the modern countries averages 1.5 children per woman, 28 percent below the replacement level. The European rate, astonishingly, is 1.34 children per woman—radically below replacement level. The Japanese rate is similar. The United States is the exceptional country in the current demographic scene.

As a whole, the nations of the Western world will soon be less populous, and a substantially smaller fraction of the world population. Demographer Samuel Preston estimates that even if European fertility rates jump back to replacement level immediately (which won't happen) the continent would still lose 100 million people by 2060. Should the rate not level off fairly soon, the ramifications are incalculable, or, as the Italian demographer Antonio Golini likes to mutter at demographic meetings, "unsustainable . . . unsustainable." (Shockingly, the current Italian fertility rate is 1.2 children per woman, and it has been at or below 1.5 for 20 years—a full generation.)

The modern countries of the world, the bearers of Western civilization, made up one third of the global population in 1950, and one fifth in 2000, and are projected to represent one eighth by 2050. If we end up in a world with nine competing civilizations, as Samuel Huntington maintains, this will make it that much harder for Western values to prevail in the cultural and political arenas.

The good news is that fertility rates have also plunged in the less developed countries—from 6 children in 1970 to 2.9 today. By the middle to end of this century, there should be a rough global convergence of fertility rates and population growth.

≈⦿≈

Since September 11, immigration has gotten bad press in America. The terrorist villains, indeed, were foreigners. Not only in the U.S. but in many other nations as well, governments are suddenly cracking down on illegal entry. This is understandable for the moment. But an enduring turn away from legal immigration would be foolhardy for America and its allies.

If America doesn't continue to take in immigrants, it won't continue to grow in the long run. If the Europeans and Japanese don't start to accept more immigrants they will evaporate. Who will empty the bedpans in Italy's retirement homes? The only major pool of immigrants available to Western countries hails from the less developed world, i.e., non-white, and non-Western countries.

The West as a whole is in a deep demographic ditch. Accordingly, Western countries should try to make it easier for couples who want to have children. In America, the advent of tax credits for children (which went from zero to $1,000 per child per year over the last decade) is a small step in the direction of fertility reflation. Some European nations are enacting similar pro-natal policies. But their fertility rates are so low, and their economies so constrained, that any such actions can only be of limited help.

That leaves immigration. I suggest America should make immigration safer (by more carefully investigating new entrants), but not cut it back. It may even be wise to make a small increase in our current immigration rate. America needs to keep growing, and we can fruitfully use both high- and low-skill immigrants. Pluralism works here, as it does in Canada and Australia.

Can pluralism work in Europe? I don't know, and neither do the Europeans. They hate the idea, but they will depopulate if they don't embrace pluralism, via immigration. Perhaps our example can help Europeans see that pluralism might work in the admittedly more complex European context. Japan is probably a hopeless case; perhaps the Japanese should just change the name of their country to Dwindle.

Our non-pluralist Western allies will likely diminish in population, relative power, and influence during this century. They will become much grayer. Nevertheless, by 2050 there will still be 750 million of them left, so the U.S. needs to keep the Western alliance strong. For all our bickering, let us not forget that the European story in the second half of the twentieth century was a wonderful one; Western Europeans stopped killing each other. Now they are joining hands politically. The next big prize may be Russia. If the Russians choose our path, we will see what Tocqueville saw: that America and Russia are natural allies.

We must enlist other allies as well. America and India, for instance, are logical partners—pluralist, large, English-speaking, and democratic. We must tell our story. And our immigrants, who come to our land by choice, are our best salesmen. We should extend our radio services to the Islamic world, as we have to the unliberated nations of Asia through Radio Free Asia. The people at the microphones will be U.S. immigrants.

We can lose the contest of civilizations if the developing countries don't evolve toward Western values. One of the best forms of "public diplomacy" is immigration. New immigrants send money home, bypassing corrupt governments—the best kind of foreign aid there is. They go back home to visit and tell their families and friends in the motherland that American modernism, while not perfect, ain't half-bad. Some return home permanently, but they bring with them Western expectations of open government, economic efficiency, and personal liberty. They know that Westernism need not be restricted to the West, and they often have an influence on local politics when they return to their home countries.

Still, because of Europe and Japan, the demographic slide of Western civilization will continue. And so, America must be prepared to go it alone. If we keep admitting immigrants at our current levels there will be almost 400 million Americans by 2050. That can keep us strong enough to defend and perhaps extend our views and values. And the civilization we will be advancing may not just be Western, but even more universal: American.

POSTSCRIPT

Is Third World Immigration a Threat to America's Way of Life?

$\mathbf{F}$ormer representative Silvio Conte (R-Massachusetts) said at a citizenship ceremony, "You can go to France, but you will never be a Frenchman. You can go to Germany but you will never be a German. Today you are all Americans, and that is why this is the greatest country on the face of the earth." At one time America's open door to immigrants was one of the prides of America. For some people, like Wattenberg, it still is. He thinks that an integrated, multicultural society is a culturally rich society and that immigration is making America stronger. Many people disagree because they fear the consequences of today's immigration. Buchanan worries that, although the new immigrants may want to assimilate, they have reached such a critical mass that the United States has lost the ability to absorb everyone into its own, slowly dissipating culture. The result is that immigrants are encouraged to maintain and promote the cultures that they arrive with, which further dilutes the original culture of America. The issue is based on what one thinks will happen as America becomes more diverse. Buchanan sees America as coming apart and Wattenberg sees America as leading the world.

Stanley Lieberson and Mary C. Waters, in *From Many Strands* (Russell Sage Foundation, 1988), argue that ethnic groups with European origins are assimilating, marrying outside their groups, and losing their ethnic identities. Richard D. Alba's study "Assimilation's Quiet Tide," *The Public Interest* (Spring 1995) confirms these findings.

Several major works debate whether or not immigrants, on average, economically benefit America and can assimilate. Sources that argue that immigrants largely benefit America include Julian L. Simon, *The Economic Consequences of Immigration*, 2d ed. (University of Michigan Press, 1999) and *Immigration: The Demographic and Economic Facts* (Cato Institute, 1995).

Sources that argue that immigrants have more negative than positive impacts include George Borjas, *Heaven's Door: Immigration Policy and the American Economy* (Princeton University Press, 1999); Roy Beck, *The Case Against Immigration* (W. W. Norton, 1996); and Patrick Buchanan, *The Death of the West: How Dying Populations and Immigrant Invasions Imperil Our Country and Civilization* (Thomas Dunne Books, 2002). For a more even-handed discussion, see *Not Just Black and White: Historical and Contemporary Perspectives on Immigration, Race, and Ethnicity in the United States* (Russell Sage Foundation, 2004) edited by Nancy Foner and *America's Newcomers and the Dynamics of Diversity* (Russell Sage Foundation, 2003) by Frank D. Bean and Gilian Stevens. On the issue of

Mexican immigration, see Douglas S. Massey, Jorge Durand, and Nolan J. Malone's *Beyond Smoke and Mirrors: Mexican Immigration in an Era of Economic Integration* (Russell Sage Foundation, 2003) and Victor Davis Hanson's *Mexifornia: A State of Becoming* (Encounter Books, 2003).

American Men's Studies Association

The American Men's Studies Association is a not-for-profit professional organization of scholars, therapists, and others interested in the exploration of masculinity in modern society.

http://mensstudies.org

American Studies Web

The American Studies Web site is an eclectic site that provides links to a wealth of resources on the Internet related to gender studies.

http://www.georgetown.edu/crossroads/asw/

Feminist Majority Foundation

The Feminist Majority Foundation Web site provides affirmative action links, resources from women's professional organizations, information for empowering women in business, sexual harassment information, and much more.

http://www.feminist.org/gateway/sdexec2.html

GLAAD: Gay and Lesbian Alliance Against Defamation

The Gay and Lesbian Alliance Against Defamation (GLAAD), formed in New York in 1985, seeks to improve the public's attitudes toward homosexuality and to put an end to discrimination against lesbians and gay men.

http://www.glaad.org/org.index.html

International Lesbian and Gay Association

The resources on the International Lesbian and Gay Association Web site are provided by a worldwide network of lesbian, gay, bisexual, and transgendered groups.

http://www.ilga.org

SocioSite: Feminism and Women's Issues

The Feminism and Women's Issues SocioSite provides insights into a number of issues that affect family relationships. It covers wide-ranging issues regarding women and men, family and children, and much more.

http://www.pscw.uva.nl/sociosite/TOPICS/Women.html

PART 2

Sex Roles, Gender, and the Family

*T*he modern feminist movement has advanced the causes of women to the point where there are now more women in the workforce in the United States than ever before. Professions and trades that were traditionally regarded as the provinces of men have opened up to women, and women now have easier access to the education and training necessary to excel in these new areas. But what is happening to sex roles, and what are the effects of changing sex roles? How have men and women been affected by the stress caused by current sex roles, male-female communication difficulties, the demand for the right to same-sex marriages, and the deterioration of the traditional family structure? The issues in this part address these sorts of questions.

- Do the New Sex Roles Burden Women More Than Men?

- Are Communication Problems Between Men and Women Largely Due to Radically Different Conversation Styles?

- Should Same-Sex Marriages Be Legally Recognized?

- Is the Decline of the Traditional Family a National Crisis?

ISSUE 4

Do the New Sex Roles Burden Women More Than Men?

YES: Jeff Grabmeier, from "The Burden Women Bear: Why They Suffer More Distress Than Men," *USA Today Magazine* (July 1995)

NO: Susan Faludi, from *Stiffed: The Betrayal of the American Man* (William Morrow and Company, 1999)

ISSUE SUMMARY

YES: Editor and author Jeff Grabmeier presents evidence showing that women experience more stress than men and then analyzes why.

NO: Author Susan Faludi argues that men have been socialized into a sex role that cannot be successfully fulfilled due to current conditions.

The publication of Betty Friedan's *The Feminine Mystique* (W. W. Norton, 1963) is generally thought of as launching the modern women's movement, and since that time significant changes have occurred in American society. Occupations and professions, schools, clubs, associations, and governmental positions that were by tradition or law previously reserved for men only are now open to women. Women are found in increasing numbers among lawyers, judges, physicians, and elected officials. In 1981 President Ronald Reagan appointed the first woman, Sandra Day O'Connor, to the Supreme Court. In 1983 the first American woman astronaut, Sally Ride, was included in the crew of a space shuttle, and women have been on more recent space shuttle missions, as well. The service academies have accepted women since 1976, and women in the military participated in the U.S. invasion of Panama in December 1989 and in the Persian Gulf War in 1990. Elizabeth Watson became the first woman to head a big-city police department when the mayor of Houston appointed her as chief of police in January 1990.

These sorts of changes—quantifiable and highly publicized—may signal a change in women's roles. Women now engage in occupations that were previously exclusive to men, and can pursue the necessary training and education required to do so. Paula Span, in "It's a Girl's World," *The Washington*

Post Magazine (June 22, 1997), quotes her daughter as saying, "Most of my girl-friends and I feel like we could do anything. . . . Being female isn't a restriction." Now most women of working age are either in school or the labor force, even those with children. As a result, the problem for women today has less to do with occupational exclusion than with the stress of inclusion.

But what about men today? To the extent that sex bias remains they are the advantaged sex. However, do they really have it made? Some would argue that they do not. Men may experience less stress as Jeff Grabmeier, author of the first selection, asserts, but they die younger. In fact, between the ages of 15 and 24, when sex roles take full hold, the death rate for men is over three times the death rate for women. Furthermore, if death by heart disease is likely to be related to stress, it should be noted that men die of heart disease at almost twice the age-adjusted death rate as women. One reason may be that men who work full time on average spend substantially more time working and commuting than women who work full time.

Neither stress data nor death-rate data can tell us the extent that sex roles affect the differential rates. Biological differences also play a role and the extent of this role is not clear. At this point, therefore, the discussion should focus on what burdens sex roles create for women and men. Current sex roles for women give them primary responsibility for household and child care so they end up with a second work shift if they choose to have a career as well as a family. According to Grabmeier, women are not too happy about this. He states that, based on his interviews with women, "well over half the women expressed anger, hostility, and resentment toward their husbands or partners for failing to share child care and household responsibilities." The aggravation is due in large part to differential sex role changes. Women's roles have changed due to the women's movement, the increasing financial need for two paychecks, and the opportunities of an expanding white-collar economy. However, the sex roles for men have not changed very much. Men's sex role problem can be seen as two-sided. One side of the problem is that men are still socialized to conform to masculine sex roles but are not given real opportunities to fulfill these roles in today's society. This is why Susan Faludi, in her selection, states that men are made to feel like failures. The other side of the problem is that men experience expectations from women to be more feminine and to increasingly perform what many men think of as women's tasks. On the one side they are failures in their own eyes and on the other side they are failures in women's eyes.

In the following selection, Grabmeier argues that women suffer a greater burden than men and uses data on stress to support his conclusions. He discusses the biological reasons for this, but emphasizes that roles for women have changed dramatically without a commensurate change in the traditional dominant roles for men. Women often blame themselves for their problems, which worsens them, according to Grabmeier. Faludi counters that men, particularly working-class men, are frustrated by a world for which their socialization has not prepared them. In combination with mortality and disease statistics, Faludi's analysis supports the conclusion that men are more burdened by modern sex roles than women.

Jeff Grabmeier

 **YES**

The Burden Women Bear: Why They Suffer More Distress Than Men

Who suffers more in life, men or women? This was a great issue to bring up around the office coffee machine or at cocktail parties because it not only made for lively conversation, it also was one of those questions that couldn't be settled simply by calling the reference desk at the local library.

Recently, though, evidence is growing that women, in fact, do suffer more than men. Blame it on biology, the stress of combining parenthood and career, living in a male-centered society, or all of the above. A study at Ohio State University by sociologists John Mirowsky and Catherine Ross shows that females experience symptoms of psychological distress—including sadness, anger, anxiety, malaise, and physical aches and pains—about 30% more often than males. Their work complements earlier research that found women about twice as likely as men to experience major clinical depression.

"Women genuinely suffered more distress than men by all the measures in our study," Mirowsky indicates. He and Ross interviewed 1,282 women and 749 men aged 18 to 90 and asked them on how many of the last seven days they had experienced various emotions. In each case, women reported more days with symptoms of distress than men. Don't assume women feel more of everything than men, however. The female participants experienced happiness 3.3% less often than the males.

In the past, assertions about women's surplus of suffering have been dismissed because they were thought to be more emotional than men. In other words, females simply complained more than males, who hid their pain behind a stoic facade. Mirowsky and Ross examined that possibility and found that women did indeed express their emotions more than men. About 68% of the males in the study agreed or strongly agreed that they kept their emotions to themselves, compared to 50% of the females who responded similarly. Even after the researchers took these differences into account, women still showed more signs of distress than men. "Women do express their emotions more, but that doesn't mean they aren't truly more depressed," Mirowsky maintains.

From Jeff Grabmeier, "The Burden Women Bear: Why They Suffer More Distress Than Men," *USA Today Magazine*, vol. 124, no. 2602 (July 1995). Copyright © 1995 by The Society for the Advancement of Education, Inc. Reprinted by permission of *USA Today Magazine*.

There is no simple explanation for why women suffer more distress than men. Most experts believe a combination of factors, including biological differences, puts females at greater risk for some psychological troubles. Scientists have discovered that imbalances of certain neurotransmitters in the brain—particularly norepinephrine and serotonin—are related to depression. Low levels of serotonin may lead to depression, anxiety, anger, eating disorders, and impulsive behavior, points out Henry Nasrallah, chairperson of psychiatry. "We don't know why, but women may have less stable brain systems for regulating these neurotransmitters. Female hormones are believed to play a role in the regulation of neurotransmitters that affect mood and that may explain why females are more likely to experience clinical depression. Fluctuations in hormone levels, for example, have been associated with the well-known premenstrual syndrome, which afflicts some women."

Just how much of a role biology plays in women's distress remains unclear. "There is usually an interplay between biological, psychological, and social factors," says Nasrallah. "Clearly there are biological factors that contribute a great deal to behavior and mood in men and women."

Blaming biology for distress can be a two-edged sword. It can help to mobilize medical resources and make physicians take such problems seriously, but also may take the focus off social factors that contribute to the situation.

This two-edged sword is painfully apparent for those with a uniquely female form of distress—postpartum depression. Women suffering from this syndrome have formed national interest groups seeking, in part, to get more medical attention for their problems, notes Verta Taylor, a professor of sociology who has studied their cause. However, these women walk a fine line between looking for medical solutions and pushing for their partners to provide more help in caring for children.

For a book she is writing, Taylor interviewed more than 100 women who said they suffered emotional problems—ranging from "baby blues" to clinical depression—after the birth or adoption of a baby. This illness, which afflicts more than three-quarters of new mothers, may last weeks or, as one woman told Taylor, it "didn't end until [my son] left home for college."

Taylor indicates that the question of whether postpartum depression has biological roots is a hotly debated topic. She found that women physicians who suffered from it were more likely than male doctors to believe that the disorder is the result of a deficiency in the hormone progesterone. Accordingly, women physicians were more likely to advocate progesterone therapy to treat the biochemical basis of the illness.

Nasrallah says most medical professionals believe that postpartum depression is an illness with biochemical causes that must be treated with anti-depressants. However, the less serious postpartum blues usually can be treated with rest, family support, and reassurance.

Even women who believe their postpartum depression has a biochemical aspect don't blame their condition simply on hormonal imbalances, Taylor points out. They echo the grievances of many working mothers—with and without postpartum depression—who complain of not getting enough support from husbands and partners. "A majority of the women I interviewed saw their excessive worry and irritability as the inevitable result of trying to combine and balance the demands of a 'second shift' of child care, housework, and a marriage with a paid job. Well over half the women expressed anger, hostility, and resentment toward their husbands or partners for failing to share child care and household responsibilities."

The problem, according to history professor Susan Hartmann, is that women now have more opportunities outside the home, but still do most of the household chores. "The old norms haven't changed that much. Women are still expected to take care of the home and children. But a majority of women also have taken on the responsibility of work. They've added new roles and responsibilities without significant changes in their old ones."

Although men sometimes may help out, there usually isn't a true sharing of household and child care responsibilities in American society. When men care for their children, for instance, it often is seen as "babysitting." When women do it, that simply is part of being a mother.

There is ample evidence that women still shoulder most of the responsibility of caring for kids, housework, and day-to-day chores. Margaret Mietus Sanik, an associate professor of family resource management, conducts studies of time use in families. She has found that, in couples with a new child, mothers spend about 4.6 hours per day in infant care, compared to about 1.3 for fathers. New mothers also lose more of their leisure time—about 3.8 hours a day—than their husbands, who give up approximately one hour. The result is that women often feel overworked and underappreciated.

A recent U.S. government survey of 250,000 working women found that stress was the most mentioned problem by respondents. The number-one issue females would like to talk about with Pres. Clinton is their inability to balance work and family, the survey found.

With the often overwhelming demands of juggling a career and family, it is no wonder that employed women suffer more depression than men. That doesn't mean that full-time homemakers have it better; in fact, research suggests they actually have higher levels of psychological distress than employed women. While working women can derive satisfaction from multiple roles at home and in the workplace, stay-at-home moms have only their homemaker role, Mirowsky indicates. They may feel isolated and out of step with the rest of society because parenting apparently is not highly valued in American culture.

Moreover, whether they want to work or not, housewives are economically dependent on their husbands, which is a powerful cause of distress. "In our culture, economic independence gives you status in the eyes of the community and a sense of security and self-worth," Mirowsky explains. "Housewives don't have that economic security. What we have found is that women are psychologically better off if they are employed."

In her studies of postpartum depression, Taylor has found that society's expectations of mothers also can put a suffocating burden on women. It is expected that a new mother will be happy, overjoyed even, and more than willing to put her baby's needs above her own. "But motherhood is often difficult, and women can find that their feelings are out of sync with societal expectations. They may feel as though their negative feelings are proof that they're not being a good mother, which compounds their feelings of distress, depression, anger, anxiety, and guilt."

If the stress of work and caring for children contributes to women's higher levels of distress, what about single, childless females? According to Mirowsky, they show less evidence of distress than other women, but more than men. That is because females face more than just role overload, she maintains. Women in the U.S. are paid about 75% of what men receive, are more likely to live in poverty, face a greater threat of physical and sexual abuse, and live in a culture that often promotes near-unattainable ideals for physical perfection. "Women just face a lot of problems and obstacles that men don't have to deal with. I'm surprised women don't feel more distress."

Psychological Strategies

Adding to the situation is the fact that women tend to use psychological strategies that amplify and prolong their distress. Psychologists have found that, when females are faced with problems, they are more likely than males to think continually about troubling issues. They also are more apt to blame themselves. The result is that women can be caught in a cycle of worry and depression instead of working to find a way out. Men, on the other hand, tend to take action in dealing with problems. They are more likely to place the blame elsewhere and find activities such as sports or hobbies to distract them.

All of this ruminating about their troubles leads women to more than just depression. One of the key findings about women's distress is the amount of anger they feel, Mirowsky and Ross discovered. The stereotype has been that women get depressed and men get angry, but their study revealed that the female subjects actually experienced anger about 29% more often than the males. "Anger is depression's companion—not its substitute," Mirowsky notes.

The anger gap actually was larger than the difference in depression. The researchers found that women were more angry and anxious than men who were equally depressed. Females in the study also were more likely to express their anger through yelling at others. "We thought this was particularly interesting because yelling is crossing the line between an emotion and an action," Mirowsky says. "Our interpretation is that women are yelling at their children more often than their husbands do."

While women are at home getting angry and depressed, maybe men are handling their distress another way—by drinking alcohol and taking drugs. Research has shown that males are more likely than females to abuse alcohol and drugs, but Mirowsky doesn't think that explains the distress gap. "In one sense, if alcohol and drugs really did help eliminate distress, then our findings would make sense—it would explain why men feel less distressed than women. In actuality, there's no evidence that alcohol or drugs help people, or men in particular, feel better." One study, for instance, found that alcoholism and drug abuse increase the odds of a major depressive episode more than fourfold. "Alcohol and drug use probably produces more distress than it prevents," Mirowsky claims.

No matter how you look at the evidence, he suggests, it seems clear that women really do suffer more psychological distress. Is there anything that can be done about it? There is not much females can change concerning their biology, although serious depression often can be treated with anti-depressant drugs. Many of the problems require fundamental changes in how government, business, and society treat women. Taylor says they want their concerns taken seriously. Because females traditionally have been seen as emotional, their problems haven't been given much weight. "Whatever causes higher rates of distress in women, it's not treated. If women feel it and suffer from it, then it should be seen as real."

One thing they are doing is organizing to make their voices heard. Some groups, such as the National Organization for Women, are well-known for their efforts to improve the lot of females. Taylor notes that women with postpartum depression have organized two national groups to present their issues to the public and the medical community. Their efforts, while specifically for the benefit of those with postpartum depression, really involve issues of concern to many females, she states. "The leaders of these groups argue all the time in their speeches that we need men to get more involved in parenting. Women are under this tremendous strain because they are almost solely responsible for parenting. Men have to assume a larger role, and that's a societal problem that requires changing how we structure gender roles."

Working women face special problems that need to be addressed by business and government, experts say. A recent survey by the U.S. government of 250,000 working women has put the spotlight on some of the issues women face, such as lack of adequate child care and unequal pay with men. "I think that more and more businesses are trying to recognize the needs of women in the workforce, yet the progress has been slow," Hartmann points out. "The situation for working women may get incrementally better, but I don't see any major improvements soon."

Social change is always slow and uneven, Mirowsky feels, but it is necessary if the distress gap is to be eased. "People may debate whether there's a difference in the quality of life for men and women in the United States. The evidence, however, suggests the quality of life is poorer for many women, and it's something that needs to be addressed."

NO

Susan Faludi

Stiffed: The Betrayal of the American Man

The American Century Versus the Century of the Common Man

... [A]s the nation wobbled toward the millennium, its pulse-takers seemed to agree that a domestic apocalypse was under way: American manhood was under siege. ...

If so many concurred in the existence of a male crisis, consensus collapsed as soon as anyone asked the question: Why? Not that there was a shortage of responses. Everyone proposed a favorite whipping boy—or, more often, whipping girl—and blame-seekers on all sides went after their selected culprits with righteous and bitter relish.

As a feminist and a journalist, I began investigating this crisis where you might expect a feminist journalist to begin: at the weekly meetings of a domestic-violence group. ... What did I expect to divine about the broader male condition by monitoring a weekly counseling session for batterers? ... I can see now that I was operating from an assumption both underexamined and dubious: that the male crisis in America was caused by something men were *doing* unrelated to something being done to them, and that its cure was surely to be found in figuring out how to get men to *stop* whatever it was. I had my own favorite whipping boy, suspecting that the crisis of masculinity was caused by masculinity on the rampage. If male violence was the quintessential expression of masculinity run amok, out of control and trying to control everything in its path, then a domestic-violence therapy group must be at the very heart of this particular darkness.

... The two counselors who ran the group, which was called Alternatives to Violence, worked hard to make "control" a central issue. Each new member would be asked to describe to the group what he had done to a woman, a request that was generally met with sullen reluctance, vague references to "the incident," and invariably the disclaimer "I was out of control." The counselors would then expend much energy showing him how he had, in fact, been in control the entire time. He had chosen his fists, not a knife; he had hit her in the stomach, not the face; he had stopped before landing a permanently injurious blow, and so forth. One session was devoted to reviewing "The Power and Control Wheel," a mimeographed chart that enumerated the myriad ways men could victimize their mates. No doubt the moment of physical contact for these men had grown out of a desire for supreme control fueled by a need to dominate. I cannot conceive of a circumstance that would exonerate such violence. By making the abusive spouse take responsibility for his actions, the counselors were pursuing a worthy goal. But the logic behind the violence still remained elusive.

A serviceman who had turned to nightclub bouncer jobs and pastry catering after his military base shut down seemed to confirm the counselors' position one evening shortly before his "graduation" from the group. "I denied it before," he said of the night he pummeled his girlfriend, who had also worked on the base. As he spoke he studied his massive, callused hands, lying uselessly on his lap. "I thought I'd blacked out. But looking back at that night when I beat her with an open hand, I didn't black out. I was feeling good. I was in power, I was strong, I was in control. I felt like a *man.*" But what struck me most strongly was what he said next: that moment of control had been the only one in his recent life. "That feeling of power," he said, "didn't last long. Only until they put the cuffs on. Then I was feeling again like I was no man at all."

He was typical in this regard. The men I got to know in the group had without exception lost their compass in the world. They had lost or were losing jobs, homes, cars, families. They had been labeled outlaws but felt like castoffs. Their strongest desire was to be dutiful and to belong, to adhere with precision to the roles society had set out for them as men. In this respect, they were prototypical modern wife beaters, who, demographic research suggests, are commonly ill equipped to fulfill the requirements of expected stereotypical sex roles, men who are socially isolated, afflicted with a sense of ineffectuality, and have nothing but the gender rule book to fall back on. . . .

There was something almost absurd about these men struggling, week after week, to recognize themselves as dominators when they were so clearly dominated, done in by the world. "That 'wheel' is misnamed," a laid-off engineer ruefully told the counselors. "It should be called the Powerlessness and Out-of-Control Wheel." The men had probably felt in control when they beat their wives, but their everyday experience was of feeling controlled—a feeling they had no way of expressing because to reveal it was less than masculine, would make each of them, in fact, "no man at all." For such men, the desire to be in charge was what they felt they must do to survive in a nation that *expected* them to dominate. . . .

More than a quarter century ago, women began to suspect in their own lives "a problem with no name." Even the most fortunate woman in post-war, suburban America, maneuvering her gleaming Hoovermatic across an expansive rec room, sensed that she'd been had. Eventually, this suspicion would be expressed in books—most notably Betty Friedan's *The Feminine Mystique*—that traced this uneasiness back to its source: the cultural forces of the mass media, advertising, pop psychology, and all the other "helpful" advice industries. Women began to free themselves from the box in which they were trapped by feeling their way along its contours, figuring out how it had been constructed around them, how it was shaped and how it shaped them, how their reflections on its mirrored walls distorted who they were or might be. Women were able to take action, paradoxically, by understanding how they were acted upon. "Women have been largely man-made," Eva Figes wrote in 1970 in *Patriarchal Attitudes*. What had been made by others women themselves could unmake. Once their problems could be traced to external forces generated by a male society and culture, they could see them more clearly and so challenge them.

Men feel the contours of a box, too, but they are told that box is of their own manufacture, designed to their specifications. Who are they to complain? The box is there to showcase the man, not to confine him. After all, didn't he build it—and can't he destroy it if he pleases, if he is a *man*? For men to say they feel boxed in is regarded not as laudable political protest but as childish and indecent whining. How dare the kings complain about their castles?

Women's basic grievances are seen as essentially reasonable; even the most blustery antifeminist these days is quick to say that, of course, he favors equal pay and equal opportunity. What women are challenging is something that everyone can see. Men's grievances, by contrast, seem hyperbolic, almost hysterical; so many men seem to be doing battle with phantoms and witches that exist only in their own overheated imaginations. Women see men as guarding the fort, so they don't see how the culture of the fort shapes men. Men don't see how they are influenced by the culture either; in fact, they prefer not to. If they did, they would have to let go of the illusion of control. . . .

The very paradigm of modern masculinity—that it is all about being the master of your universe—prevents men from thinking their way out of their dilemma, from taking active political steps to resolve their crisis. If they are the makers of history, not the subjects of historical forces, then how can they rise up?

. . . Yet clearly masculinity is shaped by society. Anyone wondering how mutable it is need only look at how differently it is expressed under the Taliban in Kabul or on the streets of Paris. Witness men walking with their arms wrapped around each other in Istanbul or observe the Mexican immigrant to Los Angeles whose manhood is so linked to supporting a family that any job, even a busboy's, holds a masculine pride. As anthropologist David D. Gilmore demonstrated in *Manhood in the Making*, his comprehensive crosscultural survey of masculine ideals, manliness has been expressed as laboring-class loyalty in Spain, as diligence and discipline in Japan, as dependence on life outside the home in the company of men in Cyprus, as gift-giving among Sikhs, as the restraint of temper and the expression of "creative energy" among the Gisu of Uganda, and as entirely without significance to the Tahitians. "Manliness is a symbolic script," Gilmore concluded, "a cultural construct, endlessly variable and not always necessary."

It should be self-evident that ideas of manhood vary and are contingent on the times and the culture. Despite that, contemporary discussion about what bedevils men fixes almost exclusively on the psychological and the biological. . . .

Cause Without a Rebel

A question that has plagued feminists like myself is the nature of male resistance to female change. Why are so many men so disturbed by the prospect of women's independence? Why do so many men seem to begrudge it, resent it, fear it, fight it with an unholy passion? The question launched my inquiry. But in the end, much to my surprise, it was not the question that most compelled me. It is not the question, finally, that drives this [selection]. Because the more I explored the predicament of postwar men, the more familiar it seemed to me. The more I consider what men have lost—a useful role in public life, a way of earning a decent and reliable living, appreciation in the home, respectful treatment in the culture—the more it seems that men of the late twentieth century are falling into a status oddly similar to that of women at mid-century. The fifties housewife, stripped of her connections to a wider world and invited to fill the void with shopping and the ornamental display of her ultrafeminity, could be said to have morphed into the nineties man, stripped of his connections to a wider world and invited to fill the void with consumption and a gymbred display of his ultra-masculinity. The empty compensations of a "feminine mystique" are transforming into the empty compensations of a masculine mystique; with a gentlemen's cigar club no more satisfying than a ladies' bake-off, the Nike Air Jordan no more meaningful than the Dior New Look.

And so my question changed. Instead of wondering why men resist women's struggle for a freer and healthier life, I began to wonder why men refrain from engaging in their own struggle. Why, despite a crescendo of random tantrums, have they offered no methodical, reasoned response to their predicament? Given the untenable and insulting nature of the demands placed on men to prove themselves in our culture, why don't men revolt?

Like many women, I was drawn to feminism out of a desire to challenge the silence of my sex. It has come to seem to me that, under all the rantings of men seeking to drown out the female voice, theirs is as resounding a silence. Why haven't men responded to the series of betrayals in their own lives—to the failures of their fathers to make good on their promises—with something coequal to feminism? When the frontier that their fathers offered them proved to be a wasteland, when the enemy their fathers sent them to crush turned out often to be women and children trembling in thatched huts, when the institutions their fathers claimed would buoy them downsized them, when the women their fathers said wanted their support got their own jobs, when the whole deal turned out to be a crock and it was clear that they had been thoroughly stiffed, why did the sons do nothing?

The feminine mystique's collapse a generation earlier was not just a crisis but a historic opportunity for women. Women responded to their "problem with no name" by naming it and founding a political movement, by beginning the process of freeing themselves. Why haven't men done the same? This seems to me to be the real question that lurks behind the "masculinity crisis" facing American society: not that men are fighting against women's liberation, but that they have refused to mobilize for their own— or their society's—liberation. Not that traditional male roles are endangered, but that men themselves are in danger of not acting.

Many in the women's movement and in the mass media complain that men just "don't want to give up the reins of power." But that would seem to have little applicability to the situations of most men, who individually feel not the reins of power in their hands but its bit in their mouths. What's more likely is that they are clinging to a phantom status. A number of men I interviewed, as they argued for the importance of having a male head of the household, tellingly demoted that to an honorary post: it's important, they would say, that every home have a "figurehead." But even the natural reluctance to give up a position of putative superiority, no matter how compromised, is not enough to explain a deeper male silence.

To understand why men are so reluctant to break with the codes of manhood-sanctioned in their childhood, perhaps we need to understand how strong the social constraints on them are. It's not just women who are bombarded by cultural messages about appropriate gender behavior. In the past half century, Madison Avenue, Hollywood, and the mass media have operated relentlessly on men, too. The level of mockery, suspicion, and animosity directed at men who step out of line is profound, and men respond profoundly—with acquiescence. But that is not a wholly satisfying explanation either, for haven't women, the object of such commercial and political manipulation, kicked over these traces successfully?

If men do not respond, then maybe it is because their society has proposed no route for them to venture down. Surely the culture has not offered an alternative vision of manhood. No one has: not the so-called men's movement, which clings to its dusted-off copies of *Grimms' Fairy Tales* and its caveman clichés; not conservative or liberal political leaders who call for a remilitarized model of manhood with work camps and schools run by former generals; not the Promise Keepers or Nation of Islam ministers, whose programs of male contrition and resurrection are fantasies of past fantasies; not a gay culture, which, as it gets increasingly absorbed into the larger commercial culture, becomes increasingly muted in its challenge of masculine roles; not even the women's movement, which clamors for men to change but has yet to conceptualize that change. But then, did feminists wait upon men to craft their revolution for them? Didn't the women's movement make its own way, without any assistance—no, with much resistance—from the dominant culture? So why can't men act? The ultimate answer has deep ramifications not only for men but for feminists. Eventually I came to believe that, far from being antagonists, they were each poised at this hour to be vital in the other's advance. But that answer came at the end. First I had to begin. . . .

My travels led me to a final question: Why don't contemporary men rise up in protest against their betrayal? If they have experienced so many of the same injuries as women, the same humiliations, why don't they challenge the culture as women did? Why can't men seem to act?

The stock answers that have been offered to explain men's reluctance to break out of stereotypical male models don't suffice. Men aren't simply refusing to "give up the reins of power," as some feminists have argued. The reins have already slipped from most of their hands, anyway. . . . While the pressures on men to imagine themselves in power and in control of their emotions are impediment to male revolt, a more fundamental obstacle overshadows them. If men have feared to tread where women have rushed in, then maybe that's because women have had it easier in one very simple regard: women could frame their struggle as a battle against men. . . .

Because the women who engaged in the feminist campaigns of the seventies were fighting the face of "male domination," they were able to take advantage of a ready-made model for revolt. To wage their battle, they could unfurl a well-worn map and follow a reliable strategy. Ironically, it was a male strategy—feminists grabbed hold of the blueprint for the American male paradigm and made good use of it. They had at the ready all the elements required to make that paradigm work. They had a clearly defined oppressive enemy: the "patriarchy." They had a real frontier to conquer and clear for other women: all those patriarchal institutions, both the old ones that still rebuffed women, like the U.S. Congress or U.S. Steel, and the new ones that tried to remold women, like Madison Avenue or the glamour and media-pimp kingdoms of Bert Parks and Hugh Hefner. Feminists also had their own army of "brothers": sisterhood. Each GI Jane who participated in this struggle felt she was useful. Whether she was distributing leaflets or working in a women's-health clinic, whether she was lobbying legislators to pass a child-care bill or tossing her bottles of Clairol in a "freedom trash can," she was part of a greater glory, the advancement of her entire sex. Many women whose lives were touched by feminism felt in some way that they had reclaimed an essential usefulness; together, they had charged the barricades that kept each of them from a fruitful, thriving life. Women had discovered a good fight, and a flight path to adult womanhood. Traveling along with trajectory of feminism, each "small step" for a woman would add up finally to a giant leap for womankind, not to mention humankind.

The male paradigm of confrontation, in which an enemy could be identified, contested, and defeated, was endlessly transferable. It proved useful as well to activists in the civil-rights movement and the antiwar movement, the gay-rights movement and the environmental movement. It was, in fact, the fundamental organizing principle of virtually every concerted countercultural campaign of the last half century. Yet it could launch no "men's movement." Herein lies the bedeviling paradox, and the source of male inaction: the model women have used to revolt is the exact one men not only can't use but are trapped in. The solution for women has proved the problem for men.

The male paradigm is peculiarly unsuited to mounting a challenge to men's predicament. Men have no clearly defined enemy who is oppressing them. How can men be oppressed when the culture has already identified them as the oppressors, and when they see themselves that way? As one man wrote plaintively to Promise Keepers, "I'm like a kite with a broken string, but I'm also holding the tail." In an attempt to employ the old paradigm, men have invented antagonists to make their problems visible, but with the passage of time, these culprits—scheming feminists, affirmative-action proponents, job-grabbing illegal aliens, the wife of a president—have come to seem increasingly unconvincing as explanations for their situation. Defeating such paper tigers offers no sense of victory. Nor do men have a clear frontier on which to challenge their intangible enemies. What new realms should they be gaining—the media, entertainment, and image-making institutions of corporate America? But these are institutions, they are told, that are already run by men; how can men invade their own territory? . . .

Social responsibility is not the special province of masculinity; it's the lifelong work of all citizens in a community where people are knit together by meaningful and mutual concerns. But if husbanding a society is not the exclusive calling of "husbands," all the better for men's future. Because as men struggle to free themselves from their crisis, their task is not, in the end, to figure out how to be masculine—rather, their masculinity lies in figuring out how to be human. The men who worked at the Long Beach Naval Shipyard didn't come there and learn their crafts as riggers, welders, and boilermakers to *be* masculine; they were seeking something worthwhile to *do*. Their sense of their own manhood flowed out of their utility in a society, not the other way around. Conceiving of masculinity as something to *be* turns manliness into a detachable entity, at which point it instantly becomes ornamental, and about as innately "masculine" as fake eyelashes are inherently "feminine." Michael Bernhardt was one man who came to understand this in his difficult years after he returned from Vietnam. "All these years I was trying to be all these stereotypes" of manhood, he said, "and what was the use? . . . I'm beginning to think now of not even defining it anymore. I'm beginning to think now just in terms of people." From this discovery follow others, like the knowledge that he no longer has to live by the "scorecard" his nation handed him. He can begin to conceive of other ways of being "human," and hence, of being a man.

And so with the mystery of men's nonrebellion comes the glimmer of an opening, an opportunity for men to forge a rebellion commensurate with women's and, in the course of it, to create a new paradigm for human progress that will open doors for both sexes. That was, and continues to be, feminism's dream, to create a freer, more humane world. Feminists have pursued it, particularly in the last two centuries, with great determination and passion. In the end, though, it will remain a dream without the strength and courage of men who are today faced with a historic opportunity: to learn to wage a battle against no enemy, to own a frontier of human liberty, to act in the service of a brotherhood that includes us all.

POSTSCRIPT

Do the New Sex Roles Burden Women More Than Men?

Sex roles are currently in transition. At the moment both men and women face challenges in fulfilling their sex roles. Much of this has to do with the pace of life. Both men and women are overwhelmed because they are short on time and loaded with choices and demands. But notice that most people do not want to go back to earlier days. A few men may long for frontier challenges and many women want to stay home while their children are young, but most want sex roles to continue to evolve in the direction they are going. The major influence on the changes in sex roles has been feminism and the women's movement.

Over the past 30 years, there has been a deluge of books, articles, and periodicals devoted to expounding feminist positions. Important recent statements by feminist leaders are Barbara A. Crow ed., *Radical Feminism: A Documentary Reader* (New York University Press, 2000); Gloria Steinem's book, *Outrageous Acts and Everyday Rebellions,* 2d ed. (Henry Holt, 1995) and article "Revving Up for the Next 25 Years," *Ms.* magazine (September/October 1997); and Patricia Ireland, *What Women Want* (Penguin, 1996). For a history of the women's movement see Kathleen C. Berkeley, *The Women's Liberation Movement in America* (Greenwood Press, 1999). For the impact of the women's movement on American society and culture see Cassandra L. Langer, *A Feminist Critique: How Feminism Has Changed American Society, Culture, and How We Live From the 1940's to the Present* (IconEditions, 1996); Ruth Rosen, *The World Split Open: How the Modern Women's Movement Changed America* (Viking, 2000); and Sara M. Evans, *Tidal Wave: How Women Changed America at Century's End* (Free Press, 2003). For some recent discussions of the demands of work and family on women see Arlie Russell Hochschild, *The Second Shift* (Penguin Books, 2003); Daphne Spain and Suzanne M. Bianchi, *Balancing Act: Motherhood, Marriage, and Employment Among American Women* (Russell Sage Foundation, 1996); Nancy Kaltreider ed., *Dilemmas of a Double Life: Women Balancing Careers and Relationships* (Jason Aronson, 1997), and Anna Fels, *Necessary Dreams: Ambition in Women's Changing Lives* (Pantheon Books, 2004). For some analyses of the sex role problems of men see Michael S. Kimmel, *Manhood in America: A Cultural History* (Free Press, 1996); Stephen Wicks, *Warriors and Wildmen: Men, Masculinity, and Gender* (Bergin & Carvey, 1996); Joseph A. Kuypers, ed., *Men and Power* (Prometheus Books, 1999); John MacInnes, *The End of Masculinity: The Confusion of Sexual Genesis and Sexual Difference in Modern Society* (Open University Press, 1998); Warren Farrell, *The Myth of Male Power* (Simon & Schuster, 1993); and Martin Anthony Summers, *Manliness and Its Discontents: The Black Middle Class and the Transformation of Masculinity, 1900–1930*

(University of North Carolina Press, 2004). Perhaps the final resolution of this issue is described in Pepper Schwartz' *Peer Marriage: How Love Between Equals Really Works* (Free Press, 1994). For a broad treatment of sex role issues, see Michael S. Kimmel's *Gendered Society,* 2nd edition (Oxford University Press, 2004). For worldwide changes in gender roles and inequality, see Ronald Inglehart's *Rising Tide: Gender Equality and Cultural Change around the World* (Cambridge University Press, 2003).

ISSUE 5

Are Communication Problems Between Men and Women Largely Due to Radically Different Conversation Styles?

YES: Philip Yancey, from "Do Men and Women Speak the Same Language?" *Marriage Partnership* (Fall 1993)

NO: Mary Crawford, from *Talking Difference: On Gender and Language* (Sage Publications, 1995)

ISSUE SUMMARY

YES: Author Philip Yancey argues that men and women have strikingly different communication styles because they grow up in different cultures. A man is usually concerned about enhancing or maintaining status as he communicates, while a woman will usually communicate in ways that gain or maintain closeness.

NO: Professor of psychology Mary Crawford contends that the thesis that men and women have radically different communication styles is greatly exaggerated in the media and is based on simplistic stereotypes.

In 1992 John Gray published his best-selling book *Men Are From Mars, Women Are From Venus* (HarperCollins), which promises greatly improved relationships between men and women if they understand that men and women are different and if they accept rather than resent their differences. Here are some selections from the book:

> One of the biggest differences between men and women is how they cope with stress. Men become increasingly focused and withdrawn while women become increasingly overwhelmed and emotionally involved. At these times, a man's needs for feeling good are different from a woman's. He feels better by solving problems while she feels better by talking about problems. Not understanding and accepting these differences creates unnecessary friction in our relationships (p. 29).

When a Martian gets upset he never talks about what is bothering him. He would never burden another Martian with his problem unless his friend's assistance was necessary to solve the problem. Instead he becomes very quiet and goes to his private cave to think about his problem, mulling it over to find a solution. When he has found a solution, he feels much better and comes out of his cave (p. 30).

When a Venusian becomes upset or is stressed by her day, to find relief, she seeks out someone she trusts and then talks in great detail about the problems of her day. When Venusians share feelings of being overwhelmed, they suddenly feel better. This is the Venusian way.

On Venus sharing your problems with another actually is considered a sign of love and trust and not a burden. Venusians are not ashamed of having problems. Their egos are dependent not on looking "competent" but rather on being in loving relationships. . . .

A Venusian feels good about herself when she has loving friends with whom to share her feelings and problems. A Martian feels good when he can solve his problems on his own in his cave (p. 31).

Some claim to be greatly helped by Gray's message. Others find it demeaning to characterize women as irrational, passive, and overly dependent on others. Critics also feel that it counsels women to accept boorish and uncaring behavior in men, while telling men that they only have to listen to women more to make them happy. Gray's message gets a strong reaction because it addresses a very important issue: how can men and women better understand each other?

This issue fascinates sociologists because it plunges them into questions about the construction of reality, perceptions of reality, differential socialization, and power in male-female relationships. Gray himself is constructing reality as he sees it in his book, and according to his reality many difficulties between men and women are not anyone's fault but are just misunderstandings. His reality leaves power out, but a sociologist will always take it into account. In fact, sociologists would note that men and women differ not only in their socialization but also in their relative power in their relationships. The person with greater income, education, and job status will feel freer to determine when, where, how, and about what the pair talks.

The differences in male-female communication styles that Philip Yancey identifies in the following selection are similar to Gray's. He says that men are more concerned about hierarchy and that women are more concerned about relationships, but it is a matter of degree. He, like Gray, works for better understanding between men and women. In the second selection, Mary Crawford reacts strongly to the proponents of gender differences in communication because she feels that their construction of gendered reality is superficial and puts women down.

Philip Yancey

 **YES**

Do Men and Women Speak the Same Language?

For five years my wife, Janet, and I met in a small group with three other couples. Sometimes we studied the Bible, sometimes we read books together, sometimes we spontaneously discussed topics like money and sex. Almost always we ended up talking about our marriages. Finally we decided the time had come to investigate an explosive topic we had always avoided: the differences between men and women. We used the book *You Just Don't Understand* [William Morrow & Company, 1990], by Deborah Tannen, as the springboard for our discussions. That study of the different communication styles of men and women had risen to the top of The New York Times bestseller list. Books on gender differences tend to portray one party as the "right" party. Women are sensitive, compassionate, peace-loving, responsible, nurturing; men are boorish slobs whose idea of "bonding" is to slouch in front of a TV with their buddies watching other men chase little round balls. Or, men are rational, organizational geniuses who run the world because they are "hardwired" with leadership skills that women can never hope to master. But in her book, Tannen strives to avoid such bias, focusing instead on what it takes for men and women to understand each other.

She sees males as more competitive, aggressive, hierarchical and emotionally withdrawn. Females, she concludes, are quieter, more relational and mutually supportive. Naturally, any generalities about gender differences do not apply to all men or all women. Yet we found one point of commonality that helped us all: Male/female relationships represent a classic case of cross-cultural communication. The key to effective relationships is to understand the vast "cultural" gap between male and female.

Anyone who has traveled overseas knows that barriers exist between cultures, language being the most obvious. The barriers between men and women can be just as real, and just as frustrating. Typically, says Tannen, men and women don't recognize these differences; they tend to repeat the same patterns of miscommunication, only more forcefully. As a result, marriages often resemble the stereotypical tourist encounter: One party speaks loudly and slowly in a language the other does not comprehend.

The Male/Female Culture Gap

"Shared meaning" is a good, concise definition of culture. By virtue of growing up in the United States, I share the meaning of things like Bart Simpson, baseball and the Fourth of July with 250 million other people, and no one else in the world. Our couples group found that some problems come about because one spouse enters marriage with a different set of "shared meanings" than the other. Consider routine dinner conversation. For some of us, interrupting another's conversation seems an act of impoliteness or hostility; for others, it expresses friendly engagement. Angie, one of the women in our group, said, "When Greg first came to my Italian family's get-togethers he would hardly speak. We usually had a fight on the way home. We later figured out he felt shut down whenever someone interrupted him in the middle of a story or a comment. Well, in my family interrupting is a sign of involvement. It means we're listening to you, egging you on.

"Greg comes from a German family where everyone politely takes turns responding to the previous comment. I go crazy—their conversation seems so boring and stilted. It helped us both to realize there is no 'right' or 'wrong' style of conversation—we were simply acting out of different cultural styles."

Everyone grows up with "rules" or assumptions about how life is supposed to operate. Marriage forces into close contact two people with different sets of shared meanings and then requires them to negotiate a common ground. Bill and Holly told of a disagreement that nearly ruined their Christmas vacation. Bill said, "We visited Holly's family, which is huge and intimidating. That Christmas, one of the sisters bought a VCR and television to present to the parents, without consulting the rest of the family. 'You guys can chip in anything you want,' she told her siblings and in-laws. 'I'll sign the card and present the gift as being from all of us.'

"To me this looked like a set-up job," Bill continued. "I felt pressure to come up with our fair share, which was a lot more than we would have spent on our own. I felt manipulated and angry, and Holly couldn't understand my feelings. She said her sister was absolutely sincere. 'Our family doesn't keep score,' she said. 'Ellen spontaneously felt like buying a present, and she'll be content whether everyone chips in one-eighth or if no one contributes anything. It's not 'tit-for-tat' like your family.'

"Holly was probably right. My family does keep score. You send a letter, you expect one in return. You give a gift, you expect one of equal value. I'm finally coming to grasp that Holly's family doesn't operate like mine."

Another couple, Gayle and Don, identified on-timeness as their major cross-cultural disagreement. Gayle grew up in a family that didn't notice if they were 10 or 15 minutes late, but Don wears a digital watch and follows it punctually. Several times a week they clash over this common cross-cultural difference. In Germany the trains run on time; in Mexico they get there—eventually.

Cross-cultural differences may seem trivial but, as many couples learn, on small rocks great ships wreck. It helps to know in advance where the rocks are.

Cross-Gender Communication

Communication can either span—or widen—the gender gap. Research shows that boys and girls grow up learning different styles of communicating. Boys tend to play in large groups that are hierarchically structured, with a leader who tells the others what to do and how to do it. Boys reinforce status by giving orders and enforcing them; their games have winners and losers and are run by elaborate rules. In contrast, girls play in small groups or in pairs, with "best friends." They strive for intimacy, not status.

These gender patterns continue into adulthood. A man relates to the world as an individual within a hierarchy; he measures himself against others and judges success or failure by his movement up or down the ladder. A woman approaches the world as a network of many social connections. For women, writes Deborah Tannen, "conversations are negotiations for closeness in which people try to seek and give confirmation and support, and to reach consensus."

Tannen's studies of the corporate world show it to be a male-dominated culture where men tend to make pronouncements, to surround themselves with symbols of status, to position themselves against one another, and to improve their standing by opposition. Women, though, tend to seek approval from others and thereby gain their sense of worth. Women are more inclined to be givers of praise than givers of information.

Our couples group agreed that Tannen's observations about the corporate world ring true. "I feel trapped," said Gayle, a management consultant. "At work I find myself changing in order to meet male expectations. I can't be tentative or solicit other people's reactions. I have to appear strong and confident whether I genuinely feel that way or not. I feel I'm losing my femininity."

Because women rely so strongly on feedback from others, they may hesitate to express themselves in a forthright, direct manner. As one psychologist says, "A man might ask a woman, 'Will you please go the store?' where a woman might say, 'I really need a few things from the store, but I'm so tired.'" A man might judge such behavior sneaky or underhanded, but such indirectness is actually the norm in many cultures.

For example, a direct approach such as, "I want to buy that cabbage for 50 cents" will get you nowhere in a Middle Eastern or African market. Both parties expect an elaborate social dance of bluff and innuendo. "If indirectness is understood by both parties, then there is nothing covert about it," Tannen concludes. The challenge in marriage is for both parties to recognize a communication style and learn to work within it.

Battle of the Sexes

We discovered that each couple in our group had what we called a Blamer and a Blamee; two of the Blamers were husbands, two were wives. The Blamer was usually a perfectionist, very detail-and task-oriented, who expected unrealistically high standards of the spouse. "No matter what I do," said one Blamee, "I can never measure up to my husband's standard of cooking or housekeeping or reading or sex, or anything. It's like I'm constantly being graded on my performance. And it doesn't motivate me to improve. I figure I'm not going to satisfy him anyway, so why try?"

All of us would like to make a few changes in the person we live with, but attempts to coax those changes often lead to conflict. And in conflict, gender differences rise quickly to the surface. Men, who grow up in a hierarchical environment, are accustomed to conflict. Women, concerned more with relationship and connection, prefer the role of peacemaker.

In my own marriage, for example, Janet and I view conflict through different eyes. As a writer, I thrive on criticism. I exchange manuscripts with other writers, and I've learned the best editors are the least diplomatic ones. I have two friends who pepper my manuscripts with words like "Ugh!" and "Awk!", and I would hesitate to publish any book without first running it through their gauntlet. In addition, I've gotten used to receiving heated letters from readers. Complimentary letters sound alike; angry letters fascinate me.

Janet, though, tends to feel criticism as a personal attack. I have learned much by watching her manage other people. Sensitive to criticism herself, she has become masterful at communicating criticism to others. When I managed employees in an office setting I would tend to blunder in with a straightforward approach: "There are five things you're doing right and five things you're doing wrong." After numerous failures, I began to see that the goal in criticism is to help the other person see the problem and desire to change. I have learned the necessity of communicating cross-culturally in my conflicts. When dealing with gluttons for punishment like me, I can be as direct as I want. For more sensitive persons, I need to exercise the skills I've gleaned from diplomats like my wife.

As our small group discussed various styles, we arrived at the following "guidelines" for conflict:

First, identify your fighting style. We tend to learn fighting styles from the family we grow up in. In Angie's Italian family, the fighting style was obvious: yell, argue and, if necessary, punch your brother in the nose. She approached marriage much the same way, only without the punches. Meanwhile, her husband would clam up and walk away from an argument. Angie thought Greg was deliberately ignoring her, and their conflicts never got resolved until they sought counseling. There, they realized that Greg was walking away because he knew he had no chance against Angie's well-honed fighting skills. Once both of them realized the dynamics behind their dead-end conflicts, they were able to make appropriate adjustments and change the "rules of engagement."

Second, agree on rules of engagement. Every couple needs to negotiate what constitutes "fighting fair." The couples in our group agreed to avoid these things: fighting in public, straying from the topic at hand, bringing up old history, threatening divorce and using sex as a way to paper over conflict. It's also helpful to consider additional rules, such as "Don't pretend to go along with a decision and then bring it up later as a matter of blame;" and "Don't resort to 'guerrilla warfare'—getting revenge by taking cheap shots after an argument is over."

Third, identify the real issue behind the conflict. A hidden message often underlies conflict. For example, women are sometimes accused of "nagging." On the surface, their message is the specific complaint at hand: not spending enough time with the kids, not helping with housework, coming home late from work. Actually, Deborah Tannen writes, there is another message at work:

"That women have been labeled 'nags' may result from the interplay of men's and women's styles, whereby many women are inclined to do what is asked of them and many men are inclined to resist even the slightest hint that anyone, especially a woman, is telling them what to do. A woman will be inclined to repeat a request that doesn't get a response because she is convinced that her husband would do what she asks if he only understood that she really wants him to do it. But a man who wants to avoid feeling that he is following orders may instinctively wait before doing what she asked in order to imagine that he is doing it of his own free will. Nagging is the result, because each time she repeats the request, he again puts off fulfilling it."

Spouses need to ask themselves questions like, "Is taking out the garbage really the issue, or is it a husband's crusty resistance to anything that infringes on his independence?"

Man Talk, and Woman Talk

In conversation, men and women appear to be doing the same thing—they open their mouths and produce noise. However, they actually use conversation for quite different purposes. Women use conversation primarily to form and solidify connections with other people. Men, on the other hand, tend to use words to navigate their way within the hierarchy. They do so by communicating their knowledge and skill, imparting information to others.

Women excel at what Tannen calls "private speaking" or "rapport-talk." Men feel most comfortable in "public speaking" or "report talk." Even though women may have more confidence in verbal ability (aptitude tests prove their superior skill), they are less likely to use that ability in a public context. Men feel comfortable giving reports to groups or interrupting a speaker with an objection—these are skills learned in the male hierarchy. Many women might perceive the same behavior as putting themselves on display. For example, at a party the men tell stories, share their expertise and tell jokes while the women usually converse in smaller groups about more personal subjects. They are busy connecting while the men are positioning themselves.

Our couples' group discussion became heated when we brought up another female trait that commonly goes by the name "bitching" (Tanner substituted the much more respectable term "ritual lament"). "Yeah, let's talk about this!" Greg said. "I remember one ski trip when I met some of my buddies in Colorado. We spent three days together before our wives joined us. We guys were having a great time, but when the women showed up everything changed. Nothing was right: The weather was too cold and the snow too crusty, the condo was drafty, the grocery store understocked, the hot tub dirty. Every night we heard them complain about sore muscles and raw places where the ski boots rubbed.

"The guys would listen to the griping, then just look at each other and say, 'The women are here!' It was incredible. We were living and skiing in exactly the same conditions. But before the women arrived, we had peace. Afterward, we heard nothing but gripes."

Tannen's explanation is that women tend to bond in pain. Through griping, they reaffirm connections with each other. For men, the immediate response to a complaint is to fix the problem. Otherwise, why complain? Women don't necessarily want the problem solved—who can "fix" the weather, for example? They merely want to feel understood and sympathized with.

Coming Together

Over several months our couples group gained an appreciation for the profound differences between male and female, but also a respect for how difficult it can be to pin down those differences.

Mary Crawford  **NO**

Talking Difference: On Gender and Language

Talking Across the Gender Gap

People believe in sex differences. As one best-selling book puts it, when it comes to communication, *Men are from Mars, Women are from Venus* (Gray, 1992). Social scientists have helped to create and confirm that belief by conducting innumerable studies of every conceivable linguistic and stylistic variation between the sexes and by developing theories that stress differences rather than similarities and overlap (West and Zimmerman, 1985). In *Language and Woman's Place* (1975) the linguist Robin Lakoff proposed that women use a speech style that is ineffectual because it is overly polite, hesitant, and deferent. The assertiveness training movement of the 1970s and 1980s—a therapeutic fad led by psychologists whose clients were largely women—engaged perhaps hundreds of thousands of people in attempts to change their way of communicating. A rationale for the movement was that some people (especially women) suffer from poor communication skills and irrational beliefs that prevent them from expressing themselves clearly and directly. More recently, linguists and communication experts have created another conceptual bandwagon by applying theories of cross-cultural communication to women and men. According to this view, 'men from Mars' and 'women from Venus' are fated to misunderstand each other unless they recognize their deeply socialized differences.

The view of gender and language encoded in these writings and therapies is that fundamental differences between women and men shape the way they talk. The differences are conceived as located within individuals and prior to the talk—as differences in personality traits, skills, beliefs, attitudes, or goals. For the millions of people who have become acquainted with issues of gender and language through reading best-selling books telling women how to be more assertive or how to understand the 'opposite' sex, or through watching television talk shows featuring communication experts who claim that talk between women and men is cross-cultural communication, a powerful narrative frame is provided and validated: that gender is difference, and difference is static, bipolar, and categorical. Absorbing such messages, it would be very difficult *not* to believe that women and men are indeed opposite sexes when it comes to talk. . . .

Two Sexes, Two Cultures

Cross-Cultural Talk . . .

Talking Across the Gender Divide

. . . When we think of distinct female and male subcultures we tend to think of societies in which women and men spend virtually their entire lives spatially and interactionally segregated; for example, those which practice purdah. In Western societies, however, girls and boys are brought up together. They share the use of common space in their homes; eat, work, and play with their siblings of both sexes; generally attend co-educational schools in which they are aggregated in many classes and activities. Both sexes are supervised, cared for, and taught largely by women in infancy and early childhood, with male teachers and other authority figures becoming more visible as children grow older. Moreover, they see these social patterns mirrored and even exaggerated in the mass media. How can the talk of Western women and men be seen as talk across cultures?

The two-cultures model was first applied to the speech of North American women and men by Daniel Maltz and Ruth Borker, who proposed that difficulties in cross-sex and cross-ethnic communication are 'two examples of the same larger phenomenon: cultural difference and miscommunication' (1982: 196). Maltz and Borker acknowledge the argument that American women and men interact with each other far too much to be characterized as living in different subcultures. However, they maintain that the social rules for friendly conversation are learned between the ages of approximately 5 and 15, precisely the time when children's play groups are maximally segregated by sex. Not only do children voluntarily choose to play in same-sex groups, they consciously exaggerate differences as they differentiate themselves from the other sex. Because of the very different social contexts in which they learn the meanings and goals of conversational interaction, boys and girls learn to use language in different ways.

Citing research on children's play, Maltz and Borker (1982) argue that girls learn to do three things with words:

1. to create and maintain relationships of closeness and equality;
2. to criticize others in acceptable (indirect) ways;
3. to interpret accurately and sensitively the speech of other girls.

In contrast, boys learn to do three very different things with words:

1. to assert one's position of dominance;
2. to attract and maintain an audience;
3. to assert oneself when another person has the floor.

The Two-Cultures Approach as Bandwagon

. . . The new twist in the two-cultures model of communication is to conceive relationship difficulties not as women's deficiencies but as an inevitable result of deeply ingrained male–female differences. The self-help books that encode a two-cultures model make the paradoxical claim that difference between the sexes is deeply socialized and/or fundamental to masculine and feminine natures, and at the same time subject to change and manipulation if the reader only follows prescribed ways of talking. Instead of catchy slogans and metaphors that stigmatize women (*Women who Love too Much*, Doris Doormat v. Agatha Aggressive) the equally catchy new metaphors glorify difference.

. . . Deborah Tannen's *You just don't Understand: Women and Men in Conversation* (1990) . . . has become a phenomenal success in the US. Acclaimed in the popular press as the 'Rosetta Stone that at last deciphers the miscommunication between the sexes' and as 'a Berlitz guidebook to the language and customs of the opposite gender [sic]' . . . Tannen claims that childhood play has shaped world views so that, when adult women and men are in relationships 'women speak and hear a language of connection and intimacy, while men speak and hear a language of status and independence' (1990: 42). The contrasting conversational goals of intimacy and independence lead to contrasting conversational styles. Women tell each other of their troubles, freely ask for information and help, and show appreciation of others' helping efforts. Men prefer to solve problems rather than talk about them, are reluctant to ask for help or advice, and are more comfortable in the roles of expert, lecturer, and teacher than learner or listener. Men are more talkative in public, women in private. These different styles are labelled 'report talk' (men's) and 'rapport talk' (women's).

Given the stylistic dichotomy between the sexes, miscommunication is almost inevitable; however, no one is to blame. Rather, another banner proclaims, 'The Key is Understanding:' 'Although each style is valid on its own terms, misunderstandings arise because the styles are different. Taking a cross-cultural approach to male–female conversations makes it possible to explain why dissatisfactions are justified without accusing anyone of being wrong or crazy' (1990: 47).

You just don't Understand makes its case for the two-cultures model skillfully and well using techniques that have become standard in popular writing about behavior: characterizations of 'most' women and men, entertaining anecdotes, and the presentation of research findings as fact. . . . Instead of advocating conversational formulae or regimented training programs for one sex, it recommends simply that people try to understand and accept sex differences and to be as flexible in style as possible. . . .

The Two-Cultures Approach: An Evaluation

Beyond Deficiencies and Blame

Proponents of the two-cultures model maintain that it is an advance over approaches that blame particular groups for miscommunication. . . .

Unlike earlier approaches, the two-cultures model does not characterize women's talk as deficient in comparison to a male norm. In contrast to the notion of an ineffectual 'female register' or the prescriptive masculine ideals of the assertiveness training movement, the two-cultures model problematizes the behavior of men as well as women. To John Gray, neither Mars nor Venus is a superior home. To Deborah Tannen, 'report talk' and 'rapport talk' are equally limiting for their users in cross-sex communication. The speech style attributed to men is no longer 'standard' speech or 'the language,' but merely one way of negotiating the social landscape.

A model of talk that transcends woman-blaming is less likely to lead to woman-as-problem research programs or to widespread attempts to change women through therapy and skills training. Moreover, ways of talking thought to characterize women can be positively revalued within this frame-work. In a chapter on gossip, Tannen notes that the negative connotation of the word reflects men's interpretation of women's ways of talking. But gossip can be thought of as 'talking about' rather than 'talking against.' It can serve crucial functions of establishing intimacy and rapport. . . .

Doing Gender, Doing Power

The two-cultures approach fails to theorize how power relations at the structural level are recreated and maintained at the interactional level. The *consequences* of 'miscommunication' are not the same for powerful and powerless groups. As Deborah Cameron (1985: 150) points out, 'The right to represent and stereotype is not mutual.' Stereotypes of less power-ful groups (immigrants, people of color) as inadequate speakers serve to ensure that no one need take seriously what these people say. People of color may have their own set of negative stereotypes of white people, but 'these are the ideas of people without power. They do not serve as a base for administrative procedures and decisions, nor do they get expressed routinely in mass media.' Recent research on the relationship between power and stereotyping suggests that people in power stereotype others partly as a cognitive 'shortcut' that minimizes the need to attend to them as individuals. People without power, of course, must attend carefully to their 'superiors' in order to avoid negative judgment or actual harm and cannot afford to use schematic shortcuts (Fiske, 1993).

'Negotiating status' is an evaluatively neutral term for interpersonal behaviors that consolidate power and maintain dominance. Ignoring the enactment of power and how it connects to structural power in gender relations does a disservice to sociolinguistics, distorting its knowledge base and undermining other more legitimate research approaches (Freed, 1992). Moreover, it badly misrepresents communication phenomena. Nancy Henley and Cheris Kramarae (1991) provide a detailed analysis of six 'cultural differences' in female–male speech styles taken from Maltz and Borker (1982), showing that they may be more plausibly interpreted as manifestations and exercises of power. For example, men's tendency to interpret questions as requests for information, and problem-sharing as an opportunity to give expert advice, can be viewed as prerogatives of power.

In choosing these speech strategies, men take to themselves the voice of authority.

This failure to recognize structural power and connect it with international power has provoked the strongest criticisms of the two-cultures approach. In a review of *You just don't Understand,* Senta Troemel-Ploetz (1991) pointed out that if the majority of relationships between women and men in our society were not fundamentally asymmetrical to the advantage of men,

> we would not need a women's liberation movement, women's commissions, houses for battered women, legislation for equal opportunity, antidiscrimination laws, family therapy, couple therapy, divorce . . . If you leave out power, you do not understand any talk, be it the discussion after your speech, the conversation at your own dinner-table, in a doctor's office, in the back yards of West Philadelphia, in an Italian village, on a street in Turkey, in a court room or in a day-care center, in a women's group or at a UN conference. It is like saying Black English and Oxford English are just two different varieties of English, each valid on its own; it just so happens that the speakers of one variety find themselves in high-paying positions with a lot of prestige and power of decision-making, and the others are found more in low-paying jobs, or on the streets and in prisons. They don't always understand each other, but they both have the best intentions; if they could only learn a bit from each other and understand their differences as a matter of style, all would be well. (Troemel-Ploetz, 1991: 497–8)

No one involved in debating the two-cultures approach denies that men have more social and political power than women. Maltz and Borker (1982: 199) acknowledge that power differentials 'may make some contribution' to communication patterns. However, they do not theorize the workings of power in interaction or advocate structural changes to reduce inequity.

The Bandwagon Revisited

There is no inherent limitation to the two-cultures approach that would prevent its development as a theory of difference *and* dominance, a theory that could encompass the construction of gendered subjectivities, the reproduction of inequality in interaction, and the role of interaction in sustaining gendered social structures. It is therefore the more disappointing that in the popularized versions that have influenced perhaps millions of people, it is flattened into an account of sex dichotomies. And this is why the model has been so harshly evaluated by feminist scholars. Perhaps unfortunately, the more egregious versions have been largely ignored and the more scholarly one attacked. Deborah Tannen's critics have charged that, despite the absence of overt women-blaming and the positive evaluation of 'feminine' modes of talk, the interpretations she offers often disguise or gloss over inequity, and privilege men's interpretations (Freed, 1992; Troemel-Ploetz, 1991). They have accused her of being an apologist for men, excusing their insensitivity, rudeness, and dominance as mere stylistic quirks, and encouraging women to make the adjustments when needs conflict (Freed, 1992). Indeed, the interpretations Tannen offers for the many anecdotes that enliven her book often read as though the past two decades of women's studies scholarship had never occurred, and there were no feminist analyses available with which to contextualize gendered behavior (Troemel-Ploetz, 1991).

You just don't Understand is apolitical—a choice which is in itself a political act, and a significant one at that, given that the book has sold well over a million copies. Like the popular psychology of the assertiveness training movement, it does not threaten the status quo (Troemel-Ploetz, 1991). Like its pop-psychology companions on the bookstore shelves, it offers something to both the powerful and those over whom they have power: to men, a compelling rationale of blame-free difference and to women a comforting promise of mutual accommodation.

Let us consider [two] examples, from [two] types of conversational setting, to illustrate how the accounts of interaction in *You just don't Understand* might be reinterpreted in light of research on women and gender. The first is an anecdote about Josh and Linda. When an old friend calls Josh at work with plans for a visit nearby on business, Josh invites him to spend the weekend and makes plans to go out with him Friday night. These plans are made without consulting with Linda, who protests that Josh should have checked with her, especially since she will be returning from a business trip herself that day. Tannen's explanation of the misunderstanding is in terms of an autonomy/intimacy dichotomy. Linda likes to have her life entwined with Josh's, to consult and be consulted about plans. Josh feels that checking with her implies a loss of independence. 'Linda was hurt because she sensed a failure of closeness in their relationship . . . he was hurt because he felt she was trying to control him and limit his freedom' (1990: 27).

No resolution of the conflict is provided in the anecdote; the implication is that Josh's plans prevail. Interpreting this story in terms of women's needs for intimacy and men's for autonomy glosses the fact that Josh has committed mutual resources (living space, food, the time and work required to entertain a houseguest) on behalf of himself and his partner without acknowledgement that the partner should have a voice in that decision. His behavior seems to reflect the belief that the time and energy of others (women) are to be accommodated to men. As a test of the fairness of his behavior, imagine that Josh were living with a male housemate. To invite a mutual weekend guest without consulting the housemate would be considered overtly rude. The housemate (but not the woman in a heterosexual couple) would be warranted in refusing to cooperate, because he is seen as entitled to make his own plans and control his own resources. A sense of entitlement to act entirely on one's own and make decisions unilaterally is 'part of the social empowerment that men enjoy. It has precious little to do with communicative style or language' (Freed, 1992: 4). . . .

In a section titled 'First Me, Then Me,' Tannen describes her own experience of discourse in a professional setting. Seated at a faculty dinner next to a woman, she enjoyed a mutually informative and pleasant discussion in which each talked about her research and explored connections and overlaps. Turning to a male guest, she initiated a conversation in a similar way.

However, the conversation proceeded very differently:

> During the next half hour, I learned a lot about his job, his research, and his background. Shortly before the dinner ended there was a lull, and he asked me what I did. When I said I was a linguist, he became excited and told me about a research project he had conducted that was related to neurolinguistics. He was still telling me about his research when we all got up to leave the table. (1990: 126)

Lecturing, says Tannen, is part of a male style. And women let them get away with it. Because women's style includes listening attentively and not interrupting, they do not jump in, challenge, or attempt to deflect the lecturer. Men assume that if their partner had anything important to say, she would say it. The two styles interact to produce silent women, who nod and smile although they are bored, and talkative men, who lecture at length though they themselves may be bored and frustrated by the lack of dialogue. Thus, apparent conversational dominance is not something men deliberately do to women. Neither is it something women culpably permit. The imbalance is created by 'habitual styles.'

The stylistic interpretation discounts the possibility that the male academic in this example did not want to hear about his female dinner companion's research because he did not care about it. That women and what they do are valued less than men and what they do is one of the fundamental insights of feminism. The history of women in the professions provides ample evidence of exclusion, discrimination, and marginalization. Methods vary: plagiarizing women's work (Spender, 1989), denigrating them as unfeminine while stealing their ideas (Sayre, 1975), denying them employment (Crawford, 1981; Scarborough and Furumoto, 1987) and recognition (Nochlin, 1971). When women compete successfully in male domains, they are undermined by sexual harassment (Gutek, 1985) and by being represented as sex objects (a long-running 1980s ad campaign featured female physicians and attorneys making medical rounds and appearing in court in their underwear) (Lott, 1985). In short, there is not yet much reason to believe that women in the professions are routinely taken as seriously as their male peers. And the academy is no exception. What Tannen explains as mere stylistic differences have the effect of keeping women and their work invisible, and have had documented consequences on women's hiring, promotion, and tenure (Caplan, 1993). . . .

A Rhetoric of Reassurance

The rhetoric of difference makes everyone—and no one—responsible for interpersonal problems. Men are not to blame for communication difficulties; neither is a social system in which gender governs access to resources. Instead, difference is reified: 'The culprit, then is not an individual man or even men's styles alone, but the difference between women and men's styles' (Tannen, 1990: 95).

One of the most striking effects achieved in these books is to reassure women that their lot in heterosexual relationships is normal. Again and again, it is stressed that no one is to blame, that miscommunication is inevitable, that unsatisfactory results may stem from the best of intentions. As these explanations dominate the public realm of discourse about gender, they provide 'one more pseudo-explanation' and 'one more ingenious strategy for not tackling the root causes of women's subordinate status' (Cameron, in press).

Its very ubiquity has made inequality of status and power in heterosexual relationships seem unremarkable, and one of the most important contributions of feminist research has been to make it visible (Wilkinson and Kitzinger, 1993). In the discourse of miscommunication the language feminists have developed to theorize status and power is neutralized. Concepts such as sexism, sex discrimination, patriarchy, and gender inequity are barely mentioned, and conversational strategies that have the effect of silencing women are euphemized as stylistic 'asymmetries.' For example, Tannen explains that when men do most of the talking in a group, it is not because they intend to prevent women from speaking or believe that women have nothing important to say. Rather, they see the women as *equals,* and expect them to compete in the same style they themselves use. Thus, an inequity that feminists have conceptualized in terms of power differentials is acknowledged, but explained as an accidental imbalance created by style and having little to do with a gendered social order.

Power dynamics in heterosexual relationships are obscured by the kinds of intentions imputed to speakers. Both books presume an innocence of communicative intent. In the separate and simplistic worlds of Martians and Venusians, women just want to be cherished and men just want to be needed and admired. In the separate worlds of 'report talk' and 'rapport talk', the goal may be sex-specific but the desire is the same: to be understood and responded to in kind. In *You just don't Understand,* each anecdote is followed by an analysis of the intentions of *both* speakers, a practice that Tannen (1992) feels reflects her fairness to both sexes. But this symmetry is false, because the one kind of intention that is never imputed to any speaker is the intent to dominate. Yet people are aware of such intentions in their talk, and, when asked, can readily describe the verbal tactics they use to 'get their own way' in heterosexual interactions (Falbo, 1982; Falbo and Peplau, 1980; Kelley et al., 1978). Tannen acknowledges the role of power in conversational dynamics (cf. p. 283, 'We enact and create our gender, and our inequality, with every move we make'). But the rhetorical force of the anecdotes is about difference. When an anecdote seems obviously explainable in terms of dominance strategies, the possibility of such an account is often acknowledged but discounted. The characteristics that the two-cultures model posit for females' speech are ones appropriate to friendly conversation, while the characteristics posited for men's speech are not neutral, but indicate uncooperative, dominating and disruptive interaction (Henley and Kramarae, 1991). Whose needs are being served when intent to dominate is ruled out *a priori* in accounting for cross-sex conversation?

Many of the most compelling anecdotes describe situations in which a woman is hurt, frustrated or angered by a man's apparently selfish or dominating behavior, only to find that her feelings were unwarranted because the man's intentions were good. This is psychologically naive. There is no reason to believe that *post hoc* stated intentions are a complete and sufficient description of conversational motives. . . .

The emphasis on interpreting a partner's intentions is problematic in other ways as well. As Nancy Henley and Cheris Kramarae (1991: 42) point out, '[F]emales are required to develop special sensitivity to interpret males' silence, lack of emotional expressiveness, or brutality, and to help men express themselves, while men often seem to be trained deliberately to misinterpret much of women's meaning.' Young girls are told that hitting, teasing, and insults are to be read as signs of boys' 'liking.' Adolescent girls are taught to take responsibility for boys' inexpressiveness by drawing them out in conversation, steering talk to topics that will make them feel comfortable, and being a good listener. . . .

Analyzing conversation in terms of intentions has a very important implication: it deflects attention from *effects,* including the ways that everyday action and talk serve to recreate and maintain current gender arrangements.

POSTSCRIPT

Are Communication Problems Between Men and Women Largely Due to Radically Different Conversation Styles?

One of Crawford's concerns is the demeaning picture of women that the literature on gender differences in communication styles often suggests. Men are problem solvers and stand on their own two feet, while women are people pleasers and dependent. Men, however, could also feel put down. According to the theory, men are predominantly interested in defending and advancing their status, even to the point of stepping on toes and jeopardizing closeness. This makes men out to be rather immoral. Self-promotion and the need to dominate others is not sanctioned by most religions or appreciated much by most people. Women come closer to religious and popular ideals than men do. To their credit, they bond, love, and share more through communication than men do, and women do so without necessarily sacrificing their competence in the process.

Many issues regarding gender differences in communication styles remain murky. Everyone, including Crawford, acknowledges that there are talking differences between genders, but how big are these differences? This relates to the large question of how different men and women are on other significant dimensions. What causes these differences? To what extent are they biological and hormonal, and to what extent are they due to differential socialization and different positions in society? How changeable are these differences? Should they be changed?

The past two decades have produced considerable research on gender differences in communication styles, which is reflected in several readers and academic works. Deborah Tannen is prominent in this literature, see Tannen's *You Just Don't Understand: Women and Men in Conversation* (Ballantine Books, 1991); and *Gender and Discourse* (Oxford University Press, 1994). See also Deborah Cameron, ed., *The Feminist Critique of Language: A Reader,* 2d ed. (Routledge, 1998); Jennifer Coates, ed., *Language and Gender: A Reader* (Blackwell, 1998); Mary Bucholtz, A. C. Liang, and Laurel A. Sutton, eds., *Reinventing Identities: The Gendered Self in Discourse* (Oxford University Press, 1999); Judith Baxter, *Positioning Gender in Discourse: a Feminist Methodology* (Palgrave Macmillan, 2003); Robert Hopper, *Gendering Talk* (Michigan State University Press, 2003); and Jennifer Coates, *Men Talk: Stories in the Making of Masculinities* (Blackwell, 2003).

ISSUE 6

Should Same-Sex Marriages Be Legally Recognized?

YES: Lambda Legal Defense and Education Fund, from "Talking about the Freedom to Marry: Why Same-Sex Couples Should Have Equality in Marriage," LLDEF website (June 20, 2001)

NO: Sam Schulman, from "Gay Marriage—and Marriage," *Commentary* (November 2003)

ISSUE SUMMARY

YES: The Lambda Legal Defense and Education Fund, which is a national advocacy group for gay rights, has presented the major arguments for same-sex marriage in a position statement.

NO: Writer Sam Schulman argues that traditions have great value, and the negative consequences of redefining marriage would be serious. For one thing, to allow gay marriages would judicially open the door for all kinds of marriages including polygamous and incestual marriages.

In 1979 in Sioux Falls, South Dakota, Randy Rohl and Grady Quinn became the first acknowledged homosexual couple in America to receive permission from their high school principal to attend the senior prom together. The National Gay Task Force hailed the event as a milestone in the progress of human rights. It is unclear what the voters of Sioux Falls thought about it, since it was not put up to a vote. However, if their views were similar to those of voters in Dade County, Florida; Houston, Texas; Wichita, Kansas; and various localities in the state of Oregon, they probably were not pleased. In referenda held in these and other areas, voters have reversed decisions by legislators and local boards that banned discrimination by sexual preference.

Yet the attitude of Americans toward the rights of homosexuals is not easy to pin down. Voters have also defeated resolutions such as the one in California in 1978 that would have banned the hiring of homosexual schoolteachers, or the one on the Oregon ballot in 1992 identifying homosexuality as "abnormal, wrong, unnatural and perverse." In some states, notably Colorado, voters have approved initiatives widely perceived as antihomosexual. But, almost invariably, these resolutions have been carefully worded so as to appear to oppose "special" rights for homosexuals. In general, polls show that a large majority of Americans believe that homosexuals should have equal rights with heterosexuals with regard to job opportunities. On the other hand, many view homosexuality as morally wrong.

Currently, same-sex marriages are not legally recognized by Congress. In the Defense of Marriage Act of 1996, Congress defined marriage as heterosexual. A state does not have to recognize another state's nonheterosexual marriage. The legal situation is constantly changing. Several states have legalized same-sex civil unions, and San Francisco and Massachusetts have legalized same-sex marriages. These developments have prompted President Bush to propose a Constitutional Amendment limiting marriage to the union of a man and a women.

The issue of same-sex marriage fascinates sociologists because it represents a basic change in a major social institution and is being played out on several fields: legal, cultural/moral, and behavioral. The legal debate will be decided by courts and legislatures; the cultural/moral debate is open to all of us; and the behavioral debate will be conducted by the activists on both sides. In the readings that follow, the Lambda Legal Defense and Education Fund presents the major arguments for same-sex marriages, and Sam Schulman argues that marriage must remain heterosexual.

 **YES**

Talking About the Freedom to Marry: Why Same-Sex Couples Should Have Equality in Marriage

Today, same-sex couples are not allowed to marry in any state—no matter how long they have been together, no matter how committed they are to their relationship or their children, no matter how much they have already assumed the same responsibilities as different-sex married couples, and no matter how much their families need the protections and benefits that come with civil marriage.

Same-sex couples want the right to marry for the same reasons different-sex couples do.

Same-sex couples want to get married for the same variety of reasons as any other couple: they seek the security and protection that come from a legal union both for themselves and for any children they may have; they want the recognition from family, friends and the outside world that comes with a marriage; and they seek the structure and support for their emotional and economic bonds that a marriage provides. All gay people, whether in a relationship today or not, whether they would choose marriage or not, deserve to have the same choice that all heterosexuals have.

The government should fully recognize same-sex couples as it does different-sex couples.

Marriage is a civil right that belongs to everyone. Loving, committed same-sex couples form families and provide emotional and economic support for each other and for their children just like other couples do. When different-sex couples apply for a marriage license, the state does not ask them whether their relationship is worthy of its recognition, because the government has no business deciding whom a person should marry. That is a completely private, personal choice that every individual has the right to make for him or herself—a basic principle that should be as true for same-sex couples as for other couples.

> *This inequality in access to marriage should end, just as our nation has abolished prior discriminatory exclusions.*

This is not the first instance of unlawful governmental interference with the freedom to marry. Less than forty years ago, many states prohibited interracial couples from legally marrying. In *Loving v. Virginia,* a married interracial couple was arrested in Virginia and faced up to five years in prison. The state court upheld their conviction because it found interracial relationships to be "unnatural":

> "Almighty God created the races white, black, yellow, malay and red, and he placed them on separate continents. And but for the interference with his arrangement there would be no cause for such marriages. The fact that he separated the races shows that he did not intend for the races to mix."

Similar arguments are used against recognizing same-sex relationships today. But the U.S. Supreme Court held in its 1967 decision in the case that restricting marriage to same-race couples was unlawful discrimination. The government's restriction of marriage to different-sex couples is discriminatory as well. The choice of a marriage partner belongs to each individual, not to the state.

Responses to Some Possible Concerns and Comments

> *"Tradition" is not a reason to deny marriage to same-sex couples.*

Marriage was "traditionally" defined as a union of two people of the same religion or the same race, or one in which wives were the property of their husbands. Those "traditional" elements of marriage changed to reflect this nation's core principles of equality for all people. Marriage should be defined to include the committed relationships of same-sex couples as well.

> *Raising children is one of many reasons for marriage, and same-sex couples do raise children.*

Marriage is not only about procreation—many people marry who cannot have or choose not to have children. Marriage is about love between two adults who want to live in a committed relationship, with or without children. The state extends the same marital protections to couples who are infertile or couples who are past childbearing age that it extends to couples intending to have multiple children. It is also a fact that more and more lesbian and gay couples are raising children together. Marriage would create automatic protections for these children that now may have to be created through adoption or elaborate legal documents.

The right to a civil marriage is not a right to a religious ceremony.

Couples who wish legal recognition for their marriage must first get a license issued by the government and then have an authorized person marry them. This is a civil marriage. Depending on the state, the person who marries the couple may be a government official (such as a justice of the peace or city hall official) or an otherwise authorized individual (such as some clergy). But if the couple asks a clergyperson to marry them, that clergyperson can always say no, meaning that the couple would have to ask some other authorized person.

- Religious groups retain the right to marry or not to marry couples, as they wish, according to their religious principles.
- Though many faiths do perform marriage ceremonies for same-sex couples, at present these marriages have no legal recognition because they have not been licensed by the government, and thus are not civil marriages.
- Religions should not dictate who gets a marriage license from the state, just as the state should not dictate which marriage any religion performs or recognizes.

For those couples desiring the full structure and status of marriage, domestic partner benefits are inadequate.

In certain cities, states or companies, there is limited recognition of relationships between unmarried partners, often including both different-sex couples and same-sex couples. As domestic partners, couples may gain access to health care coverage and certain other basic family benefits. But many couples wish to structure their families around a broader set of rights and responsibilities. For these couples, domestic partnership is no substitute for civil marriage.

Civil unions are an important step forward, but separate is still unequal.

Vermont offers "civil unions" to same-sex couples. Civil unions provide a set of rights and responsibilities within Vermont that parallels marriage. This is an important step forward. It is not marriage, however, and its implications beyond Vermont have yet to be determined by the courts. It is a separate and unequal institution, setting same-sex couples apart for second-class citizenship in the eyes of others, which will carry over into how such couples are treated in other areas of their lives. Having the choice to marry is full equality. A separate, gay-only institution is not.

The sky will not fall because of equality for same-sex couples.

When opponents are desperate for arguments, they resort to familiar "the sky will fall" claims, such as the argument that allowing same-sex couples to marry could be followed by demands to legalize polygamy. This is a scare tactic, not an argument. Same-sex *couples* want the freedom to marry that is currently taken for granted by different-sex *couples*. The issue is about legal recognition for *couples*.

Allowing same-sex couples to marry does not destabilize marriage.

Allowing all families access to marriage, if they believe the structures and protections of marriage are appropriate for them, promotes stability for communities overall. Same-sex couples build their lives together like other couples, working hard at their jobs, volunteering in their neighborhoods, and valuing the responsibilities and love that their family commitments provide to them and to the children they may have. These families have everyday concerns, like being financially sound, emotionally and physically healthy, and protected by adequate health insurance. These concerns heighten when there are children in the family. Marriage provides tangible protections that address many of these concerns. Promotion of support and security for families is a benefit to the entire community; it does not de-stabilize other families. Equal access to marriage will also emphasize equality and non-discrimination for all of society.

Gay Marriage—and Marriage

The feeling seems to be growing that gay marriage is inevitably coming our way in the U.S., perhaps through a combination of judicial fiat and legislation in individual states. Growing, too, is the sense of a shift in the climate of opinion. The American public seems to be in the process of changing its mind—not actually in favor of gay marriage, but toward a position of slightly revolted tolerance for the idea. Survey results suggest that people have forgotten why they were so opposed to the notion even as recently as a few years ago.

It is curious that this has happened so quickly. With honorable exceptions, most of those who are passionately on the side of the traditional understanding of marriage appear to be at a loss for words to justify their passion; as for the rest, many seem to wish gay marriage had never been proposed in the first place, but also to have resigned themselves to whatever happens. In this respect, the gay-marriage debate is very different from the abortion debate, in which few with an opinion on either side have been so disengaged.

I think I understand why this is the case: as someone passionately and instinctively opposed to the idea of homosexual marriage, I have found myself disappointed by the arguments I have seen advanced against it. The strongest of these arguments predict measurable harm to the family and to our arrangements for the upbringing and well-being of children. I do not doubt the accuracy of those arguments.[1] But they do not seem to get at the heart of the matter.

To me, what is at stake in this debate is not only the potential unhappiness of children, grave as that is; it is our ability to maintain the most basic components of our humanity. I believe, in fact, that we are at an "Antigone moment." Some of our fellow citizens wish to impose a radically new understanding upon laws and institutions that are both very old and fundamental to our organization as individuals and as a society. As Antigone said to Creon, we are being asked to tamper with "unwritten and unfailing laws, not of now, nor of yesterday; they always live, and no one knows their origin in time." I suspect, moreover, that everyone knows this is the case, and that, paradoxically, this very awareness of just how much is at stake is what may have induced, in defenders of those same "unwritten and unfailing laws," a kind of paralysis.

Admittedly, it is very difficult to defend that which is both ancient and "unwritten"—the arguments do not resolve themselves into a neat parade of documentary evidence, research results, or citations from the legal literature. Admittedly, too, proponents of this radical new understanding have been uncommonly effective in presenting their program as something that is not radical at all but as requiring merely a slight and painless adjustment in our customary arrangements. Finally, we have all learned to practice a certain deference to the pleas of minorities with a grievance, and in recent years no group has benefited more from this society-wide dispensation than homosexuals. Nevertheless, in the somewhat fragmentary notes that follow, I hope to re-articulate what I am persuaded everyone knows to be the case about marriage, and perhaps thereby encourage others with stronger arguments than mine to help break the general paralysis.

Let us begin by admiring the case *for* gay marriage. Unlike the case for completely unrestricted abortion, which has come to be something of an embarrassment even to those who advance it, the case for gay marriage enjoys the decided advantage of appealing to our better moral natures as well as to our reason. It deploys two arguments. The first centers on principles of justice and fairness and may be thought of as the civil-rights argument. The second is at once more personal and more utilitarian, emphasizing the degradation and unhappiness attendant upon the denial of gay marriage and, conversely, the human and social happiness that will flow from its legal establishment. . . .

The civil-rights argument goes like this. Marriage is a legal state conferring real, tangible benefits on those who participate in it: specifically, tax breaks as well as other advantages when it comes to inheritance, property ownership, and employment benefits. But family law, since it limits marriage to heterosexual couples over the age of consent, clearly discriminates against a segment of the population. It is thus a matter of simple justice that, in Sullivan's words, "all public (as opposed to private) discrimination against homosexuals be ended and that every right and responsibility that heterosexuals enjoy as public citizens be extended to those who grow up and find themselves emotionally different." Not to grant such rights, Sullivan maintains, is to impose on homosexuals a civil deprivation akin to that suffered by black Americans under Jim Crow.

The utilitarian argument is more subtle; just as the rights argument seems aimed mainly at liberals, this one seems mostly to have in mind the concerns of conservatives. In light of the disruptive, anarchic, violence-prone behavior of many homosexuals (the argument runs), why should we *not* encourage the formation of stable, long-term, monogamous relationships that will redound to the health of society as a whole? In the apt words of a letter-writer in COMMENTARY in 1996:

> [H]omosexual marriage . . . preserves and promotes a set of moral values that are essential to civilized society. Like heterosexual marriage, it sanctions loyalty, unselfishness, and sexual fidelity; it rejects the promiscuous, the self-serving, the transitory relationship. Given the choice between building family units and preventing them, any conservative should favor the former.

. . . In brief, legalizing gay marriage would, in Andrew Sullivan's summary formulation,

> offer homosexuals the same deal society now offers heterosexuals: general social approval and specific legal advantages in exchange for a deeper and harder-to-extract-yourself-from commitment to another human being. Like straight marriage, it would foster social cohesion, emotional security, and economic prudence.

The case is elegant, and it is compelling. But it is not unanswerable. And answers have indeed been forthcoming, even if, as I indicated at the outset, many of them have tended to be couched somewhat defensively. Thus, rather than repudiating the very idea of an abstract "right" to marry, many upholders of the traditional definition of marriage tacitly concede such a right, only going on to suggest that denying it to a minority amounts to a lesser hurt than conferring it would impose on the majority, and especially on children, the weakest members of our society.

Others, to be sure, have attacked the Bawer/Sullivan line more forthrightly. In a September 2000 article in COMMENTARY, "What Is Wrong with Gay Marriage," Stanley Kurtz challenged the central contention that marriage would do for gay men what it does for straights—e.g., "domesticate" their natural male impulse to promiscuity. Citing a number of academic "queer theorists" and radical gays, Kurtz wrote:

> In contrast to moderates and "conservatives" like Andrew Sullivan, who consistently play down [the] difference [between gays and straights] in order to promote their vision of gays as monogamists-in-the-making, radical gays have argued—more knowledgeably, more powerfully, and more vocally than any opponent of same-sex marriage would dare to do—that homosexuality, and particularly male homosexuality, is by its very nature incompatible with the norms of traditional monogamous marriage.

True, Kurtz went on, such radical gays nevertheless support same-sex marriage. But what motivates them is the hope of "eventually undoing the institution [of marriage] altogether," by delegitimizing age-old understandings of the family and thus (in the words of one such radical) "striking at the heart of the organization of Western culture and societies."

Nor are radical gays the only ones to entertain such destructive ambitions. Queuing up behind them, Kurtz warned, are the proponents of polygamy, polyandry, and polyamorism, all ready to argue that their threesomes, foursomes, and other "nontraditional" arrangements are entitled to the same rights as everyone else's. In a recent piece in the *Weekly Standard*, Kurtz has written that the "bottom" of this particular slippery slope is "visible from where we stand." . . .

Like other critics of same-sex marriage, Kurtz has himself been vigorously criticized, especially by Sullivan. But he is almost certainly correct as to political and legal realities. If we grant rights to one group because they have demanded it—which is, practically, how legalized gay marriage will come to pass—we will find it exceedingly awkward to deny similar rights to others ready with their own dossiers of "victimization." In time, restricting marriage rights to couples, whether straight or gay, can be made to seem no less arbitrary than the practice of restricting marriage rights to one man and one woman. Ultimately, the same must go for incestuous relationships between consenting adults—a theme to which I will return.

A different defense of heterosexual marriage has proceeded by circling the wagons around the institution itself. According to this school of thought, ably represented by the columnist Maggie Gallagher, the essential purpose of that institution is to create stable families:

> Most men and women are powerfully drawn to perform a sexual act that can and does generate life. Marriage is our attempt to reconcile and harmonize the erotic, social, sexual, and financial needs of men and women with the needs of their partner and their children.

Even childless marriages protect this purpose, writes Gallagher, by ensuring that, as long as the marriage exists, neither the childless husband nor the childless wife is likely to father or mother children outside of wedlock.

Gallagher is especially strong on the larger, social meaning of heterosexual marriage, which she calls "inherently normative":

> The laws of marriage do not create marriage, but in societies ruled by law they help trace the boundaries and sustain the public meanings of marriage. . . . Without this shared, public aspect, perpetuated generation after generation, marriage becomes what its critics say it is: a mere contract, a vessel with no particular content, one of a menu of sexual lifestyles, of no fundamental importance to anyone outside a given relationship.

Human relationships are by nature difficult enough, Gallagher reminds us, which is why communities must do all they can to strengthen and not to weaken those institutions that keep us up to a mark we may not be able to achieve through our own efforts. The consequences of not doing so will be an intensification of all the other woes of which we have so far had only a taste in our society and which are reflected in the galloping statistics of illegitimacy, cohabitation, divorce, and fatherlessness. For Gallagher, the modest request of gay-marriage advocates for "a place at the table" is thus profoundly selfish as well as utterly destructive—for gay marriage "would require society at large to gut marriage of its central presumptions about family in order to accommodate a few adults' desires." . . .

To grasp what is at the other edge of that wedge—that is, what stands to be undone by gay marriage—we have to distinguish marriage itself from a variety of other goods and values with which it is regularly associated by its defenders and its aspirants alike. Those values—love and monogamous sex and establishing a home, fidelity, childbearing and childrearing, stability, inheritance, tax breaks, and all the rest—are not the same as marriage. True, a good marriage generally contains them, a bad marriage is generally deficient in them, and in law, religion, and custom, even under the strictest of moral regimes, their absence can be grounds for ending the union. But the *essence* of marriage resides elsewhere, and those who seek to arrange a kind of marriage for the inherently unmarriageable are looking for those things in the wrong place. . . .

The truth is banal, circular, but finally unavoidable: by definition, the essence of marriage is to sanction and solemnize that connection of opposites which alone creates new life. (Whether or not a given married couple does in fact create new life is immaterial.) Men and women *can* marry only because they belong to different, opposite, sexes. In marriage, they surrender those separate and different sexual allegiances, coming together to form a new entity. Their union is not a formalizing of romantic love but represents a certain idea—a construction, an abstract thought—about how best to formalize the human condition. This thought, embodied in a promise or a contract, is what holds marriage together, and the creation of this idea of marriage marks a key moment in the history of human development, a triumph over the alternative idea, which is concubinage.

Let me try to be more precise. Marriage can only concern my connection to a woman (and not to a man) because, as my reference to concubinage suggests, marriage is an institution that is built around female sexuality and female procreativity. (The very word "marriage" comes from the Latin word for mother, *mater.*) It exists for the gathering-in of a woman's sexuality under the protective net of the human or divine order, or both. This was so in the past and it is so even now, in our supposedly liberated times, when a woman who is in a sexual relationship without being married is, and is perceived to be, in a different state of being (not just a different legal state) from a woman who is married.

Circumstances have admittedly, changed. Thanks to contraception, the decision to marry no longer precedes sexual intercourse as commonly as it did 50 years ago, when, for most people, a fully sexual relationship could begin only with marriage (and, when, as my mother constantly reminds me, one married *for* sex). Now the decision can come later; but come it almost certainly must. Even with contraception, even with feminism and women's liberation, the feeling would appear to be nearly as strong as ever that, for a woman, a sexual relationship must either end in marriage, or end.

This is surely understandable, for marriage *benefits* women, again not just in law but essentially. A woman can control who is the father of her children only insofar as there is a civil and private order that protects her from rape; marriage is the bulwark of that order. . . .

For a woman, the fundamental advantage of marriage is thus not to regulate her husband but to empower herself—to regulate who has access to her person, and to marshal the resources of her husband and of the wider community to help her raise her children. . . .

Why should I not be able to marry a man? The question addresses a class of human phenomena that can be described in sentences but nonetheless cannot be. However much I might wish to, I cannot be a father to a pebble—I cannot be a brother to a puppy—I cannot make my horse my consul. Just so, I cannot, and should not be able to, marry a man. If I want to be a brother to a puppy, are you abridging my rights by not permitting it? I may say what I please; saying it does not mean that it can be.

In a gay marriage, one of two men must play the woman, or one of two women must play the man. "Play" here means travesty—burlesque. Not that their love is a travesty; but their participation in a ceremony that apes the marriage bond, with all that goes into it, is a travesty. Their taking-over of the form of this crucial and fragile connection of opposites is a travesty of marriage's purpose of protecting, actually and symbolically, the woman who enters into marriage with a man. To burlesque that purpose weakens those protections, and is essentially and profoundly anti-female. . . .

Marriage, to say it for the last time, is what connects us with our nature and with our animal origins, with how all of us, heterosexual and homosexual alike, came to be. It exists not because of custom, or because of a conspiracy (whether patriarchal or matriarchal), but because, through marriage, the *world* exists. Marriage is how we are connected backward in time, through the generations, to our Creator (or, if you insist, to the primal soup), and forward to the future beyond the scope of our own lifespan. It is, to say the least, bigger than two hearts beating as one.

Severing this connection by defining it out of existence—cutting it down to size, transforming it into a mere contract between chums—sunders the natural laws that prevent concubinage and incest. Unless we resist, we will find ourselves entering on the path to the abolition of the human. The gods move very fast when they bring ruin on misguided men.

Note

1. For a summary of the scant research on children raised in homes with same-sex parents as of six or seven years ago, see James Q. Wilson, "Against Homosexual Marriage," in Commentary, March 1996.

POSTSCRIPT

Should Same-Sex Marriages Be Legally Recognized?

The issue of the rights of homosexuals creates a social dilemma. Most people would agree that all members of society should have equal rights. However, the majority may disapprove of the lifestyles of a minority group and pass laws against some of their behaviors. The question is: When do these laws violate civil rights? Are laws against same-sex marriage such a violation?

There is a considerable literature on homosexuality and the social and legal status of homosexuals. Recent works on gay marriage include David Moats, *Civil Wars: A Battle for Gay Marriage* (Harcourt, 2004); Evan Gerstmann, *Same-Sex Marriage and the Constitution* (Cambridge University Press, 2004); *Marriage and Same-Sex Unions: A Debate* edited by Lynn D. Wardle, et al. (Praeger, 2003); Martin Dupuis, *Same-Sex Marriage, Legal Mobilization, and the Politics of Rights* (Peter Lang, 2002); and Kevin Bourassa, *Just Married: Gay Marriage and the Expansion of Human Rights* (University of Wisconsin Press, 2002). Recent works on the history of the gay rights movement include Dudley Clendinen and Adam Nagourney, *Out for Good: The Struggle to Build a Gay Rights Movement in America* (Simon & Schuster, 1999); Ronald J. Hunt, *Historical Dictionary of the Gay Liberation Movement* (Scarecrow Press, 1999); JoAnne Myers, *Historical Dictionary of the Lesbian Liberation Movement: Still the Rage* (Scarecrow Press, 2003); and John Loughery, *The Other Side of Silence: Men's Lives and Gay Identities: A Twentieth-Century History* (Henry Holt, 1998). For broad academic works on homosexuality see Kath Weston, *Long Slow Burn: Sexuality and Social Science* (Routledge, 1998); and Michael Ruse, *Homosexuality: A Philosophical Inquiry* (Blackwell, 1998). Recent works that focus on homosexual rights include David A. J. Richards, *Identity and the Case for Gay Rights* (University of Chicago Press, 1999); Daniel R. Pinello, *Gay Rights and American Law* (Cambridge University Press, 2003); Carlos A. Ball, *The Morality of Gay Rights: An Exploration in Political Philosophy* (Routledge, 2003); Brette McWhorter Sember, *Gay and Lesbian Rights: A Guide for GLBT Singles, Couples, and Families* (Sphinx Publishing, 2003); and Nan D. Hunter, *The Rights of Lesbians, Gay Men, Bisexuals, and Transgender People: The Authoritative ACLU Guide to a Lesbian, Gay, Bisexual, or Transgender Person's Rights*, 4th edition (Southern Illinois University Press, 2004).

ISSUE 7

Is the Decline of the Traditional Family a National Crisis?

YES: David Popenoe, from "The American Family Crisis,"
National Forum: The Phi Kappa Phi Journal (Summer 1995)

NO: Stephanie Coontz, from "The American Family," *Life*
(November 1999)

ISSUE SUMMARY

YES: Sociologist David Popenoe contends that families play
important roles in society but how the traditional family functions in these roles has declined dramatically in the last several
decades, with very adverse effects on children.

NO: Family historian Stephanie Coontz argues that current discussion of family decline includes a false idealization of the
traditional family of the past and misleading interpretations of
current data on families. She finds that the trends are both
positive and negative.

The state of the American family deeply concerns many Americans.
About 40 percent of marriages end in divorce, and only 27 percent of children born in 1990 are expected to be living with both parents by the time
they reach age 17. Most Americans, therefore, are affected personally or are
close to people who are affected by structural changes in the family. Few
people can avoid being exposed to the issue: violence in the family and
celebrity divorces are standard fare for news programs, and magazine articles decrying the breakdown of the family appear frequently. Politicians
today try to address the problems of the family. Academics have affirmed
that the family crisis has numerous significant negative effects on children,
spouses, and the rest of society.

Sociologists pay attention to the role that the family plays in the functioning of society. For a society to survive, its population must reproduce (or
take in many immigrants), and its young must be trained to perform adult
roles and to have the values and attitudes that will motivate them to contribute to society. Procreation and socialization are two vital roles that families

traditionally have performed. In addition, the family provides economic and emotional support for its members, which is vital to their effective functioning in society.

Today the performance of the family is disappointing in all of these areas. Procreation outside of marriage has become common, and it has been found to lead to less than ideal conditions for raising children. The scorecard on American family socialization is hard to assess, but there is concern about such issues as parents' declining time with and influence on their children and latchkey children whose parents work and who must therefore spend part of the day unsupervised. The economic performance of two-parent families is improving because more mothers are entering the labor force, but this gain is often related to a decline in emotional support. Single-parent families tend to perform less well on both counts. Overall, the high divorce rate and the frequency of child and spousal abuse indicate that the modern family fails to provide adequate social and emotional support.

Although most experts agree that the American family is in crisis, there is little agreement about what, if anything, should be done about it. After all, most of these problems result from the choices that people make to try to increase their happiness. People end unhappy marriages. Married women work for fulfillment or financial gain. Unwed mothers decide to keep their children. The number of couples who choose to remain childless is growing rapidly. These trends cannot be changed unless people start choosing differently. As yet there is no sign of this happening in a big way. Does this mean that the weakening of the family is desirable? Few would advocate such an idea, but perhaps some weakening must be accepted as the consequence of embracing other cherished values.

In the selections that follow, David Popenoe argues that the family is the key institution in society. Since it plays many important roles, its functional decline, which is largely due to cultural trends, has many adverse social impacts, including greatly harming children. He concludes by suggesting what needs to be done to strengthen families and family life. Stephanie Coontz provides a much different assessment of the present state of the family as compared with earlier times. She maintains that the family crisis thesis ignores the many strengths of American families today, overemphasizes certain negative trends, and misinterprets several of them. She tries to set the record straight and to counter much of the misinformation that the media produces.

David Popenoe  **YES**

The American Family Crisis

Throughout our nation's history, we have depended heavily on the family to provide both social order and economic success. Families have provided for the survival and development of children, for the emotional and physical health of adults, for the special care of the sick, injured, handicapped, and elderly, and for the reinforcement of society's values. Today, America's families face growing problems in each of these areas, and by many measures are functioning less well than ever before—less well, in fact, than in other advanced, industrialized nations.

The most serious negative effects of the functional decline of families have been on children. Evidence suggests that today's generation of children is the first in our nation's history to be less well-off psychologically and socially than their parents were at the same age. Alarming increases have occurred in such pathologies as juvenile delinquency, violence, suicide, substance abuse, eating disorders, nonmarital births, psychological stress, anxiety, and unipolar depression.

Such increases are especially troubling because many conditions for child well-being have improved. Fewer children are in each family today; therefore, more adults are theoretically available to care for them. Children are in some respects healthier and materially better off; they have completed more years in school, as have their parents. Greater national concern for children's rights, for child abuse, and for psychologically sound childrearing practices is also evident.

Family Origins and History

As the first social institution in human history, the family probably arose because of the need for adults to devote a great amount of time to childrearing. Coming into the world totally dependent, human infants must, for a larger portion of their lives than for any other species, be cared for and taught by adults. To a unique degree, humans nurture, protect, and educate their offspring. It is hard to conceive of a successful society, therefore, that does not have families that are able to raise children to become adults who have the capacity to love and to work, who are committed to such positive social values as honesty, respect, and responsibility, and who pass these values on to the next generation.

Infants and children need, at minimum, one adult to care for them. Yet, given the complexities of the task, childrearing in all societies until recent years has been shared by many adults. The institutional bond of marriage between biological parents, with the essential function of tying the father to the mother and child, is found in virtually every society. Marriage is the most universal social institution known; in no society has nonmarital childbirth, or the single parent, been the cultural norm. In all societies the biological father is identified where possible, and in almost all societies he plays an important role in his children's upbringing, even though his primary task is often that of protector and breadwinner.

In the preindustrial era, however, adult family members did not necessarily consider childrearing to be their primary task. As a unit of rural economic production, the family's main focus typically was economic survival. According to some scholars, rather than the family being for the sake of the children, the children, as needed workers, were for the sake of the family. One of the most important family transitions in history was the rise in industrial societies of what we now refer to as the "traditional nuclear family": husband away at work during the day and wife taking care of the home and children full time. This transition took place in the United States beginning in the early 1800s. The primary focus of this historically new family form was indeed the care and nurturing of children, and parents dedicated themselves to this effort.

Over the past thirty years, the United States (along with other modern societies) has witnessed another major family transformation—the beginning of the end of the traditional nuclear family. Three important changes have occurred:

- The divorce rate increased sharply (to a level currently exceeding 50 percent), and parents increasingly decided to forgo marriage, with the consequence that a sizable number of children are being raised in single-parent households, apart from other relatives.
- Married women in large numbers left the role of full-time mother and housewife to go into the labor market, and the activities of their former role have not been fully replaced.
- The focus of many families shifted away from childrearing to the psychological well-being and self-development of their adult members. One indication of this latter focus is that, even when they have young children to raise, parents increasingly break up if their psychological and self-fulfillment needs are unmet in the marriage relationship.

We can never return to the era of the traditional nuclear family, even if we wanted to, and many women and men emphatically do not. The conditions of life that generated that family form have changed. Yet the one thing that has not changed through all the years and all the family transformations is the need for children to be raised by mothers and fathers. Indeed, in modern, complex societies in which children need an enormous amount of education and psychological security to succeed, active and nurturing relationships with adults may be more critical for children than ever.

Unfortunately, the amount of time children spend with adults, especially their parents, has been dropping dramatically. Absent fathers, working mothers, distant grandparents, anonymous schools, and transient communities have become hallmarks of our era. Associated with this trend in many families, and in society as a whole, is a weakening of the fundamental assumption that children are to be loved and valued at the highest level of priority.

The Individualism Trend

To understand fully what has happened to the family, we must look at the broader cultural changes that have taken place, especially changes in the values and norms that condition everyday choices. Over recent centuries in industrialized and industrializing societies, a gradual shift has occurred from a "collectivist" culture (I am using this term with a cultural and not a political meaning) toward an individualistic culture. In the former, group goals take precedence over individual ones. "Doing one's duty," for example, is more important than "self-fulfillment," and "social bonds" are more important than "personal choice." In individualistic cultures, the welfare of the group is secondary to the importance of such personal goals as self-expression, independence, and competitiveness.

Not surprisingly, individualistic societies rank higher than collectivist societies in political democracy and individual development. But the shift from collectivism to individualism involves social costs as well as personal gains—especially when it proceeds too far. Along with political democracy and individual development, individualistic societies tend to have high rates of individual deviance, juvenile delinquency, crime, loneliness, depression, suicide, and social alienation. In short, these societies have more free and independent citizens but less social order and probably a lower level of psychological well-being.

"Communitarian" Individualism

The United States has long been known as the world's most individualistic society. Certainly, we place a high value on this aspect of our society, and it is a major reason why so many people from other countries want to come here. Yet for most of our history, this individualism has been balanced, or tempered, by a strong belief in the sanctity of accepted social organizations and institutions, such as the family, religion, voluntary associations, local communities, and even the nation as a whole. While individualistic in spirit, people's identities were rooted in these social units, and their lives were directed toward the social goals that they represented. Thus, the United States has been marked for much of its history, not by a pure form of individualism, but by what could be termed a "communitarian" or balanced individualism.

"Expressive" Individualism

As the individualism trend has advanced, however, a more radical or "expressive" individualism has emerged, one that is largely devoted to "self-indulgence" or "self-fulfillment" at the expense of the group. Today, we see a large number of people who are narcissistic or self-oriented, and who show concern for social institutions only when these directly affect their own well-being. Unfortunately, these people have a tendency to distance themselves from the social and community groupings that have long been the basis for personal security and social order. Since the 1950s, the number of people being married, visiting informally with others, and belonging to voluntary associations has decreased, and the number of people living alone has increased.

In turn, the traditional community groupings have been weakened. More people are viewing our once accepted social institutions with considerable skepticism. As measured by public opinion polls, confidence in such public institutions as medicine, higher education, the law, the press, and organized religion has declined dramatically. As measured by people voting with their feet, trust in the institution of marriage also had declined dramatically. And, as we see almost every night on the news, our sense of cultural solidarity seems to be diminishing.

The highly disturbing actions of inner-city residents that we have witnessed in the urban riots of recent years could be considered less a departure from everyday American cultural reality than a gross intensification of it. Few social and cultural trends found in the inner city are not also present in the rest of the nation. Indeed, with respect to the family, the characteristics of the African American family pronounced by President Lyndon Johnson in 1965 to be in a state of "breakdown" are very similar to the family characteristics of America as a whole in 1994!

In summary, for the good of both the individual and society, the individualism trend in the United States has advanced too far. The family holds the key. People need strong families to provide them with the identity, belonging, discipline, and values that are essential for full individual development. The social institutions of the surrounding community depend on strong families to teach those "civic" values—honesty, trust, self-sacrifice, personal responsibility, respect for others—that enable them to thrive. But let us not forget that strong families depend heavily on cultural and social supports. Family life in an unsupportive community is always precarious and the social stresses can be overwhelming.

Not to Forget the Gains

While I have presented a fairly grim picture in describing these cultural changes, it is important to add that not every aspect of our society has deteriorated. In several key areas, this nation has seen significant social progress. For instance, we are a much more inclusive society today—segregation and racism have diminished, and we now accept more African

Americans, Hispanics, and other minority groups into the mainstream. The legal, sexual, and financial emancipation of women has become a reality as never before in history. With advances in medicine, we have greater longevity and, on the whole, better physical health. And our average material standard of living, especially in the possession of consumer durables, has increased significantly.

The Nuclear Family and Marriage

Given our nation's past ability to accept positive social change, we can have some confidence in our capacity to solve the problem of family decline. In seeking solutions, we should first consider what family structure is best able to raise children who are autonomous and socially responsible, and also able to meet adult needs for intimacy and personal attachment. Considering the available evidence, as well as the lessons of recent human experience, unquestionably the family structure that works best is the nuclear family. I am not referring to the traditional nuclear family, but rather to the nuclear family that consists of a male and a female who marry and live together and share responsibility for their children and for each other.

Let us look, for a moment, at other family forms. No advanced, Western society exists where the three-generation extended family is very important and where it is not also on the wane. Some scholars suggest that a new extended family has emerged with the trend toward "step" and "blended" families. "Isn't it nice," they say, "that we now have so many new relatives!" The final verdict is not yet in on stepfamilies, but preliminary evidence from the few empirical studies that have been done sends quite the opposite message, and it is a chilling one. For example, a recent British study of 17,000 children born in 1958 concluded that "the chances of stepchildren suffering social deprivation before reaching twenty-one are even greater than those left living after divorce with a lone parent." Similar findings are turning up in the United States.

How are the single-parent families doing? Accumulating evidence on the personal and social consequences of this family type paints an equally grim picture. A 1988 survey by the National Center for Health Statistics found, for example, that children from single-parent families are two to three times more likely to have emotional and behavioral problems than children from intact families, and reduced family income is by no means the only factor involved. In their new book *Growing Up With a Single Parent,* Sara McLanahan and Gary Sandefur, after examining six nationally representative data sets containing over 25,000 children from a variety of racial and social class backgrounds, conclude that "children who grow up with only one of their biological parents are disadvantaged across a broad array of outcomes . . . they are twice as likely to drop out of high school, 2.5 times as likely to become teen mothers, and 1.4 times as likely to be idle—out of school and out of work—as children who grow up with both parents." The loss of economic resources, they report, accounts for only about 50 percent of the disadvantages associated with single parenthood.

Toward Solutions

Of course, many people have no other choice than to live in step- and single-parent families. These families can be successful, and their members deserve our continuing support. Nevertheless, the benefits that strong nuclear families bring to a high-achieving, individualistic, and democratic society are absolutely clear. For example, a committed marriage, which is the basis of the strong nuclear family, brings enormous benefits to adults. It is ironic in this age of self-fulfillment, when people are being pulled away from marriage, that a happy marriage seems to provide the best source of self-fulfillment. By virtually every measure, married individuals are better off than single individuals.

Another reason for supporting strong nuclear families is that society gains enormously when a high percentage of men are married. While unmarried women take relatively good care of themselves, unmarried men often have difficulty in this regard. In general, every society must be wary of the unattached male, for he is universally the cause of numerous social ills. Healthy societies are heavily dependent on men being attached to a strong moral order, which is centered in families, both to discipline sexual behavior and to reduce competitive aggression. Men need the moral and emotional instruction of women more than vice versa. Family life, especially having children, is for men a civilizing force of no mean proportions.

We should be seriously concerned, therefore, that men currently spend more time living apart from families than at probably any other time in American history. About a quarter of all men aged twenty-five to thirty-four live in nonfamily households, either alone or with an unrelated individual. In 1960, average Americans spent 62 percent of their adult lives with spouse and children, which was the highest in our history; by 1980, they spent 43 percent, the lowest in our history. This trend alone may help to account for the high and rising crime rates over the past three decades. During this period, the number of reported violent crimes per capita, largely committed by unattached males, increased by 355 percent.

Today, a growing portion of American men are highly involved in child care, providing more help with the children than their own fathers did. Yet, because they did not stay with or marry the mothers of their children, or because of divorce, a large number of men have abandoned their children entirely.

Between 1960 and 1990 the percentage of children living apart from their biological fathers more than doubled, from 17 percent to 36 percent. In general, childrearing women have become increasingly isolated from men. This is one of the main reasons why nothing would benefit the nation more than a national drive to promote strong marriages.

The New Familism: A Hopeful Trend

One bright spot in this picture is what some of us have called "the new familism," a growing realization in America that, "yes, the family really is in trouble and needs help." Public opinion polls indicate that nearly two-thirds of Americans believe "family values have gotten weaker in the United States." Both major political parties and our President now seem to be in agreement.

Two primary groups are involved in this cultural mini-shift: the maturing baby boomers, now at the family stage of their life cycle, and the "babyboom echo" children of the divorce revolution. The middle-aged baby boomers, spurred by growing evidence that children have been hurt by recent family changes, have been instrumental in shifting the media in a profamily direction. And many of the echo children of the 1970s, with their troubled childhoods, are coming into adulthood with a resolve not to repeat their parents' mistakes. They tend to put a high premium on marital permanence, perhaps because they have been unable to take the family for granted as many of their parents—the children of the familistic 1950s—did. But one concern is this: will they have the psychological stability to sustain an intimate relationship, or will their insecure childhoods make it impossible for them to fulfill their commitment to a lasting marriage?

Unfortunately, studies of the long-term effects of divorce on children and adolescents provide no optimism in this regard.

A couple of other factors seem to be working in a profamily direction. One is AIDS, which has now noticeably slowed the sexual revolution. As one entertainment figure recently said (with obvious dismay), "dating in Hollywood just isn't what it used to be." Neither, I must add, is dating what it used to be on the college campus, but the changes so far have not been very remarkable. Another factor is that cultural change is often reflected in cycles, and some cycles of change are patterned in generational terms. We know that not all cultural values can be maximized simultaneously. What one generation comes to value because they have less of it, their parents' generation rejected. This factor leads us to believe that the nation as a whole may be primed in the 1990s to run away from the values of radical individualism and more fully embrace the ideals of family and other social bonds.

Conclusion

In thinking about how to solve America's family crisis, we should keep the following considerations uppermost in mind:

- As a society, we cannot return to the era of the traditional nuclear family. But, we must do everything possible to strengthen the husband-wife nuclear family that stays together and takes responsibility for its children. Every child both wants—and needs—a mother and a father.
- Fundamental to strengthening the nuclear family is a renewed emphasis on the importance of marriage, which is the social institution designed primarily to hold men to the mother-child unit. It is extremely important for our children, and for our society, that men are attached to childrearing families.
- With even the strongest of marriages, parents have great difficulty raising children in an unsupportive and hostile environment. We

must seek to renew the sinews of community life that can support families, maintain social order, and promote the common good. We should give as much attention to recreating a "family culture" as we are now giving to strengthening a "work culture."

- As an overall approach to promoting family life, nothing is more important than trying to diminish and even turn back the trend toward radical individualism. Social bonds, rather than personal choice, and community needs, rather than individual autonomy, must be accorded a higher priority in our culture—and in our lives.

The American Family

As the century comes to an end, many observers fear for the future of America's families. Our divorce rate is the highest in the world, and the percentage of unmarried women is significantly higher than in 1960. Educated women are having fewer babies, while immigrant children flood the schools, demanding to be taught in their native language. Harvard University reports that only 4 percent of its applicants can write a proper sentence.

There's an epidemic of sexually transmitted diseases among men. Many streets in urban neighborhoods are littered with cocaine vials. Youths call heroin "happy dust." Even in small towns, people have easy access to addictive drugs, and drug abuse by middle-class wives is skyrocketing. Police see 16-year-old killers, 12-year-old prostitutes, and gang members as young as 11.

America at the end of the 1990s? No, America at the end of the 1890s.

The litany of complaints may sound familiar, but the truth is that many things were worse at the start of this century than they are today. Then, thousands of children worked full-time in mines, mills and sweatshops. Most workers labored 10 hours a day, often six days a week, which left them little time or energy for family life. Race riots were more frequent and more deadly than those experienced by recent generations. Women couldn't vote, and their wages were so low that many turned to prostitution.

In 1900 a white child had one chance in three of losing a brother or sister before age 15, and a black child had a fifty-fifty chance of seeing a sibling die. Children's-aid groups reported widespread abuse and neglect by parents. Men who deserted or divorced their wives rarely paid child support. And only 6 percent of the children graduated from high school, compared with 88 percent today.

Why do so many people think American families are facing worse problems now than in the past? Partly it's because we compare the complex and diverse families of the 1990s with the seemingly more standard-issue ones of the 1950s, a unique decade when every long-term trend of the 20th century was temporarily reversed. In the 1950s, for the first time in 100 years, the divorce rate fell while marriage and fertility rates soared, creating a boom in nuclear-family living. The percentage of foreign-born individuals in the country decreased. And the debates over social and cultural issues that had divided Americans for 150 years were silenced, suggesting a national consensus on family values and norms.

Some nostalgia for the 1950s is understandable: Life looked pretty good in comparison with the hardship of the Great Depression and World War II. The GI Bill gave a generation of young fathers a college education and a subsidized mortgage on a new house. For the first time, a majority of men could support a family and buy a home without pooling their earnings with those of other family members. Many Americans built a stable family life on these foundations.

But much nostalgia for the 1950s is a result of selective amnesia—the same process that makes childhood memories of summer vacations grow sunnier with each passing year. The superficial sameness of 1950s family life was achieved through censorship, coercion and discrimination. People with unconventional beliefs faced governmental investigation and arbitrary firings. African Americans and Mexican Americans were prevented from voting in some states by literacy tests that were not administered to whites. Individuals who didn't follow the rigid gender and sexual rules of the day were ostracized.

Leave It to Beaver did not reflect the real-life experience of most American families. While many moved into the middle class during the 1950s, poverty remained more widespread than in the worse of our last three recessions. More children went hungry, and poverty rates for the elderly were more than twice as high as today's.

Even in the white middle class, not every woman was as serenely happy with her lot as June Cleaver was on TV. Housewives of the 1950s may have been less rushed than today's working mothers, but they were more likely to suffer anxiety and depression. In many states, women couldn't serve on juries or get loans or credit cards in their own names.

And not every kid was as wholesome as Beaver Cleaver, whose mischievous antics could be handled by Dad at the dinner table. In 1955 alone, Congress discussed 200 bills aimed at curbing juvenile delinquency. Three years later, LIFE reported that urban teachers were being terrorized by their students. The drugs that were so freely available in 1900 had been outlawed, but many children grew up in families ravaged by alcohol and barbiturate abuse.

Rates of unwed childbearing tripled between 1940 and 1958, but most Americans didn't notice because unwed mothers generally left town, gave their babies up for adoption and returned home as if nothing had happened. Troubled youths were encouraged to drop out of high school. Mentally handicapped children were warehoused in institutions like the Home for Idiotic and Imbecilic Children in Kansas, where a woman whose sister had lived there for most of the 1950s once took me. Wives routinely told pollsters that being disparaged or ignored by their husbands was a normal part of a happier-than-average marriage.

Denial extended to other areas of life as well. In the early 1900s, doctors refused to believe that the cases of gonorrhea and syphilis they saw in young girls could have been caused by sexual abuse. Instead, they reasoned, girls could get these diseases from toilet seats, a myth that terrified generations of mothers and daughters. In the 1950s, psychiatrists dismissed incest reports as Oedipal fantasies on the part of children.

Spousal rape was legal throughout the period and wife beating was not taken seriously by authorities. Much of what we now label child abuse was accepted as a normal part of parental discipline. Physicians saw no reason to question parents who claimed that their child's broken bones had been caused by a fall from a tree.

There are plenty of stresses in modern family life, but one reason they seem worse is that we no longer sweep them under the rug. Another is that we have higher expectations of parenting and marriage. That's a good thing. We're right to be concerned about inattentive parents, conflicted marriages, antisocial values, teen violence and child abuse. But we need to realize that many of our worries reflect how much better we *want* to be, not how much better we *used* to be.

AMERICAN MIRROR

Muncie, Ind. (pop. 67,476), calls itself America's Hometown. But to generations of sociologists it is better known as America's Middletown— the most studied place in the 20th century American landscape. "Muncie has nothing extraordinary about it," says University of Virginia professor Theodore Caplow, which is why, for the past 75 years, researchers have gone there to observe the typical American family. Muncie's averageness first drew sociologists Robert and Helen Lynd in 1924. They returned in 1935 (their follow-up study was featured in a LIFE photo essay by Margaret Bourke-White). And in 1976, armed with the Lynds' original question-naires, Caplow launched yet another survey of the town's citizens.

Caplow discovered that family life in Muncie was much healthier in the 1970s than in the 1920s. Not only were husbands and wives com-municating more, but unlike married couples in the 1920s, they were also shopping, eating out, exercising and going to movies and concerts together. More than 90 percent of Muncie's couples characterized their marriages as "happy" or "very happy." In 1929 the Lynds had described partnerships of a drearier kind, "marked by sober accommodation of each partner to his share in the joint undertaking of children, paying off the mortgage and generally 'getting on.' "

Caplow's five-year study, which inspired a six-part PBS series, found that even though more moms were working outside the home, two thirds of them spent at least two hours a day with their children; in 1924 fewer than half did. In 1924 most children expected their mothers to be good cooks and housekeepers, and wanted their fathers to spend time with them and respect their opinions. Fifty years later, expectations of fathers were unchanged, but children wanted the same—time and respect—from their mothers.

—*Sora Song*

Fathers in intact families are spending more time with their children than at any other point in the past 100 years. Although the number of hours the average woman spends at home with her children has declined since the early 1900s, there has been a decrease in the number of children per family and an increase in individual attention to each child. As a result, mothers today, including working moms, spend almost twice as much time with each child as mothers did in the 1920s. People who raised children in the 1940s and 1950s typically report that their own adult children and grand-children communicate far better with their kids and spend more time helping with homework than they did—even as they complain that other parents today are doing a worse job than in the past.

Despite the rise in youth violence from the 1960s to the early 1990s, America's children are also safer now than they've ever been. An infant was four times more likely to die in the 1950s than today. A parent then was three times more likely than a modern one to preside at the funeral of a child under the age of 15, and 27 percent more likely to lose an older teen to death.

If we look back over the last millennium, we can see that families have always been diverse and in flux. In each period, families have solved one set of problems only to face a new array of challenges. What works for a family in one economic and cultural setting doesn't work for a family in another. What's helpful at one stage of a family's life may be destructive at the next stage. If there is one lesson to be drawn from the last millennium of family history, it's that families are always having to play catch-up with a changing world.

Take the issue of working mothers. Families in which mothers spend as much time earning a living as they do raising children are nothing new. They were the norm throughout most of the last two millennia. In the 19th century, married women in the United States began a withdrawal from the workforce, but for most families this was made possible only by sending their children out to work instead. When child labor was abolished, married women began reentering the workforce in ever large numbers.

For a few decades, the decline in child labor was greater than the growth of women's employment. The result was an aberration: the male-breadwinner family. In the 1920s, for the first time, a bare majority of American children grew up in families where the husband provided all the income, the wife stayed home full-time, and they and their siblings went to school instead of work. During the 1950s, almost two thirds of children grew up in such fami-lies, an all-time high. Yet that same decade saw an acceleration of workforce participation by wives and mothers that soon made the dual-earner family the norm, a trend not likely to be reversed in the next century.

What's new is not that women make half their families' living, but that for the first time they have substantial control over their own income, along with the social freedom to remain single or to leave an unsatisfactory marriage. Also new is the declining proportion of their lives that people devote to rearing children, both because they have fewer kids and because they are living longer. Until about 1940, the typical marriage was broken by the death of one partner within a few years after the last child left home. Today, couples can look forward to spending more than two decades together after the children leave.

The growing length of time partners spend with only each other for company has made many individuals less willing to put up with an unhappy marriage, while women's economic independence makes it less essential for them to do so. It is no wonder that divorce has risen steadily since 1900. Disregarding a spurt in 1946, a dip in the 1950s and another peak around 1980, the divorce rate is just where you'd expect to find it, based on the rate of increase from 1900 to 1950. Today, 40 percent of all marriages will end in divorce before a couple's 40th anniversary. Yet despite this high divorce rate, expanded life expectancies mean that more couples are reaching that anniversary than ever before.

Families and individuals in contemporary America have more life choices than in the past. That makes it easier for some to consider dangerous or unpopular options. But it also makes success easier for many families that never would have had a chance before—interracial, gay or lesbian, and single-mother families, for example. And it expands horizons for most families.

Women's new options are good not just for themselves but for their children. While some people say that women who choose to work are selfish, it turns out that maternal self-sacrifice is not good for children. Kids do better when their mothers are happy with their lives, whether their satisfaction comes from being a full-time homemaker or from having a job.

Largely because of women's new roles at work, men are doing more at home. Although most men still do less housework than their wives, the gap has been halved since the 1960s. Today, 49 percent of couples say they share childcare equally, compared with 25 percent of 1985.

Men's greater involvement at home is good for their relationships with their parents, and also good for their children. Hands-on fathers make better parents than men who let their wives do all the nurturing and child-care: They raise sons who are more expressive and daughters who are more likely to do well in school, especially in math and science.

In 1900, life expectancy was 47 years, and only 4 percent of the population was 65 or older. Today, life expectancy is 76 years, and by 2025, about 20 percent of Americans will be 65 or older. For the first time, a generation of adults must plan for the needs of both their parents and their children. Most Americans are responding with remarkable grace. One in four households gives the equivalent of a full day a week or more in unpaid care to an aging relative, and more than half say they expect to do so in the next 10 years. Older people are less likely to be impoverished or incapacitated by illness than in the past, and they have more opportunity to develop a relationship with their grandchildren.

Even some of the choices that worry us the most are turning out to be manageable. Divorce rates are likely to remain high, but more non-custodial parents are staying in touch with their children. Child-support receipts are up. And a lower proportion of kids from divorced families are exhibiting problems than in earlier decades. Stepfamilies are learning to maximize children's access to supportive adults rather than cutting them of from one side of the family.

Out-of-wedlock births are also high, however, and this will probably continue because the age of first marriage for women has risen to an all-time high of 25, almost five years above what it was in the 1950s. Women who marry at an older age are less likely to divorce, but they have more years when they are at risk—or at choice—for a nonmarital birth.

Nevertheless, births to teenagers have fallen from 50 percent of all nonmarital births in the late 1970s to just 30 percent today. A growing proportion of women who have a nonmarital birth are in their twenties and thirties and usually have more economic and educational resources than unwed mothers of the past. While two involved parents are generally better than one, a mother's personal maturity, along with her educational and economic status, is a better predictor of how well her child will turn out than her marital status. We should no longer assume that children raised by single parents face debilitating disadvantages.

As we begin to understand the range of sizes, shapes and colors that today's families come in, we find that the differences *within* family types are more important than the differences *between* them. No particular family form guarantees success, and no particular form is doomed to fail. How a family functions on the inside is more important than how it looks from the outside.

The biggest problem facing most families as this century draws to a close is not that our families have changed too much but that our institutions have changed too little. America's work policies are 50 years out of date, designed for a time when most moms weren't in the workforce and most dads didn't understand the joys of being involved in childcare. Our school schedules are 150 years out of date, designed for a time when kids needed to be home to help with the milking and haying. And many political leaders feel they have to decide whether to help parents stay home longer with their kids or invest in better childcare, preschool and afterschool programs, when most industrialized nations have long since learned it's possible to do both.

So America's social institutions have some Y2K bugs to iron out. But for the most part, our families are ready for the next millennium.

POSTSCRIPT

Is the Decline of the Traditional Family a National Crisis?

Popenoe admits that there are many positive aspects to the recent changes that have affected families, but he sees the negative consequences, especially for children, as necessitating actions to counter them. He recommends a return to family values and speaks out against the individualistic ethos. Coontz contends that the traditional family form that people like Popenoe are nostalgic for was atypical in American history and cannot be re-created. Furthermore, a closer look at the data indicates that the institution of the family is not in crisis. While admitting that many marriages fail, Coontz asserts that many families are strong.

Support for Coontz's point of view can be found in E. L. Kain, *The Myth of Family Decline* (D. C. Heath, 1990); J. F. Gubrium and J. A. Holstein, *What Is a Family?* (Mayfield, 1990); and Rosalind C. Barnett and Caryl Rivers, *She Works/He Works: How Two-Income Families Are Happier, Healthier, and Better Off* (HarperCollins, 1997). Recent works describing the weakening of the family and marriage include Richard T. Gill, *Posterity Lost: Progress, Ideology, and the Decline of the American Family* (Rowman & Littlefield, 1997); Dana Mack, *The Assault on Parenthood: How Our Culture Undermines the Family* (Simon & Schuster, 1997); Maggie Gallagher, *The Abolition of Marriage: How We Destroy Lasting Love* (Regnery, 1996); and Barbara Dafoe Whitehead, *The Divorce Culture: How Divorce Became an Entitlement and How It Is Blighting the Lives of Our Children* (Alfred A. Knopf, 1997). The work dealing with divorce and its consequences that is currently in the spotlight is Judith Wallerstein, *The Unexpected Legacy of Divorce* (Hyperion, 2000). In contrast E. Mavis Hetherington and John Kelly argue that most children in divorced families adjust well in the long run in *For Better or for Worse: Divorce Reconsidered* (W.W. Norton, 2002). David Popenoe and Jean Bethke Elshtain's book *Promises to Keep: Decline and Renewal of Marriage in America* (Rowman & Littlefield, 1996) discusses the decline but also signs of renewal of marriage.

Works that analyze changes in marriage and the family include; Betty Farrell's *Family: The Making of an Idea, an Institution, and a Controversy in American Culture* (Westview Press, 1999); Karla B. Hackstaff's *Marriage in a Culture of Divorce* (Temple University Press, 1999); Jessica Weiss's *To Have and to Hold: Marriage, the Baby Boom, and Social Change* (University of Chicago Press, 2000); Barbara J. Risman's *Gender Vertigo: American Families in Transition* (Yale University Press, 1998); Ronald D. Taylor and Margaret C. Wang, eds., *Resilience Across Contexts: Family, Work, Culture, and Community* (Lawrence Erlbaum, 2000); Linda J. Waite and Maggie Gallagher, *The Case for Marriage: Why Married People Are Happier, Healthier, and Better Off Financially* (Doubleday, 2000);

and Lynne M. Casper and Suzanne M. Bianchi, *Continuity and Change in the American Family* (Sage, 2002). For council on how to strengthen marriages, see David P. Gushee, *Getting Marriage Right: Realistic Counsel for Saving and Strengthening Relationships* (Baker Books, 2004).

For three major works on aspects of familial changes, see David Blankenhorn, *Fatherless America: Confronting Our Most Urgent Social Problem* (Basic Books, 1995); Sara McLanahan and Gary Sandefur, *Growing up With a Single Parent: What Hurts and What Helps* (Harvard University Press, 1994); and David Popenoe, *Life without Father: Compelling New Evidence That Fatherhood and Marriage Are Indispensable for the Good of Children and Society* (Harvard University Press, 1999).

The issue of the tension between family and work is recently receiving much attention. See Jerry A. Jacobs, *The Time Divide: Work, Family, and Gender Inequality* (Harvard University Press, 2004); Harriet B. Presser, *Working in a 24/7 Economy: Challenges for American Families* (Russell Sage Foundation, 2003); Arlie Russell Hochschild, *The Commercialization of Intimate Life* (University of California Press, 2003); and Janet C. Gornick and Marcia K. Meyers, *Families that Work Policies for Reconciling Parenthood and Employment* (Russell Sage Foundation, 2003). Brid Featherstone points out that government policies can reduce this stress in *Family Life and Family Support: A Feminist Analysis* (Palgrave Macmillan, 2004).

On the Internet . . .

Statistical Resources on the Web: Sociology

This Statistical Resources on the Web site provides links to data on poverty in the United States. Included is a link that contains both current and historical poverty data.

`http://www.lib.umich.edu/govdocs/stats.html`

Institute for Research on Poverty (IRP)

The Institute for Research on Poverty researches the causes and consequences of social inequality and poverty in the United States. This Web site includes frequently asked questions about poverty and links to other Internet resources on the subject.

`http://www.ssc.wisc.edu/irp/`

About.com: Affirmative Action

About com's Web site on affirmative action contains information about resources and organizations that focus on affirmative action policies and current events. This site also enables you to search other topics related to race relations.

`http://www.racerelations.about.com/cs/affirmativeaction`

Yahoo! Full Coverage: Affirmative Action

This Web site links you to the Yahoo! search engine for the topic of affirmative action.

`http://fullcoverage.yahoo.com/fc/US/AffirmativeAction`

PART 3

Stratification and Inequality

*W*_{hy} *is there so much poverty in a society as rich as ours? Why has there been such a noticeable increase in inequality over the past quarter century? Although the ideal of equal opportunity for all is strong in the United States, many charge that the American political and economic system is unfair. Does extensive poverty demonstrate that policymakers have failed to live up to United States egalitarian principles? Are American institutions deeply flawed in that they provide fabulous opportunities for the educated and rich and meager opportunities for the uneducated and poor? Is the American stratification system at fault or are the poor themselves at fault? And what about the racial gap? The civil rights movement and the Civil Rights Act have made America more fair than it was, so why does a sizeable racial gap remain? Various affirmative action programs have been implemented to remedy unequal opportunities, but some argue that this is discrimination in reverse. In fact, California passed a referendum banning affirmative action. Where should America go from here? Social scientists debate these questions in this part.*

- Is Increasing Economic Inequality a Serious Problem?

- Is the Underclass the Major Threat to American Ideals?

- Has Affirmative Action Outlived Its Usefulness?

ISSUE 8

Is Increasing Economic Inequality a Serious Problem?

YES: Christopher Jencks, from "Does Inequality Matter?" *Daedalus* (Winter 2002)

NO: Christopher C. DeMuth, from "The New Wealth of Nations," *Commentary* (October 1997)

ISSUE SUMMARY

YES: Christopher Jencks, professor of social policy at the Kennedy School at Harvard University, presents data on how large the income inequality is in the United States and describes the consequences of this inequality.

NO: Christopher C. DeMuth, president of the American Enterprise Institute for Public Policy Research, argues that the "recent increase in income inequality . . . is a very small tick in the massive and unprecedented leveling of material circumstances that has been proceeding now for almost three centuries and in this century has accelerated dramatically."

The cover of the January 29, 1996, issue of *Time* magazine bears a picture of 1996 Republican presidential candidate Steve Forbes and large letters reading: "DOES A FLAT TAX MAKE SENSE?" During his campaign Forbes expressed his willingness to spend $25 million of his own wealth in pursuit of the presidency, with the major focus of his presidential campaign being a flat tax, which would reduce taxes substantially for the rich. It seems reasonable to say that if the rich pay less in taxes, others would have to pay more. Is it acceptable for the tax burden to be shifted away from the rich in America? Forbes believed that the flat tax would benefit the poor as well as the rich. He theorized that the economy would surge ahead because investors would shift their money from relatively nonproductive, but tax-exempt, investments to productive investments. Although Forbes has disappeared from the political scene, his basic argument still thrives today. It is an example of the trickle-down theory, which states that helping the rich stimulates the economy, which helps the poor. In fact, the trickle-down theory is the major rationalization for the view that great economic inequality benefits all of society.

Inequality is not a simple subject. For example, America is commonly viewed as having more social equality than the more hierarchical societies of Europe and Japan, but America has more income inequality than almost all other industrial societies. This apparent contradiction is explained when one recognizes that American equality is not in income but in the opportunity to obtain higher incomes. The issue of economic inequality is further complicated by other categories of equality/inequality, which include political power, social status, and legal rights.

Americans believe that everyone should have an equal opportunity to compete for jobs and awards. This belief is backed up by free public school education, which provides poor children with a ladder to success, and by laws that forbid discrimination. Americans, however, do not agree on many specific issues regarding opportunities or rights. For example, should society compensate for handicaps such as disadvantaged family backgrounds or the legacy of past discrimination? This issue has divided the country. Americans do not agree on programs such as income-based scholarships, quotas, affirmative action, or the Head Start compensatory education program for poor preschoolers.

America's commitment to political equality is strong in principle, though less strong in practice. Everyone over 18 years old gets one vote, and all votes are counted equally. However, the political system tilts in the direction of special interest groups; those who do not belong to such groups are seldom heard. Furthermore, as in the case of Forbes, money plays an increasingly important role in political campaigns.

The final dimension of equality/inequality is status. Inequality of status involves differences in prestige, and it cannot be eliminated by legislation. Ideally, the people who contribute the most to society are the most highly esteemed. To what extent does this principle hold true in the United States?

The Declaration of Independence proclaims that "all men are created equal," and the Founding Fathers who wrote the Declaration of Independence went on to base the laws of the land on the principle of equality. The equality they were referring to was equality of opportunity and legal and political rights for white, property-owning males. In the two centuries following the signing of the Declaration, nonwhites and women struggled for and won considerable equality of opportunity and rights. Meanwhile, income gaps in the United States have been widening.

In the readings that follow, Christopher Jencks points out how extreme the inequality has become and how bad off the lowest fifth of the country is. He is cautious in asserting what the impacts are of extreme inequality because he requires hard data that is difficult to get. Nevertheless, he concludes, "My bottom line is that the social consequences of economic inequality are sometimes negative, sometimes neutral, but seldom—as far as I can discover—positive." Christopher C. DeMuth admits that incomes have become more unequally distributed, but he argues that consumption, a better indicator of living conditions, has become much more equally distributed.

Christopher Jencks  **YES**

Does Inequality Matter?

The economic gap between rich and poor has grown dramatically in the United States over the past generation and is now considerably wider than in any other affluent nation. This increase in economic inequality has no recent precedent, at least in America. The distribution of family income was remarkably stable from 1947 to 1980. We do not have good data on family incomes before 1947, but the wage gap between skilled and unskilled workers narrowed dramatically between 1910 and 1947, which probably means that family incomes also became more equal. The last protracted increase in economic inequality occurred between 1870 and 1910.

The gap between the rich and the rest of America has widened steadily since 1979. The Census Bureau, which is America's principal source of data on household incomes, does not collect good data from the rich, but the Congressional Budget Office (CBO) has recently combined census data with tax records to track income trends near the top of the distribution. Figure 1 shows that the share of after-tax income going to the top 1 percent of American households almost doubled between 1979 and 1997. The top 1 percent included all households with after-tax incomes above $246,000 in 1997. The estimated purchasing power of the top 1 percent rose by 157 percent between 1979 and 1997, while the median household's purchasing power rose only 10 percent. The gap between the poorest fifth of American households and the median household also widened between 1979 and 1997, but the trend was far less dramatic. . . .

Some of the potential costs and benefits of inequality emerge when we contrast the United States with other rich democracies. One simple way to describe income inequality in different countries is to compute what is called the "90/10 ratio." To calculate this ratio we rank households from richest to poorest. Then we divide the income of the household at the ninetieth percentile by the income of the household at the tenth percentile. (Comparing the ninetieth percentile to the tenth percentile is better than, say, comparing

Excerpted from Christopher Jencks, "Does Inequality Matter?" *Daedalus* (Winter 2002), pp. 49–53, 55–60, 64–65. Copyright © 2002 by Christopher Jencks. Reprinted by permission of the author. Notes omitted.

Figure 1

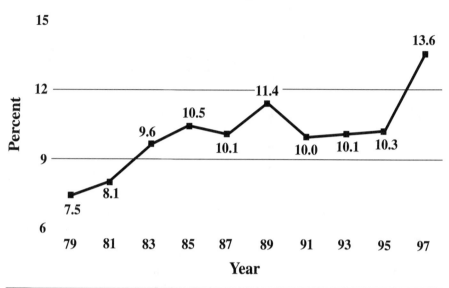

Percent of Household Income Going to the Richest One Percent

Changes in the percent of household income going to the richest 1 percent of American households, 1979–1977.
Source: Congressional Budget Office, *Historical Effective Tax Rates, 1979–1977.* September 2001, Table G-1C.

the ninety-ninth percentile to the first percentile, because few countries collect reliable data on the incomes of either the very rich or the very poor.)

The Luxembourg Income Study (LIS), which is the best current source of data on economic inequality in different countries, has calculated 90/10 ratios for fourteen rich democracies in the mid-1990s. Table 1 shows the results. To keep differences between these fourteen countries in perspective I have also included data on two poorer and less democratic countries, Mexico and Russia. If we set aside Mexico and Russia, the big English-speaking democracies are the most unequal, the Scandinavian democracies are the most equal, and Western European democracies fall in the middle. (Italy looks more unequal than the other continental democracies, but the Italian data is somewhat suspect.) Within the English-speaking world the United States is the most unequal of all. The 90/10 ratio in the United States is twice that in Scandinavia. But even the United States is nothing like as unequal as Russia, Mexico, or many other Latin American countries.

America's unusually high level of inequality is not attributable to its unusually diverse labor force. Years of schooling are more equally distributed in the United States than in the European countries for which we have comparable data (Sweden, the Netherlands, and Germany). Adult test scores are more un-equally distributed in the United States than Europe, partly because American immigrants score so poorly on tests given in English. But disparities in cognitive skills turn out to play a tiny role in explaining cross-national

Table 1

Income Inequality and Economic Output in Various Countries During the 1990s

Country (and year of the ninetieth to the tenth percentile)	Ratio of household income at the 90th to 10th percentile[a]	GDP per capita as a percent of U.S. level in 1998[b]	Life expectancy at birth (1995 est.)[c]
Scandinavia[d]	2.8	75	77.2
Sweden (1995)	2.6	68	78.9
Finland (1995)	2.7	68	76.6
Norway (1995)	2.8	85	77.8
Denmark (1992)	2.9	79	75.4
Western Europe	3.6	73	77.5
Nether. (1994)	3.2	75	77.5
Germany (1994)	3.2	71	76.6
Belgium (1996)	3.2	74	76.4
France (1994)	3.5	66	78.4
Switz. (1992)	3.6	84	78.5
Italy (1995)	4.8	67	77.6
Brit. Com.	4.3	73	77.7
Canada (1994)	4.0	78	78.2
Australia (1994)	4.3	75	78.0
U.K. (1995)	4.6	67	77.0[e]
U.S. (1997)	5.6	100	75.7
Middle-income nations			
Russia (1995)	9.4	21(?)	65.0
Mexico (1998)	11.6	25	NA

[a]From http://lisweb.ceps.lu/key/figures/inqtable.htm.
[b]From U.S. Bureau of the Census *Statistical Abstract of the United States,* 2000, Government Printing Office, Table 1365. GDP is converted to $U.S. using purchasing power parity.
[c]National Center for Health Statistics, *Health, United States,* 2000, Government Printing Office 2000, Table 27.
[d]All area averages are unweighted arithmetic means.
[e]England and Wales.

differences in the distribution of earnings. If one compares American workers with the same test scores and the same amount of schooling, the Americans' wages vary more than the wages of *all* Swedish, Dutch, or German workers.

Almost everyone who studies the causes of economic inequality agrees that by far the most important reason for the differences between rich democracies is that their governments adopt different economic policies. There is no agreement about *which* policies are crucial, but there is a fairly standard list of suspects. A number of rich countries have centralized wage bargaining, which almost always compresses the distribution of earnings. Many rich democracies also make unionization easy, which also tends to compress the wage distribution. Some rich democracies transfer a lot of money to people who are retired, unemployed, sick, or permanently disabled, while others are far less generous. The United States is unusually unequal partly because it makes little effort to limit wage inequality: the minimum wage is low, and American law makes unionization relatively difficult. In addition, the United States transfers less money to those who are not working than most other rich democracies.

The fact that the American government makes so little effort to reduce economic inequality may seem surprising in a country where social equality is so important. American politicians present themselves to the public as being just like everyone else, and once they step outside their offices, Americans all wear jeans. The way Americans talk and the music they listen to are also affected by egalitarian impulses. But while the tenor of American culture may be democratic, Americans are also far more hostile to government than the citizens of other rich democracies. Since egalitarian economic policies require governmental action, they win far less support in the United States than in most other rich democracies. . . .

Conservatives often blame American poverty on the existence of an "underclass" that rejects mainstream social norms, does little paid work, and has children whom neither parent can support. It is certainly true that poor American households include fewer working adults than affluent American households. This is true in every rich country for which we have data. But when Lars Osberg, an economist at Dalhousie University, compared poor households in the United States, Canada, Britain, Sweden, France, and Germany, he found that the poor American households worked far more hours per year than their counterparts in the other five countries. This finding suggests that what distinguishes the United States from the other rich democracies is not the idleness of the American poor but the anger that idleness inspires in more affluent Americans, which helps explain the stinginess of the American welfare state. . . .

❧❀❧

Up to this point I have been focusing exclusively on what people can afford to buy. While economic goods and services are obviously important, many people believe that inequality also affects human welfare in ways that are independent of any given household's purchasing power. Even if my family income remains constant, the distribution of income in my neighborhood or my nation may influence my children's educational opportunities, my life expectancy, my chance of being robbed, the probability that I will vote, and perhaps even my overall happiness. The remainder of this article tries to summarize what we know about such effects.

Educational opportunities. Increases in economic inequality have raised the value of a college degree in the United States. If all else had remained equal, making a college degree more valuable should increase both teenagers' interest in attending college and their parents' willingness to pay for college. But the growth of economic inequality in America has been accompanied by a change in the way we finance public higher education. Tax subsidies play a smaller role than they once did, and tuition plays a larger role. Since 1979 tuition at America's public colleges and universities has risen faster than most parents' income.

. . . [S]tudents are likely to be far more sensitive to changes in tuition than to a change in the hypothetical lifetime value of a BA. Tuition is easily observed and has to be paid now. The lifetime value of a BA is always

Table 2

Purchasing Power of Households at the 10th and 90th Percentiles of Each Nation's Distribution Relative to Households at the Same Percentile in the United States in the Same Year, 1992–1997

Country (and year)	Purchasing power as a percent of the U.S. level in the same year		
	10th percentile	90th percentile	Average of all percentiles
Scandinavia	112	57	77
Sweden (1995)	103	49	67
Finland (1995)	105	53	73
Norway (1995)	128	68	88
Denmark (1995)	110	59	80
Western Europe	119	73	88
Neth. (1994)	110	64	76
Germany (1994)	113	67	82
Belgium (1996)	121	73	80
France (1994)	110	71	84
Switz. (1992)	141	89	116
Commonwealth	94	73	80
Canada (1994)	105	80	92
U.K. (1995)	85	68	72
Australia (1994)	87	71	76
U.S. (1997)	100	100	100

Source: Columns 1 and 2 are from Timothy Smeeding and Lee Rainwater, "Comparing Living Standards Across Countries: Real Incomes at the Top, the Bottom, and the Middle" (paper prepared for a conference on "What Has Happened to the Quality of Life in America and Other Advanced Industrial Nations?" Levy Institute, Bard College, Annandale-on-Hudson, N.Y., June 2001). Local currencies were converted to dollars using their estimated purchasing power parity. Area averages are unweighted arithmetic means. Column 3 is calculated from the national means of the logarithms of after-tax household income, using data provided by Rainwater.

uncertain and cannot be realized for a long time. Among students who pay their own bills, higher tuition could easily reduce college attendance even when the long-run returns of a college degree are rising.

Table 3 is taken from work by two economists, David Ellwood at Harvard and Thomas Kane at UCLA. It shows changes between 1980–1982 and 1992 in the fraction of high-school graduates from different economic backgrounds entering four-year colleges. Among students from the most affluent families, the proportion entering a four-year college rose substantially. Among students from middle-income families, whose families often help with children's college expenses but seldom pay the whole bill, attendance rose more modestly. Students from the poorest quartile were no more likely to attend a four-year college in 1992 than in 1980–1982. . . .

Life expectancy.   People live longer in rich countries than in poor countries, but the relationship flattens out as national income rises. Indeed, the statistics in Table 1 show that life expectancy and GDP per capita are not strongly related in rich democracies. In particular, life expectancy is lower in the United States than in almost any other rich democracy.

Table 3

Percent of High-School Graduates Enrolling in a 4-year-College or Some Other Form of Postsecondary Education Within 20 months of Graduation, by Income Quartile: 1980–1982 and 1992

Income quartile	Entered a 4-year college			Entered some other form of post-secondary education		
	1980–82	1992	Change	1980–82	1992	Change
Lowest	29	28	–1	28	32	4
Second	33	38	5	30	32	2
Third	39	48	9	33	32	–1
Highest	55	66	11	26	24	–2
All	39	45	6	29	30	1

Source: David Ellwood and Thomas Kane, "Who Is Getting a College Education? Family Background and the Growing Gaps in Enrollment," in Sheldon Danziger and Jane Waldfogel, eds., *Securing the Future* (New York: Russell Sage, 2000).

Within any given country people with higher incomes also live longer. This relationship flattens out near the top of the income distribution, but the gap between richer and poorer families does not seem to narrow when everyone's standard of living rises. Despite both rising incomes and the introduction of Medicare and Medicaid, for example, the effects of both income and education on mortality increased in the United States between 1960 and 1986. . . .

In 1992 Richard Wilkinson wrote an influential article arguing that a more equal distribution of income improved life expectancy in rich countries. Subsequent work showed that mortality was also lower in American states and metropolitan areas where incomes were more equal. . . .

Wilkinson and his followers believe that inequality also lowers life expectancy independent of its effect on any given household's income, because it changes the social context in which people live. According to Wilkinson, inequality erodes the social bonds that make people care about one another and accentuates feelings of relative deprivation (the social-science term for what people used to call envy). Other epidemiologists take what they call a "materialist" position, arguing that inequality kills because it affects public policy, altering the distribution of education, health care, environmental protection, and other material resources. . . .

❧

I began this inquiry by arguing that American does less than almost any other rich democracy to limit economic inequality. As a result, the rich can buy a lot more in America than in other affluent democracies, while the poor can buy a little less. If you evaluate this situation by Rawlsian standards, America's policies are clearly inferior to those of most rich European countries. If you evaluate the same situation using a utilitarian calculus, you are likely to conclude that most American consumers do better than their counterparts in other large democracies. Much of this advantage is due to the fact that Americans spend more time working than Europeans do, but that may not be the whole story.

I also looked at evidence on whether economic inequality affects people's lives independent of its effects on their material standard of living. At least in the United States, the growth of inequality appears to have made more people attend college but also made educational opportunities more unequal. Growing inequality may also have lowered life expectancy, but the evidence for such an effect is weak and the effect, if there was one, was probably small. There is some evidence that changes in equality affect happiness in Europe, but not much evidence that this is the case in the United States. If inequality affects violent crime, these effects are swamped by other factors. There is no evidence that changes in economic inequality affect political participation, but declining political participation among the less affluent may help explain why American politicians remained so passive when inequality began to grow after 1980.

My bottom line is that the social consequences of economic inequality are sometimes negative, sometimes neutral, but seldom—as far as I can discover—positive. The case for inequality seems to rest entirely on the claim that it promotes efficiency, and the evidence for that claim is thin. All these judgments are very tentative, however, and they are likely to change as more work is done. Still, it is worthwhile to ask what they would imply about the wisdom of trying to limit economic inequality if they were, in fact, correct.

Readers' answers to that question should, I think, depend on four value judgments. First, readers need to decide how much weight they assign to improving the lot of the least advantaged compared with improving the average level of well-being. Second, they need to decide how much weight they assign to increasing material well-being compared with increasing "family time" or "leisure." Third, they need to decide how much weight they assign to equalizing opportunities for the young as against maximizing the welfare of adults. Fourth, they need to decide how much value they assign to admitting-more people from poor countries such as Mexico to the United States, since this almost inevitably makes the distribution of income more unequal.

If you are a hard-core Rawlsian who thinks that society's sole economic goal should be to improve the position of the least advantaged, European experience suggests that limiting inequality can benefit the poor. If you are a hard-core utilitarian, European experiences suggests—though it certainly does not prove—that limiting inequality lowers consumption. But European experience also suggests that lowering inequality reduces consumption partly by encouraging people to work fewer hours, which many Europeans see as a good thing. If you care more about equal opportunity for children than about consumption among adults, limiting economic inequality among parents probably reduces disparities in the opportunities open to their children.

All things considered, the case for limiting inequality seems to me strong but not overwhelming. That is one reason why most rich societies are deeply divided about the issue. Yet given the centrality of redistribution in modern politics, it is remarkable how little effort rich societies have made to assemble the kinds of evidence they would need to assess the costs and benefits of limiting inequality. Even societies that redistribute a far larger fraction of their GDP than the United States spend almost nothing on answering questions of this kind. Answering such questions would require collecting better evidence, which costs real money. It would also require politicians to run the risk of being proven wrong. Nonetheless, moral sentiments uninformed by evidence have done incalculable damage over the past few centuries, and their malign influence shows no sign of abating. Rich democracies can do better if they try.

Christopher C. DeMuth  **NO**

The New Wealth of Nations

The Nations of North America, Western Europe, Australia, and Japan are wealthier today than they have ever been, wealthier than any others on the planet, wealthier by far than any societies in human history. Yet their governments appear to be impoverished—saddled with large accumulated debts and facing annual deficits that will grow explosively over the coming decades. As a result, government spending programs, especially the big social-insurance programs like Social Security and Medicare in the United States, are facing drastic cuts in order to avert looming insolvency (and, in France and some other European nations, in order to meet the Maastricht treaty's criteria of fiscal rectitude). American politics has been dominated for several years now by contentious negotiations over deficit reduction between the Clinton administration and the Republican Congress. This past June, first at the European Community summit in Amsterdam and then at the Group of Eight meeting in Denver, most of the talk was of hardship and constraint and the need for governmental austerity ("Economic Unease Looms Over Talks at Denver Summit," read the *New York Times* headline).

These bloodless problems of governmental accounting are said, moreover, to reflect real social ills: growing economic inequality in the United States; high unemployment in Europe; an aging, burdensome, and medically needy population everywhere; and the globalization of commerce, which is destroying jobs and national autonomy and forcing bitter measures to keep up with the bruising demands of international competitiveness.

How can it be that societies so surpassingly wealthy have governments whose core domestic-welfare programs are on the verge of bankruptcy? The answer is as paradoxical as the question. We have become not only the richest but also the freest and most egalitarian societies that have ever existed, and it is our very wealth, freedom, and equality that are causing the welfare state to unravel.

That we have become very rich is clear enough in the aggregate. That we have become very equal in the enjoyment of our riches is an idea strongly resisted by many. Certainly there has been a profusion of reports in the media and political speeches about increasing income inequality: the rich, it is said, are getting richer, the poor are getting poorer, and the middle and working classes are under the relentless pressure of disappearing jobs in manufacturing and middle management.

Although these claims have been greatly exaggerated, and some have been disproved by events, it is true that, by some measures, there has been a recent increase in income inequality in the United States. But it is a very small tick in the massive and unprecedented leveling of material circumstances that has been proceeding now for almost three centuries and in this century has accelerated dramatically. In fact, the much-noticed increase in measured-income inequality is in part a result of the increase in real social equality. Here are a few pieces of this important but neglected story.

• First, progress in agriculture, construction, manufacturing, and other key sectors of economic production has made the material necessities of life— food, shelter, and clothing—available to essentially everyone. To be sure, many people, including the seriously handicapped and the mentally incompetent, remain dependent on the public purse for their necessities. And many people continue to live in terrible squalor. But the problem of poverty, defined as material scarcity, has been solved. If poverty today remains a serious problem, it is a problem of individual behavior, social organization, and public policy. This was not so 50 years ago, or ever before.

• Second, progress in public health, in nutrition, and in the biological sciences and medical arts has produced dramatic improvements in longevity, health, and physical well-being. Many of these improvements—resulting, for example, from better public sanitation and water supplies, the conquest of dread diseases, and the abundance of nutritious food—have affected entire populations, producing an equalization of real personal welfare more powerful than any government redistribution of income.

The Nobel prize-winning economist Robert Fogel has focused on our improved mastery of the biological environment—leading over the past 300 years to a doubling of the average human life span and to large gains in physical stature, strength, and energy—as the key to what he calls "the egalitarian revolution of the 20th century." He considers this so profound an advance as to constitute a distinct new level of human evolution. Gains in stature, health, and longevity are continuing today and even accelerating. Their outward effects may be observed, in evolutionary fast-forward, in the booming nations of Asia (where, for example, the physical difference between older and younger South Koreans is strikingly evident on the streets of Seoul).

• Third, the critical *source* of social wealth has shifted over the last few hundred years from land (at the end of the 18th century) to physical capital (at the end of the 19th) to, today, human capital—education and cognitive ability. This development is not an unmixed gain from the standpoint of economic equality. The ability to acquire and deploy human capital is a function of intelligence, and intelligence is not only unequally distributed but also, to a significant degree, heritable. As Charles Murray and the late Richard J. Herrnstein argue in *The Bell Curve,* an economy that rewards sheer brainpower replaces one old source of inequality, socioeconomic advantage, with a new one, cognitive advantage.

◦◦◉◦◦

But an economy that rewards human capital also tears down far more artificial barriers than it erects. For most people who inhabit the vast middle range of the bell curve, intelligence is much more equally distributed than land or physical capital ever was. Most people, that is, possess ample intelligence to pursue all but a handful of specialized callings. If in the past many were held back by lack of education and closed social institutions, the opportunities to use one's human capital have blossomed with the advent of universal education and the erosion of social barriers.

Furthermore, the material benefits of the knowledge-based economy are by no means limited to those whom Murray and Herrnstein call the cognitive elite. Many of the newest industries, from fast food to finance to communications, have succeeded in part by opening up employment opportunities for those of modest ability and training—occupations much less arduous and physically much less risky than those they have replaced. And these new industries have created enormous, widely shared economic benefits in consumption; I will return to this subject below.

- Fourth, recent decades have seen a dramatic reduction in one of the greatest historical sources of inequality: the social and economic inequality of the sexes. Today, younger cohorts of working men and women with comparable education and job tenure earn essentially the same incomes. The popular view would have it that the entry of women into the workforce has been driven by falling male earnings and the need "to make ends meet" in middle-class families. But the popular view is largely mistaken. Among married women (as the economist Chinhui Juhn has demonstrated), it is wives of men with high incomes who have been responsible for most of the recent growth in employment.

- Fifth, in the wealthy Western democracies, material needs and desires have been so thoroughly fulfilled for so many people that, for the first time in history, we are seeing large-scale voluntary reductions in the amount of time spent at paid employment. This development manifests itself in different forms: longer periods of education and training for the young; earlier retirement despite longer life spans; and, in between, many more hours devoted to leisure, recreation, entertainment, family, community and religious activities, charitable and other nonremunerative pursuits, and so forth. The dramatic growth of the sports, entertainment, and travel industries captures only a small slice of what has happened. In Fogel's estimation, the time devoted to nonwork activities by the average male head of household has grown from 10.5 hours per week in 1880 to 40 hours today, while time per week at work has fallen from 61.6 hours to 33.6 hours. Among women, the reduction in work (including not only outside employment but also household work, food preparation, childbearing and attendant health problems, and child rearing) and the growth in nonwork have been still greater.

There is a tendency to overlook these momentous developments because of the often frenetic pace of modern life. But our busy-ness actually demonstrates the point: time, and not material things, has become the scarce and valued commodity in modern society.

⟡

One implication of these trends is that in very wealthy societies, income has become a less useful gauge of economic welfare and hence of economic equality. When income becomes to some degree discretionary, and when many peoples' incomes change from year to year for reasons unrelated to their life circumstances, *consumption* becomes a better measure of material welfare. And by this measure, welfare appears much more evenly distributed: people of higher income spend progressively smaller shares on consumption, while in the bottom ranges, annual consumption often exceeds income. (In fact, government statistics suggest that in the bottom 20 percent of the income scale, average annual consumption is about twice annual income—probably a reflection of a substantial underreporting of earnings in this group.) According to the economist Daniel Slesnick, the distribution of consumption, unlike the distribution of reported income, has become measurably *more* equal in recent decades.

If we include leisure-time pursuits as a form of consumption, the distribution of material welfare appears flatter still. Many such activities, being informal by definition, are difficult to track, but Dora Costa of MIT has recently studied one measurable aspect—expenditures on recreation—and found that these have become strikingly more equal as people of lower income have increased the amount of time and money they devote to entertainment, reading, sports, and related enjoyments.

Television, videocassettes, CD's, and home computers have brought musical, theatrical, and other entertainments (both high and low) to everyone, and have enormously narrowed the differences in cultural opportunities between wealthy urban centers and everywhere else. Formerly upper-crust sports like golf, tennis, skiing, and boating have become mass pursuits (boosted by increased public spending on parks and other recreational facilities as well as on environmental quality), and health clubs and full-line book stores have become as plentiful as gas stations. As some of the best things in life become free or nearly so, the price of pursuing them becomes, to that extent, the "opportunity cost" of time itself.

The substitution of leisure activities for income-producing work even appears to have become significant enough to be contributing to the recently much-lamented increase in inequality in measured income. In a new AEI study, Robert Haveman finds that most of the increase in earnings inequality among U.S. males since the mid-1970's can be attributed not to changing labor-market opportunities but to voluntary choice—to the free pursuit of nonwork activities at the expense of income-producing work.

Most of us can see this trend in our own families and communities. A major factor in income inequality in a wealthy knowledge economy is age—many people whose earnings put them at the top of the income curve in their late fifties were well down the curve in their twenties, when they were just getting out of school and beginning their working careers. Fogel again: today the average household in the top 10 percent might consist of a professor or accountant married to a nurse or secretary, both in their peak years of earning. As for the stratospheric top 1 percent, it includes not only very rich people like Bill Cosby but also people like Cosby's fictional Huxtable family: an obstetrician married to a corporate lawyer. All these individuals would have appeared well down the income distribution as young singles, and that is where their young counterparts appear today.

That more young people are spending more time in college or graduate school, taking time off for travel and "finding themselves," and pursuing interesting but low- or non-paying jobs or apprenticeships before knuckling down to lifelong careers is a significant factor in "income inequality" measured in the aggregate. But this form of economic inequality is in fact the social equality of the modern age. It is progress, not regress, to be cherished and celebrated, not feared and fretted over.

POSTSCRIPT

Is Increasing Economic Inequality a Serious Problem?

This debate can be posed in terms of contradictory statements by the two authors: "The economic gap between rich and poor has grown dramatically in the United States over the past generation and is now considerably wider than in any other affluent nation" (Jencks). "We have become very equal in the enjoyment of our riches" (DeMuth). Both authors support their statements with indicators that measure trends, but they select different indicators. The reader has to decide which set of indicators better describes his or her idea of inequality.

Inequality, stratification, and social mobility are central concerns of sociology, and they are addressed by a large literature. Important discussions of income inequality are Barry Bluestone and Bennett Harrison, *Growing Prosperity: The Battle for Growth With Equity in the Twenty-First Century* (Houghton Mifflin, 2000); D. G. Champernowne and F. A. Cowell, *Economic Inequality and Income Distribution* (Cambridge University Press, 1998); Sheldon Danziger and Peter Gottschalk, *America Unequal* (Harvard University Press, 1995); Richard B. Freeman, *When Earnings Diverge: Causes, Consequences, and Cures for the New Inequality in the U.S.* (National Policy Association, 1997); Andrew Hacker, *Money: Who Has How Much and Why* (Scribner's Reference, 1997); Frank Levy, *The New Dollars and Dreams: American Income and Economic Change* (Russell Sage Foundation, 1998); Paul Ryscavage, *Income Inequality in America: An Analysis of Trends* (M. E. Sharpe, 1999); Edward N. Wolff, *Top Heavy: The Increasing Inequality of Wealth in America and What Can Be Done about It* (New Press, 2002); *The Causes and Consequences of Increasing Inequality*, edited by Finis Welch (University of Chicago Press, 2001); *Inequality in America: What Role for Human Capital Policies?*, edited by James J. Heckman and Alan B. Krueger (MIT Press, 2003); and *Social Inequality*, edited by Kathryn Neckernam (Russell Sage Foundation, 2004). A big part of the inequality picture is the conditions of the working poor, which is analyzed by Lawrence Mishel et al. *The State of Working America, 2002–2003* (Cornell University Press, 2003); *Low-Wage America: How Employers Are Reshaping Opportunity in the Workplace*, edited by Eileen Appelbaum et al. (Russell Sage Foundation, 2003); and David K. Shipler, *The Working Poor: Invisible in America* (Knopf, 2004). For a poignant ethnographic study of the poor and their disadvantages, see Elliot Liebow, *Tell Them Who I Am: The Lives of Homeless Women* (Free Press, 1993).

ISSUE 9

Is the Underclass the Major Threat to American Ideals?

YES: Charles Murray, from "And Now for the Bad News," *Society* (November/December 1999)

NO: Barry Schwartz, from "Capitalism, the Market, the 'Underclass,' and the Future," *Society* (November/December 1999)

ISSUE SUMMARY

YES: Author Charles Murray describes destructive behavior among the underclass. Murray asserts that this type of behavior will result in serious trouble for society even though, according to statistics, the number of crimes committed has decreased.

NO: Psychology professor Barry Schwartz states that the underclass is not the major threat to American ideals. He counters that "the theory and practice of free-market economics have done more to undermine traditional moral values than any other social force."

$\mathbf{T}$he Declaration of Independence proclaims the right of every human being to "life, liberty, and the pursuit of happiness." It never defines happiness, but Americans tend to agree that happiness includes doing well financially, getting ahead in life, and maintaining a comfortable standard of living.

The fact is that millions of Americans do not do well and do not live comfortably. They are mired in poverty and seem unable to get out. On the face of it, this fact poses no contradiction to America's commitment to the pursuit of happiness. To pursue is not necessarily to catch.

The real difficulty in reconciling the American ideal with American reality is not the problem of income differentials but the *persistence* of poverty from generation to generation. There are two basic explanations for this problem. One largely blames the poor and the other largely blames the circumstances of the poor and, thus, society.

The explanation that blames the poor is most strongly identified with the culture-of-poverty thesis, according to which a large segment of the poor does not really try to get out of poverty. In its more extreme form this view portrays the poor as lazy, stupid, or base. Poverty is not to be blamed on defects of American society but on personal defects. After all, many successful Americans have worked their way up from humble beginnings, and many immigrant groups have made progress in one generation. Therefore, some believe that the United States provides ample opportunities for those who work hard.

According to this view, available opportunities are ignored by the portion of the poor that embraces what is known as the *culture of poverty*. In other words, the poor have a culture all their own that is at variance with middle-class culture and that hinders their success. Although it may keep people locked into what seems to be an intolerable life, some would assert that this culture nevertheless has its own compensations and pleasures. It does not demand that people postpone pleasure, save money, or work hard.

However, the culture of poverty does not play a major role in today's version of the poor-are-to-blame theory. According to recent versions of this theory, having children out of wedlock, teenage pregnancy, divorce, absent fathers, crime, welfare dependency, and child abuse are what contribute to poverty. The culture of poverty contributes to these practices by being permissive or even condoning. This culture, however, is not antithetical to but is rather shared in part by much of the middle class. The difference is that in the middle class its consequences are usually not as extreme.

According to the second explanation of poverty, the poor have few opportunities and many obstacles to overcome to climb out of poverty. Most of the poor will become self-supporting if they are given the chance. Their most important need is for decent jobs that have the potential for advancement. Many poor people cannot find jobs, and when they do, the jobs are degrading or lack further opportunity.

These two perspectives are expressed in the two selections that follow. Charles Murray blames a segment of the poor that he calls the underclass for their poverty and for much of the harm done to society. Barry Schwartz blames the functioning of capitalism and the stock market for creating obstacles to the poor for getting ahead. Values such as sympathy, fairness, and self control, which sustain a productive and humane society, are undermined, according to Schwartz.

Charles Murray

And Now for the Bad News

Good news is everywhere. Crime rates are falling; welfare rolls are plunging; unemployment is at rock bottom; teenage births are down. Name an indicator, economic or social, and chances are it has taken a turn in the right direction. This happy story is worth celebrating. It is also a story that begs to be disentangled. For what is happening to the nation as a whole is not happening to the sub-population that we have come to call the underclass.

To make the case, I return to three indicators I first selected in the late 1980s to track the course of the underclass: criminality, dropout from the labor force among young men, and illegitimate births among young women. Then and now, these three seemed to me key outcroppings of what we mean by the underclass: people living outside the mainstream, often preying on the mainstream, in a world where the building blocks of a life—work, family and community—exist in fragmented and corrupt forms. Crime offers the most obvious example of a story that needs disentangling. After seven straight years of decline, the crime rate is at its lowest in a quarter-century. Almost everyone feels safer, especially in big cities. But suppose we ask not how many crimes are committed, but how many Americans demonstrate chronic criminality. That number is larger than ever. We don't notice, because so many of the chronically criminal are in jail.

Off the Street

For the past 20 years the United States has engaged in a massive effort to take criminals off the street. As of 1997, more than 1.8 million people were in prisons, jails and juvenile facilities. It has not been an efficient process— many who should be behind bars aren't and vice versa—but the great majority of prisoners are there because they have been a menace to their fellow citizens. To see how our appraisal of the crime problem depends on the imprisonment binge, suppose that in 1997 we imprisoned at the same rate relative to crime that we did in 1980, the year that the crime rate hit its all-time high. At the 1980 rate, 567,000 people would have been incarcerated in 1997, roughly 1.3 million fewer than the actual number. Now suppose that tomorrow we freed 1.3 million prisoners. Recent scholarly estimates of the average number of crimes prevented per year of incarceration range from 12 to 21. Even if these numbers are too high, it is clear that if we set free 1.3 million people now in prison, we would no longer be bragging about a falling crime rate. The only uncertainty is how sky-high the crime rate would be. It is a major accomplishment that crime has gone down. It has been achieved not by socializing the underclass, but by putting large numbers of its members behind bars.

Unemployment is another success story for the nation as a whole. Unemployment rates have dropped for just about any group of people who have been in the labor market, including blacks, and young black males in particular. Suppose we turn instead to a less-publicized statistic, but one of the most significant in trying to track the course of the underclass, the percentage of young males not in the labor force. When large numbers of young men neither work nor look for work, most are living off the underground economy or are dependent on handouts, perhaps moving into the labor force periodically, getting a job, and then quitting or getting fired a few weeks later, consigning themselves to a life at the margins of the economy.

Sudden and unexpected increases in the labor force dropout rates of young black males in the mid-1960s heralded the deterioration of the inner city. The 1990s have seen a new jump in dropout from the labor force that is just as ominous. The increased dropout has occurred selectively, among a subgroup that should have virtually 100% labor-force participation: young men who are no longer in school. The increase in labor force dropout is largest among young black males. Among 16- to 24-year-old black males not in school, the proportion who are not working or looking for work averaged 17% during the 1980s. It first hit 20% in 1992. As of 1997, it stood at 23%. The magnitude of dropout among white males the same age not in school is smaller, 9% in 1997. But the proportional increase since 1990 is substantial, up 25% overall, and concentrated among white teenagers (up 33% since 1990). That these increases in labor-force dropout have occurred despite a sustained period of high demand for workers at all skill levels is astonishing and troubling.

As for illegitimacy, confusion reigns. Headlines declare that "Illegitimacy is Falling," but the referent is birthrates, illegitimate births per 1,000 unmarried women. The referent for the headlines is also usually blacks, because that's where the dramatic change has occurred: The black illegitimate birth rate for women 15 to 44 fell 18% from 1990 to 1996; the black teenage birth rate fell by even more. But what is happening to the illegitimacy *ratio*—the percentage of babies who are born to unmarried women? The two measures need not track with each other, as the black experience vividly illustrates. Birthrates for unmarried black women and for black teenagers did not begin to drop in 1990. They dropped further and for much longer from 1960 to 1985. But the black illegitimacy ratio rose relentlessly throughout that period. The ratio also rose from 1990 to 1994 as birth rates fell. The good news about the black illegitimacy ratio is that it has since leveled off, even dropping a percentage point—meaning that as of 1997 it stood at a catastrophic 69% instead of a catastrophic 70%.

Most analysts, including me, have focused on the ratio rather than the rate because it is the prevalence of mother-only homes that determines the nature of a neighborhood and the socialization of the next generation. But when we turn from blacks to the national numbers for all races, it doesn't make much difference which measure you think is important. The rate and ratio have both risen substantially over the past few decades. Since 1994 the rate has fallen slightly, while the ratio has been flat at 32%. That is, almost one out of three American babies is now born to an unmarried woman.

The problems associated with illegitimacy have not really leveled off. Because the illegitimacy ratio is so much higher today than 18 years ago, the proportion of American children under 18 who were born to unmarried women will continue to increase. The problems associated with illegitimacy will also continue to increase well into the next century as the babies born in the 1990s grow up. That illegitimacy has stopped rising is a genuinely hopeful sign, but for practical purposes we are at the peak of the problem.

The size of the welfare population was not one of my 1989 indicators for tracking the underclass (it tends to double-count the role of illegitimacy), but recent success on this front has been so dramatic that it should be acknowledged. By "welfare reform" I mean the movement that began in the states in the early 1990s and culminated in the national welfare reform law of 1996. The change has been stunning: In 1993, slightly more than five million families were on welfare. By 1998, that number had dropped to about three million—a 40% drop in five years. The economy gets only a modest part of the credit. During the two preceding booms, welfare soared (in the 1960s) and declined fractionally (in the 1980s).

But once again, disentangling is crucial. For years, liberals defending welfare stressed that half of all women who ever go on welfare exit within a few years (and thus are ordinary women who have hit a rough patch), while conservatives attacking welfare stressed that half the welfare caseload at any point in time consists of women who have been on the rolls for many years (and thus are likely candidates for the underclass). So the crucial question is: How has the 40% reduction in caseload split between the two groups? No one yet knows. Past experience with workfare programs has been that the effect is concentrated on women who fit the profile of the short-term recipient. Answers about the current situation should be forthcoming soon.

The more profound question is what difference it makes if single mothers go to work. Is a community without fathers importantly different just because more mothers are earning a paycheck? One line of argument says yes. Jobs provide regularity, structure and dignity to family life, even if the father is not around. But we know from recent research that the bad effects of single parenting persist for women not on welfare. No counterbalancing body of research demonstrates that it is good for children when a single mother works (rather the opposite). I like to think children who see their mothers working for a living grow up better equipped to make their way in the world than children who watch their mothers live off a welfare check, even if there are no fathers in their lives. But this is a hope, not a finding.

In net, the underclass is as large as or larger than it has ever been. It is probably still growing among males, level or perhaps falling among females.

We know for sure that the underclass today is substantially larger than it was at any time in the 1980s when the Reagan administration was being excoriated for ignoring the underclass. Yet the underclass is no longer a political issue. Why? I propose an ignoble explanation. Whatever we might tell ourselves, mainstream Americans used to worry about the underclass primarily insofar as it intruded on our lives. Busing sent children from the wrong side of the tracks into our schools; the homeless infested our public spaces; the pervasive presence of graffiti, street hustlers and clusters of glowering teenagers made us anxious. Most of all, high crime rates twisted urban life into a variety of knots.

It took the better part of three decades, but we dealt with those intrusions. Busing is so far in the past that the word has an archaic ring to it. Revitalized vagrancy laws and shelters took most homeless off the streets. Most of all, we figured out what to do with criminals. Innovations in policing helped, but the key insight was an old one: lock 'em up.

Why is the underclass no longer an issue? Because what bothered us wasn't that the underclass existed, but that it was in our face. Now it is not. So we can forget about it. "For the time being" is the crucial hedge. What about the long term? Can the United States retain its political and social culture in the presence of a permanent underclass? The answer is certainly yes, if an underclass is sufficiently small. As long as it is only a fragment, the disorganization and violence of its culture do not spill over into the mainstream. The answer is certainly no if the underclass is sufficiently large. Trying to decide where the American underclass stands on that continuum raises two questions without clear answers.

First, how much has the culture of the underclass already spilled over into the mainstream? So far, the American underclass has been predominantly urban and black. Urban black culture has been spilling over into mainstream American culture for more than a century now, to America's great advantage. But during the past three decades it has increasingly been infiltrated by an underclass subculture that celebrates a bastardized social code— predatory sex and "getting paid." The violence and misogyny that pervade certain forms of popular music reflect these values. So does the hooker look in fashion, and the flaunting of obscenity and vulgarity in comedy.

Perhaps most disturbing is the widening expression, often approving, of underclass ethics: Take what you want. Respond violently to anyone who antagonizes you. Despise courtesy as weakness. Take pride in cheating (stealing, lying, exploiting) successfully. I do not know how to measure how broadly such principles have spread, but it's hard to deny that they are more openly espoused in television, films and recordings than they used to be. Among the many complicated explanations for this deterioration in culture, cultural spill-over from the underclass is implicated.

Implicated—that's all. There are many culprits behind the coarsening of American life. It should also go without saying that vulgarity, violence and the rest were part of mainstream America before the underclass came along. But these things always used to be universally condemned in public discourse. Now they are not. It is not just that America has been defining deviancy down, slackening old moral codes. Inner-city street life has provided an alternative code and it is attracting converts.

The converts are mainly adolescents, which makes sense. The street ethics of the underclass subculture are not "black." They are the ethics of male adolescents who haven't been taught any better. For that matter, the problem of the underclass itself is, ultimately, a problem of adolescents who haven't been taught any better. There are a lot more white adolescents than black ones, leading to the second question: How fast will the white underclass grow?

National statistics tell us that in the past decade white criminality has not only increased but gotten more violent, that white teenage males are increasingly dropping out of the labor force, and that white illegitimacy has increased rapidly. Anecdotal evidence about changes in white working-class neighborhoods points to increased drug use, worse school performance and a breakdown of neighborhood norms—recalling accounts of black working-class neighborhoods three decades ago. (Systematic documentation of these trends is still lacking.)

Looking ahead, much depends on whether illegitimacy among whites has already reached critical mass—the point at which we can expect accelerated and sustained growth in white crime, labor force dropout and illegitimacy rates. The good news is that the growth in the white illegitimacy ratio has slowed. The bad news is that it stands at 26%–22% for non-Latino whites—which, judging from the black experience in the early 1960s, may be near that point of critical mass. No one knows, of course, whether the subsequent trajectory of events for whites will be the same as it was for blacks, but there is ample cause for worry. European countries with high white illegitimacy ratios offer no comfort. Juvenile crime is increasing rapidly across Europe, along with other indicators of social deterioration in low-income groups.

Jamesian Directions

The most striking aspect of the current situation, and one that makes predictions very dicey, is the degree to which the United States is culturally compartmentalizing itself. America in the 1990s is a place where the local movie theater may play *Sense and Sensibility* next door to *Natural Born Killers*. Brian Lamb (on C-SPAN) is a few channels away from Jerry Springer. Formal balls are in vogue in some circles; mosh pits in others. Name just about any aspect of American life, and a case can be made that the country is going in different directions simultaneously, some of them Jamesian, others Hogarthian.

The Jamesian elements are not confined to a cultured remnant. Broad swaths of American society are becoming more civil and less vulgar, more responsible and less self-indulgent. The good news is truly good, and it extends beyond the statistics. What's more, the bad news may prove manageable. One way to interpret the nation's success in re-establishing public order is that we have learned how to cope with our current underclass. One may then argue that the size of the underclass is stabilizing, meaning that we can keep this up indefinitely. It requires only that we set aside moral considerations and accept that the huge growth of the underclass since 1960 cannot now be reversed.

Welfare reform and the growing school-voucher movement are heartening signs that many are not ready to accept the status quo. But they struggle against a larger movement toward what I have called "custodial democracy," in which the mainstream subsidizes but also walls off the underclass. In effect, custodial democracy takes as its premise that a substantial portion of the population cannot be expected to function as citizens.

At this moment, elated by falling crime rates and shrinking welfare rolls, we haven't had to acknowledge how far we have already traveled on the road to custodial democracy. I assume the next recession will disabuse us. But suppose that our new *modus vivendi* keeps working? We just increase the number of homeless shelters, restore the welfare guarantee, build more prison cells, and life for the rest of us goes on, pleasantly. At some point we will be unable to avoid recognizing that custodial democracy has arrived. This will mark a fundamental change in how we conceive of America. Will anyone mind?

Capitalism, the Market, the "Underclass," and the Future

I share Charles Murray's concern that there is bad news lurking in the shadows of what seems to be unalloyed prosperity in millennial America. I share his concerns about urban crime, employment, the fragility of the family, and the coarseness of the culture. But I am also angry. I am angry at the resolute refusal of conservatives like Murray, William Bennett, and James Q. Wilson to face squarely what their colleague Pat Buchanan is willing to face, when he writes:

> Reaganism and its twin sister, Thatcherism, create fortunes among the highly educated, but in the middle and working classes, they generate anxiety, insecurity and disparities. . . . Tax cuts, the slashing of safety nets and welfare benefits, and global free trade . . . unleash the powerful engines of capitalism that go on a tear. Factories and businesses open and close with startling speed. . . . As companies merge, downsize and disappear, the labor force must always be ready to pick up and move on. . . . The cost is paid in social upheaval and family breakdown. . . . Deserted factories mean gutted neighborhoods, ghost towns, ravaged communities and regions that go from boom to bust . . . Conservatism is being confronted with its own contradictions for unbridled capitalism is an awesome destructive force.

Murray's message is that things have not been working nearly as well as we think they have. Crime is down only because we have locked all the hardened criminals away; the tendency to commit crime has not changed. Unemployment is down, but those who remain unemployed are contemptuous of work. Illegitimate births are down, but legitimate births are down even more, as growing numbers of people seem disdainful of marriage. All these signs of moral decay Murray traces to the underclass, and he is especially worried because the middle class seems increasingly to approve of what he calls "underclass ethics." He says that "among the many complicated explanations for this deterioration in culture, cultural spill-over [from the underclass to the rest of us] is implicated."

But Murray also says this: "There are many culprits behind the coarsening of American life. It should also go without saying that vulgarity, violence and the rest were part of mainstream America before the underclass came along. But these things always used to be universally condemned in public discourse. Now they are not. It is not just that America has been defining deviancy down, slackening old moral codes. Inner-city street life has provided an alternative code and it is attracting converts."

The idea that middle America needs to look at the underclass for examples of coarseness is preposterous. It turns a willful blind eye to what the conservative revolution has brought us. The conservatism that captured America's fancy in the 1980s was actually two distinct conservatisms. It was an *economic* conservatism committed to dismantling the welfare state and turning as many facets of life as possible over to the private sector. And it was a *moral* conservatism committed to strengthening traditional values and the social institutions that foster them. These two conservatisms corresponded to the economic and social agendas that guided the policies of both the Reagan and the Bush administrations. These Presidents and their supporters seemed to share not only the belief that free-market economics and traditional moral values are good, but that they go together.

This has proven to be a serious mistake. The theory and practice of free-market economics have done more to undermine traditional moral values than any other social force. It is not permissive parents, unwed mothers, undisciplined teachers, multicultural curricula, fanatical civil libertarians, feminists, rock musicians, or drug pushers who are the primary sources of the corrosion that moral conservatives are trying to repair. Instead, it is the operation of the market system itself, along with an ideology that justifies the pursuit of economic self-interest as the "American way." And so, I acknowledge that Murray's concerns about the "problem of the underclass" are not being solved by our current prosperity. But I insist that they will never be solved unless we face up squarely to what causes them. And what causes them, I believe, is in large part what is responsible for our current prosperity.

I am not going to argue here that the evils of market capitalism demand that we all gather to storm the barricades and wrest the means of production out of the hands of evil capitalists and turn them over to the state. As everyone says, "the Cold War is over, and we won." State ownership of the means of production is a non-issue. We are all capitalists now. The issues before us really are two. First, what kind of capitalism? Is it the capitalism of Reagan and Thatcher—of unregulated markets and privatization of everything, with government involvement viewed as a cause of waste and inefficiency? Or is it the capitalism of John Maynard Keynes and of Franklin Roosevelt, with significant state regulation of the market and state guarantees of life's necessities? I'm going to argue for the latter—old-fashioned capitalism. The boom we are in the midst of has created perhaps the greatest degree of income inequality in the history of the developed world. What the free market teaches us is that what *anyone* can have not *everyone* can have, often with very painful consequences for the have-nots. And second, if we must live with capitalism, what are we prepared to do to correct the moral corrosion that it brings as a side effect? For in addition to asking what free-market capitalism does *for* people, we must ask what it does *to* people. And I will suggest that it turns people into nasty, self-absorbed, self-interested competitors—that it demands this of people, and celebrates it.

The Market and Inequality

One would think that if the problem is the underclass, the solution—or *a* solution—is to reduce its numbers. What do we know about the great economic "boom" we are living in the midst of? The income of the average wage-earning worker in 1997 was 3.1% lower than it was in 1989. Median family income was $1000 less in 1997 than in 1989. The typical couple worked 250 more hours in 1997 than in 1989. So to the extent that average people have been able to hold their own at all, it is because they worked harder. The median wage of high school graduates fell 6% between 1980 and 1996 while the median wage of college graduates rose 12%.

And this picture looks worse if you include benefits. Benefits used to be the "great equalizer," distributed equally among employees despite huge disparities in salary. For example, the $20,000/year employee and the $500,000/year employee got the same $4000 medical insurance. But despite IRS efforts to prevent differential benefits based on income (by making such benefits taxable), employers have invented all kinds of tricks. They have introduced lengthy employment "trial periods" with no benefits. They have resorted to hiring temporary workers who get no benefits. The result is that while 80% of workers received paid vacations and holidays in 1996, less than 10% in the bottom tenth of the income distribution did. The result is that while 70% of workers have some sort of employer funded pension, less than 10% of those in the bottom tenth of the income distribution do. The result is that while 90% of high wage employees have health insurance, only 26% of low wage employees do. All told, about 40 million Americans have no health insurance. The picture looks still worse if you consider *wealth* rather than income. The richest 1% of Americans have almost 50% of the nation's wealth. The next 9% have about a third. And the remaining 90% have about a sixth.

America now has the greatest wealth and income inequality in the developed world, and it is getting bigger every day. Efforts to implement even modest increases in the minimum wage are met with intense resistance. Further, as pointed out in a recent analysis in the *Left Business Observer,* the United States has the highest poverty rate of any developed nation, and uses government income transfers to reduce poverty less than any developed nation. Our two main rivals in these categories are Thatcher's England, and postcommunist, gangster-capitalist Russia.

Is this massive inequality an accident—an imperfection in an otherwise wonderful system? I don't think so. Modern capitalism depends on inequality. Modern capitalism is consumer capitalism. People have to buy things. In 1997, $120 billion was spent in the United States on advertising, more than was spent on all forms of education. Consumer debt, excluding home mortgages, exceeded $1 trillion in 1995—more than $10,000 per household. But people also need to save, to accumulate money for investment, especially now, in these days of ferocious global competition. How can you save and spend at the same time? The answer is that some must spend while others save. Income and wealth inequality allow a few to accumulate, and invest, while most of us spend—even more than we earn. And this is not an accident, but a structural necessity. There must be some people who despite society-wide exhortation to spend just cannot spend all they make. These people will provide the capital for investment.

Perhaps this kind of inequality is just the price we pay for prosperity. Concentrating wealth in the hands of the few gives them the opportunity to invest. This investment "trickles down" to improve the lives of all, by improving the products we buy and creating employment opportunities. There is no question that the current political leadership in the U.S.—of both parties—thinks that keeping Wall Street happy is essential to the nation's financial well-being. By encouraging people to buy stocks we put money in the hands of investors who then produce innovation and improvement in economic efficiency. Thus, we reduce capital gains taxes. And we eliminate the deficit to make Wall Street happy, even if it means neglecting the social safety net.

But who gains? It is true that what's good for Wall Street is good for America? On investment, more than 90% of all stock market trades involve just shuffling of paper as shares move from my hands to yours, or vice versa. Almost none of the activity on Wall Street puts capital in the hands of folks who invest in plant and equipment. Similarly, most corporate debt is used to finance mergers and acquisitions, or to buy back stock that later goes to chief executives as performance bonuses.

Why is it that when a company announces major layoffs, its stock goes up? The answer is that layoffs signal higher profits, good news for investors. Why is it that when unemployment rates go down, stock prices go down? The answer is that low unemployment signals potential inflation, bad news for investors. Why is it that banks bailed out a highly speculative hedge fund—for rich folks only—that was able to invest borrowed money (20 times its actual assets) while at the same time lobbying to crack down on personal bankruptcy laws, when the overwhelming majority of those facing personal bankruptcy make less than $20,000/year? The evidence is clear and compelling: the stock market operates to benefit the few at the expense of the many.

So if, as Murray contends (correctly, I think), the underclass is a social problem for America that is not going away, why isn't Murray demanding a set of policies that make it smaller rather than larger? Why isn't he demanding a minimum wage that is a *living* wage, so that parents can *afford* to take care of their children? And in addition, why isn't he demanding high-quality day care, so that the children of single mothers, or of two worker households, won't be neglected? How is it that a set of economic policies that has made the underclass bigger glides by free of Murray's wrath, as he chooses to condemn instead the nation's growing enthusiasm for underclass values?

The Market and Morality

. . . [R]ecent thinkers have realized that we can't take the bourgeois values that support capitalism for granted. Indeed, as Karl Polanyi, in *The Great*

Transformation, and Fred Hirsch, in *Social Limits to Growth* argue persuasively, not only can we not take these values for granted, but market capitalism—the very thing that so desperately depends on them—actively undermines them. This, I believe, is the lesson that Murray and his cohort refuses to accept. The so-called "underclass" may threaten the comfort and safety of the middle class, but it is the overclass that threatens the stability and the future prospects of society.

One sees this dramatically in James Q. Wilson's . . . book *The Moral Sense.* In that book, Wilson argues for a biologically based moral sense in human beings—a sense that almost guarantees such moral traits as sympathy, duty, self-control, and fairness. . . .

Having made the sweeping claim that the market contributes more to the erosion of our moral sense than any other modern social force, I want to defend that claim with some more specific arguments. In particular, I want to discuss the market's negative effects on some of the moral sentiments that Wilson emphasizes and on some of the social institutions that nurture those sentiments.

One of the moral sentiments that is central to Wilson's argument is sympathy, the ability to feel and understand the misfortune of others and the desire to do something to ameliorate that misfortune. Wilson notes correctly that other-regarding sentiments and actions, including sympathy and altruism, are extremely common human phenomena, notwithstanding the efforts of many cynical social scientists to explain them away as subtle forms of self-interested behavior. What the literature on sympathy and altruism have made clear is that they depend on a person's ability to take the perspective of another (to "walk a mile in her shoes"). This perspective-taking ability in turn depends on a certain general cognitive sophistication, on familiarity with the other, and on proximity to the other. What does the market do to sympathy? Well, the market thrives on anonymity. One of its great virtues is that buyers are interchangeable with other buyers and sellers with other sellers. All that matters is price and quality and the ability to pay. Increasingly, in the modern market, transactions occur over long distances. Indeed, increasingly, they occur over telephone lines, as "e-commerce" joins the lexicon. Thus, the social institution that dominates modern American society is one that fosters, both in principle and in fact, social relations that are distant and impersonal—social relations that are the antithesis of what sympathy seems to require.

A second moral sentiment that attracts Wilson's attention is fairness. He correctly notes (as any parent will confirm) that concern about fairness appears early in human development and that it runs deep. Even four-year-olds have a powerful, if imperfect conception of what is and is not fair. What does fairness look like in adults?

[Professors] Daniel Kahneman, Jack Knetsch, and Richard Thaler asked this question by posing a variety of hypothetical business transactions to randomly chosen informants and asking the informants to judge whether the transactions were fair. What these hypothetical transactions had in common was that they all involved legal, profit-maximizing actions that were of questionable moral character. What these researchers found is that the overwhelming majority of people have a very strong sense of what is fair. While people believe that business people are entitled to make a profit, they do not think it fair for producers to charge what the market will bear (for example, to price gouge during shortages) or to lower wages during periods of slack employment. In short, most people think that concerns for fairness should be a constraint on profit-seeking. So far, so good; this study clearly supports Wilson's contention that fairness is one of our moral sentiments.

But here's the bad news. Another investigator posed these same hypotheticals to students in a nationally prominent MBA program. The overwhelming majority of these informants thought that anything was fair, as long as it was legal. Maximizing profit was the point; fairness was irrelevant. In another study, these same hypotheticals were posed to a group of CEOs. What the authors of the study concluded was that their executive sample was less inclined than those in the original study to find the actions posed in the survey to be unfair. In addition, often when CEOs did rate actions as unfair, they indicated in unsolicited comments that they did not think the actions were unfair so much as they were unwise, that is, bad business practice. . . .

To summarize, people care about fairness, but if they are participants in the market, or are preparing to be participants in the market, they care much less about fairness than others do. Is it the ideology of relativism that is undermining this moral sentiment or the ideology of the market?

Another of the moral sentiments Wilson discusses is self-control. What does the market do to self-control? As many have pointed out, modern corporate management is hardly a paradigm of self-control. The combination of short-termism and me-first management that have saddled large companies with inefficiency and debt are a cautionary tale on the evils of self-indulgence. Short termism is in part structural; managers must answer to shareholders, and in the financial markets, you're only as good as your last quarter. Me-first management seems to be pure greed. Some of the excesses of modern executive compensation have recently been documented by Derek Bok, in his book *The Cost of Talent.* Further, *The Economist,* in a survey of pay published in May of 1999, makes it quite clear that the pay scale of American executives is in another universe from that in any other nation, and heavily loaded with stock options that reward the executive for the company's performance in the stock market rather than the actual markets in goods and services in which the company operates. . . .

The final moral sentiment that Wilson identifies and discusses is duty, "a disposition to honor obligations even without hope of reward or fear of punishment." Wilson is quite right about the importance of duty. If we must rely on threat of punishment to enforce obligations, they become unenforceable. Punishment works only as long as most people will do the right thing most of the time even if they can get away with transgressing. . . .

The enemy of duty is free-riding, taking cost-free advantage of the dutiful actions of others. The more people are willing to be free-riders, the higher the cost to those who remain dutiful, and the higher the cost of enforcement to society as a whole. How does the market affect duty and free-riding? Well, one of the studies of fairness I mentioned above included a report of an investigation of free-riding. Economics students are more likely to be free riders than students in other disciplines. And this should come as no surprise. Free-riding is the "rational, self-interested" thing to do. Indeed, if you are the head of a company, free-riding may even be your fiduciary responsibility. So if free-riding is the enemy of duty, then the market is the enemy of duty.

. . . In my view, this is what market activity does to all the virtues that Wilson, and Murray long for—it submerges them with calculations of personal preference and self-interest.

If Wilson fails to acknowledge the influence of the market on our moral sense, where then does he look? As I said earlier, he thinks a good deal of human morality reflects innate predisposition. But that disposition must be nurtured, and it is nurtured, according to Wilson, in the family, by what might be described as "constrained socialization." The child is not a miniature adult (socialization is required), but nor is she a blank slate (not anything is possible; there are predispositions on the part of both parents and children for socialization to take one of a few "canonical" forms.) One of the primary mechanisms through which socialization occurs is imitation: "There can be little doubt that we learn a lot about how we ought to behave from watching others, especially others to whom we are strongly attached. . . .

So let us accept Wilson's position about socialization and ask what the adults who the young child will be imitating look like. I believe, following the work of [economist] Fred Hirsch, that in the last few decades there has been an enormous upsurge in what might be called the "commercialization of social relations"—that choice has replaced duty and utility maximization replaced fairness in relations among family members. . . .

Wilson seems mindful of all this. He decries the modern emphasis on rights and the neglect of duty. He acknowledges that modern society has posed a real challenge to the family by substituting labor markets for householding. And he deplores the ideology of choice as applied to the family:

> Not even the family has been immune to the ideology of choice. In the 1960s and 1970s (but less so today) books were written advocating "alternative" families and "open" marriages. A couple could choose to have a trial marriage, a regular marriage but without an obligation to sexual fidelity, or a revocable marriage with an easy exit provided by no-fault divorce. A woman could choose to have a child out of wedlock and to raise it alone. Marriage was but one of several "options" by which men and women could manage their intimate needs, an option that ought to be carefully negotiated in order to preserve the rights of each contracting party. The family, in this view, was no longer the cornerstone of human life, it was one of several "relationships" from which individuals could choose so as to maximize their personal goals.

But instead of attributing this ideology of choice to the market, from which I think it clearly arises, Wilson attributes it to the weakening of cultural standards—to relativism. Indeed he even adopts a Becker-like economic analysis of the family himself, apparently unaware that if people actually thought about their families in the way that he and [economist Gary] Becker claim they do, the family would hardly be a source of any of the moral sentiments that are important to him:

> But powerful as they are, the expression of these [familial] instincts has been modified by contemporary circumstances. When children have less economic value, then, at the margin, fewer children will be produced, marriage (and childbearing) will be postponed, and more marriages will end in divorce. And those children who are produced will be raised, at the margin, in ways that reflect their higher opportunity cost. Some will be neglected and others will be cared for in ways that minimize the parental cost in personal freedom, extra income, or career opportunities.

Let me be clear that I think Wilson is right about changes that have occurred in the family, and that he is also right about the unfortunate social consequences of those changes. His mistake is in failing to see the responsibility for these changes that must be borne by the spread of market thinking into the domain of our intimate social relations. As I have said elsewhere, there is an opportunity cost to thinking about one's social relations in terms of opportunity costs. In Wilson's terms, that opportunity cost will be paid in sympathy, fairness, and duty. Sociologist Arlie Hochschild has written that "each marriage bears the footprints of economic and cultural trends which originate far outside marriage." Wilson has emphasized the cultural and overlooked the economic. And so, alas, has Murray.

What Economies Do to People

In Arthur Miller's play, *All My Sons,* much of the drama centers around the belated discovery by a son that his father knowingly shipped defective airplane parts to fulfill a government contract during World War II. The parts were installed, some of the planes crashed, and pilots and their crews were killed. The man responsible, the father, is a good man, a kind man, a man who cares deeply about his family and would do anything to protect them and provide for them. His son simply can't imagine that a man like his father is capable of such an act—but he is. As he explains, he was under enormous pressure to deliver the goods. The military needed the parts right away, and failure to deliver would have destroyed his business. He had a responsibility to take care of his family. And anyway, there was no certainty that the parts would not hold up when in use. As the truth slowly comes out, the audience has the same incredulity as the son. How could it be? If a man like that could do a thing like that, then anyone is capable of doing anything.

This, of course, is one of the play's major points. Almost anyone *is* capable of almost anything. A monstrous system can make a monster of anyone, or perhaps more accurately, can make almost anyone do monstrous things. We see this as drama like Miller's are played out in real life, with horrifyingly tragic consequences.

- All too close to the story of *All My Sons,* military contractors have been caught knowingly making and selling defective brake systems for U.S. jet fighters, defective machine gun parts that cause the guns to jam when used, and defective fire-fighting equipment for navy ships.
- An automobile manufacturer knowingly made and sold a dangerous car, whose gas tank was alarmingly likely to explode in rear end collisions. This defect could have been corrected at a cost of a few dollars per car.
- A chemical company continued operating a chemical plant in Bhopal, India long after it knew the plant was unsafe. A gas leak killed more than 2000 people, and seriously injured more than 30,000. The $5 billion company responded to this tragedy by sending $1 million in disaster relief and a shipment of medicines sufficient for about 400 people.
- Other drug and chemical manufacturers make and sell to the Third World products known to be sufficiently dangerous that their sale is banned in the U.S.
- The asbestos industry knowingly concealed the hazardous nature of their products for years from workers who were exposed to carcinogens on a daily basis.
- Trucking companies put trucks on the road more than 30% of which would fail safety inspections and are thus hazards to their drivers as well as to other motorists.
- And of course, we all know now about the tobacco industry.

And it isn't just about dramatic death and destruction. The death and destruction can be slow and torturous:

- Firms get closed down, people put out of work, and communities destroyed, not because they aren't profitable, but because they aren't *as* profitable as other parts of the business.
- People are put to work in illegal sweatshops, or the work is sent offshore, where the working conditions are even worse, but not illegal.

Why does all this abuse occur? What makes people seek to exploit every advantage over their customers? What makes bosses abuse their employees? Do the people who do these things take pleasure from hurting their unsuspecting customers? Do they relish the opportunity to take advantage of people? It does not seem so. When bosses are challenged about their unscrupulous practices, they typically argue that "everybody does it." Understand, the argument is not that since everybody does it, it is all right. The argument is that since everybody does it, you have to do it also, in self-defense. In competitive situations, it seems inevitable that dishonest, inhumane practices will drive out the honest and humane ones; to be humane becomes a luxury that few business people can afford.

I find it unimaginable as I talk to the talented, ambitious, enthusiastic students with whom I work that any of them aspires to a future in which he or she will oversee the production of cars, drugs, chemicals, foods, military supplies, or anything else that will imperil the lives of thousands of people. I even find it unimaginable that any of them will accept such a future. They are good, decent people, as far removed from those who seek to turn human weakness and vulnerability into profit as anyone could be. And yet, I know that some of my former students already have, and some of my current students surely will accept such positions. They will also marry, have families, and raise wonderful children who won't believe their parents could ever do such things. Surely there is an urgent need to figure out what it is that makes good people do such bad things, and stop it.

The leaders of corporations tell themselves that they have only one mission—to do whatever they can to further the interests of the shareholders, the owners of the company that these leaders have been hired to manage. When the leaders of corporations say these things to themselves, they are telling themselves the truth. They work within a system that asks—even requires—them to be single-minded, no matter how much they wish they could be different. As long as the system has this character, we can expect that only the single-minded will rise to the top. Only rarely will people whose intentions are to change corporate practices go far enough to implement those intentions.

Several years ago United States Catholic Bishops drafted a position paper, a pastoral letter, on the economy. In it they said, "every perspective on economic life that is human, moral, and Christian must be shaped by two questions: What does the economy do *for* people? What does the economy do *to* people?" I have been suggesting that our economy does terrible things *to* people, even to those people who succeed. It makes them into people that they should not and do not want to be, and it encourages them to do things that they should not and do not want to do. No matter what an economy does *for* these people, it cannot be justified if it does these things *to* them. And it seems to me that in the face of massive, antisocial practices like these, blaming the underclass for teaching mainstream America the lessons of incivility is perverse.

POSTSCRIPT

Is the Underclass the Major Threat to American Ideals?

In *Reducing Poverty in America* edited by Michael R. Darby (Sage Publications, 1996), James Q. Wilson summarizes the debate on the causes of poverty as the clash between two views: "The first is incentives or objective factors: jobs, incomes, opportunities. The second is culture: single-parent families, out-of-wedlock births, and a decaying work ethic." Sociologists expect the structural versus individual explanations of poverty to be debated for a long time because both can be seen as at least partially true. The cultural explanation derives from the anthropological studies of Oscar Lewis and was proposed as a major cause of urban poverty in America by Edward Banfield in *The Unheavenly City* (Little, Brown, 1970). More recent proponents of the culture-of-poverty thesis today are Lawrence E. Harrison, who wrote *Who Prospers? How Cultural Values Shape Economic and Political Success* (Basic Books, 1992); and Theodore Dalrymple, *Life at the Bottom: The Worldview that Makes the Underclass* (Ivan R. Dee, 2001). In *The Dream and the Nightmare: The Sixties' Legacy to the Underclass* (William Morrow, 1993), Myron Magnet blames the culture of the underclass for their poverty, but he also blames the upper classes for contributing greatly to the underclass's culture.

The counter to the cultural explanation of poverty is the structural explanation. Its most current version focuses on the loss of unskilled jobs. This is the thrust of William Julius Wilson's analysis of the macroeconomic forces that impact so heavily on the urban poor in *The Truly Disadvantaged* (University of Chicago Press, 1987) and in *When Work Disappears: The World of the New Urban Poor* (Alfred A. Knopf, 1996). If Jeremy Rifkin's analysis in *The End of Work: The Decline of the Global Labor Force and the Dawn of the Post-Market Era* (Putnam, 1995) is correct, then this situation will get worse. A recent treatment of structural factors is Garth L. Mangum, *The Persistence of Poverty in the United States* (Johns Hopkins University Press, 2003).

As the Schwartz reading above points out, capitalism and its culture have serious negative social consequences for America. This position is supported by Joel Bakan, *The Corporation: The Pathological Pursuit of Profit and Power* (Free Press, 2004); and Guy B. Adams, *Unmasking Administrative Evil* (M.E. Sharpe, 2004).

ISSUE 10

Has Affirmative Action Outlived Its Usefulness?

YES: Curtis Crawford, from "Racial Preference Versus Nondiscrimination," *Society* (March/April 2004)

NO: Ann Rosegrant Alvarez, from "Are Affirmative-Action Policies Increasing Equality in the Labor Market?" *Controversial Issues in Social Policy* (Allyn and Bacon, 2003)

ISSUE SUMMARY

YES: Curtis Crawford, editor of the website www.DebatingRacial-Preferences.org, explores all possible options for bettering the situation of disadvantaged minorities in a truly just manner. He argues that the right of everyone, including white males, to nondiscrimination clearly is superior to the right of minorities to affirmative action.

NO: Ann Rosegrant Alvarez, professor of social work at Wayne State University, argues that affirmative action policies are increasing equality in the labor market, and they are still necessary because inequality of opportunity still exists.

In America, equality is a principle as basic as liberty. "All men are created equal" is perhaps the most well known phrase in the Declaration of Independence. More than half a century after the signing of the Declaration, the French social philosopher Alexis de Tocqueville examined democracy in America and concluded that its most essential ingredient was the equality of condition. Today we know that the "equality of condition" that Tocqueville perceived did not exist for women, blacks, Native Americans, and other racial minorities, nor for other disadvantaged social classes. Nevertheless, the ideal persisted.

When slavery was abolished after the Civil War, the Constitution's newly ratified Fourteenth Amendment proclaimed, "No State shall . . . deny to any person within its jurisdiction the equal protection of the laws." Equality has been a long time coming. For nearly a century after the abolition of slavery, American blacks were denied equal protection by law in some states and by social practice nearly everywhere. One-third of the states either

164

permitted or forced schools to become racially segregated, and segregation was achieved elsewhere through housing policy and social behavior. In 1954 the Supreme Court reversed a 58-year-old standard that had found "separate but equal" schools compatible with equal protection of the law. A unanimous decision in *Brown v. Board of Education* held that separate is *not* equal for the members of the discriminated-against group when the segregation "generates a feeling of inferiority as to their status in the community that may affect their hearts and minds in a way unlikely ever to be undone." The 1954 ruling on public elementary education has been extended to other areas of both governmental and private conduct, including housing and employment.

Even if judicial decisions and congressional statutes could end all segregation and racial discrimination, would this achieve equality—or simply perpetuate the status quo? Consider that the unemployment rate for blacks today is much higher than that of whites. Disproportionately higher numbers of blacks experience poverty, brutality, broken homes, physical and mental illness, and early deaths, while disproportionately lower numbers of them reach positions of affluence and prestige. It seems possible that much of this inequality has resulted from 300 years of slavery and segregation. Is termination of this ill treatment enough to end the injustices? No, say the proponents of affirmative action.

Affirmative action—the effort to improve the educational and employment opportunities for minorities—has had an uneven history in U.S. federal courts. In *Regents of the University of California v. Allan Bakke* (1978), which marked the first time the Supreme Court dealt directly with the merits of affirmative action, a 5–4 majority ruled that a white applicant to a medical school had been wrongly excluded in favor of a less qualified black applicant due to the school's affirmative action policy. Yet the majority also agreed that "race-conscious" policies may be used in admitting candidates—as long as they do not amount to fixed quotas. The ambivalence of *Bakke* has run through the Court's treatment of the issue since 1978. In 2003 the Supreme Court found the University of Michigan's admissions policy discriminatory but the University of Michigan Law School's admissions policy nondiscriminatory. As a result, race can still be used as one factor among many to create a diverse student body, but the weight of that factor must be far less than some universities had been using.

In the following selections, Curtis Crawford and Ann Rosegrant Alvarez debate the merits of affirmative action. Crawford carefully lays out the options and arguments and balances the various rights and values involved. In the end, he argues, we must hold fast to the principle that the right to not be discriminated against supercedes all other values in this case and will produce the best results. Alvarez counters that discrimination against minorities still exists, and affirmative actions—if not egregious—are still needed to bring about greater justice in society.

Curtis Crawford  **YES**

Racial Preference versus Nondiscrimination

After a 25-year silence on the subject, the Supreme Court has pronounced on the constitutionality of race-based affirmative action in university admissions. Those who had hoped that the issues would be wisely clarified and weighed must have been greatly disappointed. The two cases accepted for review, *Grutter v. Bollinger* and *Gratz v. Bollinger,* provided valuable information on how universities actually implement preferential admissions. . . .

The litigation of these two cases revealed large racial inequalities in the treatment of applicants with similar academic credentials. For example, at the trial in federal district court, the Michigan Law School admission grid for 1995 (the year Ms. Grutter was rejected) was offered in evidence. For all applicants, identified by race but not by name, the grid included data on their Undergraduate Grade Point Average (UGPA), Law School Aptitude Test score (LSAT), and admission or rejection. Each cell of the grid combined a small range of grades and scores. . . .

The size of the preference is indicated by the gap between the rates of admission for Favored Minorities and for Other Applicants. In the cell containing the median grade and score for all applicants (UGPA 3.25–3.49, LSAT 161–163), all Favored Minorities were admitted but only 5% of Other Applicants. . . . Down at the 30th percentile (applicants with grades and scores below 70% of their rivals), 83% of Favored Minorities but just 1% of Other Applicants gained admission. . . . In sum, Favored Minorities in the 10th percentile cell had a slightly better chance of admission than Other Applicants in the median cell, while Favored Minorities in the median cell had a slightly better chance than Other Applicants in the top cell. . . .

Racial affirmative action began almost forty years ago with efforts to make sure that people were not being treated unequally because of their race. It soon developed into programs conferring special treatment based on race, especially in higher education and employment. Decisions typically affected have been admission to college and graduate school; and hiring, promotion and training for private and government jobs. The groups now regularly designated for favorable treatment based on race or ethnicity are blacks, Latinos and Native Americans. Asians sometimes receive it; whites,

From *Society*, March/April 2004, pp. 51–58. Copyright © 2004 by Transaction Publishers, Inc. Reprinted by permission.

almost never. The advantage is usually conferred by applying a double standard, whereby the requirements for selection are less exacting for members of the favored group.

These programs have been upheld as a remedy for past injustice, yet condemned as an instrument of present injustice. They have been praised for increasing minority access to business and professional careers, and blamed for debasing standards in the process. They are supposed by some to have raised and by others to have undermined the self-esteem of their recipients and the value placed on them by others. The controversy is fierce, partly because people on both sides believe that their position is what justice requires. But contrary views cannot both be right. We must dig deeper than usually occurs in public discussion to uncover and disentangle the relevant standards for moral judgment.

Unequal Treatment in General

At the outset, we need to distinguish between unequal treatment in general, and unequal treatment based on race. The latter may or may not be a special case, with special rules. Unequal treatment is simply treatment that favors one person over another. People are treated unequally for so many reasons, in so many contexts, that the existence of a general moral rule may seem impossible. But I suggest that we have such a rule. Ask yourself if and when you think that treating people unequally is the right thing to do. Is it all right when there is no reason for it? That would be arbitrary. Is it morally permissible if there is a good reason? For example, is it permissible to favor one applicant over another if they differ in ability, character, training, experience, and the like? Of course. Concerning something as important as the opportunity for education or employment, should people ever be treated unequally without good reason? No. But if there is a good reason, is it morally permissible to treat them unequally? It is not only permissible, it may be required.

What if the individual difference on which special treatment is based has nothing to do with an applicant's ability or need? Suppose that a public university gives an admissions preference to in-state residents, or a scholarship preference for veterans. Does the rule still hold, that unequal treatment is morally permissible when it is reasonable? The reasons commonly offered are, in the first case, that a state university is financed by, and owes a primary educational responsibility to, the residents of the state; in the second case, that such scholarships are both reward and incentive for service in the armed forces. The reasons seem good to me, and my sense of right and wrong does not bar the unequal treatment in either example. Others may think the reasons poor and the treatment wrong. In either view, whether unequal treatment is permissible depends on whether there is a good reason for it.

Preferential admission to a private university for the children of alumni is supposed to strengthen the school's relationship with its former students, thereby solidifying their continued interest and financial support, without which the quality and even the survival of the school might be jeopardized. Whether these are good reasons is disputed, but again the point is that, if one thinks the reasons good, one does not consider the preference immoral.

Supporters of racial preference think that the reasons for it are good: better, indeed, than for many kinds of preference that are generally accepted. Hence they conclude that there is nothing morally wrong with the unequal treatment they advocate. This conclusion is valid, if the rule for unequal treatment based on race is the same as the rule for unequal treatment in general. But are the rules the same?

Does the rule, that unequal treatment is morally permissible when there is good reason, still hold when it is based on race? During the campaign to overthrow American discrimination against blacks and others, it was never suggested that if the discriminators had good reason, their actions would be morally acceptable. The legislatures, schools, professions, businesses and unions that practiced racial discrimination were not asked about their reasons; they were simply told to quit. Any claims that their policies were "reasonable means to legitimate ends" were rejected as rationalizations for racial injustice. The overriding conviction was that racial discrimination was morally out of bounds, no matter what reasons the discriminators might offer.

Based on this moral principle, laws were enacted between 1940 and 1970 at the local, state and national levels, barring unequal treatment in voting, housing, health care, public accommodations, public facilities, education and employment. These statutes established the right not to be discriminated against, and the corresponding duty not to discriminate, on account of "race, color or national origin." Rights are not absolute: they may be overridden by superior rights or by public necessity. But when unequal treatment on a particular basis is barred *as a matter of right*, people are not free to discriminate on that basis simply because they have good reasons. The right not to be racially discriminated against was not reserved for members of particular groups, but ascribed equally to every person in the United States.

Was the moral principle behind this legislation mistaken? For blacks it can be seen as a two-edged sword, banning adverse discrimination to be sure, but also prohibiting any discrimination in their favor. The antidiscrimination statutes left blacks with two important disadvantages. They were still held back by deficiencies in ability, training and motivation attributable at least in part to past discrimination; and they faced the prospect that discrimination against them in the future, though illegal, would often occur. No one doubts that the social and economic condition of American blacks would be better, absent their history of racial oppression. A plausible remedy would be racial preference, until both the effects of past, and the practice of current, anti-black discrimination had dissipated. But such a remedy would require important exceptions to the general ban on racial discrimination.

Any society that decides to end an era of discrimination faces the same moral dilemma. If everyone is granted the right not to be discriminated against on account of race, the possibility of helping the victims of past discrimination through racial preference is lost. If members of the previously excluded groups are favored on the basis of race, the right of others not to suffer racial discrimination is denied.

There is a way to slice through the dilemma, which would assist many disadvantaged individuals. Instead of racial preference, a program could assist those who had suffered specific, oppressive treatment, such as chronic and substantial racial discrimination. Any person, regardless of race, who could demonstrate such treatment in his own case would be eligible for the assistance. Such a program would satisfy the racial nondiscrimination rule, since the basis for assistance would be individual injury, not racial identity. But it would help only a fraction of those who currently benefit from race-based affirmative action.

Are there superior rights or public necessities that might override the right to racial nondiscrimination? The right to racial nondiscrimination, though momentous, is not the only care of the republic. Other (sometimes conflicting) rights and interests must also be protected. The moral dilemma of racial preference for some *versus* racial nondiscrimination for all might be avoided if, in certain circumstances, the right to racial nondiscrimination were superseded by a higher right or by public necessity.

Equity and Compensation

Some argue that there is a right to equal participation for racial groups, which overrides the individual right to nondiscrimination. According to this view, 'equal participation' means equal success in wealth, status, and achievement, not for every individual, but for the average person in each group, as compared with the average American. A belief in this right is often the moral basis for affirmative-action goals, adopted for the purpose of increasing the percentage of "underrepresented" minorities in the higher echelons of education and employment, to match their share of the general population. If such a right exists, it would conflict with the right to nondiscrimination, and might overrule it. . . .

If individuals who have been subjected to racial discrimination can be given compensatory help without running afoul of the nondiscrimination rule, why not an entire racial group? Could we thus escape from our moral dilemma? Is it possible that all we need is a finding by the national legislature that discrimination against certain racial groups has been and continues to be so pervasive that every member of the group is entitled to compensatory preference? Many proponents of affirmative action proceed as if such a finding had occurred, in their own minds if not in the legislative process. This helps them to think of racial preference as compensation, rather than discrimination.

A legislative finding of this sort, though based on evidence of injury to some, would be mere supposition concerning others. But the right of just compensation requires proof of specific injury to the person who invokes it. A legislative decision to compensate an entire racial group could not meet this criterion; it would be discrimination masquerading as compensation. Moreover, a legislature permitted to stereotype racial groups sympathetically would be free to do the contrary. Based on data that discrimination against Blacks is much more frequent than against whites, it would declare every black a victim. Based on statistics that crime by Blacks is much more frequent than by Whites, it could declare every Black a criminal. . . .

A Public Necessity to Achieve Diversity?

Some, giving a broader definition to public necessity, uphold two propositions, (a) that racial diversity in education and employment is a public necessity, and (b) that racial preference is essential to achieve such diversity. If by "diversity" they simply mean difference or variety, proposition (a) may be true, but proposition (b) is manifestly untrue. In a society composed of many different groups, all one needs in order to ensure racial and ethnic variety in colleges and workplaces is not to discriminate. But among supporters of race-based affirmative action, "diversity" often means having a larger number from "underrepresented groups" than would occur without racial preference. Using this definition, proposition (b) is true, but proposition (a) is false. There is no public necessity that racial groups be represented in education or employment in proportions higher than warranted by the fitness of their members, individually and impartially assessed.

A Need to Reduce Bias against Minorities?

Some argue that racial preference helps to prevent racial discrimination. They believe that unlawful discrimination against nonwhites in education and employment is common, since those in power are mostly white; they argue that when decision-makers have to meet goals for increasing minority participation, antiminority discrimination is effectively prevented. Racial goals and quotas are therefore imposed, by institutions over their officials or by courts over institutions, to ensure that people who might discriminate will not do so.

Paradoxically, this policy prevents violations of the right to racial nondiscrimination by making certain that they occur. . . .

The Right to Racial Nondiscrimination

We have found that, if we recognize a general moral right to racial nondiscrimination, racial preference cannot be justified as serving a superior right or a public necessity. The supposed rights and necessities either do not exist, or do not conflict with the right to nondiscrimination. Is there another approach that might clear the way for racial preference?

The moral right to racial nondiscrimination could be expunged or limited. One could (1) scrap the right altogether, (2) define the right more narrowly, (3) exempt education and employment from the nondiscrimination rule, (4) permit discrimination favorable to blacks, or (5) permit discrimination favorable to all "underrepresented" minorities. Should the United States have chosen (or now choose) one of these options?

1. Scrap the Right Entirely?

This option would require us to repeal our antidiscrimination laws and to reject the moral principle on which they are based. No one advocates this. . . .

Wherever practiced, racial discrimination generates racial oppression, hostility and violence. Nondiscrimination is not easy, but it is the only standard to which members of every racial and ethnic group might agree, since it is the only standard that places no one at a disadvantage because of his group membership. . . .

2. Redefine Wrongful Discrimination?

Instead of forbidding all unequal treatment based on race, we might bar such treatment only when it is motivated by racial prejudice or hostility. This would clear the way for "benign" discrimination in behalf of a previously excluded group, without sacrificing anyone's right to be free from "malign" discrimination.

A principal disadvantage to this approach is the extensive harm that it would legalize. A major reason for antidiscrimination laws is to protect people from being deprived of products, services, and opportunities by discriminatory acts. But this deprivation is just as great, whether the discrimination is motivated by prejudice or not. Discrimination is not benign to the person it injures. . . .

3. Exempt Education and Employment?

No one contends that racial discrimination should be outlawed in every kind of decision; to bar it in choosing a friend, a spouse, or a legislative representative would be invasive or unenforceable. Why not, then, withdraw the prohibition from the two areas in which preferential treatment might be most helpful for members of a previously excluded group, by bringing them more quickly into prestigious occupations and encouraging their fellows to aim higher and work harder?

A decision to exempt education and employment from the ban on discrimination would place both society and government in moral contradiction with themselves. The society, having decided that racial discrimination in general is wrong, would nevertheless be treating it in crucial areas as beneficial. The government, in its roles as educator and employer, would freely practice here that which elsewhere it must prosecute and punish. Such broad contradictions are fatal to the public consensus that racial discrimination is ordinarily unjust, a consensus that is necessary for general adherence to antidiscrimination laws. . . .

4. Favor Blacks Only?

This would respond forthrightly to the moral dilemma posed early in this essay, by making Blacks an exception to the nondiscrimination rule. The exception could apply to all areas of life that are covered by the rule, including housing, business, finance, voter registration, shopping, entertainment, criminal and civil justice, *etc.*, as well as education, employment, and government contracting. But an exception this large, which could easily sink the rule, has no champions. What is proposed instead is to limit the exception primarily to employment and higher education.

The exception faces two ways: Blacks would gain the privilege of favorable discrimination, by themselves or in their behalf; while all others would lose the right not to racially discriminated against when blacks are the beneficiaries.

A major argument against this option is the absence of a principled basis for making blacks the only beneficiaries of racial discrimination. If, when the nation decided to ban racial discrimination, blacks were the only group to have suffered it in the past, a basis for this exception would be clear. But Blacks were not alone. American Indians; Mexicans, Puerto Ricans, and other Latinos; Japanese, Chinese, and other Asians; Poles, Italians, Slavs, Arabs, Jews, and other whites could all point to group wounds from past discrimination. . . .

5. Favor "Underrepresented" Minorities?

It may be argued that this, in effect, is the option we have chosen, not by amending the nondiscrimination statutes, but by creating affirmative-action programs. Under them, Blacks, Latinos, and Native Americans receive racial preference and are supposedly not discriminated against; whites do not receive preference and are often discriminated against; Asians are sometimes the beneficiaries, sometimes the victims. That many whites and Asians have lost their right to racial nondiscrimination in these areas is not made explicit. But it is surely implied, by the view that racial preference at their expense is morally permissible when serving a good purpose, and by the argument that they have no more reason to complain when disadvantaged by racial preference, than if the preference had been based on place of residence or family connections. . . .

Supporters of racial preference for black, Hispanic and Native Americans in education and employment typically invoke principles of racial justice, such as the right to compensation for past injury and/or a right to equal racial success. We have argued above that the latter right does not exist and the former right, properly applied, does not require special treatment based on race. We have argued also that the plea of public necessity is unfounded. . . .

Our inquiry began with a moral dilemma. If all have the right not to be subject to racial discrimination, no one may be assisted via racial preference; if racial preference is authorized for some, the right not to suffer racial discrimination is thereby denied to others. Two ways out of the dilemma were examined.

May the right to racial nondiscrimination, especially in education and employment, though belonging to everyone, be overridden by certain higher rights or public necessities? By a right to equal success for racial groups, or to just compensation for past discrimination? Or by a public necessity for racial preference as a means to racial peace, to racial diversity, or to the prevention of discrimination? These supposed rights and necessities were found to be either non-existent, or not in conflict with the right to racial nondiscrimination, and therefore incapable of overriding it.

Should we rescind or limit the right to racial nondiscrimination, in order to make racial preference available? Five options were considered. The nondiscrimination rule could be scrapped altogether, redefined to cover only prejudiced or hostile acts, dropped from education and employment, or modified in these areas to allow preference for blacks only or for all "under-represented" minorities. The arguments against these limits were in every case preponderant.

We cannot have the individual and social benefits of the nondiscrimination rule if we decline to obey it. We cannot teach our children that racial discrimination is wrong if we persistently discriminate. We cannot preserve the right to nondiscrimination by systematically violating it. But, without breaking or bending the rule, we can respond to many people who need and deserve help. The racial nondiscrimination rule does not preclude compensation for specific injury. It does not bar special assistance, by the public or private sector, to persons who labor under social, cultural, or economic disadvantages, provided that the purpose of the help and the criteria for eligibility are colorblind.

Besides excluding racial preference, there are other important respects in which a desirable assistance program would not imitate current affirmative action. It would help people increase their ability to meet regular standards, instead of lowering standards to accommodate inferior ability. The role of government would be primarily determined by the legislative branch, not the bureaucracy or the judiciary. The participation of the private sector would be voluntary or contractual, not compulsory. The rules and operation of the program would be honestly described and freely accessible to public scrutiny. These guidelines are not mandates of the nondiscrimination rule, just counsels of good sense. They will be easier to meet in a racial policy that we really believe is right.

Ann Rosegrant Alvarez  **NO**

Are Affirmative-Action Policies Increasing Equality in the Labor Market? Yes

Americans are not noted for their interest in policy. Indeed, most U.S. Americans perceive matters of policy as boring, as well as largely irrelevant to their daily lives. The exception is affirmative-action policies, which evoke a strong response from the American public. Witness the lively and frequent attention to this topic in the academic disciplines, including social work, sociology, public policy, political science, economics, and education, . . . as well as generous coverage by news media and on numerous Web sites devoted to the topic. Everyone, it appears, has an opinion on affirmative action.

Why? In part, many Americans believe that they or their loved ones have been affected by these policies. This gives almost everyone a vested interest in the implementation and results of such policies. In addition, in a country in which issues of gender and—particularly—race are incendiary and omnipresent, it offers an arena to discuss, debate, and exert an impact on the retention, or the reform and dissolution of, racist and sexist norms and practices.

I assert that affirmative-action policies are increasing equality in the labor market. In this article, I briefly address the issues of why such policies were initially put into place. The subsequent discussion examines the three primary arguments used against affirmative-action policies: (1) They are unnecessary; (2) they are discriminatory or otherwise detrimental; and (3) they are not effective. My conclusion emphasizes the social-justice perspective with regard to affirmative-action policies.

Background: The Development of Affirmative-Action Policies

Despite constitutional provisions and civil-rights laws guaranteeing equality and certain rights to all U.S. Americans, racial discrimination, inequality, and the resulting problems—including poverty—have remained prominent issues nationally and locally. During the 1960s, with civil rights at the forefront of the nation's consciousness, inequities in employment and promotion practices made access to jobs an obvious area for intervention. In 1961, President John F. Kennedy issued Executive Order 10925. The order established the Committee on Equal Employment Opportunity and for the first time required affirmative action to ensure nondiscrimination in employment. In 1965, President Lyndon B. Johnson directly addressed these issues in Executive Order 11246, later amended in 1967 to include gender discrimination. Johnson outlined the directive to "take affirmative action" in a stirring oratory in 1965, when he declared, "We seek not just freedom but opportunity—not just legal equity but human ability—not just equality as a right and a theory, but equality as a fact and as a result." . . .

The concept of affirmative action has broadened during the intervening years, both in terms of the populations included and the settings and venues targeted. . . . Affirmative-action battles are raging in courts, human-resource departments, and admissions offices. A consideration of some of the important questions surrounding this issue may help to assess the value and efficacy of affirmative-action policies.

Is Affirmative Action Necessary?

To answer the question, "Is affirmative action necessary?" let's consider similarities between unions and affirmative-action policies. Labor unions arose from members' desire to change inequitable and unjust employment practices, including hiring, promoting, and firing on grounds other than qualifications and seniority. Affirmative-action policies were similarly designed to address inequities, but with a focus on those related to gender and race or ethnicity.

Many opponents of affirmative-action policies argue that circumstances no longer warrant such intervention (if they ever did), because inequality of opportunities and participation does not exist. For example, Sally Pipes, president of the Pacific Research Institute, contends that women hold more than half of all professional positions . . . and "nearly half of all managerial and executive positions." . . . However, data either do not support these claims or are highly subject to interpretation.

The U.S. Equal Employment Opportunity Commission [EEOC] reports that in 1999, women constituted 51 percent of those in the workforce defined as "Professionals." . . . Yet this category includes such traditionally female occupations as nurse, teacher, and librarian. These occupations typically include many women while offering low pay and low status relative to many other professional jobs in male-dominated fields. . . . In addition, no corroboration exists of Pipes' and her coauthor's contention regarding "managerial and executive positions." . . . In fact, within the semantically closest category reported on by the EEOC—"Officials & Managers"—female participation drops to only 33.2 percent. . . . The unevenness revealed in statistics by race . . . is even more striking. Though all "minorities" combined account for 28.4 percent of overall employment participation, the category of "Professional" employment has only 18.2 percent minority participation. Just 13.7 percent minority participation is reported for positions classified as "Officials & Managers." The work of the Federal Glass Ceiling Commission also refutes the claims of those who attempt to minimize existing inequalities and the need to address them. This bipartisan body, created by the Civil Rights Act of 1991, released extensive findings corroborating inequities in the participation of women and minorities in leadership positions in U.S. corporations. Their findings included the following:

- Of senior-level male managers in Fortune 1000 industrial and Fortune 500 service industries, almost 97 percent were white, 0.6 percent African American, 0.3 percent Asian, and 0.4 percent Hispanic. . . .
- Compared to the earnings of white males, African American men with professional degrees earned only 79 percent, and African American women with professional degrees earned only 60 percent. . . .
- Based on surveys and reports, 95–97 percent of senior managers in Fortune 1500 companies are men; of these, 97 percent are white. In 1994, only two women were CEOs of Fortune 1000 companies. . . .

This and other data demonstrate that women and people of color are not represented proportionately in the most highly ranked and highly paid jobs. Given that approximately proportional representation is a potential outcome of affirmative action, current employment statistics confirm an ongoing need for policies (and enforcement) to equalize hiring processes and patterns.

Going beyond this, Bergmann presents and evaluates data on wages, employment patterns, and occupational segregation. After extensive analysis, she concludes that "the argument that affirmative action programs have already accomplished so much that we no longer need any programs of this . . . type in the workplace cannot seriously be made by anyone who has examined the evidence of what is currently going on in the workplace."

Returning to the example of unions, let me point out that they are not universally beloved or respected. Clearly, many people believe that they promote abuses of the system, as well as further inequities. However, they still protect the rights of people who otherwise would be subjected to the arbitrary whims of employers. Many people believe that these safeguards are necessary, owing to human nature and the general tendency of people to want to hire, work with, and promote people with whom they are comfortable. Comfort comes from commonalities—including similarities of gender and race.

This point has important implications for affirmative-action policies. Current statistics suggest an ongoing necessity for such policies as well as a future need. This need will continue until or unless people change the way they evaluate and select applicants for jobs or schools, including committing to eliminating bias in the selection process.

Are Affirmative-Action Policies Discriminatory or Detrimental?

To label "discriminatory" something that is designed to oppose and remedy the effects of discrimination smacks of circular reasoning. Behind affirmative action is the assumption—borne out by history—that a policy of "no intervention" creates discriminatory practice. But many people confuse reducing the unfair advantage traditionally enjoyed by some groups with creating an unfair advantage for others.

Peebles-Wilkins points out the inconsistency of those who contend that affirmative action unfairly advantages African Americans and who suggest that such privilege is unique to "minority" groups: "As a member of the African-American community, I have always been aware that preferential treatment and special privileges have existed for the children of the influential and wealthy, for recipients of political patronage, and for individuals with white or light-colored skin." Reducing such preferential treatment and privilege should not be confused with discrimination.

Nevertheless, many Americans believe that affirmative-action policies promote a "double standard" and "reverse discrimination" that unjustly penalize some people while furthering the interests of others who either do not deserve or have no special claim to or need for this "favoritism." That these beliefs persist is supported by the work of Kick and Fraser, who present research findings that examine three themes underlying the beliefs that affirmative action is discriminatory. They cite Wilson and Bobo and Kluegel in defining "self-interest" as the primary perspective among whites that race-targeted programs limit their own opportunities and impose "costs such as support for non-white educational and employment opportunities." . . . A second theme—"racial attitudes"—originates in "beliefs about the inherent inferiority of blacks and correspondingly prejudicial treatment of them." Finally, "stratification beliefs" represent a point of view that a true meritocracy exists, with unlimited opportunities for all, and with low accomplishment seen as a product of low ability, effort, or merit.

Even some African Americans, who might be presumed to have reason to favor affirmative-action policies, dispute their value. For example, many African American conservative columnists, including Armstrong Williams, Ken Hamblin, and Walter Williams, argue against such policies on various grounds, contending that they are paternalistic and debilitating to blacks. These policies, they maintain, promote a "victim" mindset that only exacerbates inequalities and performance differences along racial lines.

Noted African American social-work educator Peebles-Wilkins also expresses concerns about the potential and actual consequences of affirmative-action policies, including a stigmatizing impact on African Americans who others assume have been installed in positions for which they are unqualified. However, she ultimately asserts that although existing policies are imperfect, the United States needs some version of them. With respect to affirmative-action policies in educational settings, she concludes, "In summary, the very nature of our patriarchal, racially stratified society dictates that race and sex should be considered in faculty hiring and students admissions."

Finally, some scholars argue that affirmative-action policies create a diversity that benefits not only the obvious targets but society as a whole. For example, Bergmann cites the value of the "differing points of view, insights, values, and knowledge of the world that members of various groups bring to their roles."

Are Affirmative-Action Policies Effective?

Clearly, equality in the labor market has increased over time and since the implementation of affirmative-action policies. For example, Ong reports that the representation of women in the U.S. labor force increased from 24.7 percent in 1940 to 46.1 percent in 1995. For California, the corresponding increase was from 25.5 percent to 44.7 percent. In the broadcasting industry, women constituted 23.3 percent of full-time employees in 1971, and 41 percent by 1997. People of color increased their participation in this field as well, showing an increase from 9 percent of full-time broadcasting employees in 1971 to 20 percent in 1997. . . .

Wages of women compared to men, and wages of people of color compared to whites, reveal further good news. For example, the female-to-male average-earnings ratios for full-time workers in California, adjusted for education and experience, increased from 57 percent in 1959 to 70 percent in 1989. . . . The comparable ratio by race for men in California—that is, adjusted minority-to-white annual earnings ratios—shows the following changes between 1959 and 1989: for blacks, an increase from 68 percent to 74 percent; for Latinos, an increase from 86 percent to 88 percent; and for Asian Americans, an increase from 80 percent to 94 percent. . . . Nationally, the median employment earning for women in 1965 (when affirmative action was being implemented) was 40 percent of that of men; by 1999, that had risen to 62 percent. . . .

What has caused these changes? This question is difficult to answer. One possible solution is to estimate the potential impact of eliminating affirmative-action efforts. Following a careful analysis of the impact of affirmative action on public-sector employment, Badgett refrained from making large generalizations about the extent of change that could result from the elimination of public-sector affirmative-action programs in California. However, she did conclude that "the direction of change—a loss of opportunities for women and people of color—is clear, even if the magnitude of the change is not."

This issue of the extent of the change merits a closer look. Even among those who support the concept and goals of affirmative action, some have reservations. They contend that affirmative action has had such negligible impact that it should be either revised or abandoned altogether. I believe that even if the extensive efforts to date have not produced the *intended* degree of change, reducing or eliminating these efforts would severely curtail the gains toward equality that *have* been made.

In defense of existing policies, Chestang argues that although data may not confirm enormous gains for women and minorities as a result of affirmative-action policies, we must still consider the manner and strength of the implementation when assessing their impact. Chestang points out that rather than blaming affirmative-action policies for continuing inequalities, "it is more reasonable to assume that vigorous implementation of affirmative action policies might have resulted in greater gains for African Americans." . . .

Comedian George Burns responded to a query about how he felt about growing older by stating: "Considering the alternative, it's not too bad at all." . . . Given our current situation, do we have anything better to propose? Various authors and social critics have considered this question. . . . Their suggestions include focusing on certain professions, targeting all those who are economically deprived, enhancing competitive skills among those who currently benefit from affirmative action, intervening within organizational contexts, and broadening exposure to and positive experiences with affirmative action.

Within corporate settings, a number of strategies have been implemented. Some seem to be effective in changing the profile of those in executive ranks. These include mentoring programs; "succession planning," in which top executives select and develop women and minority replacement candidates for their positions; and the provision of special seminars or training opportunities, such as those provided through WOMEN Unlimited, that teach "how to succeed in a male-dominated environment." . . .

These approaches may have merit and, in the case of some, may have created positive change. But in the end, I think they would be most useful in conjunction with current affirmative-action policies, rather than as replacement strategies. In agreeing with this, Bergmann argues against a variety of potential alternative approaches based on improving education and training, providing assistance to all who come from economically disadvantaged backgrounds, and offering apprenticeship programs. While acknowledging the value of these different strategies in a supplementary role, she points out that they do not ultimately address the root causes of the problem: discrimination, in the form of racism and sexism.

Conclusion

Affirmative-action policies are not a matter purely for academic discourse, but are relevant and meaningful to the daily lives of many people. Of course, the debate around these issues can grow emotional and intense. Such issues tap into some of our most deeply felt beliefs about what is fair; who we are; and how we are perceived, judged, and valued. Affirmative-action proponents and opponents alike will use the same data and draw different conclusions—although each side may think that the preponderance of evidence supports its case.

To be sure, many thoughtful and well-intentioned people oppose affirmative-action policies for the reasons mentioned, and probably for others as well. I believe that either these opponents are not fully informed on the issues and do not fully appreciate the circumstances surrounding affirmative action, or that their motives are suspect. Both data and accompanying narratives establish that (1) there is a continuing need for affirmative action, (2) it is not discriminatory, and any negative side effects are outweighed by its benefits, and (3) it has been effective, although it has not made as much of a difference to date as its proponents originally hoped for.

Moreover, a social-justice perspective ultimately mandates the continuation of affirmative-action policies and efforts. Chestang advocates from this perspective, exhorting that "affirmative action should be supported because it is right, it is ethical, it is fair, and it is in the best of American tradition." It seems specious or naive to argue against this approach, when reports document that "prejudice against minorities and white women continues to be the single most important barrier to their advancement." . . . If this is true— and I believe there is overwhelmingly evidence that it is—then we cannot expect huge gains in equality from programs designed to increase individual potential through improvements in education, from diversity training in the workplace, or from a laissez-faire approach. Instead, the most effective approach is to continue with a variety of supplementary efforts, but with an aggressive and progressive implementation of existing affirmative-action policies at the center of those efforts. . . .

POSTSCRIPT

Has Affirmative Action Outlived Its Usefulness?

Crawford and Alvarez approach the issue of affirmative action from different directions. Alvarez starts with the end or goal of fairness to disadvantaged minorities and argues that affirmative action is a necessary means to that end. Crawford starts with the means and argues that affirmative action as morally unjustifiable. On the other hand, compensation for individuals who have been discriminated against is morally justifiable, but most of the people who benefit from affirmative action programs are not in this category. This argument would not persuade anyone who is passionate about justice for disadvantaged minorities, because our laws already allow discrimination victims to seek redress in the courts and that has not stopped or compensated for discrimination. Many believe that something more is needed, and affirmative action properly conducted is the best means.

The writings on this subject are diverse and numerous. For an in-depth discussion of the legal standing of affirmative action, see Girardeau A. Spann, *The Law of Affirmative Action: Twenty-Five Years of Supreme Court Decisions on Race and Remedies* (New York University Press, 2000). For a review of affirmative action programs, see M. Ali Raza et al., *The Ups and Downs of Affirmative Action Preferences* (Greenwood, 1999). William G. Bowen and Derek Bok review affirmative action in college admissions in *The Shape of the River: Long-Term Consequences of Considering Race in College and University Admissions* (Princeton University Press, 1998). Robert K. Fullinwider and Judith Lichtenberg provide a more recent assessment in *Leveling the Playing Field: Justice, Politics, and College Admissions* (Rowman & Littlefield, 2004) and Patricia Gurin et al. defend affirmative action at the University of Michigan in *Defending Diversity: Affirmative Action at the University of Michigan* (University of Michigan Press, 2004). For a history of affirmative action, see Philip F. Rubio, *A History of Affirmative Action* (University Press of Mississippi, 2001). The need for affirmative action or another effective means to address racial and gender inequality is provided in *Problem of the Century: Racial Stratification in the United States,* edited by Elijah Anderson and Douglas S. Massey (Russell Sage Foundation); Andrew Hacker, *Mismatch: The Growing Gulf between Women and Men* (Scribner, 2003); and David Neumark, *Sex Differences in Labor Markets* (Routledge, 2004). The debate on affirmative action is covered by Carl Cohen and James P. Sterba in *Affirmative Action and Racial Preference: A Debate* (Oxford University Press, 2003). Recently an anti-affirmative action movement has mobilized. Three works that try to counter this movement are Fred L. Pincus, *Reverse Discrimination: Dismantling the Myth* (Lynne Rienner, 2003); Faye J. Crosby, *Affirmative Action Is Dead: Long Live Affirmative Action* (Yale University Press,

2004); and Lee Cokorinos, *The Assault on Diversity: An Organized Challenge to Racial and Gender Justice* (Rowman & Littlefield, 2003). Andrew Hacker argues that affirmative action has relatively minor adverse consequences for whites in *Two Nations: Black and White, Separate, Hostile, Unequal* (Charles Scribner's Sons, 1992). Dinesh D'Souza, in *The End of Racism* (Free Press, 1995), argues that white racism has pretty much disappeared in the United States. The opposite is argued by Joe R. Feagin and Hernan Vera in *White Racism: The Basics* (Routledge, 1995) and by Stephen Steinberg in *Turning Back* (Beacon Press, 1995). For international comparisons see Thomas Sowell, *Affirmative Action around the World: An Empirical Study* (Yale University Press, 2004).

Economic Report of the President

The Economic Report of the President Web site includes current and anticipated trends in the United States and annual numerical goals concerning topics such as employment, production, real income, and federal budget outlays. The database notes employment objectives for significant groups of the labor force, annual numeric goals, and a plan for carrying out program objectives.

`http://www.library.nwu.edu/gpo/help/econr.html`

National Center for Policy Analysis

Through the National Center for Policy Analysis site you can read discussions that are of major interest in the study of American politics and government from a sociological perspective.

`http://www.ncpa.org`

Speakout.com

The Speakout.com Web site contains a library of online information and links related to public policy issues, primarily those in the United States. The issues are organized into topics and subtopics for easy searching.

`http://www.speakout.com/activism/issues`

Policy.com

Visit Policy.com, the site of the "policy community," to examine major issues related to social welfare, welfare reform, social work, and many other topics. The site includes substantial resources for researching issues online.

`http://www.policy.com`

PART 4

Political Economy
and Institutions

Are political power and economic power merged within a "power elite" that dominates the U.S. political system? The first issue in this part explores that debate. The second issue concerns the proper role of government in the economy. Some believe that the government must correct for the many failures of the market, while others think that the government usually complicates the workings of the free market and reduces its effectiveness. The next debate concerns public policy: What is the impact of the end of the Federal AFDC program? The fourth issue examines alternative educational policies for significantly improving public education. Finally, the last issue in this part looks at doctor-assisted suicide for terminally ill patients.

- Is Government Dominated by Big Business?

- Should Government Intervene in a Capitalist Economy?

- Has Welfare Reform Benefited the Poor?

- Is Competition the Solution to the Ills of Public Education?

- Should Doctor-Assisted Suicide Be Legalized for the Terminally Ill?

ISSUE 11

Is Government Dominated by Big Business?

YES: G. William Domhoff, from *Who Rules America? Power and Politics in the Year 2000,* 3rd ed. (Mayfield Publishing, 1998)

NO: Jeffrey M. Berry, from "Citizen Groups and the Changing Nature of Interest Group Politics in America," *The Annals of the American Academy of Political and Social Science* (July 1993)

ISSUE SUMMARY

YES: Political sociologist G. William Domhoff argues that the "owners and top-level managers in large income-producing properties are far and away the dominant power figures in the United States" and that they have inordinate influence in the federal government.

NO: Jeffrey M. Berry, a professor of political science, contends that public interest pressure groups that have entered the political arena since the end of the 1960s have effectively challenged the political power of big business.

$\mathbf{S}$ince the framing of the U.S. Constitution in 1787, there have been periodic charges that America is unduly influenced by wealthy financial interests. Richard Henry Lee, a signer of the Declaration of Independence, spoke for many Anti-Federalists (those who opposed ratification of the Constitution) when he warned that the proposed charter shifted power away from the people and into the hands of the "aristocrats" and "moneyites."

Before the Civil War, Jacksonian Democrats denounced the eastern merchants and bankers who, they charged, were usurping the power of the people. After the Civil War, a number of radical parties and movements revived this theme of antielitism. The ferment—which was brought about by the rise of industrial monopolies, government corruption, and economic hardship for western farmers—culminated in the founding of the People's Party at the beginning of the 1890s. The Populists, as they were more commonly called, wanted economic and political reforms aimed at transferring power away from the rich and back to "the plain people."

By the early 1900s the People's Party had disintegrated, but many writers and activists have continued to echo the Populists' central thesis: that the U.S. democratic political system is in fact dominated by business elites. Yet the thesis has not gone unchallenged. During the 1950s and the early 1960s, many social scientists subscribed to the *pluralist* view of America.

Pluralists argue that because there are many influential elites in America, each group is limited to some extent by the others. There are some groups, like the business elites, that are more powerful than their opponents, but even the more powerful groups are denied their objectives at times. Labor groups are often opposed to business groups; conservative interests challenge liberal interests, and vice versa; and organized civil libertarians sometimes fight with groups that seek government-imposed bans on pornography or groups that demand tougher criminal laws. No single group, the pluralists argue, can dominate the political system.

Pluralists readily acknowledge that American government is not democratic in the full sense of the word; it is not driven by the majority. But neither, they insist, is it run by a conspiratorial "power elite." In the pluralist view, the closest description of the American form of government would be neither majority rule nor minority rule but *minorities* rule. (Note that in this context, "minorities" does not necessarily refer to race or ethnicity but to any organized group of people with something in common—including race, religion, or economic interests—not constituting a majority of the population.) Each organized minority enjoys some degree of power in the making of public policy. In extreme cases, when a minority feels threatened, its power may take a negative form: the power to derail policy. When the majority—or, more accurately, a coalition of other minorities—attempts to pass a measure that threatens the vital interests of an organized minority, that group may use its power to obstruct their efforts. (Often cited in this connection is the use of the Senate filibuster, which is the practice of using tactics during the legislative process that cause extreme delays or prevent action, thus enabling a group to "talk to death" a bill that threatens its vital interests.) But in the pluralist view negative power is not the only driving force: when minorities work together and reach consensus on certain issues, they can institute new laws and policy initiatives that enjoy broad public support. Pluralism, though capable of producing temporary gridlock, ultimately leads to compromise, consensus, and moderation.

Critics of pluralism argue that pluralism is an idealized depiction of a political system that is in the grip of powerful elite groups. Critics fault pluralist theory for failing to recognize the extent to which big business dominates the policy-making process. In the selections that follow, G. William Domhoff supports this view, identifies the groups that compose the power elite, and details the way they control or support social, political, and knowledge-producing associations and organizations that advance their interests. Jeffrey M. Berry, in opposition, argues that, thanks to new consumer, environmental, and other citizen groups, big business no longer enjoys the cozy relationship it once had with Washington policymakers.

G. William Domhoff

 **YES**

Who Rules America?

Power and Class in the United States

| . . . [T]he owners and top-level managers in large income-producing proper-
ties are far and away the dominant power figures in the United States. Their
corporations, banks, and agribusinesses come together as a *corporate community* that dominates the federal government in Washington. Their real estate,
construction, and land development companies form *growth coalitions* that
dominate most local governments. Granted, there is competition within
both the corporate community and the local growth coalitions for profits
and investment opportunities, and there are sometimes tensions between
national corporations and local growth coalitions, but both are cohesive on
policy issues affecting their general welfare, and in the face of demands by
organized workers, liberals, environmentalists, and neighborhoods.

As a result of their ability to organize and defend their interests, the
owners and managers of large income-producing properties have a very great
share of all income and wealth in the United States, greater than in any other
industrial democracy. Making up at best 1 percent of the total population, by
the early 1990s they earned 15.7 percent of the nation's yearly income and
owned 37.2 percent of all privately held wealth, including 49.6 percent of all
corporate stocks and 62.4 percent of all bonds. Due to their wealth and the
lifestyle it makes possible, these owners and managers draw closer as a common social group. They belong to the same exclusive social clubs, frequent
the same summer and winter resorts, and send their children to a relative
handful of private schools. Members of the corporate community thereby
become a *corporate rich* who create a nationwide *social upper class* through
their social interaction. . . . Members of the growth coalitions, on the other
hand, are *place entrepreneurs,* people who sell locations and buildings. They
come together as local upper classes in their respective cities and sometimes
mingle with the corporate rich in educational or resort settings.

The corporate rich and the growth entrepreneurs supplement their
small numbers by developing and directing a wide variety of nonprofit
organizations, the most important of which are a set of tax-free charitable
foundations, think tanks, and policy-discussion groups. These specialized
nonprofit groups constitute a *policy-formation network* at the national level.

Chambers of commerce and policy groups affiliated with them form similar policy-formation networks at the local level, aided by a few national-level city development organizations that are available for local consulting.

Those corporate owners who have the interest and ability to take part in general governance join with top-level executives in the corporate community and the policy-formation network to form the *power elite*, which is the leadership group for the corporate rich as a whole. The concept of a power elite makes clear that not all members of the upper class are involved in governance; some of them simply enjoy the lifestyle that their great wealth affords them. At the same time, the focus on a leadership group allows for the fact that not all those in the power elite are members of the upper class; many of them are high-level employees in profit and nonprofit organizations controlled by the corporate rich. . . .

The power elite is not united on all issues because it includes both moderate conservatives and ultraconservatives. Although both factions favor minimal reliance on government on all domestic issues, the moderate conservatives sometimes agree to legislation advocated by liberal elements of the society, especially in times of social upheaval like the Great Depression of the 1930s and the Civil Rights Movement of the early 1960s. Except on defense spending, ultraconservatives are characterized by a complete distaste for any kind of government programs under any circumstances—even to the point of opposing government support for corporations on some issues. Moderate conservatives often favor foreign aid, working through the United Nations, and making attempts to win over foreign enemies through patient diplomacy, treaties, and trade agreements. Historically, ultraconservatives have opposed most forms of foreign involvement, although they have become more tolerant of foreign trade agreements over the past thirty or forty years. At the same time, their hostility to the United Nations continues unabated.

Members of the power elite enter into the electoral arena as the leaders within a *corporate-conservative coalition,* where they are aided by a wide variety of patriotic, antitax, and other single-issue organizations. These conservative advocacy organizations are funded in varying degrees by the corporate rich, direct-mail appeals, and middle-class conservatives. This coalition has played a large role in both political parties at the presidential level and usually succeeds in electing a conservative majority to both houses of Congress. Historically, the conservative majority in Congress was made up of most Northern Republicans and most Southern Democrats, but that arrangement has been changing gradually since the 1960s as the conservative Democrats of the South are replaced by even more conservative Southern Republicans. The corporate-conservative coalition also has access to the federal government in Washington through lobbying and the appointment of its members to top positions in the executive branch. . . .

Despite their preponderant power within the federal government and the many useful policies it carries out for them, members of the power elite are constantly critical of government as an alleged enemy of freedom and economic growth. Although their wariness toward government is expressed in terms of a dislike for taxes and government regulations, I believe their underlying concern is that government could change the power relations in the private sphere by aiding average Americans through a number of different avenues: (1) creating government jobs for the unemployed; (2) making health, unemployment, and welfare benefits more generous; (3) helping employees gain greater workplace rights and protections; and (4) helping workers organize unions. All of these initiatives are opposed by members of the power elite because they would increase wages and taxes, but the deepest opposition is toward any government support for unions because unions are a potential organizational base for advocating the whole range of issues opposed by the corporate rich. . . .

Where Does Democracy Fit In?

. . . [T]o claim that the corporate rich have enough power to be considered a dominant class does not imply that lower social classes are totally powerless. *Domination* means the power to set the terms under which other groups and classes must operate, not total control. Highly trained professionals with an interest in environmental and consumer issues have been able to couple their technical information and their understanding of the legislative and judicial processes with well-timed publicity, lobbying, and lawsuits to win governmental restrictions on some corporate practices. Wage and salary employees, when they are organized into unions and have the right to strike, have been able to gain pay increases, shorter hours, better working conditions, and social benefits such as health insurance. Even the most powerless of people— the very poor and those discriminated against—sometimes develop the capacity to influence the power structure through sit-ins, demonstrations, social movements, and other forms of social disruption, and there is evidence that such activities do bring about some redress of grievances, at least for a short time.

More generally, the various challengers to the power elite sometimes work together on policy issues as a *liberal-labor coalition* that is based in unions, local environmental organizations, some minority group communities, university and arts communities, liberal churches, and small newspapers and magazines. Despite a decline in membership over the past twenty years, unions are the largest and best-financed part of the coalition, and the largest organized social force in the country (aside from churches). They also cut across racial and ethnic lines more than any other institutionalized sector of American society. . . .

The policy conflicts between the corporate-conservative and liberal-labor coalitions are best described as *class conflicts* because they primarily concern the distribution of profits and wages, the rate and progressivity of taxation, the usefulness of labor unions, and the degree to which business should be regulated by government. The liberal-labor coalition wants corporations to pay higher wages to employees and higher taxes to government. It wants government to regulate a wide range of business practices, including many that are related to the environment, and help employees to organize unions. The corporate-conservative coalition resists all these policy objectives to a greater or lesser degree, claiming they endanger the freedom of individuals and the efficient workings of the economic marketplace. The conflicts these disagreements generate can manifest themselves in many different ways: workplace protests, industrywide boycotts, massive demonstrations in cities, pressure on Congress, and the outcome of elections.

Neither the corporate-conservative nor the liberal-labor coalition includes a very large percentage of the American population, although each has the regular support of about 25–30 percent of the voters. Both coalitions are made up primarily of financial donors, policy experts, political consultants, and party activists. . . .

Pluralism

The main alternative theory [I] address . . . claims that power is more widely dispersed among groups and classes than a class-dominance theory allows. This general perspective is usually called *pluralism,* meaning there is no one dominant power group. It is the theory most favored by social scientists. In its strongest version, pluralism holds that power is held by the general public through the pressure that public opinion and voting put on elected officials. According to this version, citizens form voluntary groups and pressure groups that shape public opinion, lobby elected officials, and back sympathetic political candidates in the electoral process. . . .

The second version of pluralism sees power as rooted in a wide range of well-organized "interest groups" that are often based in economic interests (e.g., industrialists, bankers, labor unions), but also in other interests as well (e.g., environmental, consumer, and civil rights groups). These interest groups join together in different coalitions depending on the specific issues. Proponents of this version of pluralism sometimes concede that public opinion and voting have only a minimal or indirect influence, but they see business groups as too fragmented and antagonistic to form a cohesive dominant class. They also claim that some business interest groups occasionally join coalitions with liberal or labor groups on specific issues, and that business-dominated coalitions sometimes lose. Furthermore, some proponents of this version of pluralism believe that the Democratic Party is responsive to the wishes of liberal and labor interest groups.

In contrast, I argue that the business interest groups are part of a tightly knit corporate community that is able to develop classwide cohesion on the issues of greatest concern to it: opposition to unions, high taxes, and government regulation. When a business group loses on a specific issue, it is often because other business groups have been opposed; in other words, there are arguments within the corporate community, and these arguments are usually settled within the governmental arena. I also claim that liberal and labor groups are rarely part of coalitions with business groups and that for most of its history the Democratic Party has been dominated by corporate and agribusiness interests in the Southern states, in partnership with the growth coalitions in large urban areas outside the South. Finally, I show that business interests rarely lose on labor and regulatory issues except in times of extreme social disruption like the 1930s and 1960s, when differences of opinion between Northern and Southern corporate leaders made victories for the liberal-labor coalition possible. . . .

How the Power Elite Dominates Government

This [section] shows how the power elite builds on the ideas developed in the policy-formation process and its success in the electoral arena to dominate the federal government. Lobbyists from corporations, law firms, and trade associations play a key role in shaping government on narrow issues of concern to specific corporations or business sectors, but their importance should not be overestimated because a majority of those elected to Congress are predisposed to agree with them. The corporate community and the policy-formation network supply top-level governmental appointees and new policy directions on major issues.

Once again, as seen in the battles for public opinion and electoral success, the power elite faces opposition from a minority of elected officials and their supporters in labor unions and liberal advocacy groups. These opponents are sometimes successful in blocking ultra-conservative initiatives, but most of the victories for the liberal-labor coalition are the result of support from moderate conservatives. . . .

Appointees to Government

The first way to test a class-dominance view of the federal government is to study the social and occupational backgrounds of the people who are appointed to manage the major departments of the executive branch, such as state, treasury, defense, and justice. If pluralists are correct, these appointees should come from a wide range of interest groups. If the state autonomy theorists are correct, they should be disproportionately former elected officials or longtime government employees. If the class-dominance view is correct, they should come disproportionately from the upper class, the corporate community, and the policy-formation network.

There have been numerous studies over the years of major governmental appointees under both Republican and Democratic administrations, usually focusing on the top appointees in the departments that are represented in the president's cabinet. These studies are unanimous in their conclusion that most top appointees in both Republican and Democratic administrations are corporate executives and corporate lawyers—and hence members of the power elite. . . .

Conclusion

This [section] has demonstrated the power elite's wide-ranging access to government through the interest-group and policy-formation processes, as well as through its ability to influence appointments to major government positions. When coupled with the several different kinds of power discussed in earlier [sections] this access and involvement add up to power elite domination of the federal government.

By *domination,* as stated in the first [section], social scientists mean the ability of a class or group to set the terms under which other classes or groups within a social system must operate. By this definition, domination does not mean control on each and every issue, and it does not rest solely on involvement in government. Influence over government is only the final and most visible aspect of power elite domination, which has its roots in the class structure, the corporate control of the investment function, and the operation of the policy-formation network. If government officials did not have to wait for corporate leaders to decide where and when they will invest, and if government officials were not further limited by the general public's acceptance of policy recommendations from the policy-formation network, then power elite involvement in elections and government would count for a lot less than they do under present conditions.

Domination by the power elite does not negate the reality of continuing conflict over government policies, but few conflicts, it has been shown, involve challenges to the rules that create privileges for the upper class and domination by the power elite. Most of the numerous battles within the interest-group process, for example, are only over specific spoils and favors; they often involve disagreements among competing business interests.

Similarly, conflicts within the policy-making process of government often involve differences between the moderate conservative and ultraconservative segments of the dominant class. At other times they involve issues in which the needs of the corporate community as a whole come into conflict with the needs of specific industries, which is what happens to some extent on tariff policies and also on some environmental legislation. In neither case does the nature of the conflict call into question the domination of government by the power elite.

. . . Contrary to what pluralists claim, there is not a single case study on any issue of any significance that shows a liberal-labor victory over a united corporate-conservative coalition, which is strong evidence for a class-domination theory on the "Who wins?" power indicator. The classic case studies frequently cited by pluralists have been shown to be gravely deficient as evidence for their views. Most of these studies reveal either conflicts among rival groups within the power elite or situations in which the moderate conservatives have decided for their own reasons to side with the liberal-labor coalition. . . .

More generally, it now can be concluded that all four indicators of power introduced in [the first section] point to the corporate rich and their power elite as the dominant organizational structure in American society. First, the wealth and income distributions are skewed in their favor more than in any other industrialized democracy. They are clearly the most powerful group in American society in terms of "Who benefits?" Second, the appointees to government come overwhelmingly from the corporate community and its associated policy-formation network. Thus, the power elite is clearly the most powerful in terms of "Who sits?"

Third, the power elite wins far more often than it loses on policy issues resolved in the federal government. Thus, it is the most powerful in terms of

"Who wins?" Finally, as shown in reputational studies in the 1950s and 1970s, . . . corporate leaders are the most powerful group in terms of "Who shines?" By the usual rules of evidence in a social science investigation using multiple indicators, the owners and managers of large income-producing properties are the dominant class in the United States.

Still, as noted at the end of the first [section], power structures are not immutable. Societies change and power structures evolve or crumble from time to unpredictable time, especially in the face of challenge. When it is added that the liberal-labor coalition persists in the face of its numerous defeats, and that free speech and free elections are not at risk, there remains the possibility that class domination could be replaced by a greater sharing of power in the future.

NO

Jeffrey M. Berry

Citizen Groups and the Changing Nature of Interest Group Politics in America

ABSTRACT: The rise of liberal citizen groups that began in the 1960s has had a strong impact on the evolution of interest group advocacy. The success of these liberal organizations was critical in catalyzing the broader explosion in the numbers of interest groups and in causing the collapse of many subgovernments. New means of resolving policy conflicts had to be established to allow for the participation of broader, more diverse policy communities. Citizen groups have been particularly important in pushing policymakers to create new means of structuring negotiations between large numbers of interest group actors. The greater participation of citizen groups, the increased numbers of all kinds of interest groups, and change in the way policy is made may be making the policymaking process more democratic.

Many protest movements have arisen in the course of American history, each affecting the political system in its own way. The social movements that took hold in the 1960s had their own unique set of roots but seemed to follow a conventional life span. The civil rights and antiwar groups that arose to protest the injustices they saw were classic social movements. Their views were eventually absorbed by one of the political parties, and, after achieving their immediate goals, their vitality was sapped. The antiwar movement disappeared, and black civil rights organizations declined in power. The most enduring and vital citizen groups born in this era of protest were never protest oriented. Consumer groups, environmental groups, and many other kinds of citizen lobbies have enjoyed unprecedented prosperity in the last 25 years. Never before have citizen groups been so prevalent in American politics, and never before have they been so firmly institutionalized into the policymaking process.

The rise of citizen groups has not only empowered many important constituencies, but it has altered the policymaking process as well. This article focuses on how citizen groups have affected interest group politics in general and how these organizations have contributed to the changing nature of

From THE ANNALS OF THE AMERICAN ACADEMY OF POLITICAL AND SOCIAL SCIENCE, July 2003. Copyright © 2003 by Sage Publications, Inc. Reprinted by permission.

public policymaking. A first step is to examine the initial success of liberal advocacy organizations as well as the conservative response to this challenge. Next, I will look at the impact of this growth of citizen group politics on the policymaking process. Then I will turn to how Congress and the executive branch have tried to cope with a dense population of citizen groups and the complex policymaking environment that now envelops government.

Finally, I will speculate as to how all of this has affected policymaking in terms of how democratic it is. The popular perception is that the rise of interest groups along with the decline of political parties has had a very negative impact on American politics. Analysis of the decline of parties will be left to others, but a central point here is that the growth in the numbers of citizen groups and of other lobbying organizations has not endangered the political system. There are some unfortunate developments, such as the increasing role of political action committees in campaign financing, but the rise of citizen groups in particular has had a beneficial impact on the way policy is formulated. The overall argument may be stated succinctly: the rise of liberal citizen groups was largely responsible for catalyzing an explosion in the growth of all types of interest groups. Efforts to limit the impact of liberal citizen groups failed, and the policymaking process became more open and more participatory. Expanded access and the growth in the numbers of competing interest groups created the potential for gridlock, if not chaos. The government responded, in turn, with institutional changes that have helped to rationalize policymaking in environments with a large number of independent actors.

The Rise of Citizen Groups

The lobbying organizations that emerged out of the era of protest in the 1960s are tied to the civil rights and antiwar movements in two basic ways. First, activism was stimulated by the same broad ideological dissatisfaction with government and the two-party system. There was the same feeling that government was unresponsive, that it was unconcerned about important issues, and that business was far too dominant a force in policymaking. Second, the rise of liberal citizen groups was facilitated by success of the civil rights and antiwar movements. More specifically, future organizers learned from these social movements. They learned that aggressive behavior could get results, and they saw that government could be influenced by liberal advocacy organizations. Some activists who later led Washington-based citizen lobbies cut their teeth as volunteers in these earlier movements.

For liberal consumer and environmental groups, an important lesson of this era was that they should not follow the protest-oriented behavior of the civil rights and antiwar movements. There was a collective realization that lasting influence would come from more conventional lobbying inside the political system. For consumer and environmental organizers, "power to the people" was rejected in favor of staff-run organizations that placed little emphasis on participatory democracy. This is not to say that these new organizations were simply copies of business lobbies; leaders of these groups like Ralph Nader and

John Gardner placed themselves above politics-as-usual with their moralistic rhetoric and their attacks against the established political order.

While there was significant support for these groups from middle-class liberals, a major impetus behind their success was financial backing from large philanthropic foundations. The foundations wanted to support social change during a time of political upheaval, but at the same time they wanted responsible activism. This early support, most notably from the Ford Foundation's program in public interest law, was largely directed at supporting groups relying on litigation and administrative lobbying. The seed money for these organizations enabled them to flourish and provided them with time to establish a track record so that they could appeal to individual donors when the foundation money ran out. Other groups emerged without the help of foundations, drawing on a combination of large donors, dues-paying memberships, and government grants. Citizen lobbies proved remarkably effective at raising money and at shifting funding strategies as the times warranted.

Citizen groups emerged in a variety of areas. In addition to consumer and environmental groups, there were organizations interested in hunger and poverty, governmental reform, corporate responsibility, and many other issues. A number of new women's organizations soon followed in the wake of the success of the first wave of citizen groups, and new civil rights groups arose to defend other groups such as Hispanics and gays. As has been well documented, the rise of citizen groups was the beginning of an era of explosive growth in interest groups in national politics. No precise baseline exists, so exact measurement of this growth is impossible. Yet the mobilization of interests is unmistakable. One analysis of organizations represented in Washington in 1980 found that 40 percent of the groups had been started since 1960, and 25 percent had begun after 1970.

The liberal citizen groups that were established in the 1960s and 1970s were not simply the first ripples of a new wave of interest groups; rather, they played a primary role in catalyzing the formation of many of the groups that followed. New business groups, which were by far the most numerous of all the groups started since 1960, were directly stimulated to organize by the success of consumer and environmental groups. There were other reasons why business mobilized, but much of their hostility toward the expanded regulatory state was directed at agencies strongly supported by liberal citizen groups. These organizations had seemingly seized control of the political agenda, and the new social regulation demanded increased business mobilization. New conservative citizen lobbies, many focusing on family issues such as abortion and the Equal Rights Amendment, were also begun to counter the perceived success of the liberal groups.

The swing of the ideological pendulum that led to a conservative takeover of the White House in 1980 led subsequently to efforts to limit the impact of liberal citizen groups. The Reagan administration believed that the election of 1980 was a mandate to eliminate impediments to economic growth. Environmental and consumer groups were seen as organizations that cared little about the faltering American economy; President Reagan referred to liberal public interest lawyers as "a bunch of ideological ambulance chasers." Wherever possible, liberal citizen groups were to be removed from the governmental process. . . .

The Reagan administration certainly succeeded in reducing the liberal groups' access to the executive branch. On a broader level, however, the conservative counterattack against the liberal groups was a failure. The reasons go far beyond the more accommodating stance of the Bush administration or the attitude of any conservative administrations that may follow. These organizations have proved to be remarkably resilient, and they are a strong and stable force in American politics. Most fundamentally, though, the Reagan attempt failed because the transformation of interest group politics led to large-scale structural changes in the public policymaking process.

Consequences

The rise of citizen groups and the rapid expansion of interest group advocacy in general have had many important long-term consequences for the way policy is formulated by the national government. Most important, policymaking moved away from closed subgovernments, each involving a relatively stable and restricted group of lobbyists and key government officials, to much broader policymaking communities. Policymaking in earlier years is typically described as the product of consensual negotiations between a small number of back-scratching participants.

Policymaking is now best described as taking place within issue networks rather than in subgovernments. An issue network is a set of organizations that share expertise in a policy area and interact with each other over time as relevant issues are debated. As sociologist Barry Wellman states, "The world is composed of networks, not groups." This is certainly descriptive of Washington policymaking. Policy formulation cannot be portrayed in terms of what a particular group wanted and how officials responded to those demands. The coalitions within networks, often involving scores of groups, define the divisions over issues and drive the policymaking process forward. Alliances are composed of both old friends and strange bedfellows; relationships are built on immediate need as well as on familiarity and trust. Organizations that do not normally work in a particular issue network can easily move into a policymaking community to work on a single issue. The only thing constant in issue networks is the changing nature of the coalitions.

The result of issue network politics is that policymaking has become more open, more conflictual, and more broadly participatory. What is crucial about the role of citizen groups is that they were instrumental in breaking down the barriers to participation in subgovernments. Building upon their own constituency support and working with allies in Congress, citizen groups made themselves players. They have not been outsiders, left to protest policies and a system that excluded them. Rather, they built opposition right into the policymaking communities that had previously operated with some commonality of interest. Even conservative administrators who would prefer to exclude these liberal advocacy groups have recognized that they have to deal with their opponents in one arena or another. The Nuclear Regulatory Commission, the epitome of an agency hostile to liberal advocacy groups, cannot get away with ignoring groups like the Union of Concerned Scientists. The consensus over nuclear power has long been broken. Critics and advocacy groups like the Union of Concerned Scientists have the technical expertise to involve themselves in agency proceedings, and they have the political know-how to get themselves heard on Capitol Hill and in the news media.

Issue networks are not simply divided between citizen groups on one side and business groups on another. Organizations representing business usually encompass a variety of interests, many of which are opposed to each other. As various business markets have undergone rapid change and become increasingly competitive, issue networks have found themselves divided by efforts of one sector of groups to use the policymaking process to try to gain market share from another sector of the network. Citizen groups, rather than simply being the enemy of business, are potential coalition partners for different business sectors. A characteristic of the culture of interest group politics in Washington is that there are no permanent allies and no permanent enemies.

Citizen groups are especially attractive as coalition partners because they have such a high level of credibility with the public and the news media. All groups claim to represent the public interest because they sincerely believe that the course of action they are advocating would be the most beneficial to the country. Since they do not represent any vocational or business interest, citizen groups may be perceived by some to be less biased—though certainly not unbiased—in their approach to public policy problems. This credibility is also built around the high-quality research that many citizen groups produce and distribute to journalists and policymakers in Washington. Reports from advocacy organizations such as Citizens for Tax Justice or the Center for Budget and Policy Priorities are quickly picked up by the media and disseminated across the country. Most business groups would love to have the respect that these citizen groups command in the press. For all the financial strength at the disposal of oil lobbyists, no representative of the oil industry has as much credibility with the public as a lobbyist for the Natural Resources Defense Council.

Despite the growth and stability of citizen groups in national politics, their reach does not extend into every significant policymaking domain. In the broad area of financial services, for example, citizen groups have played a minor role at best. There are some consumer groups that have been marginally active when specific issues involving banks, insurance companies, and securities firms arise, but they have demonstrated little influence or staying power. There is, however, a vital consumer interest at stake as public policymakers grapple with the crumbling walls that have traditionally divided different segments of the financial services market. Defense policy is another area where citizen groups have been relatively minor actors. But if citizen groups are conspicuous by their absence in some important areas, their overall reach is surprisingly broad. They have become major actors in policy areas where they previously had no presence at all. In negotiations over a free trade agreement with Mexico, for example, environmental groups became central players in the bargaining. These groups were concerned that increased U.S. investment in Mexico would result in increased pollution there from unregulated manufacturing, depleted groundwater supplies, and other forms of environmental degradation. To its dismay, the Bush White House found that the only practical course was to negotiate with the groups.

The increasing prominence of citizen groups and the expanding size of issue networks change our conception of the policymaking process. The basic structural attribute of a subgovernment was that it was relatively bounded with a stable set of participants. Even if there was some conflict in that subgovernment, there were predictable divisions and relatively clear expectations of what kind of conciliation between interest groups was possible. In contrast, issue networks seem like free-for-alls. In the health care field alone, 741 organizations have offices in Washington or employ a representative there. Where subgovernments suggested control over public policy by a limited number of participants, issue networks suggest no control whatsoever. Citizen groups make policymaking all the more difficult because they frequently sharpen the ideological debate; they have different organizational incentive systems from those of the corporations and trade groups with which they are often in conflict; and they place little emphasis on the need for economic growth, an assumption shared by most other actors.

This picture of contemporary interest group politics may make it seem impossible to accomplish anything in Washington. Indeed, it is a popular perception that Congress has become unproductive and that we are subject to some sort of national gridlock. Yet the policymaking system is adaptable, and the relationship between citizen groups and other actors in issue networks suggests that there are a number of productive paths for resolving complicated policy issues.

Complex Policymaking

The growth of issue networks is not, of course, the only reason why the policymaking process has become more complex. The increasingly technical nature of policy problems has obviously put an ever higher premium on expertise. Structural changes are critical, too. The decentralization of the House of Representatives that took place in the mid-1970s dispersed power and reduced the autonomy of leaders. Today, in the House, jurisdictions between committees frequently overlap and multiple referrals of bills are common. When an omnibus trade bill passed by both houses in 1987 was sent to conference, the House and the Senate appointed 200 conferees, who broke up into 17 subconferences. The growth of the executive branch has produced a similar problem of overlapping jurisdictions. In recent deliberations on proposed changes in wetlands policy, executive branch participants included the Soil Conservation Service in the Agriculture Department, the Fish and Wildlife Service in Interior, the Army Corps of Engineers, the Environmental Protection Agency (EPA), the Office of Management and

Budget, the Council on Competitiveness, and the President's Domestic Policy Council.

Nevertheless, even though the roots of complex policymaking are multifaceted, the rise of citizen groups has been a critical factor in forcing the Congress and the executive branch to focus more closely on developing procedures to negotiate settlements of policy disputes. The quiet bargaining of traditional subgovernment politics was not an adequate mechanism for handling negotiations between scores of interest groups, congressional committees, and executive branch agencies.

Citizen groups have been particularly important in prompting more structured negotiations for a number of reasons. First, in many policy areas, citizen groups upset long-standing working arrangements between policymakers and other interest groups. Citizen groups were often the reason subgovernments crumbled; under pressure from congressional allies and public opinion, they were included in the bargaining and negotiating at some stage in the policymaking process.

Second, citizen groups could not be easily accommodated in basic negotiating patterns. It was not a matter of simply placing a few more chairs at the table. These groups' entrance into a policymaking community usually created a new dividing line between participants. The basic ideological cleavage that exists between consumer and environmental interests and business is not easy to bridge, and, consequently, considerable effort has been expended to devise ways of getting mutual antagonists to negotiate over an extended period. As argued above, once accepted at the bargaining table, citizen groups could be attractive coalition partners for business organizations.

Third, . . . citizen groups typically have a great deal of credibility with the press. Thus, in negotiating, they often have had more to gain by going public to gain leverage with other bargainers. This adds increased uncertainty and instability to the structure of negotiations.

Fourth, citizen groups are often more unified than their business adversaries. The business interests in an issue network may consist of large producers, small producers, foreign producers, and companies from other industries trying to expand into new markets. All these business interests may be fiercely divided as each tries to defend or encroach upon established market patterns. The environmentalists in the same network, while each may have its own niche in terms of issue specialization, are likely to present a united front on major policy disputes. In a perverse way, then, the position of citizen groups has been aided by the proliferation of business groups. (Even without the intrusion of citizen lobbies, this sharp rise in the number of business groups would have irretrievably changed the nature of subgovernments.) . . .

Conclusion

Citizen groups have changed the policymaking process in valuable and enduring ways. Most important, they have broadened representation in our political system. Many previously unrepresented or underrepresented constituencies now have a powerful voice in Washington politics. The expanding numbers of liberal citizen groups and their apparent success helped to stimulate a broad mobilization on the part of business. The skyrocketing increase in the numbers of interest groups worked to break down subgovernments and led to the rise of issue networks.

Issue networks are more fragmented, less predictable policymaking environments. Both Congress and the executive branch have taken steps to bring about greater centralized control and coherence to policymaking. Some of these institutional changes seem aimed directly at citizen groups. Negotiated regulations, for example, are seen as a way of getting around the impasse that often develops between liberal citizen groups and business organizations. Centralized regulatory review has been used by Republican administrations as a means of ensuring that business interests are given primacy; regulators are seen as too sympathetic to the citizen groups that are clients of their agencies.

Although government has established these and other institutional mechanisms for coping with complex policymaking environments, the American public does not seem to feel that the government copes very well at all. Congress has been portrayed as unproductive and spineless, unwilling to tackle the tough problems that require discipline or sacrifice. At the core of this criticism is that interest groups are the culprit. Washington lobbies, representing every conceivable interest and showering legislators with the political action committee donations they crave, are said to be responsible for this country's inability to solve its problems.

Although it is counterintuitive, it may be that the increasing number of interest groups coupled with the rise of citizen groups has actually improved the policymaking system in some important ways. More specifically, our policymaking process may be more democratic today because of these developments. Expanded interest group participation has helped to make the policymaking process more open and visible. The closed nature of subgovernment politics meant not only that participation was restricted but that public scrutiny was minimal. The proliferation of interest groups, Washington media that are more aggressive, and the willingness and ability of citizen groups in particular to go public as part of their advocacy strategy have worked to open up policymaking to the public eye.

The end result of expanded citizen group advocacy is policy communities that are highly participatory and more broadly representative of the public. One can argue that this more democratic policymaking process is also one that is less capable of concerted action; yet there is no reliable evidence that American government is any more or less responsive to pressing policy problems than it has ever been. There are, of course, difficult problems that remain unresolved, but that is surely true of every era. Democracy requires adequate representation of interests as well as institutions capable of addressing difficult policy problems. For policymakers who must balance the demand for representation with the need for results, the key is thinking creatively about how to build coalitions and structure negotiations between large groups of actors.

POSTSCRIPT

Is Government Dominated by Big Business?

One of the problems for any pluralist is the danger that many people may not be properly represented. Suppose, for example, that business and environmental groups in Washington compromise their differences by supporting environmental legislation but passing the costs along to consumers. The legislation may be good, even necessary, but have the consumer's interests been taken into account? There are, of course, self-styled consumer groups, but it is hard to determine whether or not they really speak for the average consumer. The challenge for pluralists is to make their system as inclusive as possible.

The key issue is how dominant is corporate power in influencing government policies and their administration on issues that concern them. The dominant view is that neither the public nor mobilized non-corporate interests can effectively counterpose corporate interests. Two political scientists who have advocated this view in a lifetime of publications are G. William Domhoff and Thomas R. Dye. Domhoff's latest power elite work offers hope that fighting against corporate power may not be futile. See his *Changing the Powers that Be: How the Left Can Stop Losing and Win* (Rowman and Littlefield, 2003). Two of Dye's recent books are *Who's Running America?: The Bush Restoration* (Prentice Hall, 2003) and *Top Down Policymaking* (Chatham House, 2001). Other works supporting this view are Charles Perrow, *Organizing America: Wealth, Power, and the Origins of Corporate America* (Princeton University Press, 2002); Peter Kobrak, *Cozy Politics: Political Parties, Campaign Finance, and Compromised Governance* (Lynne Rienner, 2002); Arianna Stassinopoulos Huffington, *Pigs at the Trough: How Corporate Greed and Political Corruption Are Undermining America* (Crown, 2003); Ted Nace, *Gangs of America: The Rise of Corporate Power and the Disabling of Democracy* (Berrett-Koehler, 2003); Dan Clawson et al. *Dollars and Votes: How Business Campaign Contributions Subvert Democracy* (Temple University Press, 1998); and John B. Parrott, *Being Like God: How American Elites Abuse Politics and Power* (University Press of America, 2003). According to David C. Korten in *When Corporations Rule the World,* 2nd edition (Kumarian Press, 2001), American corporations also rule the world.

For some pluralist arguments, see David Vogel, *Fluctuating Fortunes: The Political Power of Business in America* (Basic Books, 1989) and *Kindred Strangers: The Uneasy Relationship Between Politics and Business in America* (Princeton University Press, 1996); John P. Heinz, Edward O. Laumann, Robert L. Nelson, and Robert H. Salisbury, *The Hollow Core: Private Interests in National Policy Making* (Harvard University Press, 1993); Susan Herbst, *Numbered Voices: How Opinion Polls Shape American Politics* (University of Chicago Press, 1993); Kevin Danaher, *Insurrection: Citizen Challenges to Corporate Power* (Routledge, 2003); and

Battling Big Business: Countering Greenwash, Infiltration, and Other Forms of Corporate Bullying (Common Courage Press, 2002). Recently the pluralist view is being reworked into political process theory. See Andrew S. McFarland, *Neopluralism: The Evolution of Political Process Theory* (University Press of Kansas, 2004).

ISSUE 12

Should Government Intervene in a Capitalist Economy?

YES: Robert Kuttner, from *Everything for Sale: The Virtues and Limits of Markets* (Alfred A. Knopf, 1997)

NO: John Stossel, "The Real Cost of Regulation," *Imprimis* (May 2001)

ISSUE SUMMARY

YES: Robert Kuttner, professor of economics and co-editor of *The American Prospect*, argues that the market has vices as well as virtues. Government must intervene "to promote development, to temper the market's distributive extremes, to counteract its unfortunate tendency to boom-and-bust, to remedy its myopic failure to invest to little in public goods, and to invest too much in processes that harmed the human and natural environment."

NO: John Stossel, a TV news reporter and producer of one-hour news specials, argues that regulations have done immense damage and do not protect us as well as market forces.

The expression "That government is best which governs least" sums up a deeply rooted attitude of many Americans. From early presidents Thomas Jefferson and Andrew Jackson to America's most recent leaders, George Bush, Bill Clinton, and George W. Bush, American politicians have often echoed the popular view that there are certain areas of life best left to the private actions of citizens.

One such area is the economic sphere, where people make their living by buying, selling, and producing goods and services. The tendency of most Americans is to regard direct government involvement in the economic sphere as both unnecessary and dangerous. The purest expression of this view is the economic theory of *laissez-faire,* a French term meaning "let be" or "let alone." The seminal formulation of *laissez-faire* theory was the work of eighteenth-century Scottish philosopher Adam Smith, whose treatise *The Wealth of Nations* appeared in 1776. Smith's thesis was that each individual, pursuing his or her own selfish interests in a competitive market, will be "led by an invisible hand to promote an end which was no part of his intention." In other words, when people singlemindedly seek profit, they actually serve the community because sellers must keep prices down and quality up if they are to meet the competition of other sellers.

Laissez-faire economics was much honored (in theory, if not always in practice) during the nineteenth and early twentieth centuries. But as the nineteenth century drew to a close, the Populist Party sprang up. The Populists denounced eastern bankers, Wall Street stock manipulators, and rich "moneyed interests," and they called for government ownership of railroads, a progressive income tax, and other forms of state intervention. The Populist Party died out early in the twentieth century, but the Populist message was not forgotten. In fact, it was given new life after 1929, when the stock market collapsed and the United States was plunged into the worst economic depression in its history.

By 1932 a quarter of the nation's workforce was unemployed, and most Americans were finding it hard to believe that the "invisible hand" would set things right. Some Americans totally repudiated the idea of a free market and embraced socialism, the belief that the state (or "the community") should run all major industries. Most stopped short of supporting socialism, but they were now prepared to welcome some forms of state intervention in the economy. President Franklin D. Roosevelt, elected in 1932, spoke to this mood when he pledged a "New Deal" to the American people. "New Deal" has come to stand for a variety of programs that were enacted during the first eight years of Roosevelt's presidency, including business and banking regulations, government pension programs, federal aid to the disabled, unemployment compensation, and government-sponsored work programs. Side by side with the "invisible hand" of the marketplace was now the very visible hand of an activist government.

Government intervention in the economic sphere increased during World War II as the government fixed prices, rationed goods, and put millions to work in government-subsidized war industries. Activist government continued during the 1950s, but the biggest leap forward occurred during the late 1960s and early 1970s, when the federal government launched a variety of new welfare and regulatory programs: the multibillion-dollar War on Poverty, new civil rights and affirmative action mandates, and new laws protecting consumers, workers, disabled people, and the environment. These, in turn, led to a proliferation of new government agencies and bureaus, as well as shelves and shelves of published regulations. Proponents of the new activism conceded that it was expensive, but they insisted that activist government was necessary to protect Americans against pollution, discrimination, dangerous products, and other effects of the modern marketplace. Critics of government involvement called attention not only to its direct costs but also to its effect on business activity and individual freedom.

In the following selections, Robert Kuttner is aware that regulations can go too far, but over two decades of privatization, deregulation, and government downsizing has swung the pendulum too far, and tighter regulations or government interventions are needed for the public good. John Stossel can only imagine greater harm coming from an expanded role of government if the past is our guide.

207

YES

Everything for Sale: The Virtues and Limits of Markets

The ideal of a free, self-regulating market is newly triumphant. The historical lessons of market excess, from the Gilded Age to the Great Depression, have all but dropped from the collective memory. Government stands impeached and impoverished, along with democratic politics itself. Unfettered markets are deemed both the essence of human liberty, and the most expedient route to prosperity.

In the United States, the alternative to laissez-faire has never been socialism. Rather, the interventionist party, from Hamilton and Lincoln, through the Progressive era, Franklin Roosevelt and Lyndon Johnson, sponsored what came to be known as a "mixed economy." The idea was that market forces could do many things well—but not everything. Government intervened to promote development, to temper the market's distributive extremes, to counteract its unfortunate tendency to boom-and-bust, to remedy its myopic failure to invest too little in public goods, and to invest too much in processes that harmed the human and natural environment.

Since the constitutional founding, however, the libertarian strain in American life has often overwhelmed the impulse toward collective betterment. Today, after two decades of assault by the marketizers, even the normal defenders of the mixed economy are defensive and uncertain. The last two Democratic presidents have been ambivalent advocates for the mixed economy. Mostly, they offered a more temperate call for the reining in of government and the liberation of the entrepreneur. The current vogue for deregulation began under Jimmy Carter. The insistence of budget balance was embraced by Bill Clinton, whose pledge to "reinvent government" soon became a shared commitment merely to reduce government. And much of the economics profession, after an era of embracing the mixed economy, has reverted to a new fundamentalism cherishing the virtues of markets.

America, in short, is in one of its cyclical romances with a utopian view of laissez-faire. Free markets are famous for overshooting. Real-estate bubbles, tulip manias, and stock-market euphorias invariably lead to crowd psychologies and painful mornings-after. The same, evidently, is true of ideological fashions.

So this is a good moment for a sober sorting out. How does the market, whose first principle is one-dollar/one-vote, properly coexist with a political democracy whose basic rule is "one person/one vote"? When does the market run riot? What are the proper boundaries of market principles? What should not be for sale?

Even in a capitalist economy, the marketplace is only one of several means by which society makes decisions, determines worth, allocates resources, maintains a social fabric, and conducts human relations. Actual capitalist nations display a wide variation in the blend of market and nonmarket. A basically capitalist system is clearly superior to a command economy. But the nations where markets have the freest rein do not invariably enjoy the most reliable prosperity, let alone the most attractive society.

In this age of the resurgent market, we are promised that technology, ingenuity, and freedom from the dead hand of government will revive economic efficiency and material progress. Yet, despite the triumph of market principles, market society is no Utopia. Compared with the golden era of the postwar boom and the mixed economy, this is a time of broad economic unease. As society becomes more marketized, it is producing stagnation of living standards for most people, and a fraying of the social fabric that society's best-off are all too able to evade. One thing market society does well is to allow its biggest winners to buy their way out of its pathologies.

Even as the market enjoys new prestige, ordinary people are uneasy with many of the results. With greater marketization comes not just opportunity but opportunism; a society that prizes risk also reaps insecurity. Taken to an extreme, markets devalue and diminish extra-market values and norms—on which viable capitalism depends.

The promise of growth has also run into questions of sustainability. Even mainstream economists wonder about the effect on the natural environment if the third world were to enjoy even half the living standards and the claim on natural systems of the United States and Europe. The standard economic calculus does not know how to measure the costs of depletion of natural systems, since these are not accurately captured in current prices. And in market logic, by definition, what is not reflected in the price system does not exist.

All of this should cast serious doubt on the presumption, so fashionable of late, that the natural form of capitalism is laissez-faire. Beyond a certain point, excessive marketization may not be efficient *even for economic life*. In this article, I seek to explore where that point lies; to search for criteria to understand better where the market is best left alone and where it needs help; to reclaim a defensible middle ground; and to suggest the policy implications that follow, in several realms. . . .

This article begins with the working hypothesis that a capitalist system is a superior form of economic organization, but even in a market economy there are realms of human life where markets are imperfect, inappropriate, or unattainable. Many forms of human motivation cannot be reduced to the market model of man. . . .

The Market's Magic

Markets accomplish much superbly. They offer consumers broad choices; they promote and reward innovation. They bring investors together with entrepreneurs. Markets force producers to search for greater efficiency and ruthlessly purge the economy of failures. Market systems are far better than command systems at determining rough economic worth. As economists since Adam Smith have observed, the great paradox of the market is that the individual pursuit of self-interest aggregates to an efficient general good.

At the very core of the market system is the price mechanism. Prices indicate what millions of individual goods and services are "worth" to willing sellers and willing buyers. Prices thereby function to apportion economic resources efficiently: they signal sellers what to produce; consumers how to buy; capitalists where to invest.

When economists speak of the market's efficiency, they generally have in mind the efficiency of *allocation*. Prices steer resources to the uses that maximize output in the form of products and services, relative to the available input of capital and human labor. Prices do so via the discipline of supply and demand. So far so good.

The genius of market pricing is its malleability. Prices can rise or fall instantly and change continually, as they adjust to shifting tastes and costs. Markets, therefore, can claim to embody and express freedom of choice, as well as efficient allocation of scarce resources. Markets epitomize decentralized, atomized decision-making. This concept of ongoing and reasoned refinement of preferences, prices, and quantities is central to the picture of satisfied economic man dwelling in an efficient marketplace. . . .

. . . [S]upermarkets are not perfectly efficient. Retail grocers operate on thin profit margins, but the wholesale part of the food-distribution chain is famous for enormous markups. A farmer is likely to get only ten cents out of a box of cornflakes that retails for $3.99. National conglomerates like Procter & Gamble or RJR Nabisco collectively spend billions on advertising and packaging to promote brand loyalty. These expenditures manipulate tastes, but beyond a point add little to the consumer's welfare. Food manufacturers proliferate brands far beyond any rational need to give the consumer choices. At my local supermarket, I counted more than 150 brands of breakfast cereal. This proliferation occurs not because shoppers demand so many choices. Rather, companies like Kellogg's and Post keep complicating consumer choices to grab shelf space and brand loyalty from each other. In the process, they add to their own overhead costs, those of the supermarket, and ultimately those of the economy. The fact that these overhead costs are roughly comparable among different food wholesalers and different supermarkets doesn't mean that consumers "want" 150 brands of cereal; it only means that the price mechanism is not competent to squeeze out this particular inefficiency.

Second, though they are subject to intense price discipline, even supermarkets are far from perfectly free markets. Their hygiene is regulated by government inspectors, as is almost all of the food they sell. Government regulations mandate the format and content of nutritional labeling. They require clear, consistent unit-pricing, to rule out a variety of temptations of deceptive marketing. Moreover, many occupations in the food industry, such as meat-cutter and checkout clerk, are substantially unionized; so the labor market is not a pure free market either. Much of the food produced in the United States is grown by farmers who benefit from a variety of interferences with a laissez-faire market, contrived by government to prevent ruinous fluctuations in prices. The government also subsidizes education and technical innovation in agriculture. Economists debate whether this interference with agricultural markets is a net gain or loss to efficiency.

Still, as a roughly efficient free marketplace, the supermarket is close enough—and evidently good enough. It is interesting that a modicum of regulation is entirely compatible with the basic discipline of supply and demand, and probably enhances its efficiency by making for better-informed consumers and less opportunistic sellers, and by placing off-limits the market's most self-cannibalizing tendencies. Real (inflation-adjusted) prices of food keep declining over time. Consumer choice keeps increasing. . . .

When the Market Fails

Consider a market profoundly different from the market for retail groceries—the market for health care. This is no small, special case, since it consumes 15 percent of the entire economy, roughly as much as food does. . . . Health care is anything but a textbook free market, yet market forces and profit motives in the health industry are rife.

On the supply side, the health industry violates several conditions of a free market. Unlike the supermarket business, there is not "free entry." You cannot simply open a hospital, or hang out your shingle as a doctor. This gives health care providers a degree of market power that compromises the competitive model—and raises prices. On the demand side, consumers lack the special knowledge to shop for a doctor the way they buy a car, and lack a perfectly free choice of health-insurer. Since society has decided that nobody shall perish for lack of medical care, we partly de-link effective demand from private purchasing power, which is also inflationary.

Health care also offers substantial "positive externalities"—diffused benefits not calculated in the instant transaction. The value to society of mass vaccinations far exceeds the profits that can be captured by the doctor or drug company. If vaccinations and other public-health measures were left to private supply-and-demand, society would seriously underinvest. The health system also depends heavily on extra-market norms. Physicians and nurses are guided by ethical constraints and professional values that limit the opportunism that their specialized knowledge and power might otherwise invite.

The fact that health care is a far cry from a perfect market sets up a chain of perverse incentives. In ordinary markets, sellers maximize profits by minimizing costs. But in health care, the profit maximizer's object is to maximize insurance reimbursement. The more complex the procedure and the more inflated the cost base, the more money can be billed to the insurance company. In recent years, private and government insurers have tried to crack down—by intensively reviewing what doctors and hospitals do, publishing book-length schedules of permissible procedures and reimbursements. Providers have fought back, by further complicating their own billing. All this inflates the cost of the whole system.

Worse, the insurance industry's efforts to reduce inflation (in a highly imperfect market) have created a second-order set of inefficiencies. Increasingly, consumers lack the ability to shop around for doctors or insurance plans. Often, they are locked in either because they get health insurance through their jobs, or because a "pre-existing condition" makes them unattractive to other insurers. They then become easy prey for insurance plans that seek to save costs by denying them care that they need, and to which they are ostensibly entitled.

Increasingly, too, insurance companies seek to minimize costs simply by refusing to insure people likely to become sick. This process of risk selection and segmentation, known as medical underwriting, is itself very expensive. So is the endless point-counterpoint of complex preapprovals and reviews of treatments. And so is the proliferation of paperwork. The providers and the insurers are each behaving "rationally" as profit maximizers, but their behavior does not yield a general good; the result is irrational for the system as a whole.

Thus, health care violates all the premises of an efficient free market—perfect competition, perfect information, mobility of factors, and so on. Yet, unless we want people dying from preventable diseases for lack of private purchasing power, the cure does not lie in liberation of the health "market." . . .

The Market's Assaults

In a mixed economy, the state intervenes to protect citizens from a variety of assaults that laissez-faire forces would otherwise produce. These include the spewing of pollutants into the air and water, the manufacture of dangerous products, the coercive power of private business to condition employment on unsafe working conditions, and other "contracts of desperation" that do not reflect truly voluntary transactions.

Many such abuses are the consequence not just of price inaccuracies but of imbalances in private knowledge and bargaining power. The consumer can't be expected to know with precision if her hamburger is poisoned, if the lawnmower will cut his foot off, if the water is safe to drink. The factory worker can't know whether an industrial compound risks producing cancer ten years into the future. The individual citizen doesn't have the basis to insist that the local public utility burn cleaner fuel or develop lower-polluting technology—except via government regulation. . . .

In the pricing of pollutants and employee or consumer injuries, the market's inability to price accurately is the norm. The remedy for these and kindred abuses entails broad public-policy goals, not mere corrections of narrow, isolated "market failure." Policy goals here flow from a recognition that society as a whole may choose to award itself certain common minima—clean drinking water, wholesome working environments, presumptively safe prescription drugs and foodstuffs—that market forces neglect or even deliberately frustrate to save short-run costs. A still broader goal is to vouchsafe the environment to future generations, or to achieve high living standards at lower overall environmental cost. These are civic goals that myopic markets cannot identify. So the purpose of public policy in this realm is not just to compensate passively for market imperfections, but to ratify public values and stimulate social learning. . . .

The wave of social regulation that began in the late 1960s resulted from a new public consciousness about the deteriorating natural environment. The consensus was remarkably broad. Most of the landmark environmental bills were signed by a Republican president, Richard Nixon, with bipartisan support. There seemed no other area where it was so widely agreed that market forces, left to themselves, yielded intolerable and unsustainable outcomes. This shift resulted from a change in social values rather than private "tastes"—a broad acceptance that environmental degradation was cumulative, that the air and water could no longer be treated as a free sink, and that employees need not bear a disproportionate share of industry's hazards. By the time the wave crested, in the mid-1970s, Congress had added new systems for regulating clean air and water, toxic substances, food and drugs, the workplace, and consumer products generally. . . .

Regulating Conditions of Work

The issue of employee health and safety nicely illustrates the limits of markets and even of "marketlike" regulation. One doesn't have to be Marxist to notice a pervasive imbalance of bargaining power between a wage or salary worker and the owner of an enterprise. Commentators since Adam Smith have observed that most ordinary employees have little savings to fall back on. A worker out of a job for a more than a few weeks will starve. "Many workmen could not subsist a week, few could subsist a month, and scarce any a year without employment," Smith wrote. "In the long run the workman may be as necessary to his master as his master is to him, but the necessity is not so immediate." In 1995, economist Edward Wolff confirmed that little had changed in more than two centuries. The median member of the work force, Wolff calculated, was about three months away from destitution if he lost his job. . . .

In the Progressive era, reformist exposés documented appalling rates of industrial accident and disease. One study in 1908 estimated that 35,000 workers were killed and 536,000 injured every year, out of a work force of about 30 million. Between 1907 and 1912, industrial accidents caused nearly 10 percent of all deaths of male Americans, 23 percent of deaths among miners, and 49 percent of deaths among electrical linemen. . . .

Enter OSHA

As enacted in 1970, OSHA required employers generally to furnish employment "free from recognized hazards so as to provide safe and healthful working conditions." It authorized a rule-making process, empowering OSHA to set standards, on both a routine and an emergency basis. It established a process for workplace inspections, with fines for noncompliance, and allowed the secretary of labor to shut down plants in cases of imminent hazard. It created a number of new employee rights, including the right to participate in inspections, the monitoring of hazards, and access to information about inspectors' findings. The law also set up a National Institute of Occupational Safety and Health, and a national commission on the reform of workers'-compensation laws. One of its most far-reaching provisions, criticized by many economists as ignoring cost, required OSHA to set standards that assure "to the extent feasible, on the basis of the best available evidence, that no employee will suffer material impairment of health or functional capacity even if such employee has regular exposure to the hazard . . . for the period of his working life." In writing this language, Congress explicitly rejected efforts by the steel and chemical industries to water down the language to refer to "economic" feasibility. In upholding OSHA's cotton-dust standard, the Supreme Court later found that Congress had not intended to set up a narrow cost-benefit test, but to mandate a threshold level of safety. . . .

Regulation as Mother of Invention

Opponents of investments in health and safety tend to overstate the cost of compliance with OSHA standards, and understate the benefits. For example, the textile industry bitterly opposed OSHA's imposition of tough standards on cotton dust, which had caused acute byssinosis ("brown-lung disease") in eighty-four thousand active workers at the time the standard was adopted in 1978, as well as disability in another thirty-five thousand former textile workers no longer employed. Before the final cotton-dust standard was issued, industry estimates of the compliance costs ranged from $875 million to nearly $2 billion. Five years later, OSHA concluded that the actual capital costs will total about $245 million.

Textile workers are exposed to cotton dust in the early, more labor-intensive stages of textile production—opening, cleaning, and carding the raw cotton and then drawing out the fibers—prior to the more mechanized process of spinning the cleaned and blended cotton into yarn, spooling the yarn, and finally weaving in into cloth. Automation was already under way at the more modern plants, but it was accelerated by the OSHA cotton-dust standard. Whereas the caricature of health-and-safety compliance portrays it as a purely extraneous function and cost, tacked on to a production process that is already—by definition—as efficient as it can be, in practice greater health and safety measures are typically "designed in" to new generations of production technology. According to a study for the Office of Technology Assessment, the textile industry came into compliance with OSHA's cotton-dust standard by modernizing and automating the dirtiest phases of the manufacturing process. . . .

In early 1996, EPA, responding to a Congressional mandate, dutifully prepared a 392-page cost benefit analysis of the 1970 Clean Air Act. The costs of compliance, EPA found, were approximately $436 billion over 20 years.

The benefits, to improved health, reductions in lost work days, agricultural productivity, and reduced clean-up benefits, were between $2.3 trillion and $14 trillion. The pricing of pollution by free markets simply was not capable of this calculus.

The system in which the private market operates is inevitably structured by law and by democratic choices. Those choices can contrive a relatively efficient, or inefficient, brand of mixed economy. But the quest for a perfectly pure free market, or an economy free of political influences, is an illusion.

The Inevitability of Politics

Our tour of the virtues and limits of markets necessarily takes us back to politics. Even a fervently capitalist society, it turns out, requires prior rules. Rules govern everything from basic property rights to the fair terms of engagement in complex mixed markets such as health care and telecommunications. Even the proponents of marketlime incentives—managed competition in health care, tradable emissions permits for clean air, supervised deregulation of telecommunications, compensation mandates to deter unsafe workplace practices—depend, paradoxically, on discerning, public-minded regulation to make their incentive schemes work. As new, unimagined dilemmas arise, there is no fixed constitution that governs all future cases. As new products and business strategies appear and markets evolve, so necessarily does the regime of rules.

The patterns of market failure, our tour reveals, are more pervasive than most market enthusiasts acknowledge. Generally, they are the result of the immutable structural characteristics of certain markets and the ubiquity of both positive and negative spillovers. Unfettered opportunism is more widespread in economic life than free-market theory admits. In much of the economy, sellers are not reliably held accountable by buyers. In markets where the consumer is not effectively sovereign (telecommunications, public utilities, banking, airlines, pure food and drugs), or where the reliance on market verdicts would lead to socially intolerable outcomes (health care, pollution, education, gross inequality of income, the buying of office or purchase of professions), a recourse purely to ineffectual market discipline would leave both consumer and society worse off than the alternative of a mix of market forces and regulatory interventions.

Another paradox: markets are rather stronger and more resourceful than their champions admit. The basic competitive discipline of a capitalist economy can coexist nicely with diverse extra-market forces; the market can even be rendered more efficient by them. These include both explicit regulatory interventions and the cultivation of extra-market norms, most notably trust, civility, and long-term reciprocity. As we have seen in markets as varied as banking, public utilities, and health care, entrepreneurs do not sicken and expire when faced with "contoured competition"; they simply revise their competitive strategy and go right on competing. Norms that commit society to resist short-term opportunism can make both the market and the society a healthier place. Pure markets, in contrast, commend and invite opportunism, and depress trust.

We have also seen, contrary to the theory of perfect markets, that much of economic life is not the mechanical satisfaction of exogenous preferences or the pursuit of a first-best equilibrium. On the contrary, many paths are possible—many blends of different values, many mixes of market and social, many possible distributions of income and wealth—all compatible with tolerably efficient getting and spending. The grail of a perfect market, purged of illegitimate and inefficient distortions, is a fantasy—and a dangerous one.

The marketizers make one powerful point: everything cannot be regulated. But neither can everything be deregulated. So the practical task is to determine when regulation improves efficiency, what sort of regulatory strategies to pursue, which regulations take precedence over others, and where is the point of diminishing returns. The real world displays a very broad spectrum of actual markets with diverse structural characteristics, and different degrees of separation from the textbook, libertarian ideal. Some need little regulation, some a great deal—either to make the market mechanism work efficiently or to solve problems that the market cannot fix. Someone has to make such determinations, or we end up in a world very far from even the available set of second bests.

Rules require rule-setters. In a democracy, that enterprise entails democratic politics, competent public administration, and reliable courts. . . .

If markets are not perfectly self-correcting, then the only check on their excesses must be extra-market institutions. These reside in values other than market values, and in affiliations that transcend mere hedonism and profit maximization. To temper the market, one must reclaim civil society and government, and make clear that government and civic vitality are allies, not adversaries. . . .

No real-world society has attained the ideal the libertarians commend. The closer ours gets to that vision, the more resistance is likely to set in. A society that was a grand auction block would not be a political democracy worth having. And it would be far less attractive economically than its enthusiasts imagine. We must beware this utopia, as we have been properly wary of others. Everything must not be for sale.

NO

The Real Cost of Regulation

The following is an abridged version of Mr. Stossel's speech delivered on February 20, 2001, in Fort Myers, Florida, at a Hillsdale College seminar.

When I started 30 years ago as a consumer reporter, I took the approach that most young reporters take today. My attitude was that capitalism is essentially cruel and unfair, and that the job of government, with the help of lawyers and the press, is to protect people from it. For years I did stories along those lines—stories about Coffee Association ads claiming that coffee "picks you up while it calms you down," or Libby-Owens-Ford Glass Company ads touting the clarity of its product by showing cars with their windows rolled down. I and other consumer activists said, "We've got to have regulation. We've got to police these ads. We've got to have a Federal Trade Commission." And I'm embarrassed at how long it took me to realize that these regulations make things worse, not better, for ordinary people.

The damage done by regulation is so vast, it's often hard to see. The money wasted consists not only of the taxes taken directly from us to pay for bureaucrats, but also of the indirect cost of all the lost energy that goes into filling out the forms. Then there's the distraction of creative power. Listen to Jack Faris, president of the National Federation of Independent Business: "If you're a small businessman, you have to get involved in government or government will wreck your business." And that's what happens. You have all this energy going into lobbying the politicians, forming the trade associations and PACs, and trying to manipulate the leviathan that's grown up in Washington, D.C. and the state capitals. You have many of the smartest people in the country today going into law, rather than into engineering or science. This doesn't create a richer, freer society. Nor do regulations only depress the economy. They depress the spirit. Visitors to Moscow before the fall of communism noticed a dead-eyed look in the people. What was that about? I don't think it was about fear of the KGB. Most Muscovites didn't have intervention by the secret police in their daily lives. I think it was the look that people get when they live in an all-bureaucratic state. If you go to Washington, to the Environmental Protection Agency, I think you'll see the same thing.

One thing I noticed that started me toward seeing the folly of regulation was that it didn't even punish the obvious crooks. The people selling the breast-enlargers and the burn-fat-while-you-sleep pills got away with it. The Attorney General would come at them after five years, they would hire lawyers to gain another five, and then they would change the name of their product or move to a different state. But regulation *did* punish *legitimate* businesses.

When I started reporting, all the aspirin companies were saying they were the best, when in fact aspirin is simply aspirin. So the FTC sued and demanded corrective advertising. Corrective ads would have been something like, "Contrary to our prior ads, Excedrin does not relieve twice as much pain." Of course these ads never ran. Instead, nine years of costly litigation finally led to a consent order. The aspirin companies said, "We don't admit doing anything wrong, but we won't do it again." So who won? Unquestionably the lawyers did. But did the public? Aspirin ads are more honest now. They say things like, "Nothing works better than Bayer"—which, if you think about it, simply means, "We're all the same." But I came to see that the same thing would have happened without nearly a decade of litigation, because markets police themselves. I can't say for certain *how* it would have happened. I think it's a fatal conceit to predict how markets will work. Maybe Better Business Bureaus would have gotten involved. Maybe the aspirin companies would have sued each other. Maybe the press would have embarrassed them. But the truth would have gotten out. The more I watched the market, the more impressed I was by how flexible and reasonable it is compared to government-imposed solutions.

Market forces protect us even where we tend most to think we need government. Consider the greedy, profit-driven companies that have employed me. CBS, NBC, and ABC make their money from advertisers, and they've paid me for 20 years to bite the hand that feeds them. Bristol-Myers sued CBS and me for $23 million when I did the story on aspirin. You'd think CBS would have said, "Stossel ain't worth that." But they didn't. Sometimes advertisers would pull their accounts, but still I wasn't fired. Ralph Nader once said that this would never happen except on public television. In fact the opposite is true: Unlike PBS, almost every local TV station has a consumer reporter. The reason is capitalism: More people watch stations that give honest information about their sponsors' products. So although a station might lose some advertisers, it can charge the others more. Markets protect us in unexpected ways.

Alternatives to the Nanny State

People often say to me, "That's okay for advertising. But when it comes to health and safety, we've got to have OSHA, the FDA, the CPSC" and the whole alphabet soup of regulatory agencies that have been created over the past several decades. At first glance this might seem to make sense. But by interfering with free markets, regulations almost invariably have nasty side effects. Take the FDA, which saved us from thalidomide—the drug to prevent morning sickness in pregnant women that was discovered to cause birth defects. To be accurate, it wasn't so much that the FDA saved us, as that it was so slow in studying thalidomide that by the end of the approval process, the drug's awful effects were being seen in Europe. I'm glad for this. But since the thalidomide scare, the FDA has grown ten-fold in size, and I believe it now does more harm than good. If you want to get a new drug approved today, it costs about $500 million and takes about ten years. This means that there are drugs currently in existence that would improve or even save lives, but that are being withheld from us because of a tiny chance they contain carcinogens. Some years ago, the FDA held a press conference to announce its long-awaited approval of a new beta-blocker, and predicted it would save 14,000 American lives per year. Why didn't anybody stand up at the time and say, "Excuse me, doesn't that mean you killed 14,000 people last year by not approving it?" The answer is, reporters don't think that way.

Why, in a free society, do we allow government to perform this kind of nanny-state function? A reasonable alternative would be for government to serve as an information agency. Drug companies wanting to submit their products to a ten-year process could do so. Those of us who choose to be cautious could take only FDA-approved drugs. But others, including people with terminal illnesses, could try non-approved drugs without sneaking off to Mexico or breaking the law. As an added benefit, all of us would learn something valuable by their doing so. I'd argue further that we don't need the FDA to perform this research. As a rule, government agencies are inefficient. If we abolished the FDA, private groups like the publisher of *Consumer Reports* would step in and do the job better, cheaper, and faster. In any case, wouldn't that be more compatible with what America is about? Patrick Henry never said, "Give me absolute safety or give me death!"

Lawyers and Liability

If we embrace the idea of free markets, we have to accept the fact that trial lawyers have a place. Private lawsuits could be seen as a supplement to Adam Smith's invisible hand: the invisible fist. In theory they should deter bad behavior. But because of how our laws have evolved, this process has gone horribly wrong. It takes years for victims to get their money, and most of the money goes to lawyers. Additionally, the wrong people get sued. A Harvard study of medical malpractice suits found that most of those getting money don't deserve it, and that most people injured by negligence don't sue. The system is a mess. Even the cases the trial lawyers are most proud of don't really make us safer. They brag about their lawsuit over football helmets, which were thin enough that some kids were getting head injuries. But now the helmets are so thick that kids are butting each other and getting other kinds of injuries. Worst of all, they cost over $100 each. School districts on the margin can't afford them, and as a result some are dropping their football programs. Are the kids from these schools safer playing on the streets? No.

An even clearer example concerns vaccines. Trial lawyers sued over the Diphtheria-Pertussis-Tetanus Vaccine, claiming that it wasn't as safe as it might have been. Although I suspect this case rested on junk science, I don't know what the truth is. But assuming these lawyers were right, and that they've made the DPT vaccine a little safer, are we safer? When they sued, there were twenty companies in America researching and making vaccines. Now there are four. Many got out of the business because they said, "We don't make that much on vaccines. Who needs this huge liability?" Is America better off with four vaccine makers instead of twenty? No way.

These lawsuits also disrupt the flow of information that helps free people protect themselves. For example, we ought to read labels. We should read the label on tetracycline, which says that it won't work if taken with milk. But who reads labels anymore? I sure don't. There are 21 warning labels on stepladders—"Don't dance on stepladders wearing wet shoes," etc.—because of the threat of liability. Drug labels are even crazier. If anyone were actually to read the two pages of fine print that come with birth control pills, they wouldn't need to take the drug. My point is that government and lawyers don't make us safer. Freedom makes us safer. It allows us to protect *ourselves*. Some say, "That's fine for us. We're educated. But the poor and the ignorant need government regulations to protect them." Not so. I sure don't know what makes one car run better or safer than another. Few of us are automotive engineers. But it's hard to get totally ripped off buying a car in America. The worst car you can find here is safer than the best cars produced in planned economies. In a free society, not everyone has to be an expert in order for markets to protect us. In the case of cars, we just need a few car buffs who read car magazines. Information gets around through word-of-mouth. Good companies thrive and bad ones atrophy. Freedom protects the ignorant, too.

Admittedly there are exceptions to this argument. I think we need some environmental regulation, because now and then we lack a market incentive to behave well in that area. Where is the incentive for me to keep my waste-treatment plant from contaminating your drinking water? So we need some rules, and some have done a lot of good. Our air and water are cleaner thanks to catalytic converters. But how much regulation is enough? President Clinton set a record as he left office, adding 500,000 new pages to the Federal Register—a whole new spiderweb of little rules for us to obey. How big should government be? For most of America's history, when we grew the fastest, government accounted for five percent or less of GDP. The figure is now 40 percent. This is still less than Europe. But shouldn't we at least have an intelligent debate about how much government should do? The problem is that to have such a debate, we need an informed public. And here I'm embarrassed, because people in my business are not helping that cause.

Fear-Mongering: A Risky Business

A turning point came in my career when a producer came into my office excited because he had been given a story by a trial lawyer—the lazy reporter's best friend—about Bic lighters spontaneously catching fire in people's pockets. These lighters, he told me, had killed four Americans in four years. By this time I'd done some homework, so I said, "Fine. I'll do the exploding lighter story after I do stories on plastic bags, which kill 40 Americans every four years, and five-gallon buckets, which kill 200 Americans (mostly children) every four years." This is a big country, with 280 million people. Bad things happen to some of them. But if we frighten all the rest about ant-sized dangers, they won't be prepared when an elephant comes along. The producer stalked off angrily and got Bob Brown to do the story. But several years later, when ABC gave me three hour-long specials a year in order to keep me, I insisted the first one be called, "Are We Scaring Ourselves to Death?" In it, I ranked some of these risks and made fun of the press for its silliness in reporting them.

Risk specialists compare risks not according to how many people they kill, but according to how many days they reduce the average life. The press goes nuts over airplane crashes, but airplane crashes have caused fewer than 200 deaths per year over the past 20 years. That's less than one day off the average life. There is no proof that toxic-waste sites like Love Canal or Times Beach have hurt anybody at all, despite widely reported claims that they cause 1,000 cases of cancer a year. (Even assuming they do, and assuming further that all these cancer victims die, that would still be less than four days off the average life.) House fires account for about 4,500 American deaths per year—18 days off the average life. And murder, which leads the news in most towns, takes about 100 days off the average life. But to bring these risks into proper perspective, we need to compare them to far greater risks like driving, which knocks 182 days off the average life. I am often asked to do scare stories about flying—"The Ten Most Dangerous Airports" or "The Three Most Dangerous Airlines"—and I refuse because it's morally irresponsible. When we scare people about flying, more people drive to Grandma's house, and more are killed as a result. This is statistical murder, perpetuated by regulators and the media.

Even more dramatic is the fact that Americans below the poverty line live seven to ten fewer years than the rest of us. Some of this difference is self-induced: poor people smoke and drink more. But most of it results from the fact that they can't afford some of the good things that keep the rest of us alive. They drive older cars with older tires; they can't afford the same medical care; and so on. This means that when bureaucrats get obsessed about flying or toxic-waste sites, and create new regulations and drive up the cost of living in order to reduce these risks, they shorten people's lives by making them poorer. Bangladesh has floods that kill 100,000 people. America has comparable floods and no one dies. The difference is wealth. Here we have TVs and radios to hear about floods, and cars to drive off in. Wealthier is healthier, and regulations make the country poorer. Maybe the motto of OSHA should be: "To save four, kill ten."

Largely due to the prevalence of misleading scare stories in the press, we see in society an increasing fear of innovation. Natural gas in the home kills 200 Americans a year, but we accept it because it's old. It happened before we got crazy. We accept coal, which is awful stuff, but we're terrified of nuclear power, which is probably cleaner and safer. Swimming pools kill over 1,000 Americans every year, and I think it's safe to say that the government wouldn't allow them today if they didn't already exist. What about vehicles that weigh a ton and are driven within inches of pedestrians by 16-year-olds, all while spewing noxious exhaust? Cars, I fear, would never make it off the drawing board in 2001.

What's happened to America? Why do we allow government to make decisions for us as if we were children? In a free society we should be allowed to take risks, and to learn from them. The press carps and whines about our exposure to dangerous new things—invisible chemicals, food additives, radiation, etc. But what's the result? We're living longer than ever. A century ago, most people my age were already dead. If we were better informed, we'd realize that what's behind this longevity is the spirit of enterprise, and that what gives us this spirit—what makes America thrive—isn't regulation. It's freedom.

POSTSCRIPT

Should Government Intervene in a Capitalist Economy?

$\mathbf{A}$s with most good debates, the issue of the rightness of government intervention is difficult to decide. Part of the difficulty is that it involves the trade-off of values that are in conflict in real situations, and part of the difficulty is that it involves uncertain estimations of the future consequences of policy changes. Both experts and interested parties can differ greatly on value trade-offs and estimations of impacts. Government regulations and other interventions cost money for both administration and compliance. Nevertheless, Kuttner argues that certain government actions will provide benefits that greatly exceed the costs, and Stossel argues the contrary view that the costs will be far greater than Kuttner expects and probably will have net negative results. Part of the strength of Stossel's argument is that regulations often fail to do what they are designed to do. Part of the strength of Kuttner's argument is that there are many observable problems that need to be addressed, and for some of these government action seems to be the only viable option.

One aspect of the issue is the morality of businesses. Most commentators have a low opinion of business ethics and the way corporations use their power, and point to the recent corporate scandals as confirmation. Thus it is easy to conclude that since they will not do what is right, they must be made to do what is right. For support of this view see Joel Bakan, *The Corporation: The Pathological Pursuit of Profit and Power* (Free Press, 2004); Justin O"Brien, *Wall Street on Trial: A Corrupted State?* (Wiley, 2003); Steve Tombs and Dave Whyte, *Unmasking the Crimes of the Powerful: Scrutinizing States and Corporations* (P. Lang, 2003); Jamie Court, *Corporateering: How Corporate Power Steals Your Personal Freedom—and What You Can Do about It* (Jeremy P. Tarcher/ Putnam, 2003); and Victor Perlo, *Superprofits and Crisis: Modern U.S. Capitalism* (International Publishers, 1988). Some commentators, however, defend businesses in a competitive capitalistic market.

Philosopher Michael Novak contends that the ethic of capitalism transcends mere moneymaking and is (or can be made) compatible with Judeo-Christian morality. See *The Spirit of Democratic Capitalism* (Madison Books, 1991) and *The Catholic Ethic and the Spirit of Capitalism* (Free Press, 1993). Another broad-based defense of capitalism is Peter L. Berger's *The Capitalist Revolution: Fifty Propositions About Prosperity, Equality and Liberty* (Basic Books, 1988). For a feminist critique of capitalism, see J. K. Gibson-Graham, *The End of Capitalism (As We Know It): A Feminist Critique of Political Economy* (Blackwell, 1996). For a mixed view of capitalism, see Charles Wolf, Jr., *Markets or Governments: Choosing Between Imperfect Alternatives* (MIT Press, 1993). A strong attack on government interventions in the market is Jonathan Rauch, *Demosclerosis: The Silent Killer of American Government* (Times Books, 1994).

For an in-depth understanding of the way that markets work and the role that institutions maintained by the state, including property rights, function to maintain markets, see Neil Fligstein, *The Architecture of Markets: An Economic Sociology of Twenty-First Century Capitalist Societies* (Princeton University Press, 2001). An interesting role of government is its bailing-out failed corporations. See *Too Big to Fail: Policies and Practices in Government Bailouts* edited by Benton E. Gup (Praeger, 2004) and David G. Mayes et al. *Who Pays for Bank Insolvency?* (Palgrave Macmillan, 2004). Often self-regulation is better than government regulation. See Virgina Haufler, *A Public Role for the Private Sector: Industry Self-Regulation in a Global Economy* (Carnegie Endowment for International Peace, 2001).

ISSUE 13

Has Welfare Reform Benefited the Poor?

YES: Editors of *The Economist*, from "Welfare Reform: America's Great Achievement," *The Economist* (August 25, 2001)

NO: Sharon Hayes, from "Off the Rolls: The Ground-Level Results of Welfare Reform," *Dissent* (Fall 2003)

ISSUE SUMMARY

YES: The editors of the *Economist* present the facts on the declining welfare rolls and the dramatic increase in employment for welfare mothers, and they argue that many of these changes are due to the changes in the welfare laws and not simply a strong economy.

NO: Sharon Hayes, professor of sociology at the University of Virginia, got to know many welfare mothers and learned what happened to them since the welfare reform. Her article points out that while quite a few mothers have left welfare since the reform, many cannot hold on to a job and are now worse off than before.

In his 1984 book *Losing Ground: American Social Policy, 1950–1980* (Basic Books), policy analyst Charles Murray recommends abolishing Aid to Families with Dependent Children (AFDC), the program at the heart of the welfare debate. At the time of the book's publication this suggestion struck many as simply a dramatic way for Murray to make some of his points. However, 14 years later this idea became the dominant idea in Congress. In 1996 President Bill Clinton signed into law the Work Opportunity Reconciliation Act and fulfilled his 1992 campaign pledge to "end welfare as we know it." Murray's thesis that welfare hurt the poor had become widely accepted. In "What to Do About Welfare," *Commentary* (December 1994), Murray argues that welfare contributes to dependency, illegitimacy, and the number of absent fathers, which in turn can have terrible effects on the children involved. He states that workfare, enforced child support, and the abolition of welfare would greatly reduce these problems.

One reason why Congress ended AFDC was the emergence of a widespread backlash against welfare recipients. Much of the backlash, however, was misguided. It often rested on the assumptions that welfare is generous and that most people on welfare are professional loafers. In fact, over the previous two decades payments to families with dependent children eroded considerably relative to the cost of living. Furthermore, most women with dependent children on welfare had intermittent periods of work, were elderly, or were disabled. Petty fraud may be common since welfare payments are insufficient to live on in many cities, but "welfare queens" who cheat the system for spectacular sums are so rare that they should not be part of any serious debate on welfare issues. The majority of people on welfare are those whose condition would become desperate if payments were cut off. Although many believe that women on welfare commonly bear children in order to increase their benefits, there is no conclusive evidence to support this conclusion.

Not all objections to AFDC can be easily dismissed, however. There does seem to be evidence that in some cases AFDC reduces work incentives and increases the likelihood of family breakups. But there is also a positive side to AFDC—it helped many needy people get back on their feet. When all things are considered together, therefore, it is not clear that welfare, meaning AFDC, was bad enough to be abolished. But it was abolished on July 1, 1997, when the Work Opportunity Reconciliation Act went into effect. Now the question is whether the new policy is better than the old policy.

It is too soon to obtain an accurate assessment of the impacts of the act. Nevertheless, AFDC rolls have declined since the act was passed, so many conclude that it is a success rather than a failure. Of course, the early leavers are the ones with the best prospects of succeeding in the work world; the welfare-to-work transition gets harder as the program works with the more difficult cases. The crucial question is whether or not the reform will benefit those it affects. Already many working former welfare recipients are better off. But what about the average or more vulnerable recipient?

In the readings that follow, the editors of the *Economist* call welfare reform "America's great achievement" because employment statistics went up dramatically for welfare mothers and welfare rolls went down dramatically. In the second selection, Sharon Hayes acknowledges that welfare rolls have declined but challenges—with stories of ex-welfare mothers—the assumption that most lives have improved as a result. The lives of many vulnerable women have become much more unmanageable. Thus the consequences of the welfare reform are mixed.

Welfare Reform: America's Great Achievement

August 22nd marked a milestone in American social policy. On that day, five years ago, Bill Clinton, having promised to "end welfare as we know it", signed into law the Personal Responsibility and Work Opportunity Reconciliation Act, otherwise known as welfare reform. This ended welfare as an entitlement, available to all the parents who qualified, and required recipients—mostly single mothers—to look for work. Rather than simply paying up on demand, the federal government switched to a "block grant" programme, handing over a fixed sum to states ($16.5 billion a year), to disburse as they wished, within limits. There are now, in effect, 51 different plans—one in each state plus a central set of guidelines.

One of those guidelines stipulated that poor people with dependent children would get federal payments for only five years over a lifetime. Their time is up, so payments to parents who have been on the rolls since then should stop. In fact, things should not change much. No one is sure how many of today's 2m welfare families have been on the rolls for the maximum period. Not many probably, because the states have already pushed some recipients off the lists; and the 1996 law also allowed them to exempt up to a fifth of welfare recipients from the five-year time limit. More generally, federal payments now make up a smaller portion of the welfare system than payments from states and local governments.

Still, the beginning of the end of federal welfare funding marks a natural point of reflection for "the most sweeping social change in America in more than half a century" (as Tommy Thompson, one of the reform's pioneers and now its overseer as secretary for health and human services, has put it). Congress must also reauthorise the law next year. What has welfare reform achieved? And can it be improved?

When the reform became law, welfare rolls were near their all-time high. The "revolutionary" Republican Congress of Newt Gingrich tried to turn several social programmes—including Medicaid, the part-state, part-federal health care system for the poor—into block grants. Welfare was the only Republican plan Bill Clinton did not veto. And he signed it in the teeth of vociferous Democratic opposition.

Welfare is only part of the country's poverty-reduction system, which includes public housing, food stamps, day-care subsidies, Medicaid and the Child Health Insurance Programme. But it has long been the most notorious part, not just because of its scale (in the mid-1990s, one in seven children was on welfare) but because it supposedly bred a culture of dependency.

The first aim of the 1996 law was to break that culture by moving people off welfare and into jobs. Before the reform, states gave out about 80% of the federal money that they dispensed in cash benefits. Now only half goes in cash. The rest goes on job searches, education, training and day-care for children of working mothers. Welfare offices have turned from cash-dispensing machines into job-centres, all using different sticks and carrots to push welfare recipients into work.

Critics on the left predicted disaster: unskilled welfare recipients would be unprepared for the discipline of work. In fact, welfare rolls have fallen more than even supporters predicted: from 5.1m families at the peak in 1994 to just over 2m now (see chart 1). In Wisconsin, where Mr Thompson was governor, Florida and Mississippi the rolls fell by more than 75%. Around two-thirds of those who left welfare are still working. Of the large minority, some returned to welfare, some subsist on other forms of government support and a few—an unknown number—have fallen through the cracks.

The unemployment rate for single mothers had been stuck at around 43% for most of the 1980s and early 1990s. After reform, the rate fell to 28% by 1999. The unemployment rate of never-married mothers fell even faster, from just over half in 1996 to one-third three years later. In the early 1990s, the average stay on welfare had been more than eight years: dependency, indeed. Now, the stay is probably less than half that. In the narrowest sense of the law's aim, it has been a triumph.

This has not been achieved merely by skimming the cream: the worry was that the employable minority would find jobs quickly, leaving behind an unemployable residue who would not find work, even if their benefits were cut off. At some point, presumably, the law of diminishing returns must set in. But that point has not been reached yet.

Studies by the Urban Institute, a Washington think-tank, show that the most recent batch of welfare leavers (those who left in 1997–99) have similar levels of employment and wages as the first batch (who left in 1995–97). And they suffer less hardship than the earlier group, with "only" 41% living below the poverty line, compared with 48% in 1997. There has been no build-up of the worst cases on the rolls. Welfare recipients seem far more employable than critics feared.

It's Not the Economy, Stupid

The reforms took place at a time of unprecedented economic growth. Some wonder whether their success has been enhanced by transient economic factors that have begun to change. Just before the economic slowdown became apparent there was a rise in the caseload between July and September 2000—a mere 8,000 families, but the first time that more than a handful of states had seen the numbers rise.

Figure 1

A New Deal

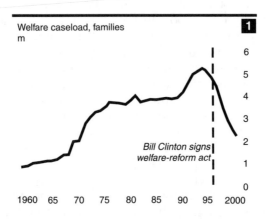

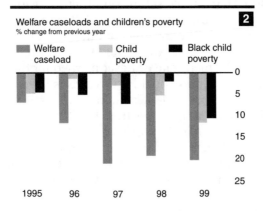

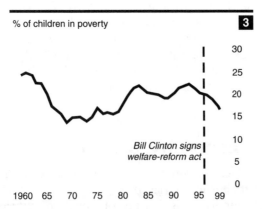

Source: Congressional Research Service; Department of Health and Human Services; Census Bureau

Yet the connection between welfare rolls and the economy is less firm than you would expect. During the 1980s, when America added 20m new jobs, welfare rolls grew by over 500,000 families. Rolls also rose quickly at the beginning of the economic recovery of the early 1990s. The good news did not begin until 1994—when welfare reform began experimentally in some states. It was strongest in those, such as Wisconsin, that went furthest with their own reform measures.

A review by the Urban Institute shows that six studies before 1996 all gave more weight to the economy than policy. Two even found the economy accounted for three-quarters of the change in caseloads. But the two more recent studies of effects after 1996 placed policy above the economy by a ratio of at least four to one.

This hardly settles the argument conclusively. The success so far must owe something to the economy—and a downturn will, at the very least, affect the pace of improvement. On the other hand, worries about the economy should not be allowed to denigrate the achievement. Reform has left recipients better off than they would otherwise have been.

"Better off", however, does not mean much. The first aim of reform was to get people into jobs; the second was to improve the income of the poor. Here reform has been less successful. Reductions in poverty have occurred, but at a slower rate than reductions in welfare rolls (chart 2).

In terms of wages, poor parents improved their lot (albeit at miserable levels). Annual wages for the bottom fifth of single-mother households rose from $1,350 in 1993 to $2,400 in 1999—a nominal rise of more than 80%. Earnings for the next 20% of wage earners increased even more, from $4,800 to $9,600.

Employed, but Not Richer

The trouble is that for every dollar gained in extra earnings, people lost around 40 cents in benefits. The poorest 40% of single-mother households increased earnings by about $3,000 between 1993 and 1999. But their disposable incomes rose by only about $1,850. The poorest of all have been hit hardest. According to Wendell Primus, a former Clinton administration official, and Ron Haskins of the Brookings Institution, 700,000 families are worse off under reform than they were before; and the child-poverty gap—the total amount that would be needed to bring all children up to the poverty line—fell only slightly in 1993–99, from $59.8 billion to $56.3 billion.

That still marks an improvement in the number of children escaping poverty. Until the mid-1990s, the proportion of children living in poverty had been rising erratically (see chart 3). Since then, the trend reversed sharply. In 1999, the child-poverty rate was back to its lowest since 1979 and poverty among black children was at its lowest level ever. Using a broader measure of poverty, the decline in poverty has been comparable to the big gains of the 1960s and was more than twice as great as during the 1980s.

Yet the fact remains: poor parents have seen less improvement in incomes than in their chance of a job. This gets more troubling when you look at wider benefits to children (such as higher school grades and keeping out of trouble with the law.) Such things, according to a study of 11 different welfare schemes by the Manpower Development Research Corporation, improve significantly only when the reforms boost both jobs and income.

But breaking the culture of dependency had wider goals than these. If you read the early pages of the welfare-reform bill, it is startling to find how often the word "marriage" appears. Welfare reform, for many of its proponents, was not to be judged by economic statistics. Rather, as one commentator, Mickey Kaus, says, it was about taking a "culture characterised by welfare dependence, a high rate of births out of wedlock, high male unemployment, and crime and replac[ing] it with a new, more virtuous social dynamic." Marriage is the best indicator of this complex change—and it is here that the most surprising good news is to be found.

For decades before welfare reform there had been a relentless rise in the number of out-of-wedlock births (from 18% in 1980 to 33% in 1999). The number of children living with single mothers was especially marked among the poor and among blacks. Yet in about 1996, these apparently unstoppable trends stopped. According to a study by the Centre for Budget and Policy Priorities (CBPP), the share of children living with single mothers on less than twice the poverty rate fell from 34.2% in 1995 to 32.8% in 2000. This group includes most welfare recipients.

The revival of the nuclear family in the past few years has been driven by many things (from education to a new long-lasting injectible contraceptive). But it has been particularly notable amongst welfare beneficiaries. The proportion of black children living with their married parents rose from 35% in 1995 to 39% in 2000—a rise almost three times bigger than that in the whole population. And a welfare programme in Minnesota which rewarded married couples has yielded startling results. After three years, married couples on the scheme were considerably more likely to stay together than comparable couples on other programmes. Single parents joining the programme were also slightly more likely to get hitched.

One of the authors of the CBPP study, Mr Primus, resigned from the Clinton administration in protest at the decision to sign welfare reform. He now credits that change for creating this most unexpected good news on the family. "Whatever we have been doing over the last five years," he says, "we ought to keep going." That depends on Congress, which has to reauthorise the welfare laws by October 2002.

There is no constituency for a radical overhaul. Welfare hardly merited a mention in the presidential election last year—a remarkable testament to the way in which success in the field has produced political consensus out of controversy in five years. However, there is still room for Congress both to mess things up and improve them.

The big danger, inevitably, involves money. Some congressmen cite the plummeting welfare rolls as a reason to chop the block grant. Yet part of the success of the block-grant system is that, as those falling rolls have left behind the harder cases, it has increased the amount of money available to find jobs for each of those people. That virtuous circle would turn vicious if the money were reduced. Indeed, the possibility of recession suggests that the $2 billion contingency fund—which provides extra money for hard-hit states—should be both increased and made easier to tap. At the moment, states virtually have to declare bankruptcy to get the cash.

The problems to do with "ancillary benefits" (like food stamps) fortunately do not require Congress to authorise more money, just to simplify the rules. Fewer than half the working mothers who leave welfare continue to get food stamps, even though they are entitled to them. Cutting red tape—both at state and federal levels—would do more than any single thing to boost the disposable incomes of welfare-leavers and to reduce child poverty.

The third tricky area is how much welfare reform can be used to promote marriage. This is mostly a matter for the states, and at least two—Oklahoma and Arizona—have set up ambitious programmes that are supposed to boost marriage rates among the poor (including marriage-training classes). Congress could set up additional matching funds to encourage such programmes. Perhaps more important, it could end the marriage penalties in its own tax code, especially in the earned-income tax credit. A study by the Urban Institute found that if a single working mother on the minimum wage marries a man earning $8 an hour, she loses a staggering $8,060 in annual benefits.

These problems are mere sun spots. It is rare enough that any government policy, let alone one dealing with poverty, is so near an unambiguous success as welfare reform has been. For decades, the underclass has loomed as America's deepest social problem. In just five years, reform has halved the size of the problem and made it possible to move on to the next stage. Pray that Congress doesn't blow it.

Off the Rolls: The Ground-Level Results of Welfare Reform

It's hard to date it precisely, but I think my severe case of cognitive dissonance set in on a summer evening in 1999. As part of my research on welfare reform, I'd spent the afternoon playing on the floor with Sammy, the four-year-old son of a welfare recipient. I was struck by his intelligence and creativity and imagined that if his mom were middle-class, she'd soon be having him tested and charting the gifted and talented programs he'd attend.

But Sammy's mom, Celia, had other things on her mind. Cradling her infant daughter, she told me that she had been recently diagnosed with cancer. Her doctor wanted her to start treatments immediately. Although she'd been working at a local Fotomart for three months, the welfare office still helped her with the costs of child care—costs she couldn't otherwise manage on her $6 per hour pay. When she asked her boss about flexible hours to manage the cancer treatments, he told her she was just too easily replaced. She'd also checked with her welfare caseworkers; they told her that if she lost her job she'd have to quickly find another or risk being cut off the welfare rolls. I talked to her about the Social Security Disability program, even though I knew that she had only a slim chance of getting help there. Celia had an eighth-grade education, no financial assets, few job skills, and no extended family members with sufficient resources to see her through. And she needed those cancer treatments now.

Under the old welfare system, she could have simply returned to full welfare benefits. Yet, knowing what I did from my research into the worlds of low-wage work, welfare, and disability, I was sure there was now virtually nowhere for her to turn, save all those local charities that were already incredibly overburdened. I didn't have the heart to tell her.

When I went home that night, the local television news was interviewing a smiling former welfare mother recently employed at a supermarket chain. It was a story of redemption—the triumph of individual willpower and American know-how—and the newscaster cheerfully pronounced it a marker of the "success" of welfare reform. That's when the dissonance set in. I've been suffering from it ever since.

From one point of view, it makes perfect sense that so many have celebrated the results of the 1996 Personal Responsibility Act. The welfare rolls have been cut by more than half—from twelve million recipients in 1996 to five million today. Among those who have left welfare, the majority (60 percent to 65 percent) are employed. Add to this the fact that public opinion polls show that almost no one liked the old system of welfare and most people (including most welfare recipients) agree that the principles behind reform—independence, self-sufficiency, strong families, a concern for the common good—are worthy ideals.

The problem is that there is a wide gap between the more worthy goals behind reform and the ground-level realities I found in the welfare office. There is also a tremendous amount of diversity hidden in those large-scale statistical accountings of the results of reform—and much of it is a great deal more disheartening than it first appears. After three years of ethnographic research inside two (distant and distinct) welfare offices, after interviewing more than 50 caseworkers and about 130 welfare mothers, and after five years of poring over policy reports on reform, it is clear to me that the majority of the nation's most desperately poor citizens are in worse shape now than they would have been had the Personal Responsibility Act never been passed.

Between Success and Failure

Political speeches, policy reports, and the popular media all cite the declining rolls and the employment of former recipients as the central evidence of the success of welfare reform. By these standards, Celia and her children would count as a success.

Of course there are genuine success stories. Take Sally. With a good job at the phone company, medical benefits, sick leave and vacation leave, a nine-to-five schedule, possibilities for advancement, and enough income to place her and her two kids above the poverty line, she was better off than she'd ever been on welfare benefits or in any of the (many) low-wage, no-benefit jobs she'd had in the past. And there was no question that the supportive services that came with reform had helped her to achieve that success. She got her job through a welfare-sponsored training program offered by the phone company. Welfare caseworkers had helped her out with clothing for work, bus vouchers, and a child care subsidy that got her through the training. "I think welfare's better now," she told me. "They've got programs there to help you. They're actually giving you an opportunity. I'm working and I feel like I can make it on my own." . . .

About one-half of the welfare mothers I met experienced at least temporary successes like these. Yet under the terms of reform, the long-term outlook for the majority is not so positive. And in many cases it is difficult to distinguish the successes from the failures.

Proponents of reform would mark Andrea, for instance, as "successful." When I met her, she was earning $5.75 an hour, working thirty-five hours a week at a Sunbelt City convenience store. After paying rent, utility bills, and food costs for her family of three, she was left with $50 a month to cover the costs of child care, transportation, clothing, medical bills, laundry, school costs, furniture, appliances, and cleaning supplies. Just four months off the welfare rolls. Andrea was already in trouble. Her phone had been turned off the month before, and she was unsure how she'd pay this month's rent. Her oldest daughter was asking for new school clothes, her youngest had a birthday coming soon, and Andrea couldn't take her mind off the upcoming winter utility bills. If she were single, she told me, she would manage somehow. But with children to worry about, she knew she couldn't make it much longer.

National-level accountings of reform would also place Teresa and her three children in the plus column. When I met her, she had a temporary (three-month) job at a collection agency. Thanks to public housing and the time-limited child care subsidy offered by the welfare office, she was making ends meet. Teresa was smart and capable, but had only a high school diploma and almost no work experience. She'd spent most of her adult life outside the mainstream economy—first married to a drug dealer, then working as a street-level prostitute, and finally, drug free, on welfare. As much as Teresa thought she was doing better than ever and spoke of how happy she was to be getting dressed up every morning and going out to work, she was still concerned about the future. The child care costs for her three kids would amount to nearly three-quarters of her paycheck if she had to cover them herself. And her job, like that child care subsidy, was only temporary. Given her résumé, I wondered just what career ladder she might find to offer her sufficient income and stability to stay off the welfare rolls and successfully juggle her duties as both primary caregiver and sole breadwinner for those three kids.

The cycle of work and welfare implied by these cases is the most common pattern among the welfare-level poor. It is a cycle of moving from welfare to low-wage jobs to mounting debts and problems with child care, husbands, boyfriends, employers, landlords, overdue utility bills, broken-down cars, inadequate public transportation, unstable living arrangements, job layoffs, sick children, disabled parents, and the innumerable everyday contingencies of low-income life—any and all of which can lead a poor family back to the welfare office to repeat the cycle again. Most of the people caught up in this cycle face a number of social disadvantages from the start. Welfare recipients are overwhelmingly mothers (90 percent), they are disproportionately non-white (38 percent are black, 25 percent Latino, and 30 percent white), nearly half are without high-school diplomas (47 percent), the majority have experience in only unskilled jobs, about half suffer from physical or mental health disabilities, almost as many have a history of domestic violence, and all have children to care for. At the same time, most welfare recipients have work experience (83 percent), and most want to work. This was true long before welfare reform. Yet given their circumstances, and given the structure of low-wage work, it is not surprising that many have found it difficult to achieve long-term financial and familial stability.

Of those who have left the rolls since reform, a full 40 percent are without work or welfare at any given time. Of the 60 percent who do have jobs, their average wage is approximately $7 per hour. But most former recipients do not find full-time or year-round work, leaving their average annual wage estimated at just over $10,000 a year. Following this same pattern, about three-quarters of the families who left welfare are in jobs without medical insurance, retirement benefits, sick days, or vacation leave; and one-quarter work night or evening shifts. It is true that their average annual wages amount to more income than welfare, food stamps, and Medicaid combined. Yet, as Kathryn Edin and Laura Lein demonstrated in *Making Ends Meet,* taking into account the additional costs associated with employment (such as child care, transportation, clothing), working poor families like these actually suffer more material hardship than their counterparts on welfare.

The reality behind the declining welfare rolls is millions of former welfare families moving in and out of low-wage jobs. Some achieve success, most do not. Approximately one-third have found themselves back on welfare at least once since reform. Overall, two-thirds of those who have left welfare are either unemployed or working for wages that do not lift their families out of poverty. And there are still millions of families on welfare, coming in anew, coming back again, or as yet unable to find a way off the rolls.

The Personal Responsibility Act itself produced two primary changes in the lives of the working/welfare poor. On the one hand, welfare reform offered sufficient positive employment supports to allow poor families to leave welfare more quickly, and in some cases it offered just the boost that was needed to allow those families to achieve genuine long-term financial stability. On the other hand, welfare reform instituted a system of rules, punishments, and time limits that has effectively pressured the poor to steer clear of the welfare office.

A central result of welfare reform, in other words, is that a large proportion of desperately poor mothers and children are now too discouraged, too angry, too ashamed, or too exhausted to go to the welfare office. Nationwide, as the welfare rolls were declining by more than half, the rate of dire (welfare-level) poverty declined by only 15 percent. To put it another way: whereas the vast majority of desperately poor families received welfare support prior to reform (84 percent), today less than half of them do. Why are all these mothers and children now avoiding welfare? To make sense of this part of the story, one needs to understand the complicated changes that have taken place inside welfare offices across the nation. I can here offer only a glimpse.

Punishment and the Push to Work

Upon arrival at the Arbordale welfare office, the first thing one sees is a large red sign, two feet high, twelve feet long, inquiring, "HOW MANY MONTHS DO YOU HAVE LEFT?" This message is driven home by caseworkers' incessant reminders of the "ticking clock," in the ubiquity of employment brochures and job postings, and, above all, by a carefully sequenced set of demanding rules and regulations.

The pressure is intense. It includes the job search that all new clients must start immediately (forty verifiable job contacts in thirty days), the "job readiness" and "lifeskills" workshops they are required to attend, the (time-consuming and difficult) child support enforcement process in which they must agree to participate, and the constant monitoring of their eligibility for welfare and their progress toward employment. Welfare mothers who are not employed within a specified period (thirty days in Arbordale, forty-five in Sunbelt City), are required to enroll in full-time training programs or take full-time unpaid workfare placements until they can find a job. Throughout, these working, training, and job-searching welfare mothers are expected to find somewhere to place their children. Although welfare recipients are all technically eligible for federal child care subsidies, only about one-third receive them. With only a $350 welfare check (the average monthly benefit for a family of three), child care arrangements can be very difficult to manage.

In Sunbelt City the pressure to get off the welfare rolls is introduced even more directly and forcefully. As is true in about half the states nationwide, Sunbelt City has a "diversionary" program designed to keep poor mothers and children from applying for welfare in the first place. Before they even begin the application process, potential welfare clients are required to attend the diversion workshop. The three workshops I went to all focused on the importance of "self sufficiency," the demanding nature of welfare requirements, and the advantages of work—and left most of the poor mothers in attendance weary and confused.

For those who persisted through the application process, their compliance to the rules of reform was assured not just by the long-term threat of time limits, but by the more immediate threat of sanctions. Any welfare mother who fails to follow through with her job search, workfare placement, training program, child support proceedings, reporting requirements, or the myriad of other regulations of the welfare office is sanctioned. To be sanctioned means that all or part of a family's welfare benefits are cut, while the "clock" keeps ticking toward that lifetime limit. National statistics suggest that about one-quarter of welfare recipients lose their benefits as a result of sanctions.

Inside the welfare offices of Arbordale and Sunbelt City many of the women I met became so disheartened that they simply gave up and left the rolls. This included women who made it through some portion of the job search, or the employment workshops, or even took a workfare placement, but just couldn't manage the pressure. Some were sanctioned, others left on their own. Connected to these, but harder to count, were all those poor mothers who gave up before they got started. Eligibility workers in Arbordale estimated that as many as one-quarter of those who started the application process did not complete it. Caseworkers in Sunbelt City guessed that about one-third of the mothers who attended their diversion workshops were ("successfully") diverted from applying for benefits. In Arbordale, about one-quarter gave up before completing the application process.

Sarah was one example of a "diverted" potential welfare client. She was the full-time caregiver for her grandchild on a lung machine, her terminally ill father, and her own two young children. She'd been managing with the help of her father's Social Security checks and her boyfriend's help. But her boyfriend had left her, and medical bills were eating up all her father's income. Sarah discovered at her initial Arbordale welfare interview that in order to receive benefits she would need to begin a job search immediately. Because no one else was available to care for her father or grandchild, she said, it just didn't make sense for her to get a job. I met her as she conveyed this story to her friends in the Arbordale waiting room, fluctuating between tones of anger and sadness. "I have to swallow my pride, and come in here, and these people just don't want to help you no more," she told us. Leaving the office, she vowed never to return. As was true of so many others, it was unclear to me what she would do. . . .

All these women and their children have contributed to the decline of the welfare rolls. They are a central basis for the celebration of reform. They are also a central basis for my case of cognitive dissonance.

The Costs

In focusing on the hardships wrought by reform, I do not mean to suggest that the successes of welfare reform are trivial or inconsequential. Those successes matter. I also don't mean to imply that all welfare mothers are saints and victims. They aren't. But there are many other issues at stake in the reform of welfare.

Reading the daily news these days, one can't help but notice that the topic of poverty has lost its prominence, especially relative to the early days of reform. One reason for this neglect, it seems to me, has been the highly effective campaign pronouncing the triumph of the Personal Responsibility Act. Like all the information that was invisible in popular accounts of the invasion of Iraq, the ground-level hardship and human costs of reform are largely hidden from view. Yet the price tag on welfare reform is real.

By 2002, the National Governors' Association found itself begging Congress not to follow through on plans to increase the pressure on welfare offices and welfare recipients across the nation—the costs, they explained, would be far too high for already stretched state budgets to bear. The U.S. Conference of Mayors found itself pleading with the Bush administration for more financial help to manage the rising populations of the hungry and homeless in American cities. Food banks were running short on food, homeless shelters were closing their doors to new customers, and local charities were raising their eligibility requirements to contend with rising numbers of people in need. The Medicaid system was in crisis, and large numbers of poor families were no longer receiving the food stamps for which they were eligible. Half of the families who left welfare had no money to buy food; one-third have had to cut the size of meals, and nearly half have had trouble paying their rent or utility bills.

In the meantime, only a fraction of welfare families have actually hit their federal lifetime limits on welfare benefits: just 120,000 welfare mothers and children had reached their limits by 2001. Given the work/welfare cycling process, and given that many families can survive at least temporarily on below-poverty wages and pieced-together alternative resources, it will take many more years for the full impact of reform to emerge. But, over the long haul, we can expect to see rising rates of hunger, homelessness, drug abuse, and crime. More children will wind up in foster care, in substandard child care, or left to fend for themselves. More disabled family members will be left without caregivers. Mental health facilities and domestic violence shelters will also feel the impact of this law, as will all the poor men who are called upon to provide additional support for their children.

Of course, this story is not apocalyptic. The poor will manage as they have always managed, magically and mysteriously, to make do on far less than poverty-level income. Many of the most desperate among them will simply disappear, off the radar screen, off to places unknown.

In any case, assessing the results of welfare reform is not just a question of its impact on the poor. It is also a question of what this law says about our collective willingness to support the nation's most disadvantaged and about the extent to which welfare reform actually lives up to the more worthy goals it purports to champion.

POSTSCRIPT

Has Welfare Reform
Benefited the Poor?

There was considerable national agreement that the old welfare system had to be changed so that it would assist people in finding jobs and achieving self-sufficiency. Much success has been gained regarding this goal so far, but some state that numerous problems still remain. Hayes focuses on these problems, especially the inadequate supports for welfare-to-workmothers. The main problem, however, is the large number of poor-paying jobs for the bottom quarter of the labor force. If that problem were solved, the welfare-to-work program would be a great success. In fact, few would need welfare in the first place.

Michael B. Katz, in *The Undeserving Poor: From the War on Poverty to the War on Welfare* (Pantheon Books, 1989), traces the evolution of welfare policies in the United States from the 1960s through the 1980s. Charles Noble traces the evolution of welfare policies into the late 1990s and argues that the structure of the political economy has greatly limited the welfare state in *Welfare as We Knew It: A Political History of the American Welfare State* (Oxford University Press, 1997). Bruce S. Johnson criticizes welfare policies in the United States since the 1930s in *The Sixteen-Trillion-Dollar Mistake: How the U.S. Bungled Its National Priorities From the New Deal to the Present* (Columbia University Press, 2001). For discussions of welfare reform see Greg J. Duncan and P. Lindsay Chase-Lansdale, eds., *For Better and for Worse: Welfare Reform and the Well-Being of Children and Families* (Russell Sage Foundation, 2001); David E. Card and Rebecca M. Blank, eds., *Finding Jobs: Work and Welfare Reform* (Russell Sage Foundation, 2000); *Finding Jobs: Work and Welfare Reform,* edited by David Card and Rebecca M. Blank (Russell Sage Foundation, 2002); Sharon Hayes, *Flat Broke with Children: Women in the Age of Welfare Reform* (Oxford University Press, 2003); and *Work, Welfare and Politics: Confronting Poverty in the Wake of Welfare,* edited by Frances Fox Piven et al. (University of Oregon Press, 2002). A new emphasis in current welfare policy involves faith-based programs, which are discussed in Mary Jo Bane and Lawrence M. Mead, *Lifting Up the Poor: A Dialogue on Religion, Poverty, and Welfare Reform* (Brookings Institution Press, 2003) and John P. Bartkowski, *Charitable Choices: Religion, Race, and Poverty in the Post-Welfare Era* (New York University, 2003). Many recognize that the key to reducing welfare rolls is to make work profitable. To understand welfare from this perspective, see *Making Work Pay: America after Welfare: A Reader,* edited by Robert Kuttner (New York Press, 2002) and Dave Hage, *Reforming Welfare by Rewarding Work: One State's Successful Experiment* (University of Minnesota Press, 2004). Two books that offer explanations as to why welfare provision is so minimal in the United States are Linda Gordon, *Pitied but Not Entitled: Single Mothers and the History of Welfare* (Free Press, 1994) and Joel F. Handler and Yeheskel Hasenfeld, *The Moral Construction of Poverty: Welfare Reform in America* (Sage Publications, 1991).

ISSUE 14

Is Competition the Solution to the Ills of Public Education?

YES: Clint Bolick, "The Key to Closing the Minority Schooling Gap: School Choice," *The American Enterprise* (April/May 2003)

NO: Matthew Yglesias, "The Verdict on Vouchers," *The American Prospect* (February 2004)

ISSUE SUMMARY

YES: Clint Bolick, vice president of the Institute for Justice, presents the argument for school choice that competition leads to improvements and makes the case that minorities especially need school choice to improve their educational performance.

NO: Matthew Yglesias critiques the research that has been interpreted as demonstrating the benefits of school voucher programs. An honest examination of the data finds little educational benefit from school choice so the potential for stripping public schools of needed resources makes vouchers a poor gamble.

The quality of American public schooling has been criticized for several decades. Secretary of Education Richard Riley said in 1994 that some American schools are so bad that they "should never be called schools at all." The average school year in the United States is 180 days, while Japanese children attend school 240 days of the year. American schoolchildren score lower than the children of many other Western countries on certain standardized achievement tests. In 1983 the National Commission on Excellence in Education published *A Nation at Risk,* which argued that American education was a failure. Critics of *A Nation at Risk* maintain that the report produced very little evidence to support its thesis, but the public accepted it anyway. Currently, much of the public still thinks that the American school system is failing and needs to be fixed. The solution most frequently proposed today is some form of competition from charter schools to a voucher system.

Today 99 percent of children ages 6 to 13 are in school. In 1900 only about 7 percent of the appropriate age group graduated from high school, but in 1990, 86 percent did. Another success is the extraordinary improvement in the graduation rates for blacks since 1964, when it was 45 percent, to 1987, when it was 83 percent. Now this rate is almost at parity with white graduation rates. And over two-thirds of the present American population has a high school degree. No other nation comes close to these accomplishments. Nevertheless, most voices are very critical of American education.

American education reforms of the past 40 years have focused on quality and on what is taught. In the late 1950s the Soviet Union's launch of the first space satellite convinced the public of the need for more math and science in the curriculum. In the late 1960s and 1970s schools were criticized for rigid authoritarian teaching styles, and schools were made less structured. They became more open, participatory, and individualized in order to stimulate student involvement, creativity, and emotional growth. In the 1980s a crusade for the return to basics was triggered by the announcement that SAT scores had declined since the early 1960s. In the 1990s the continued problems of public schools led many to call for their restructuring by means of school choice, that is, competition.

The debate today is whether or not competition will finally make American schools succeed. The answer depends on whether or not the current structure of schools is the main reason why schools seem to be failing. Many other trends have also affected school performance, so the structure of the school system may not be the key to the problem. For example, many argue that curricula changes away from basics, new unstructured teaching techniques, and the decline of discipline in the classroom have contributed to perceived problems. Perhaps the quality of teachers needs to be raised. There is evidence that those who go into teaching score far lower on SATs than the average college student. In addition, societal trends outside the school may significantly impact school performance. Increasing breakdown of the family, more permissive childrearing, the substantial decline in the amount of time that parents spend with children, and the increased exposure of children to television are trends that many believe are adversely affecting school performance.

In the selections that follow, the costs and the benefits of school choice are debated. Clint Bolick argues that school choice applies to college education and U.S. higher education is the envy of the world. The role of competition in producing excellence in business, sports, and elsewhere is well-known. And from the moral point of view, the parents should have the right to choose. Matthew Yglesias points out that a school voucher program could have negative effects. Competition has vices as well as virtues, and one vice is the inequality that competition generates: the good schools would get richer and good students and the bad schools would get poorer and bad students. Since research has not demonstrated that vouchers produce significant educational improvements, the public schools should be strengthened and not weakened by the voucher experiment.

Clint Bolick  **YES**

The Key to Closing the Minority Schooling Gap: School Choice

In a nation supposedly committed to free enterprise, consumer choice, and equal educational opportunities, school choice should be routine. That it is not demonstrates the clout of those dedicated to preserving the government's monopoly over public education. To listen to the education establishment, one would think that school choice is a radical, scary, alien concept. Indeed, the defenders of the status quo have convinced many voters that school choice is a threat to American society.

But school choice is not threatening, and it is not new. To the contrary, it is the norm in most modern nations. . . . Even in the U.S., non-government schools have long played a key educational role, often using public funds. America's college system—the world's envy—is built on school choice: Students can use the G.I. Bill, Pell Grants, and other forms of government aid to attend either public or private schools, including religious institutions. At the other end of the age spectrum, parents of preschoolers can use child care vouchers in private and religious settings. And under federal law, tens of thousands of disabled elementary and high school age children receive schooling in private schools at public expense. It is only mainstream K-12 schools in which the government commands a monopoly over public funds.

Thomas Paine, the most prescient of our founding fathers, is credited with first suggesting a voucher system in the United States. He wanted an educated, enlightened citizenry, but the idea that the government should operate schools was an alien concept to him and his generation. Instead, Paine proposed providing citizens with financial support that they could use to purchase education in private schools.

The great portion of early American "public" education took place in private schools. Even when states started creating government schools, the teachers often were ministers. The concept of "separation of church and state" is not in the U.S. Constitution, and was certainly never applied to education.

In 1869, Vermont adopted a school choice program for communities that did not build their own public schools, and Maine followed suit in 1873. To this day, both states will pay tuition for children to attend private schools, or public schools in neighboring communities. In Vermont, 6,500 children from 90 towns attend private schools at government expense; in Maine, 5,600 children from 55 towns do so. Those programs, in existence for more than a century and a quarter, have not destroyed the local public schools; to the contrary, both states boast a well-educated population.

But the goal of universal common schooling, fueled by the ideas of Horace Mann, helped make government schools the norm in the late nineteenth century. Thereafter, private schools typically served two groups: the elite, and those seeking a religious immersion different from the Protestant theology that dominated public schools. The latter, of course, were primarily Catholic immigrants.

The rise of Catholic schools bitterly annoyed Protestant public school advocates like Senator James Blaine (R-ME). Blaine struck back in 1876. His proposed amendment to the U.S. Constitution to prohibit any government aid to religious schools came just short of securing passage in Congress. His allies, however, lobbied state legislatures and succeeded in attaching "Blaine amendments" to approximately 37 state constitutions which prohibited expenditure of public funds in "support" of sectarian (i.e., Catholic) schools. Anti-Catholic bigotry crested in an Oregon law, secured by the Ku Klux Klan, which *required* all children to attend government schools.

In the landmark 1925 decision *Pierce v. Society of Sisters,* the U.S. Supreme Court struck down that Oregon law, declaring that "The fundamental theory of liberty upon which all governments in this Union repose excludes any general power of the State to standardize its children by forcing them to accept instruction from public teachers only. The child is not the mere creature of the State; those who nurture him and direct his destiny have the right, coupled with the high duty, to recognize and prepare him for additional obligations." This principle of parental sovereignty remains a cornerstone of American law today. Though it remains constantly under attack, it continues to keep private educational options (among other rights) open to parents.

The modern case for school vouchers was first made by the Nobel laureate economist Milton Friedman in 1955. Instead of providing education as a monopoly supplier, Friedman suggested, government should just finance it. Every child would be given a voucher redeemable at a school of the parent's choice, public or private. Schools would compete to attract the vouchers. Friedman's proposal contained two insights that formed the intellectual foundations of the contemporary school choice movement: that parents, rather than government, should decide where children attend school, and that the economic rules which yield good services and products are not suspended at the schoolhouse door.

Support for school choice began to expand and diversify in the 1970s, when two liberal Berkeley law professors, Jack Coons and Steven Sugarman, began to consider school choice as a means of delivering educational equity. If forced busing plans had failed, Coons and Sugarman argued, why not give vouchers to poor and minority parents so they could choose the best education for their children? Coons and Sugarman adapted Friedman's proposal to their own ends: While Friedman advocated universal vouchers, Coons and Sugarman wanted to target them to disadvantaged populations. Friedman preferred a lightly regulated system, while Coons and Sugarman called for substantial government oversight. Still, there was the beginning of an alliance between freedom-seeking conservatives on the one hand and equality-seeking liberals on the other. That alliance eventually made the school choice programs of the 1990s a reality.

The main force generating support for vouchers, however, was the alarming decline in urban public schools. During the 1960s and 1970s, most urban public schools were ruined. Whites and middle-class blacks fled to the suburbs, leaving poor and mostly minority populations in rapidly worsening city public schools.

The problems of urban public schools were connected to a broader decline in public education. The 1983 study *A Nation at Risk* warned that large doses of mediocrity and failure had crept into American public schools. Meanwhile, starting in the 1980s, social scientists like James Coleman began showing that private and religious schools were succeeding in educating the very same poor, minority schoolchildren that government schools were failing. Many corroborating studies followed.

Also helping set the stage for a school choice movement was the 1990 Brookings Institution study by John Chubb and Terry Moe, *Politics, Markets & America's Schools*. Chubb and Moe set out to discover why suburban public schools and inner-city private schools generally produced good academic outcomes, while inner-city public schools were disasters. They found that whereas the first two types of schools were characterized by strong leaders with a clear mission and a high degree of responsiveness to parents, inner-city schools were not. Instead, urban public school districts were run by bloated bureaucracies whose principal constituencies were not parents, but politicians and unions.

A crucial factor distinguishing the successful and unsuccessful schools was the element of choice: Suburban parents could send their children to private schools, or move to different communities, if they were dissatisfied with their public schools. Private schools, obviously, were entirely dependent on satisfied parents. But inner-city public school parents were captives: They had no choice except to send their children to whatever the local government school offered. In school districts with tens or hundreds of thousands of students, they were powerless to do anything about the system.

Introducing choice in inner-city public schools, Chubb and Moe concluded—particularly giving parents the power to exit the public system altogether—would force the bureaucracy to respond to its customers rather than to politicians and special-interest groups. These findings created a scholarly foundation for school choice as a way not merely of helping children in failing government schools, but also as an essential prerequisite for reforming public school systems.

When the current school choice movement started to come together a decade or two ago, its leading protagonists could have met comfortably in a telephone booth. In an amazingly short period, it has grown into a sophisticated, passionate, and ecumenical movement. There are philanthropists, activists, public officials, clergy, lawyers, and parents, all willing to put aside ideological differences in pursuit of a common cause.

The movement's core argument is that parents, not government, should have the primary responsibility and power to determine where and how their children are educated. That this basic principle should require a vicious fight is testimony to the strength, determination, and ferocity of the reactionary forces defending today's educational status quo. Teacher unions, which form the cornerstone of our education establishment, are the most powerful special-interest group in America today. At the national level, they essentially own the Democratic Party. At the state level, they wield enormous influence over elected officials in both parties. At the local level, they frequently control school boards. They and their education allies dedicated all the resources at their disposal to defeat meaningful school choice anywhere it has presented itself.

For the education establishment, this battle is about preserving their monopolistic vise grip on American schooling. For parents—and our society—the stakes are much higher. Nearly 50 years after *Brown v. Board of Education*, vast numbers of black and Hispanic children do not graduate from high school. Many of those who do still lack the most basic skills needed for even entry-level jobs. As a result, many children in inner-city schools wind up on welfare or in jail. Children who most need the compensations of a quality education are instead regulated to dysfunctional schools. In climbing out of this morass we should not worry about whether a particular reform is too radical; we should worry about whether it is radical enough.

The school choice movement is not only a crusade to improve American education. It is also a true civil rights struggle. It is critical to the real lives of real people. The system has written off many of the people who most need choice—both the parents and their children. Minority citizens may be offered welfare payments, or racial preferences, but little is done to help them become productive, self-supporting citizens. Government schools and their liberal patrons implicitly assume that low-income children are incapable of learning. With little expected of these children, that becomes a self-fulfilling prophecy.

Meanwhile, conditions are different in most inner-city private schools. Not because they have greater resources than their public school counterparts (they typically have far fewer), or because they are selective (they usually accept all applicants), but rather because the operating philosophy is markedly different. At non-government schools, parents are not discouraged from involvement, they are *required* to play a role in the school and in their children's education. The children are expected to behave. They are expected to achieve. And research shows that they do.

Ultimately, we want school choice programs that are large and accessible enough to give government schools a serious run for their money. But initially, even a small program—publicly or privately funded—can begin to introduce inner-city parents to the previously unknown concept that there is an alternative to failure. That creates a constituency for a larger program.

Any functioning program, no matter how small, will change the debate from one about hypotheticals to one about realities. When we can show that competition helps public schools, and that families are choosing good schools rather than, say, witch-craft schools, we can begin to debunk the myths of choice adversaries. In Milwaukee, where school choice has been pioneered, public opinion polls show that support for choice is stronger the closer one is to the program. Not only inner-city parents but also suburban parents now support school choice there.

Actual experience has shown that school choice programs do not "skim the cream" of students, as our detractors like to say, leaving only hard cases in the public schools. Instead (not surprisingly), school choice programs usually attract children who are experiencing academic or disciplinary problems in government schools. Many such children are on a downward trajectory. Just arresting that trajectory is an accomplishment, even if it doesn't show up immediately in improved test scores.

Academic research by Harvard's Paul Peterson and others shows that academic gains are modest in the first year or two of a school choice program, and begin to accelerate afterward. Longitudinal studies tracking choice students over many years seem likely to find higher high school graduation and college enrollment rates, plus other measures of success. If that happens, the debate over the desirability of school choice will be over. The pioneers of school choice will have shown how to rescue individuals from otherwise dark futures, as well as how to force our larger system of public education to improve itself for the good of all students.

NO

Matthew Yglesias

The Verdict on Vouchers

School vouchers are uncomfortable for many liberals. Potential worries abound: Such programs could constitute massive de facto government financing of religion; they could also strip public schools of vital resources, and leave them stuck with the hardest-to-teach children while private schools skim the most promising students. Any large-scale voucher program, moreover, would inevitably wind up giving money to parents who would have enrolled their children in private schools anyway, thus depriving the public sector of funds in order to subsidize relatively affluent parents.

The alternative—systematic improvements of public education, perhaps combined with public choice via a system of secular charter schools—seems much more appealing. But it would take a lot more time than vouchers, which could help significant numbers of the neediest children right now instead of making them wait for a hypothetical overhaul of the country's education system.

It's a tough dilemma, and one can see why conservatives delight in forcing liberals into facing it. You'd think they might win on this point. The only problem is that the best research available—largely conducted by conservative voucher advocates—indicates that this widespread faith in vouchers simply isn't warranted.

No man alone is responsible for the state of misinformation on the subject, but if you had to pick one, Paul Peterson would be a good choice. A professor of government at Harvard, Peterson heads that university's Program on Education Policy and Governance (PEPG) from which vantage point he and his colleagues put out paper after paper cheerleading for the school-choice movement. While Peterson's title and appointment give him the appearance of being just another social scientist, the center's most recent annual report tells a rather different story, with Peterson hailing the U.S. Supreme Court's *Zelman v. Simmons-Harris* decision, giving the go-ahead to public funding of religious schools, and the No Child Left Behind Act as "giant steps forward," noting that the "PEPG has contributed to this forward march" and stating clearly its intention "[t]o help the forward movement."

This is not the typical rhetoric of a sober researcher, and, indeed, a look at the PEPG's finances reveals that much of its money comes from organizations like the Olin, Bradley, Friedman and Walton foundations, which largely fund the right's network of political think tanks and advocacy groups. Harvard is, therefore, in essence acting as a credibility launderer, taking ideological money in exchange for lending its famous name to advocates for conservative causes.

To this end, and apparently motivated by the faith of a true believer, Peterson spent several years around the turn of the millennium conducting the best-designed experiments out there on the efficacy of school vouchers. Where liberals may have feared to tread, perhaps worrying that the results would undermine their case, Peterson stepped boldly into the breach. Programs in New York City, Washington, D.C., and Dayton, Ohio, that provided vouchers to low-income students via a lottery system create an ideal opportunity for study, similar to that used in random-assignment medical testing. By comparing outcomes for students who received vouchers with those of students who applied but lost in the lottery, one can obtain a truly valid comparison between two otherwise identical groups of low-income children.

These were, by all accounts, well-designed experiments, providing the right with its best opportunity to make its case. But unfortunately for Peterson, the data didn't come out right, so he had to spin instead. The best Peterson's team was able to claim in terms of academic achievement for the Dayton results was the presence of gains that fell just short of statistical significance. When the analysis of these data was completed in 2001, it was possible to portray these results as consistent with earlier, more robust findings, and to fudge their actual inconclusiveness.

The data from Washington, however, was a bit odder. The first two years of the study indicated some test-score gains for African American students, which were publicized in papers released by the PEPG in 2000 and 2001 and cited by many conservatives, including Undersecretary of Education Eugene Hickok in congressional testimony last May. The gains, however, disappeared, and, in fact, became declines in year three, a fact that's been little noted—perhaps because Peterson pretty much buried the third-year results in a rather technical pro-vouchers 2002 book—*The Education Gap: Vouchers and Urban Schools*—that he co-wrote with William Howell, rather than touting them to journalists and policy-makers.

Only in New York did his results support the notion that vouchers can improve educational performance, especially for African Americans. (This despite Peterson's claims, in *The Education Gap*, that he found "similar results" in all three cities studied.) The New York results first became known to the general public in the midst of the 2000 presidential campaign, as Peterson made a number of TV appearances and a barrage of conservative columnists claimed that the study proved that anti-voucher Al Gore was more interested in toadying to teachers' unions than helping black kids. Peterson was distinctly less interested in publicizing the survey's more important conclusion: that in the aggregate, students as a whole did no better with vouchers than without. Nor did he make much of the striking fact that Hispanic students, those among the sample who had even worse academic performance than African Americans, did somewhat worse with the vouchers.

At a news conference last summer, Peterson proclaimed the data on black performance "the most significant finding" in his research, and as a propaganda point it certainly is. But it's hard to see what the policy implication of the study taken as a whole is supposed to be. As David Myers of Mathematica Policy Research, a well-respected company that conducted the research in partnership with Peterson's group, points out, "[B]ecause we don't have a good explanation for why we would see [improvement with vouchers] for one group and not another, it's too soon to make policy out of it." Myers put out a statement to that effect in the wake of Peterson's release of the results, but his conclusion was largely lost in the ensuing media hype. The point, however, is an important one, as the federal government is not in a position to implement a racially discriminatory vouchers policy. What would be needed to turn Peterson's results into viable policy is a good theoretical explanation of why vouchers were especially useful to African Americans. If we knew that, we could target a program at anyone, of any race, for whom vouchers would likely prove useful.

While Peterson soldiered on undeterred, Princeton University's Alan Krueger found this racial disparity curious, and he received permission from Mathematica to examine the original data. . . .

"From afar, one couldn't hope to find better research" than Peterson's, he said, but "when you start to dig into it, there were some mistakes that were made." Notably, Peterson had excluded from analysis those students— around 40 percent of the total—for whom "baseline" scores were unavailable on standardized tests taken before the lottery was held. The whole point of using a truly random sample, however, is that you don't need this kind of information. As none other than Peterson himself wrote in 1996, "Analysis of randomized experimental data does not require controls for background characteristics or test scores." The students Peterson included in the study, in other words, were essentially an arbitrary subset of the appropriate sample, and in statistics it's always possible to find some such arbitrary subgroup within which the desired hypothesis holds true. When students with missing baselines are added back in, however, the extent of the gains drops to the margins of statistical significance—not a sufficiently robust result to use as the basis of policy. Controlling for a few additional variables caused the effect to disappear altogether. . . .

There's a rather delicious irony in all this. Confident that the facts would support its case, the right boldly organized and financed a well-designed experiment to assess the impact of vouchers on student achievement only to discover that they didn't help. Even leaving aside questions about the integrity of Peterson's analysis, according to his own interpretation of the data, vouchers don't help poor children as a whole do better in school. This conclusion is also supported by a four-year study commissioned by the state of Ohio of the Cleveland voucher program. At best, there is a positive impact on African Americans that is not strong enough to improve overall performance once all racial groups are taken into consideration. This result runs contrary to the intuitive idea that private schools must be better than public ones (or else no one would pay to send their children there).

That's because not all private schools are elite institutions like Andover or St. Albans. As Richard Rothstein, a lecturer at Columbia University's Teachers College, points out, "It's not surprising that schools in low-income neighborhoods filled with disadvantaged kids get similar results whether they're public or private."

To some researchers, however, the real question still remains what effect vouchers have had on schools. And while Peterson's research may not show vouchers bringing about noteworthy improvements in student performance, there is equally little evidence that they've made things worse. Voucher advocates cite this when arguing for giving vouchers a bigger chance, saying that the real gains of choice programs would only be realized if they reach very large proportions of the student body, which should produce a "competition effect." The theory here is that creating a freer market in education would produce more efficient outcomes: good schools would prosper and bad schools would suffer, creating incentives for improvement.

Skeptics, however, like Stanford University's Martin Carnoy, point out that "when you scale up" by offering vouchers to more students, "you're going to have to bring in new schools, and that's where the problem arises." There's no guarantee that new private schools created to accommodate transferring public-school students would be as good as the ones that already exist. The best information available on this subject comes from Chile and New Zealand, which have both operated large-scale choice systems for more than a decade. In Chile, research by Patrick McEwan indicates the existence of small gains in the capital city of Santiago, which are canceled out by small negative effects in the rest of the country.

New Zealand has no national standardized test, making data collection more difficult, but the country's cultural and political similarities to the United States may make it more relevant. Helen Ladd and Edward B. Fiske attempted to circumvent this problem by measuring impact indirectly through an examination of survey data from teachers and principals in the New Zealand system. Schools where teachers reported that the reforms have succeeded in introducing competition also reported that students were performing worse. The survey of principals yielded similar results, though the effects were statistically insignificant. There is, in other words, no reason to believe that large-scale vouchers could succeed where small-scale programs have failed to improve educational outcomes for children.

The news that vouchers don't help students learn, of course, still leaves the debate far from settled. One thing vouchers do have going for them is that the more options you give parents—even if the options are all objectively bad—the happier those parents wind up being with the choice they've made. All U.S. studies clearly indicate that families that receive vouchers are more satisfied with their schools than those that lost the lottery.

Against this case, liberals argue that privatizing the school system would reduce public accountability, make it harder to maintain reasonable standards, raise the possibility of religious proselytizing with public funds, and balkanize a society that has traditionally relied on public schools to forge a common civic consciousness among a religious and ethnically diverse population. This is a debate worth having, but it should be recognized for what it is at the moment: not a fight over scientific methods but a frankly ideological dispute about the role of public institutions in civic life. The notion that the magic of the market would improve academic achievement turns out, upon examination, to be nothing but a mirage.

POSTSCRIPT

Is Competition the Solution to the Ills of Public Education?

Since school reformers have focused on school choice, the literature on it has mushroomed. The choice proposal first gained public attention in 1955 when Milton Friedman wrote about vouchers in "The Role of Government in Education," in Robert Solo, ed., *Economics and the Public Interest* (Rutgers University Press). More recent school choice advocates include Harry Brighouse, *School Choice and Social Justice* (Oxford University Press, 2000); Mark Schneider, *Choosing Schools: Consumer Choice and the Quality of American Schools* (Princeton University Press, 2000); Philip A. Woods, *School Choice and Competition: Markets in the Public Interest* (Routledge, 1998); Sol Stern, *Breaking Free: Public School Lessons and the Imperative of School Choice* (Encounter Books, 2003); Clint Bolick, *Voucher Wars: Waging the Legal Battle over School Choice* (Cato Institute, 2003); *The Future of School Choice,* edited by Paul E. Peterson *(Hoover Institution Press, 2003)*; James G. Dwyer, *Vouchers within Reason: A Child-Centered Approach to Education Reform* (Cornell University Press, 2002); and Emily Van Dunk, *School Choice and the Question of Accountability: The Milwaukee Experience* (Yale University Press, 2003). School choice is most strongly advocated for inner-city schools. See Frederick M. Hess, *Revolution at the Margins: The Impact of Competition on Urban School Systems* (Brookings Institution Press, 2002) and William G. Howell, *The Education Gap: Vouchers and Urban Schools* (Brookings Institution Press, 2002). For discussions between school choice systems, see *Public School Choice vs. Private School Vouchers,* edited by Richard D. Kahlenberg (Century Foundation, 2003). For a less partisan view see Joseph P. Viteritti, *Choosing Equality: School Choice, the Constitution, and Civil Society* (Brookings Institute Press, 1999). For comparisons of school choice with other reforms, see Margaret C. Wang and Herbert J. Walberg, eds., *School Choice or Best Systems: What Improves Education?* (L. Erlbaum Associates, 2001). Some advocates of choice would limit the choices in major ways. TimothyW. Young and Evans Clinchy, in *Choice in Public Education* (Teachers College Press, 1992), contend that there is already considerable choice in public education so they argue against a voucher system, which they feel will divert badly needed financial resources from the public schools to give further support to parents who can already afford private schools.

    Important critiques of school choice include Albert Shanker and Bella Rosenberg, *Politics, Markets, and America's Schools: The Fallacies of Private School Choice* (American Federation of Teachers, 1991); Kevin B. Smith and Kenneth J. Meier, *The Case Against School Choice: Politics, Markets, and Fools* (M. E. Sharpe, 1995); Seymour Bernard Sarason, *Questions You Should Ask about Charter Schools and Vouchers* (Heinemann, 2002); Gary Miron and Christopher Nelson, *What's Public about Charter Schools?: Lessons Learned about Choice and Accountability* (Corwin Press, 2002); R. Kenneth Godwin and Frand R. Kemerer, *School Choice Tradeoff: Liberty, Equity, and Diversity* (University of Texas Press, 2002); and *School Choice: The Moral Debate,* edited by Alan Wolfe (Princeton University Press, 2003).

ISSUE 15

Should Doctor-Assisted Suicide Be Legalized for the Terminally Ill?

YES: Richard T. Hull, from "The Case for Physician-Assisted Suicide," *Free Inquiry* (Spring 2003)

NO: Margaret Somerville, from "The Case against Physician-Assisted Suicide," *Free Inquiry* (Spring 2003)

ISSUE SUMMARY

YES: Richard T. Hull, professor of philosophy at the State University of New York at Buffalo, asserts that physician-assisted suicide for suffering, terminally ill patients is an act of compassion in providing a desperately sought service. The practice should be regulated to prevent abuse and to stop a too hasty decision by the patient. To totally outlaw it, however, is cruel.

NO: Margaret Somerville, Gale Professor of Law and professor in the Faculty of Medicine at McGill University, argues that this is a form of euthanasia, which violates the sanctity of human life, and it is likely to have severe unintended negative consequences on the practice of medicine and the public attitude toward life.

According to a recent anonymous survey of almost 2,000 doctors who regularly care for dying patients, 6 percent of physicians say they have assisted patient suicides. Only 18 percent had received such requests, and one-third of these had given the requested help. Most physicians who admitted assisting in patients' deaths said they did it only once or twice, so the practice seems to be fairly uncommon. One-third of all doctors surveyed said that they would write prescriptions for deadly doses of drugs in certain cases if the law allowed, and one-quarter would give lethal injections if it were legal. *Officially* the medical community is adamantly opposed to doctor-assisted suicide.

The issue of doctor-assisted suicide is quite complex and confusing. Part of the confusion relates to definitions. Doctor-assisted suicide does not refer to a doctor injecting a patient with a lethal drug nor assisting the suicide of someone who is not terminally ill. The most common method of doctor-assisted suicide is for the doctor to prescribe a drug and then telling the patient how much of it would be lethal. The patient then administers the drug himself or herself. Doctor-assisted suicide lies between letting patients die by removing life-support systems at their request and euthanasia. The first is legal according to the Supreme Court's 1990 decision in *Cruzan v. Director, Missouri Department of Health,* and the latter is considered murder. So the question arises whether doctor-assisted suicide is more like the legal removal of life-support systems or the illegal euthanasia.

The legal, social, and moral issues involved add to the complexity and confusion. First, doctor-assisted suicide is a hotly contested legal issue governed by laws and court decisions. The legal issue was somewhat clarified by the Supreme Court on June 26, 1997, when it unanimously decided that terminally ill people have no constitutional right to die and, therefore, no right to doctor-assisted suicide. Thus, the Supreme Court will not declare invalid state laws that prohibit this practice.

Second, doctor-assisted suicide is a complex social issue with very active groups championing both sides of the debate. Medical technologies have advanced to the point that death can be postponed for a long time after the mind has ceased to function or after the quality of life has declined deeply into the negative. This produces countless situations in which people should not go on living in the judgment of most people. But what should be done for them? The situation for some may suggest that they should be helped to die. How should such a decision be made and how should it be carried out? The patient, of course, should make such decisions, if such decisions are even allowed. Painful ambiguity still remains for those who cannot make intelligent decisions and for those who have chosen to die but may not be competent to make that decision. Furthermore, what are loved ones to do when consulted by the patient or when the patient is no longer capable of making these decisions? The high medical costs for prolonging the lives of some of these very ill people may affect loved ones' decisions regarding the care or life extension of the patient and make the purity of their motives questionable. But costs cannot be totally ignored either.

Third, doctor-assisted suicide is a divisive moral issue. There is no consensus on the norms that should apply to these situations. A strong norm against euthanasia is the belief that stopping someone's life is murder even if that person wants to die. Some people apply the same norm to assisted suicide because they see little difference between injecting a patient with a lethal drug and supplying the patient with the drug to ingest. On the other side, many believe that love and mercy demand assisted suicide or even euthanasia for the terminally ill when great suffering accompanies all other options.

The following selections provide strong arguments for and against doctor-assisted suicide. Richard T. Hull contends that the relieving of suffering and honoring the patient's wishes are the overriding concerns, which fully justify the practice in light of the absence of compelling arguments to the contrary. Margaret Somerville argues that physician-assisted suicide is wrong because it is never justified for one human to take another's life. She also contends that any benefits it provides would be negated by its overall harm to individuals and society.

Richard T. Hull

 **YES**

The Case for Physician-Assisted Suicide

In early 1997, the medical community awaited the U.S. Supreme Court's decision in *Vacco* v. *Quill.* Ultimately the high court would overturn this suit, in which doctors and patients had sought to overturn New York's law prohibiting physician-assisted suicide. But it was fascinating to see how much attention physicians suddenly paid to the question of pain management while they were waiting.

Politicians and physicians alike felt shaken by the fact that the suit had made it as far as the Supreme Court. Medical schools scrutinized their curricula to see how, if at all, effective pain management was taught. The possibility that physician-assisted suicide would be declared as much a patient's right as the withdrawal of life-sustaining technology was a clarion call that medicine needed to "houseclean" its attitudes toward providing adequate narcotics for managing pain.

The ability to demand physician aid in dying is the only resource dying patients have with which to "send a message" (as our public rhetoric is so fond of putting it) to physicians, insurers, and politicians that end-of-life care is inadequate. Far too many patients spend their last days without adequate palliation of pain. Physicians sensitive to their cries hesitate to order adequate narcotics, for fear of scrutiny by state health departments and federal drug agents. Further, many physicians view imminent death as a sign of failure in the eyes of their colleagues, or just refuse to recognize that the seemingly endless variety of tests and procedures available to them can simply translate into a seemingly endless period of dying badly. Faced with all this, the ability to demand—and receive—physician aid in dying may be severely compromised patients' only way to tell caregivers that something inhumane stalks them: the inhumanity of neglect and despair.

Many physicians tell me that they feel it is an affront to suppose that their duty to care extends to a duty to kill or assist in suicide. If so, is it not even more an affront, as dying patients and their families tell me, to have to beg for increases in pain medication, only to be told that "We don't want to make you an addict, do we?" or that "Doctor's orders are being followed, and Doctor can't be reached to revise them." If apologists for the status quo fear that a slippery slope will lead to voluntary euthanasia, then nonvoluntary euthanasia, the proponents of change already know that we've been on a slippery slope of inadequate management of suffering for decades.

Let's examine some of the stronger arguments against physician-assisted suicide—while keeping in mind that these arguments may not be the deepest reasons some people oppose it. My lingering sense is that the unspoken problem with physician-assisted suicide is that it puts power where opponents don't want it: in the hands of patients and their loved ones. I want to see if there are ways of sorting out who holds the power to choose the time and manner of dying that make sense.

1. Many severely compromised individuals, in their depression, loneliness, loss of normal life, and despair, have asked their physicians to assist them in dying. Yet later (after physicians resisted their requests and others awakened them to alternative opportunities) they have returned to meaningful lives.

No sane advocate of physician-assisted suicide would deny the importance of meeting the demand to die with reluctance and a reflective, thorough examination of alternative options. The likelihood of profound mood swings during therapy makes it imperative to distinguish between a patient's acute anguish of loss and his or her rational dismay at the prospect of long-term descent into the tubes and machines of intensive care.

But note that, in stories like the above, it is the very possibility of legal physician-assisted suicide that empowers patients to draw attention to their suffering and command the resources they need to live on. Patients who cannot demand to die can find their complaints more easily dismissed as "the disease talking" or as weakness of character.

2. Medicine would be transformed for the worse if doctors could legally help patients end their lives. The public would become distrustful, wondering whether physicians were truly committed to saving lives, or if they would stop striving as soon as it became inconvenient.

Doubtless there are physicians who, by want of training or some psychological or moral defect, lack the compassionate sensitivity to hear a demand for aid in dying and act on it with reluctance, only after thorough investigation of the patient's situation. Such physicians should not be empowered to assist patients to die. I would propose that this power be restricted to physicians whose primary training and profession is in pain management and palliation: they are best equipped to ensure that reasonable alternatives to euthanasia and suicide are exhausted. Further, patients' appeals for assisted suicide should be scrutinized by the same institutional ethics committees that already review requests for the suspension of life-sustaining technology as a protection against patient confusion and relatives' greed.

3. Euthanasia and physician-assisted suicide are incompatible with our obligations to respect the human spirit and human life.

When I hear *all* motives for euthanasia and physician-assisted suicide swept so cavalierly into the dustbin labeled Failure to Respect Human Life, I'm prompted to say, "Really? *Always?*" Those same opponents who find physician-assisted suicide appalling will typically excuse, even acclaim, self-sacrifice on behalf of others. A soldier throws himself on a grenade to save his fellows. A pedestrian leaps into the path of a truck to save a child. Firefighters remain in a collapsing building rather than abandon trapped victims. These, too, are decisions to embrace death, yet we leave them to the conscience of the agent. Why tar all examples of euthanasia and physician-assisted suicide with a common brush? Given that we do not have the power to ameliorate every disease and never will, why withhold from individuals who clearly perceive the financial and emotional burdens their dying imposes on loved ones the power to lessen the duration and extent of those burdens, in pursuit of the values they have worked to support throughout their lives?

Consider also that some suffering cannot be relieved by any means while maintaining consciousness. There are individuals, like myself, who regard conscious life as essential to personal identity. I find it nonsensical to maintain that it is profoundly morally *preferable* to be rendered comatose by drugs while awaiting life's "natural end," than to hasten death's arrival while still consciously able to embrace and welcome one's release. If I am irreversibly comatose, "I" am dead; prolongation of "my life" at that point is ghoulish, and I should not be required to undergo such indignity.

Finally the question, "What kind of life is worth living?" is highly personal. There are good reasons patients diagnosed with a wide range of conditions might not wish to live to the natural end of their diseases. How dare politicians and moralists presume to make these final judgments if they don't have to live with the results? Of course, every demand for physician-assisted suicide must be scrutinized, and determined to be fully informed. To withhold aid in dying beyond that point is, first, barbarically cruel. Second, it only increases the risk that individuals determined to end their lives will attempt to do so by nonmedical means, possibly endangering others or further magnifying their own suffering.

> 4. *The time-honored doctrine of double effect permits administering pain-relieving drugs that have the effect of shortening life, provided the intent of the physician is the relief of the pain and not the (foreseen) death of the patient. Isn't that sufficient?*

Others may find comfort in the notion that the intention of the agent, not the consequences of his or her action, is the measure of morality. I do not. In any case, preferences among ethical theories are like preferences among religious persuasions: no such preference should be legislated for all citizens. For the thinker who focuses on consequences rather than intentions, the fact that we permit terminal care regimens to shorten life *in any context* shows that the line has already been crossed. The fact that physicians must, at the insistence of the competent patient or the incompetent patient's duly appointed surrogate, withdraw life-sustaining technology shows that physicians *can* assist patient suicides and can perform euthanasia on those fortunate enough to be dependent on machines. It becomes a matter of simple justice—equal protection before the law—to permit the same privileges to other terminal patients. That the U.S. Supreme Court has ruled against this argument did not dissuade the citizens of the State of Oregon from embracing it. States like New York that have turned back such initiatives must bear the shame of having imposed religious majorities' philosophies on all who suffer.

The Case Against Euthanasia and Physician-Assisted Suicide

There are two major reasons to oppose euthanasia. One is based on principle: it is wrong for one human to intentionally kill another (except in justified self-defense, or in the defense of others). The other reason is utilitarian: the harms and risks of legalizing euthanasia, to individuals in general and to society, far outweigh any benefits.

When personal and societal values were largely consistent with each other, and widely shared because they were based on a shared religion, the case against euthanasia was simple: God or the gods (and, therefore, the religion) commanded "Thou shalt not kill." In a secular society, especially one that gives priority to intense individualism, the case for euthanasia is simple: Individuals have the right to choose the manner, time, and place of their death. In contrast, in such societies the case against euthanasia is complex.

Definitions

Definitions are a source of confusion in the euthanasia debate—some of it deli-berately engendered by euthanasia advocates to promote their case.[1] Euthanasia is "a deliberate act that causes death undertaken by one person with the primary intention of ending the life of another person, in order to relieve that person's suffering."[2] Euthanasia is not the justified withdrawing or withholding of treatment that results in death. And it is not the provision of pain relief, even if it could or would shorten life, provided the treatment is necessary to relieve the patient's pain or other serious symptoms of physical distress and is given with a primary intention of relieving pain and not of killing the patient.

Secular Arguments Against Euthanasia

1. *Impact on society.* To legalize euthanasia would damage important, foundational societal values and symbols that uphold respect for human life. With euthanasia, how we die cannot be just a private matter of self-determination and personal beliefs, because euthanasia "is an act that requires two people to make it possible and a complicit society to make it acceptable."[3] The prohibition on intentional

From Margaret Somerville, "The Case Against Physician-Assisted Suicide," *Free Inquiry* (Spring 2003). Copyright © 2003 by Margaret Somerville. Reprinted by permission of the author.

killing is the cornerstone of law and human relationships, emphasizing our basic equality.[4]

Medicine and the law are the principal institutions that maintain respect for human life in a secular, pluralistic society. Legalizing euthanasia would involve—and harm—both of them. In particular, changing the norm that we must not kill each other would seriously damage both institutions' capacity to carry the value of respect for human life.

To legalize euthanasia would be to change the way we understand ourselves, human life, and its meaning. To explain this last point requires painting a much larger picture. We create our values and find meaning in life by buying into a "shared story"—a societal-cultural paradigm. Humans have always focused that story on the two great events of each life, birth and death. Even in a secular society—indeed, more than in a religious one—that story must encompass, create space for, and protect the "human spirit." By the human spirit, I do not mean anything religious (although this concept can accommodate the religious beliefs of those who have them). Rather, I mean the intangible, invisible, immeasurable reality that we need to find meaning in life and to make life worth living—that deeply intuitive sense of relatedness or connectedness to others, the world, and the universe in which we live.

There are two views of human life and, as a consequence, death. One is that we are simply "gene machines." In the words of an Australian politician, when we are past our "best before" or "use by" date, we should be checked out as quickly, cheaply, and efficiently as possible. That view favors euthanasia. The other view sees a mystery in human death, because it sees a mystery in human life, a view that does not require any belief in the supernatural.

Euthanasia is a "gene machine" response. It converts the mystery of death to the problem of death, to which we then seek a technological solution. A lethal injection is a very efficient, fast solution to the problem of death—but it is antithetical to the mystery of death. People in postmodern societies are uncomfortable with mysteries, especially mysteries that generate intense, free-floating anxiety and fear, as death does. We seek control over the event that elicits that fear; we look for a terror-management or terror-reduction mechanism. Euthanasia is such a mechanism: While it does not allow us to avoid the cause of our fear—death—it does allow us to control its manner, time, and place—we can feel that we have death under control.

Research has shown that the marker for people wanting euthanasia is a state that psychiatrists call "hopelessness," which they differentiate from depressions[5]—these people have nothing to look forward to. Hope is our sense of connection to the future; hope is the oxygen of the human spirit.[6] Hope can be elicited by a sense of connection to a very immediate future, for instance, looking forward to a visit from a loved person, seeing the sun come up, or hearing the dawn chorus. When we are dying, our horizon comes closer and closer, but it still exists until we finally cross over. People need hope if they are to experience dying as the final great act of life, as it should be. Euthanasia converts that act to an act of death.

A more pragmatic, but nevertheless very important, objection to legalizing euthanasia is that its abuse cannot be prevented, as recent reports on euthanasia in the Netherlands have documented.[7] Indeed, as a result of this evidence some former advocates now believe that euthanasia cannot be safely legalized and have recently spoken against doing so.[8]

To assess the impact that legalizing euthanasia might have, in practice, on society, we must look at it in the context in which it would operate: the combination of an aging population, scarce health-care resources, and euthanasia would be a lethal one.

2. *Impact on medicine.*[9] Advocates often argue that euthanasia should be legalized because physicians are secretly carrying it out anyway. Studies[10] purporting to establish that fact have recently been severely criticized on the grounds that the respondents replied to questions that did not distinguish between actions primarily intended to shorten life—euthanasia—and other acts or omissions in which no such intention was present—pain-relief treatment or refusals of treatment—that are not euthanasia.[11] But even if the studies were accurate, the fact that physicians are secretly carrying out euthanasia does not mean that it is right. Further, if physicians were presently ignoring the law against murder, why would they obey guidelines for voluntary euthanasia?

Euthanasia "places the very soul of medicine on trial."[12] Physicians' absolute repugnance to killing people is necessary if society's trust in them is to be maintained. This is true, in part, because physicians have opportunities to kill not open to other people, as the horrific story of Dr. Harold Shipman, the British physician–serial killer, shows.

How would legalizing euthanasia affect medical education? What impact would physician role models carrying out euthanasia have on medical students and young physicians? Would we devote time to teaching students how to administer death through lethal injection? Would they be brutalized or ethically desensitized? (Do we adequately teach pain-relief treatment at present?) It would be very difficult to communicate to future physicians a repugnance to killing in a context of legalized euthanasia.

Physicians need a clear line that powerfully manifests to them, their patients, and society that they do not inflict death; both their patients and the public need to know with absolute certainty—and to be able to trust—that this is the case. Anything that would blur the line, damage that trust, or make physicians less sensitive to their primary obligations to protect life is unacceptable. Legalizing euthanasia would do all of these things.

Conclusion

Euthanasia is a simplistic, wrong, and dangerous response to the complex reality of human death. Physician-assisted suicide and euthanasia involve taking people who are at their weakest and most vulnerable, who fear loss of control or isolation and abandonment—who are in a state of intense "pre-mortem loneliness"[13]—and placing them in a situation where they believe their only alternative is to be killed or kill themselves.

Nancy Crick, a sixty-nine-year-old Australian grandmother, recently committed suicide in the presence of over twenty people, eight of whom were members of the Australian Voluntary Euthanasia Society. She explained: "I don't want to die alone." Another option for Mrs. Crick (if she had been terminally ill—an autopsy showed Mrs. Crick's colon cancer had not recurred) should have been to die naturally with people who cared for her present and good palliative care.

Of people who requested assisted suicide under Oregon's Death with Dignity Act, which allows physicians to prescribe lethal medication, 46 percent changed their minds after significant palliative-care interventions (relief of pain and other symptoms), but only 15 percent of those who did not receive such interventions did so.[14]

How a society treats its weakest, most in need, most vulnerable members best tests its moral and ethical tone. To set a present and future moral tone that protects individuals in general and society, upholds the fundamental value of respect for life, and promotes rather than destroys our capacities and opportunities to search for meaning in life, we must reject euthanasia.

Notes

1. Margaret Somerville, "Death Talk: The Case Against Euthanasia and Physician-Assisted Suicide" (Montreal: McGill Queen's University Press, 2001), p. xiii.
2. Ibid.
3. D. Callahan, "When Self-Determination Runs Amok," *Hastings Center Report* 1992, 22(2): 52–55.
4. House of Lords. Report of the Select Committee on Medical Ethics (London: HMSO, 1994).
5. H.M. Chochinov, K.G. Wilson, M. Enns, et al. "Depression, Hopelessness, and Suicidal Ideation in the Terminally Ill," *Psychosomatics* 39 (1998):366–70, "Desire for Death in the Terminally Ill," *American Journal of Psychiatry* 152 (1995):1185–1191.
6. Margaret Somerville, *The Ethical Canary: Science, Society and the Human Spirit* (Toronto: Viking/Penguin, 2000).
7. K. Foley and H. Hendin, editors, *The Case Against Assisted Suicide: For the Right to End-of-Life Care* (Baltimore: The Johns Hopkins University Press, 2002).
8. S.B. Nuland, "The Principle of Hope," *The New Republic* OnLine 2002: May 22.
9. This section is based on Margaret Somerville, " 'Death Talk': Debating Euthanasia and Physician-Assisted Suicide in Australia," *AMAJ* February 17, 2003.
10. H. Kuhse, P. Singer, P. Baume, et al. "End-of-Life Decisions in Australian Medical Practice," *Med J Aust* 166 (1997): 191–96.
11. D.W. Kissane, "Deadly Days in Darwin," K. Foley, H. Hendin, editors, *The Case Against Assisted Suicide: For the Right to End-of-Life Care*, pp. 192–209.
12. W. Gaylin, L. Kass, E.D. Pellegrino, and M. Siegler, "Doctors Must Not Kill," *JAMA* 1988; 259:2139–2140.
13. J. Katz, *The Silent World of Doctor and Patient* (New York: Free Press, 1984).
14. K. Foley and H. Hendin. "The Oregon Experiment," in K. Foley, H. Hendin, editors, *The Case Against Assisted Suicide: For the Right to End-of-Life Care*, p. 269.

POSTSCRIPT

Should Doctor-Assisted Suicide Be Legalized for the Terminally Ill?

$\mathbf{M}$any of us know of or can imagine terminally ill people for whom doctor-assisted suicide would be merciful. They suffer a great deal and have no periods of relief. On the other hand, imagine a case where a patient desperately wanted a doctor to assist him/her to commit suicide but later recovered for a relatively pleasant period before dying. Assisted suicide would be wrong in that case. These two types of cases point up the problem of a blanket rule for all cases. What if we were to come to the conclusion that doctor-assisted suicide is wrong in most cases when patients request it but right in a minority of cases? Maybe both sides are right at times and wrong at other times. The problem is that it is difficult to make laws that apply only sometimes. Most laws provide too little leeway to be adjusted to the peculiarities of individual cases. For example, if a man goes over the speed limit, he breaks the law, even if he is driving his wife to the hospital to deliver a baby. Fortunately, most policemen would not write this man a ticket but rather turn on their siren and escort him to the hospital. For many laws the discretion of judges and juries, like that of the policeman, provides some badly needed flexibility, but problems will always remain.

The literature on doctor-assisted suicide and the larger issue of euthanasia has mushroomed in the last decade. For arguments against these practices, see Wesley J. Smith, *Forced Exit: The Slippery Slope From Assisted Suicide to Legalized Murder* (Times Books, 1997); *The Case against Assisted Suicide: For the Right to End-of-Life Care*, edited by Kathleen Foley and Herbert Hendin (Johns Hopkins Press, 2002); Margaret A. Somerville, *Death Talk: The Case against Euthanasia and Physician-Assisted Suicide* (McGill-Queen's University Press, 2001); and Barbara A. Olevitch, *Protecting Psychiatric Patients and Others from the Assisted-Suicide Movement: Insights and Strategies* (Praeger, 2002).

For works that favor doctor-assisted suicide or euthanasia or that contain various viewpoints, see Barry Rosenfeld, *Assisted Suicide and the Right to Die: The Interface of Social Science, Public Policy, and Medical Ethics* (American Psychological Association, 2004); *Assisted Suicide: Finding Common Ground*, edited by Lois Snyder and Arthur L. Caplan (Indiana University Press, 2002); and *Physician Assisted Suicide: What Are the Issues?* edited by Loretta M. Kopelman and Kenneth A. DeVille (Kluwer Academic Publishers, 2001) and Marylin Webb, *The Good Death: The New American Search to Reshape the End of Life* (Bantam Books, 1997). For works that present or analyze the issues as debates, see Michael M. Uhlman, ed., *Last Rights? Assisted Suicide and Euthanasia Debated* (William B. Eerdmans, 1998) and Tamara Roleff, ed., *Suicide: Opposing Viewpoints* (Greenhaven Press, 1998). For multiple views on doctor-assisted suicide and euthanasia, see Melvin I. Urofsky and Philip E. Urofsky, eds., *The Right to Die: A Two-Volume Anthology of Scholarly Articles* (Garland, 1996) and Robert F. Weir et al., *Physician-Assisted Suicide* (Indiana University Press, 1997).

American Society of Criminology

The American Society of Criminology Web site is an excellent starting point for studying all aspects of criminology and criminal justice. This page provides links to sites on criminal justice in general, international criminal justice, juvenile justice, courts, the police, and the government.

http://www.bsos.umd.edu/asc/four.html

Crime Times

This Crime Times site lists research reviews and other information regarding the causes of criminal and violent behavior. It is provided by the nonprofit Wacker Foundation, publishers of Crime Times.

http://www.crime-times.org

Justice Information Center (JIC)

Provided by the National Criminal Justice Reference Service, the Justice Information Center (JIC) site connects to information about corrections, courts, crime prevention, criminal justice, statistics, drugs and crime, law enforcement, and victims, among other topics.

http://www.ncjrs.org

PART 5

Crime and Social Control

*A*ll societies label certain hurtful actions as crimes and punish those who commit them. Other harmful actions, however, are not defined as crimes, and the perpetrators are not punished. Today the definition of crime and the appropriate treatment of criminals is widely debated. Some of the major questions are: Does street crime pose more of a threat to the public's well-being than white-collar crime? Billions of dollars have been spent on the "war on drugs," but who is winning? Would legalizing some drugs free up money that could be directed to other types of social welfare programs, such as the rehabilitation of addicts?

- Is Street Crime More Harmful Than White-Collar Crime?

- Should Drug Use Be Decriminalized?

- Does the threat of Terrorism Warrant the Curtailment of Civil Liberties?

ISSUE 16

Is Street Crime More Harmful Than White-Collar Crime?

YES: David A. Anderson, from "The Aggregate Burden of Crime," *Journal of Law and Economics* XLII (2) (October 1999)

NO: Jeffrey Reiman, from *The Rich Get Richer and the Poor Get Prison: Ideology, Class, and Criminal Justice,* 5th ed. (Allyn & Bacon, 1998)

ISSUE SUMMARY

YES: David A. Anderson estimates the total annual cost of crime including law enforcement and security services. The costs exceed one trillion, with fraud (mostly white collar crime) causing about one-fifth of the total. His calculations of the full costs of the loss of life and injury comes to about half of the total costs. It is right, therefore, to view personal and violent crime as the big crime problem.

NO: Professor of philosophy Jeffrey Reiman argues that the dangers posed by negligent corporations and white-collar criminals are a greater menace to society than are the activities of typical street criminals.

The word *crime* entered the English language (from the Old French) around A.D. 1250, when it was identified with "sinfulness." Later, the meaning of the word was modified: crime became the kind of sinfulness that was rightly punishable by law. Even medieval writers, who did not distinguish very sharply between church and state, recognized that there were some sins for which punishment was best left to God; the laws should punish only those that cause harm to the community. Of course, their concept of harm was a very broad one, embracing such offenses as witchcraft and blasphemy. Modern jurists, even those who deplore such practices, would say that the state has no business punishing the perpetrators of these types of offenses.

What, then, should the laws punish? The answer depends in part on our notion of harm. We usually limit the term to the kind of harm that is tangible and obvious: taking a life, causing bodily injury or psychological trauma, and destroying property. For most Americans today, particularly those who live in cities, the word *crime* is practically synonymous with street crime. Anyone who has ever been robbed or beaten by street criminals will never forget the experience. The harm that these criminals cause is tangible, and the connection between the harm and the perpetrator is very direct.

But suppose the connection is not so direct. Suppose, for example, that A hires B to shoot C. Is that any less a crime? B is the actual shooter, but is A any less guilty? Of course not, we say; he may even be more guilty, since he is the ultimate mover behind the crime. A would be guilty even if the chain of command were much longer, involving A's orders to B, and B's to C, then on to D, E, and F to kill G. Organized crime kingpins go to jail even when they are far removed from the people who carry out their orders. High officials of the Nixon administration, even though they were not directly involved in the burglary attempt at the Democratic National Committee headquarters at the Watergate Hotel complex in 1972, were imprisoned.

This brings us to the topic of white-collar crime. The burglars at the Watergate Hotel were acting on orders that trickled down from the highest reaches of political power in the United States. Other white-collar criminals are as varied as the occupations from which they come. They include stockbrokers who make millions through insider trading, as Ivan Boesky did; members of Congress who take payoffs; and people who cheat on their income taxes, like hotel owner and billionaire Leona Helmsley. Some, like Helmsley, get stiff prison sentences when convicted, though many others (like most of the officials in the Watergate scandal) do little or no time in prison. Do they deserve stiffer punishment, or are their crimes less harmful than the crimes of street criminals?

Although white-collar criminals do not directly cause physical harm or relieve people of their wallets, they can still end up doing considerable harm. The harm done by Nixon's aides threatened the integrity of the U.S. electoral system. Every embezzler, corrupt politician, and tax cheat exacts a toll on our society. Individuals can be hurt in more tangible ways by decisions made in corporate boardrooms: Auto executives, for example, have approved design features that have caused fatalities. Managers of chemical companies have allowed practices that have polluted the environment with cancer-causing agents. And heads of corporations have presided over industries wherein workers have been needlessly killed or maimed.

Whether or not these decisions should be considered crimes is debatable. A crime must always involve "malicious intent," or what the legal system calls *mens rea*. This certainly applies to street crime—the mugger obviously has sinister designs—but does it apply to every decision made in a boardroom that ends up causing harm? And does that harm match or exceed the harm caused by street criminals? In the following selections, David A. Anderson tries to calculate all the costs of all crimes. His message is that crime costs society far more than we realize. But for the debate on the relative costs of street vs. white collar crime, his study shows that street crime costs society more than white collar crime. According to Jeffrey Reiman, white-collar crime does more harm than is commonly recognized. By his count, white-collar crime causes far more deaths, injuries, illnesses, and financial loss than street crime. In light of this, he argues, we must redefine our ideas about what crime is and who the criminals are.

271

David A. Anderson

 **YES**

The Aggregate Burden of Crime

Introduction

Distinct from previous studies that have focused on selected crimes, regions, or outcomes, this study attempts an exhaustively broad estimation of the crime burden. . . .

Overt annual expenditures on crime in the United States include $47 billion for police protection, $36 billion for corrections, and $19 billion for the legal and judicial costs of state and local criminal cases. (Unless otherwise noted, all figures are adjusted to reflect 1997 dollars using the Consumer Price Index.) Crime victims suffer $876 million worth of lost workdays, and guns cost society $25 billion in medical bills and lost productivity in a typical year. Beyond the costs of the legal system, victim losses, and crime prevention agencies, the crime burden includes the costs of deterrence (locks, safety lighting and fencing, alarm systems and munitions), the costs of compliance enforcement (non-gendarme inspectors and regulators), implicit psychic and health costs (fear, agony, and the inability to behave as desired), and the opportunity costs of time spent preventing, carrying out, and serving prison terms for criminal activity.

This study estimates the impact of crime taking a comprehensive list of the repercussions of aberrant behavior into account. While the standard measures of criminal activity count crimes and direct costs, this study measures the impact of crimes and includes indirect costs as well. Further, the available data on which crime cost figures are typically based is imprecise. Problems with crime figures stem from the prevalence of unreported crimes, inconsistencies in recording procedures among law enforcement agencies, policies of recording only the most serious crime in events with multiple offenses, and a lack of distinction between attempted and completed crimes. This research does not eliminate these problems, but it includes critical crime-prevention and opportunity costs that are measured with relative precision, and thus places less emphasis on the imprecise figures used in most other measures of the impact of crime. . . .

Previous Studies

Several studies have estimated the impact of crime; however, none has been thorough in its assessment of the substantial indirect costs of crime and the

From *Journal of Law and Economics*, October 1999. Copyright © 1999 by David A. Anderson. Reprinted with permission.

Table 1

Previous Study	Focus	Not Included	$ (billions)
Colins (1994)	General	Opportunity Costs, Miscellaneous Indirect Components	728
Cohen, Miller, and Wiersema (1995)	Victim Costs of Violent and Property Crimes	Prevention, Opportunity, and Indirect Costs	472
U.S. News (1974)	General	Opportunity Costs, Miscellaneous Indirect Components	288
Cohen, Miller, Rossman (1994)	Cost of Rape, Robbery, and Assault	Prevention, Opportunity, and Indirect Costs	183
Zedlewski (1985)	Firearms, Guard Dogs, Victim Losses, Commercial Security	Residential Security, Opportunity Costs, Indirect Costs	160
Cohen (1990)	Cost of Personal and Household Crime to Victims	Prevention, Opportunity, and Indirect Costs	113
President's Commission on Law Enforcement (1967)	General	Opportunity Costs, Miscellaneous Indirect Components	107
Klaus (1994)	National Crime and Victimization Survey Crimes	Prevention, Opportunity, and Indirect Costs	19

crucial consideration of private crime prevention expenditures. The FBI Crime Index provides a measure of the level of crime by counting the acts of murder, rape, robbery, aggravated assault, burglary, larceny, motor vehicle theft, and arson each year. The FBI Index is purely a count of crimes and does not attempt to place weights on various criminal acts based on their severity. If the number of acts of burglary, larceny, motor vehicle theft, or arson decreases, society might be better off, but with no measure of the severity of the crimes, such a conclusion is necessarily tentative. From a societal standpoint what matters is the extent of damage inflicted by these crimes, which the FBI Index does not measure.

Over the past three decades, studies of the cost of crime have reported increasing crime burdens, perhaps more as a result of improved understanding and accounting for the broad repercussions of crime than due to the increase in the burden itself. Table 1 summarizes the findings of eight previous studies. . . .

The Effects of Crime

The effects of crime fall into several categories depending on whether they constitute the allocation of resources due to crime that could otherwise be used more productively, the production of ill-favored commodities, transfers from victims to criminals, opportunity costs, or implicit costs associated with risks to life and health. This section examines the meaning and ramifications of each of these categories of crime costs.

Crime-Induced Production

Crime can result in the allocation of resources towards products and activities that do not contribute to society except in their association with crime. Examples include the production of personal protection devices, the trafficking of drugs, and the operation of correctional facilities. In the absence of crime, the time, money, and material resources absorbed by the provision of these goods and services could be used for the creation of benefits rather than the avoidance of harm. The foregone benefits from these alternatives represent a real cost of crime to society. (Twenty dollars spent on a door lock is twenty dollars that cannot be spent on groceries.) Thus, expenditures on crime-related products are treated as a loss to society.

Crimes against property also create unnecessary production due to the destruction and expenditure of resources, and crimes against persons necessitate the use of medical and psychological care resources. In each of these cases, crime-related purchases bid-up prices for the associated items, resulting in higher prices for all consumers of the goods. In the absence of crime, the dollars currently spent to remedy and recover from crime would largely be spent in pursuit of other goals, bidding-up the prices of alternative categories of goods. For this reason, the *net* impact of price effects is assumed to be zero in the present research.

Opportunity Costs

As the number of incarcerated individuals increases steadily, society faces the large and growing loss of these potential workers' productivity. . . . Criminals are risk takers and instigators—characteristics that could make them contributors to society if their entrepreneurial talents were not misguided. Crimes also take time to conceive and carry out, and thus involve the opportunity cost of the criminals' time regardless of detection and incarceration. For many, crime is a full-time occupation. Society is deprived of the goods and services a criminal would have produced in the time consumed by crime and the production of "bads" if he or she were on the level. Additional opportunity costs arise due to victims' lost workdays, and time spent securing assets, looking for keys, purchasing and installing crime prevention devices, and patrolling neighborhood-watch areas.

The Value of Risks to Life and Health

The implicit costs of violent crime include the fear of being injured or killed, the anger associated with the inability to behave as desired, and the agony of being a crime victim. Costs associated with life and health risks are perhaps the most difficult to ascertain, although a considerable literature is devoted to their estimation. The implicit values of lost life and injury are included in the list of crime costs below; those not wishing to consider them can simply subtract these estimates from the aggregate figure.

Transfers

One result of fraud and theft is a transfer of assets from victim to criminal. . . .

Numerical Findings

Crime-Induced Production

. . . Crime-induced production accounts for about $400 billion in expenditures annually. Table 2 presents the costs of goods and services that would not have to be produced in the absence of crime. Drug trafficking accounts for an estimated $161 billion in expenditure. With the $28 billion cost of prenatal drug exposure and almost $11 billion worth of federal, state, and local drug control efforts (including drug treatment, education, interdiction, research, and intelligence), the combined cost of drug-related activities is about $200 billion. Findings that over half of the arrestees in 24 cities tested positive for recent drug use and about one-third of offenders reported being under the influence of drugs at the time of their offense suggest that significant portions of the other crime-cost categories may result indirectly from drug use.

Table 2

Crime-Induced Production	$ (millions)
Drug Trafficking	160,584
Police Protection	47,129
Corrections	35,879
Prenatal Exposure to Cocaine and Heroin	28,156
Federal Agencies	23,381
Judicial and Legal Services—State & Local	18,901
Guards	17,917
Drug Control	10,951
DUI Costs to Driver	10,302
Medical Care for Victims	8,990
Computer Viruses and Security	8,000
Alarm Systems	6,478
Passes for Business Access	4,659
Locks, Safes, and Vaults	4,359
Vandalism (except Arson)	2,317
Small Arms and Small Arms Ammunition	2,252
Replacements due to Arson	1,902
Surveillance Cameras	1,471
Safety Lighting	1,466
Protective Fences and Gates	1,159
Airport Security	448
Nonlethal weaponry, e.g., Mace	324
Elec. Retail Article Surveillance	149
Theft Insurance (less indemnity)	96
Guard Dogs	49
Mothers Against Drunk Driving	49
Library Theft Detection	28
Total	**397,395**

About 682,000 police and 17,000 federal, state, special (park, transit, or county) and local police agencies account for $47 billion in expenditures annually. Thirty-six billion dollars is dedicated each year to the 895 federal and state prisons, 3,019 jails, and 1,091 state, county, and local juvenile detention centers. Aside from guards in correctional institutions, private expenditure on guards amounts to more than $18 billion annually. Security guard agencies employ 55 percent of the 867,000 guards in the U.S.; the remainder are employed in-house. While guards are expected and identifiable at banks and military complexes, they have a less conspicuous presence at railroads, ports, golf courses, laboratories, factories, hospitals, retail stores, and other places of business. The figures in this paper do not include receptionists, who often play a duel role of monitoring unlawful entry into a building and providing information and assistance. . . .

Opportunity Costs

In their study of the costs of murder, rape, robbery, and aggravated assault, Cohen, Miller, and Rossman estimate that the average incarcerated offender costs society $5,700 in lost productivity per year. Their estimate was based on the observation that many prisoners did not work in the legal market prior to their offense, and the opportunity cost of those prisoners' time can be considered to be zero. The current study uses a higher estimate of the opportunity cost of incarceration because unlike previous studies, it examines the relative savings from a *crime-free* society. It is likely that in the absence of crime including drug use, some criminals who are not presently employed in the legal workforce would be willing and able to find gainful employment. This assumption is supported by the fact that many criminals are, in a way, motivated entrepreneurs whose energy has taken an unfortunate focus. In the absence of more enticing underground activities, some of the same individuals could apply these skills successfully in the legal sector. . . .

The Value of Risks to Life and Health

Table 3 presents estimates of the implicit costs of violent crime. The value of life and injury estimates used here reflect the amounts individuals are willing to accept to enter a work environment in which their health state might change. The labor market estimates do not include losses covered by workers' compensation, namely health care costs (usually provided without dollar or time limits) and lost earnings (within modest bounds, victims or their spouses typically receive about two thirds of lost earnings for life or the duration of the injury). The values do capture perceived risks of pain, suffering,

Table 3

The Value of Risks to Life and Health	$ (millions)
Value of Lost Life	439,880
Value of Injuries	134,515
Total	574,395

and mental distress associated with the health losses. If the risk of involvement in violent crime evokes more mental distress than the risk of occupational injuries and fatalities, the labor market values represent conservative estimates of the corresponding costs of crime. Similar estimates have been used in previous studies of crime costs. . . .

The average of 27 previous estimates of the implicit value of human life as reported by W. Kip Viscusi is 7.1 million. Removing two outlying estimates of just under $20 million about which the authors express reservation, the average of the remaining studies is $6.1 million. Viscusi points out that the majority of the estimates fall between $3.7 and $8.6 million ($3 and $7 million in 1990 dollars), the average of which is again $6.1 million. The $6.1 million figure was multiplied by the 72,111 crime-related deaths to obtain the $440 billion estimate of the value of lives lost to crime. Similarly, the average of 15 studies of the implicit value of non-fatal injuries, $52,637, was multiplied by the 2,555,520 reported injuries resulting from drunk driving and boating, arson, rape, robbery, and assaults to find the $135 billion estimate for the implicit cost of crime-related injuries.

Transfers

More than $603 billion worth of transfers result from crime. After the $204 billion lost to occupational fraud and the $123 billion in unpaid taxes, the $109 billion lost to health insurance fraud represents the greatest transfer by more than a factor of two, and the associated costs amount to almost ten percent of the nations' health care expenditures. Robberies, perhaps the classic crime, ironically generate a smaller volume of transfers ($775 million) than any other category of crime. The transfers of goods and money resulting from fraud and theft do not necessarily impose a net burden on society, and may in fact increase social welfare to the extent that those on the receiving end value the goods more than those losing them. Nonetheless, as Table 4 illustrates, those on the losing side bear a $603 billion annual burden. . . .

There are additional cost categories that are not included here, largely because measures that are included absorb much of their impact. Nonetheless, several are worth noting. Thaler, Hellman and Naroff, and Rizzo estimate the erosion of property values per crime. An average of their figures, $2,024, can be multiplied by the total number of crimes reported in 1994, 13,992, to estimate an aggregate housing devaluation of $28 billion. Although this figure should reflect the inability to behave as desired in the presence of crime, it also includes psychic and monetary costs imposed by criminal behavior that are already included in this [article].

Julie Berry Cullen and Stephen D. Levitt discuss urban flight resulting from crime. They report a nearly one-to-one relationship between serious crimes and individuals parting from major cities. The cost component of this is difficult to assess because higher commuting costs must be measured against lower property costs in rural areas, and the conveniences of city living must be compared with the amenities of suburbia. Several other categories of crime costs receive incomplete representation due to insufficient data, and therefore make the estimates here conservative. These include the costs of unreported

Table 4

Transfers	$ (millions)
Occupational Fraud	203,952
Unpaid Taxes	123,108
Health Insurance Fraud	108,610
Financial Institution Fraud	52,901
Mail Fraud	35,986
Property/Casualty Insurance Fraud	20,527
Telemarketing Fraud	16,609
Business Burglary	13,229
Motor Vehicle Theft	8,913
Shoplifting	7,185
Household Burglary	4,527
Personal Theft	3,909
Household Larceny	1,996
Coupon Fraud	912
Robbery	775
Total	**603,140**

crimes (although the National Crime Victimization Survey provides information beyond that reported to the police), lost taxes due to the underground economy, and restrictions of behavior due to crime.

When criminals' costs are estimated implicitly as the value of the assets they receive through crime, the gross cost of crime (including transfers) is estimated to exceed $2,269 billion each year, and the net cost is an estimated $1,666 billion. When criminals' costs are assumed to equal the value of time spent planning and committing crimes and in prison, the estimated annual gross and net costs of crime are $1,705 and $1,102 billion respectively. Table 5 presents the aggregate costs of crime based on the more conservative, time-based estimation method. The disaggregation of this and the previous tables facilitates the creation of customized estimates based on the reader's preferred assumptions. Each of the general studies summarized in Table 1 included transfers, so the appropriate comparison is to the gross cost estimate in the

Table 5

The Aggregate Burden of Crime	$ (billions)
Crime-Induced Production	397
Opportunity Costs	130
Risks to Life and Health	574
Transfers	603
Gross Burden	**$1,705**
Net of Transfers	**$1,102**
Per Capita (in dollars)	**$4,118**

current study. As the result of a more comprehensive treatment of repercussions, the cost of crime is now seen to be more than twice as large as previously recognized.

Conclusion

Previous studies of the burden of crime have counted crimes or concentrated on direct crime costs. This paper calculates the aggregate burden of crime rather than absolute numbers, includes indirect costs, and recognizes that transfers resulting from theft should not be included in the net burden of crime to society. The accuracy of society's perspective on crime costs will improve with the understanding that these costs extend beyond victims' losses and the cost of law enforcement to include the opportunity costs of criminals' and prisoners' time, our inability to behave as desired, and the private costs of crime deterrence.

As criminals acquire an estimated $603 billion dollars worth of assets from their victims, they generate an additional $1,102 billion worth of lost productivity, crime-related expenses, and diminished quality of life. The net losses represent an annual per capita burden of $4,118. Including transfers, the aggregate burden of crime is $1,705 billion. In the United States, this is of the same order of magnitude as life insurance purchases ($1,680 billion), the outstanding mortgage debt to commercial banks and savings institutions ($1,853 billion), and annual expenditures on health ($1,038 billion).

As the enormity of this negative-sum game comes to light, so, too, will the need for countervailing efforts to redefine legal policy and forge new ethical standards. Periodic estimates of the full cost of crime could speak to the success of national strategies to encourage decorum, including increased expenditures on law enforcement, new community strategic approaches, technological innovations, legal reform, education, and the development of ethics curricula. Economic theory dictates that resources should be devoted to moral enhancement until the benefits from marginal efforts are surpassed by their costs. Programs that decrease the burden of crime by more than the cost of implementation should be continued, while those associated with negligible or positive net increments in the cost of crime should be altered to better serve societal goals.

 **NO**

A Crime by Any Other Name . . .

If one individual inflicts a bodily injury upon another which leads to the death of the person attacked we call it manslaughter; on the other hand, if the attacker knows beforehand that the blow will be fatal we call it murder. Murder has also been committed if society places hundreds of workers in such a position that they inevitably come to premature and unnatural ends. Their death is as violent as if they had been stabbed or shot. . . . Murder has been committed if society knows perfectly well that thousands of workers cannot avoid being sacrificed so long as these conditions are allowed to continue. Murder of this sort is just as culpable as the murder committed by an individual.

—Frederick Engels
The Condition of the Working Class in England

What's in a Name?

If it takes you an hour to read this chapter, by the time you reach the last page, three of your fellow citizens will have been murdered. *During that same time, at least four Americans will die as a result of unhealthy or unsafe conditions in the workplace!* Although these work-related deaths could have been prevented, they are not called murders. Why not? Doesn't a crime by any other name still cause misery and suffering? What's in a name?

The fact is that the label "crime" is not used in America to name all or the worst of the actions that cause misery and suffering to Americans. It is primarily reserved for the dangerous actions of the poor.

In the February 21, 1993, edition of the *New York Times,* an article appears with the headline: "Company in Mine Deaths Set to Pay Big Fine." It describes an agreement by the owners of a Kentucky mine to pay a fine for safety misconduct that may have led to "the worst American mining accident in nearly a decade." Ten workers died in a methane explosion, and the company pleaded guilty to "a pattern of safety misconduct" that included falsifying reports of methane levels and requiring miners to work under unsupported roofs. The company was fined $3.75 million. The acting foreman at the mine was the only individual charged by the federal government, and for his cooperation with the investigation, prosecutors were recommending that he receive the minimum sentence: probation to six months in prison. The company's president expressed regret for the tragedy that occurred. And the U.S. attorney said

Adapted from Jeffrey Reiman, *The Rich Get Richer and the Poor Get Prison: Ideology, Class, and Criminal Justice,* 5th ed. (Allyn & Bacon, 1998). Copyright © 1998 by Jeffrey Reiman. Reprinted by permission of Allyn & Bacon. Notes omitted.

he hoped the case "sent a clear message that violations of Federal safety and health regulations that endanger the lives of our citizens will not be tolerated."

Compare this with the story of Colin Ferguson, who prompted an editorial in the *New York Times* of December 10, 1993, with the headline: "Mass Murder on the 5:33." A few days earlier, Colin had boarded a commuter train in Garden City, Long Island, and methodically shot passengers with a 9-millimeter pistol, killing 5 and wounding 18. Colin Ferguson was surely a murderer, maybe a mass murderer. My question is, Why wasn't the death of the miners also murder? Why weren't those responsible for subjecting ten miners to deadly conditions also "mass murderers"?

Why do ten dead miners amount to an "accident," a "tragedy," and five dead commuters a "mass murder"? "Murder" suggests a murderer, whereas "accident" and "tragedy" suggest the work of impersonal forces. But the charge against the company that owned the mine said that they "repeatedly exposed the mine's work crews to danger and that such conditions were frequently concealed from Federal inspectors responsible for enforcing the mine safety act." And the acting foreman admitted to falsifying records of methane levels only two months before the fatal blast. Someone was responsible for the conditions that led to the death of ten miners. Is that person not a murderer, perhaps even a *mass murderer?*

These questions are at this point rhetorical. My aim is not to discuss this case but rather to point to the blinders we wear when we look at such an "accident." There was an investigation. One person, the acting foreman, was held responsible for falsifying records. He is to be sentenced to six months in prison (at most). The company was fined. But no one will be tried for *murder.* No one will be thought of as a murderer. *Why not?* . . .

Didn't those miners have a right to protection from the violence that took their lives? *And if not, why not?*

Once we are ready to ask this question seriously, we are in a position to see that the reality of crime—that is, the acts we label crime, the acts we think of as crime, the actors and actions we treat as criminal—is *created*: It is an image shaped by decisions as to *what* will be called crime and *who* will be treated as a criminal.

The Carnival Mirror

. . . The American criminal justice system is a mirror that shows a distorted image of the dangers that threaten us—an image created more by the shape of the mirror than by the reality reflected. What do we see when we look in the criminal justice mirror? . . .

He is, first of all, a *he.* Out of 2,012,906 persons arrested for FBI Index crimes [which are criminal homicide, forcible rape, robbery, aggravated assault, burglary, larceny, and motor vehicle theft] in 1991, 1,572,591, or 78 percent, were males. Second, he is a *youth.* . . . Third, he is predominantly *urban.* . . . Fourth, he is disproportionately *black*—blacks are arrested for Index crimes at a rate three times that of their percentage in the national population. . . . Finally, he is *poor:* Among state prisoners in 1991, 33 percent were unemployed prior to being arrested—a rate nearly four times that of males in the general population. . . .

This is the Typical Criminal feared by most law-abiding Americans. Poor, young, urban, (disproportionately) black males make up the core of the enemy forces in the war against crime. They are the heart of a vicious, unorganized guerrilla army, threatening the lives, limbs, and possessions of the law-abiding members of society—necessitating recourse to the ultimate weapons of force and detention in our common defense.

. . . The acts of the Typical Criminal are not the only acts that endanger us, nor are they the acts that endanger us the most. As I shall show . . . , we have as great or sometimes even a greater chance of being killed or disabled by an occupational injury or disease, by unnecessary surgery, or by shoddy emergency medical services than by aggravated assault or even homicide! Yet even though these threats to our well-being are graver than those posed by our poor young criminals, they do not show up in the FBI's Index of serious crimes. The individuals responsible for them do not turn up in arrest records or prison statistics. *They never become part of the reality reflected in the criminal justice mirror, although the danger they pose is at least as great and often greater than the danger posed by those who do!*

Similarly, the general public loses more money *by far* . . . from price-fixing and monopolistic practices and from consumer deception and embezzlement than from all the property crimes in the FBI's Index combined. Yet these far more costly acts are either not criminal, or if technically criminal, not prosecuted, or if prosecuted, not punished, or if punished, only mildly. . . . *Their faces rarely appear in the criminal justice mirror, although the danger they pose is at least as great and often greater than that of those who do. . . .*

The criminal justice system is like a mirror in which society can see the face of the evil in its midst. Because the system deals with some evil and not with others, because it treats some evils as the gravest and treats some of the gravest evils as minor, the image it throws back is distorted like the image in a carnival mirror. Thus, the image cast back is false not because it is invented out of thin air but because the proportions of the real are distorted. . . .

If criminal justice really gives us a carnival-mirror of "crime," we are doubly deceived. First, we are led to believe that the criminal justice system is protecting us against the gravest threats to our well-being when, in fact, the system is protecting us against only some threats and not necessarily the gravest ones. We are deceived about how much protection we are receiving and thus left vulnerable. The second deception is just the other side of this one. If people believe that the carnival mirror is a true mirror—that is, if they believe the criminal justice system simply *reacts* to the gravest threats to their well-being—they come to believe that whatever is the target of the criminal justice system must be the greatest threat to their well-being. . . .

A Crime by Any Other Name . . .

Think of a crime, any crime. Picture the first "crime" that comes into your mind. What do you see? The odds are you are not imagining a mining company executive sitting at his desk, calculating the costs of proper safety precautions and deciding not to invest in them. Probably what you do see with your mind's eye is one person physically attacking another or robbing something from another via the threat of physical attack. Look more closely. What does the attacker look like? It's a safe bet he (and it is a *he*, of course) is not wearing a suit and tie. In fact, my hunch is that you—like me, like almost anyone else in America—picture a young, tough lower-class male when the thought of crime first pops into your head. You (we) picture someone like the Typical Criminal described above. The crime itself is one in which the Typical Criminal sets out to attack or rob some specific person. . . .

It is important to identify this model of the Typical Crime because it functions like a set of blinders. It keeps us from calling a mine disaster a mass murder even if ten men are killed, even if someone is responsible for the unsafe conditions in which they worked and died. I contend that this particular piece of mental furniture so blocks our view that it keeps us from using the criminal justice system to protect ourselves from the greatest threats to our persons and possessions.

What keeps a mine disaster from being a mass murder in our eyes is that it is not a one-on-one harm. What is important in one-on-one harm is not the numbers but the *desire of someone (or ones) to harm someone (or ones) else.* An attack by a gang on one or more persons or an attack by one individual on several fits the model of one-on-one harm; that is, for each person harmed there is at least one individual who wanted to harm that person. Once he selects his victim, the rapist, the mugger, the murderer all want this person they have selected to suffer. A mine executive, on the other hand, does not want his employees to be harmed. He would truly prefer that there be no accident, no injured or dead miners. What he does want is something legitimate. It is what he has been hired to get: maximum profits at minimum costs. If he cuts corners to save a buck, he is just doing his job. If ten men die because he cut corners on safety, we may think him crude or callous but not a murderer. He is, at most, responsible for an *indirect harm,* not a one-on-one harm. For this, he may even be criminally indictable for violating safety regulations—but not for murder. The ten men are dead as an unwanted consequence of his (perhaps overzealous or undercautious) pursuit of a legitimate goal. So, unlike the Typical Criminal, he has not committed the Typical Crime—or so we generally believe. As a result, ten men are dead who might be alive now if cutting corners of the kind that leads to loss of life, whether suffering is specifically aimed at or not, were treated as murder.

This is my point. Because we accept the belief . . . that the model for crime is one person specifically trying to harm another, we accept a legal system that leaves us unprotected against much greater dangers to our lives and well-being than those threatened by the Typical Criminal. . . .

According to the FBI's *Uniform Crime Reports,* in 1991, there were 24,703 murders and nonnegligent manslaughters, and 1,092,739 aggravated assaults. In 1992, there were 23,760 murders and nonnegligent manslaughters, and 1,126,970 aggravated assaults. . . . Thus, as a measure of the physical harm done by crime in the beginning of the 1990s, we can say that reported crimes lead to roughly 24,000 deaths and 1,000,000 instances of serious bodily injury short of death a year. As a measure of monetary loss due to property crime, we can use $15.1 billion—the total estimated dollar losses due to property crime in 1992 according to the UCR. Whatever the shortcomings of these reported crime statistics, they are the statistics upon which public policy has traditionally been based. Thus, I will consider any actions that lead to loss of life, physical harm, and property loss comparable to the figures in the UCR as actions that pose grave dangers to the community comparable to the threats posed by crimes. . . .

In testimony before the Senate Committee on Labor and Human Resources, Dr. Philip Landrigan, director of the Division of Environmental and Occupational Medicine at the Mount Sinai School of Medicine in New York City, stated that

> . . . [I]t may be calculated that occupational disease is responsible each year in the United States for 50,000 to 70,000 deaths, and for approximately 350,000 new cases of illness.

. . . The BLS estimate of 330,000 job-related illnesses for 1990 roughly matches Dr. Landrigan's estimates. For 1991, BLS estimates 368,000 job-related illnesses. These illnesses are of varying severity. . . . Because I want to compare these occupational harms with those resulting from aggravated assault, I shall stay on the conservative side here too, as with deaths from occupational diseases, and say that there are annually in the United States approximately 150,000 job-related serious illnesses. Taken together with 25,000 deaths from occupational diseases, how does this compare with the threat posed by crime?

Before jumping to any conclusions, note that the risk of occupational disease and death falls only on members of the labor force, whereas the risk of crime falls on the whole population, from infants to the elderly. Because the labor force is about half the total population (124,810,000 in 1990, out of a total population of 249,900,000), to get a true picture of the *relative* threat posed by occupational diseases compared with that posed by crimes, we should *halve* the crime statistics when comparing them with the figures for industrial disease and death. Using the crime figures for the first years of the 1990s, . . . we note that the *comparable* figures would be

	Occupational Disease	Crime (halved)
Death	25,000	12,000
Other physical harm	150,000	500,000

. . . Note . . . that the estimates in the last chart are *only* for occupational *diseases* and deaths from those diseases. They do not include death and disability from work-related injuries. Here, too, the statistics are gruesome. The National Safety Council reported that in 1991, work-related accidents caused 9,600 deaths and 1.7 million disabling work injuries, a total cost to the economy of $63.3 billion. This brings the number of occupation-related deaths to 34,600 a year and other physical harms to 1,850,000. If, on the basis of these additional figures, we recalculated our chart comparing occupational harms from both disease and accident with criminal harms, it would look like this:

	Occupational Hazard	Crime (halved)
Death	34,600	12,000
Other physical harm	1,850,000	500,000

Can there be any doubt that workers are more likely to stay alive and healthy in the face of the danger from the underworld than in the work-world? . . .

To say that some of these workers died from accidents due to their own carelessness is about as helpful as saying that some of those who died at the hands of murderers asked for it. It overlooks the fact that where workers are careless, it is not because they love to live dangerously. They have production quotas to meet, quotas that they themselves do not set. If quotas were set with an eye to keeping work at a safe pace rather than to keeping the production-to-wages ratio as high as possible, it might be more reasonable to expect workers to take the time to be careful. Beyond this, we should bear in mind that the vast majority of occupational deaths result from disease, not accident, and disease is generally a function of conditions outside a worker's control. Examples of such conditions are the level of coal dust in the air ("260,000 miners receive benefits for [black lung] disease, and perhaps as many as 4,000 retired miners die from the illness or its complications each year"; about 10,000 currently working miners "have X-ray evidence of the beginnings of the crippling and often fatal disease") or textile dust . . . or asbestos fibers . . . or coal tars . . . ; (coke oven workers develop cancer of the scrotum at a rate five times that of the general population). Also, some 800,000 people suffer from occupationally related skin disease each year. . . .

To blame the workers for occupational disease and deaths is to ignore the history of governmental attempts to compel industrial firms to meet safety standards that would keep dangers (such as chemicals or fibers or dust particles in the air) that are outside the worker's control down to a safe level. This has been a continual struggle, with firms using everything from their own "independent" research institutes to more direct and often questionable forms of political pressure to influence government in the direction of loose standards and lax enforcement. So far, industry has been winning because OSHA [Occupational Safety and Health Administration] has been given neither the personnel nor the mandate to fulfill its purpose. It is so understaffed that, in 1973, when 1,500 federal sky marshals guarded the nation's airplanes from hijackers, only 500 OSHA inspectors toured the nation's workplaces. By 1980, OSHA employed 1,581 compliance safety and health officers, but this still enabled inspection of only roughly 2 percent of the 2.5 million establishments covered by OSHA. The *New York Times* reports that in 1987 the number of OSHA inspectors was down to 1,044. As might be expected, the agency performs fewer inspections that it did a dozen years ago. . . .

According to a report issued by the AFL-CIO [American Federation of Labor and Congress of Industrial Organizations] in 1992, "The median penalty paid by an employer during the years 1972–1990 following an incident resulting in death or serious injury of a worker was just $480." The same report claims that the federal government spends $1.1 billion a year to protect fish and wildlife and only $300 million a year to protect workers from health and safety hazards on the job. . . .

Is a person who kills another in a bar brawl a greater threat to society than a business executive who refuses to cut into his profits to make his plant a safe place to work? By any measure of death and suffering the latter is by far a greater danger than the former. Because he wishes his workers no harm, because he is only indirectly responsible for death and disability while pursuing legitimate economic goals, his acts are not called "crimes." Once we free our imagination from the blinders of the one-on-one model of crime, can there be any doubt that the criminal justice system does *not* protect us from the gravest threats to life and limb? It seeks to protect us when danger comes from a young, lowerclass male in the inner city. When a threat comes from an upper-class business executive in an office, the criminal justice system looks the other way. This is in the face of growing evidence that for every three American citizens murdered by thugs, at least four American workers are killed by the recklessness of their bosses and the indifference of their government.

Health Care May Be Dangerous to Your Health

. . . On July 15, 1975, Dr. Sidney Wolfe of Ralph Nader's Public Interest Health Research Group testified before the House Commerce Oversight and Investigations Subcommittee that there "were 3.2 million cases of unnecessary surgery performed each year in the United States." These unneeded operations, Wolfe added, "cost close to $5 billion a year and kill as many as 16,000 Americans." . . .

In an article on an experimental program by Blue Cross and Blue Shield aimed at curbing unnecessary surgery, *Newsweek* reports that

> a Congressional committee earlier this year [1976] estimated that more than 2 million of the elective operations performed in 1974 were not only unnecessary—but also killed about 12,000 patients and cost nearly $4 billion.

Because the number of surgical operations performed in the United States rose from 16.7 million in 1975 to 22.4 million in 1991, there is reason to believe that at least somewhere between . . . 12,000 and . . . 16,000 people a year still die from unnecessary surgery. In 1991, the FBI reported that 3,405 murders were committed by a "cutting or stabbing instrument." Obviously, the FBI does not include the scalpel as a cutting or stabbing instrument. If they did, they would have had to report that between 15,405 and 19,405 persons were killed by "cutting or stabbing" in 1991. . . . No matter how you slice it, the scalpel may be more dangerous than the switchblade. . . .

Waging Chemical Warfare Against America

One in 4 Americans can expect to contract cancer during their lifetimes. The American Cancer Society estimated that 420,000 Americans would die of cancer in 1981. The National Cancer Institute's estimate for 1993 is 526,000 deaths from cancer. "A 1978 report issued by the President's Council on Environmental Quality (CEQ) unequivocally states that 'most researchers agree that 70 to 90 percent of cancers are caused by environmental influences and are hence theoretically preventable.'" This means that a concerted national effort could result in saving 350,000 or more lives a year and reducing each individual's chances of getting cancer in his or her lifetime from 1 in 4 to 1 in 12 or fewer. If you think this would require a massive effort in terms of money and personnel, you are right. How much of an effort, though, would the nation make to stop a foreign invader who was killing a thousand people and bent on capturing one-quarter of the present population?

In face of this "invasion" that is already under way, the U.S. government has allocated $1.9 billion to the National Cancer Institute (NCI) for fiscal year 1992, and NCI has allocated $219 million to the study of the physical and chemical (i.e., environmental) causes of cancer. Compare this with the (at least) $45 billion spent to fight the Persian Gulf War. The simple truth is that the government that strove so mightily to protect the borders of a small, undemocratic nation 7,000 miles away is doing next to nothing to protect us against the chemical war in our midst. This war is being waged against us on three fronts:

- Pollution
- Cigarette smoking
- Food additives

. . . The evidence linking *air pollution* and cancer, as well as other serious and often fatal diseases, has been rapidly accumulating in recent years. In 1993, the *Journal of the American Medical Association* reported on research that found "'robust' associations between premature mortality and air pollution levels." They estimate that pollutants cause about 2 percent of all cancer deaths (at least 10,000 a year). . . .

A . . . recent study . . . concluded that air pollution at 1988 levels was responsible for 60,000 deaths a year. The Natural Resources Defense Council sued the EPA [Environmental Protection Agency] for its foot-dragging in implementation of the Clean Air Act, charging that "One hundred million people live in areas of unhealthy air."

This chemical war is not limited to the air. The National Cancer Institute has identified as carcinogens or suspected carcinogens 23 of the chemicals commonly found in our drinking water. Moreover, according to one observer, we are now facing a "new plague—toxic exposure." . . .

The evidence linking *cigarette smoking* and cancer is overwhelming and need not be repeated here. The Centers for Disease Control estimates that cigarettes cause 87 percent of lung cancers—approximately 146,000 in 1992. Tobacco continues to kill an estimated 400,000 Americans a year. Cigarettes are widely estimated to cause 30 percent of all cancer deaths. . . .

This is enough to expose the hypocrisy of running a full-scale war against heroin (which produces no degenerative disease) while allowing cigarette sales and advertising to flourish. It also should be enough to underscore the point that once again there are threats to our lives much greater than criminal homicide. The legal order does not protect us against them. Indeed, not only does our government fail to protect us against this threat, it promotes it! . . .

Based on the knowledge we have, there can be no doubt that air pollution, tobacco, and food additives amount to a chemical war that makes the crime wave look like a football scrimmage. Even with the most conservative estimates, it is clear that *the death toll in this war is far higher than the number of people killed by criminal homicide!* . . .

Summary

Once again, our investigations lead to the same result. The criminal justice system does not protect us against the gravest threats to life, limb, or possessions. Its definitions of crime are not simply a reflection of the objective dangers that threaten us. The workplace, the medical profession, the air we breathe, and the poverty we refuse to rectify lead to far more human suffering, far more death and disability, and take far more dollars from our pockets than the murders, aggravated assaults, and thefts reported annually by the FBI. What is more, this human suffering is preventable. A government really intent on protecting our well-being could enforce work safety regulations, police the medical profession, require that clean air standards be met, and funnel sufficient money to the poor to alleviate the major disabilities of poverty—but it does not. Instead we hear a lot of cant about law and order and a lot of rant about crime in the streets. It is as if our leaders were not only refusing to protect us from the major threats to our well-being but trying to cover up this refusal by diverting our attention to crime—as if this were the only real threat.

POSTSCRIPT

Is Street Crime More Harmful Than White-Collar Crime?

$\mathbf{I}$t is important to consider both the suffering and the wider ramifications caused by crimes. Anderson captures many of these dimensions and gives a full account of the harms of street crime. Today the public is very concerned about street crime, especially wanton violence. However, it seems relatively unconcerned about white-collar crime. Reiman tries to change that perception. By defining many harmful actions by managers and professionals as crimes, he argues that white-collar crime is worse than street crime. He says that more people are killed and injured by "occupational injury or disease, by unnecessary surgery, and by shoddy emergency medical services than by aggravated assault or even homicide!" But are shoddy medical services a crime? In the end, the questions remain: What is a crime? Who are the criminals?

A set of readings that support Reiman's viewpoint is *Corporate Violence: Injury and Death for Profit* edited by Stuart L. Hills (Rowman & Littlefield, 1987); *Unmasking the Crimes of the Powerful: Scrutinizing States and Corporations,* edited by Steve Tombs and Dave Whyte (P. Lang, 2003); Joel Bakan, *The Corporation: The Pathological Pursuit of Profit and Power* (Free Press, 2004); Hazel Croall, *Understanding White Collar Crime* (Open University Press, 2001); *Readings in White-Collar Crime,* edited by David Shichor et al. (Waveland Press, 2002); and David Weisburd, *White-Collar Crime and Criminal Career* (Cambridge University Press, 2001). Most works on crime deal mainly with theft, drugs, and violence and the injury and fear that they cause including Leslie Williams Reid, *Crime in the City: A Political and Economic Analysis of Urban Crime* (LFB Scholarly Pub., 2003); Walter S. DeKeseredy, *Under Seige: Poverty and Crime in a Public Housing Community* (Lexington Books, 2003); Alex Alverez and Ronet Bachman, *Murder American Style* (Wadsworth, 2003); Claire Valier, *Crime and Punishment in Contemporary Culture* (Routledge, 2004); Matthew B. Robinson, *Why Crime?: An Integrated Systems Theory of Antisocial Behavior* (Pearson, 2004); Ronald B. Flowers, *Male Crime and Deviance: Exploring Its Causes, Dynamics, and Nature* (C.C. Thomas, 2003); and Meda Chesney-Lind and Lisa Pasko, *The Female Offender: Girls, Women, and Crime,* 2nd edition (Sage, 2004). Two works on gangs, which are often connected with violent street crime, are Martin Sanchez Jankowski, *Islands in the Street: Gangs and American Urban Society* (University of California Press, 1991) and Felix M. Padilla, *The Gang as an American Enterprise* (Rutgers University Press, 1992). William J. Bennett, John J. DiIulio, and John P. Walters, in *Body Count: Moral Poverty—and How to Win America's War Against Crime and Drugs* (Simon & Schuster, 1996), argue that moral poverty is the root cause of crime (meaning street crime). How applicable is this thesis to white-collar crime? One interesting aspect of many corporate, or white-collar, crimes is that they involve crimes of obedience, as discussed in Herman C. Kelman and V. Lee Hamilton, *Crimes of Obedience: Toward a Social Psychology of Authority and Responsibility* (Yale University Press, 1989).

ISSUE 17

Should Drug Use Be Decriminalized?

YES: Ethan A. Nadelmann, from "Commonsense Drug Policy," *Foreign Affairs* (January/February 1998)

NO: Eric A. Voth, from "America's Longest 'War,'" *The World & I* (February 2000)

ISSUE SUMMARY

YES: Ethan A. Nadelmann, director of the Lindesmith Center, a drug policy research institute, argues that history shows that drug prohibition is costly and futile. Examining the drug policies in other countries, he finds that decriminalization plus sane and humane drug policies and treatment programs can greatly reduce the harms from drugs.

NO: Eric A. Voth, chairman of the International Drug Strategy Institute, contends that drugs are very harmful and that our drug policies have succeeded in substantially reducing drug use.

A century ago, drugs of every kind were freely available to Americans. Laudanum, a mixture of opium and alcohol, was popularly used as a pain-killer. One drug company even claimed that it was a very useful substance for calming hyperactive children, and the company called it Mother's Helper. Morphine came into common use during the Civil War. Heroin, developed as a supposedly less addictive substitute for morphine, began to be marketed at the end of the nineteenth century. By that time, drug paraphernalia could be ordered through Sears and Roebuck catalogues, and Coca-Cola, which contained small quantities of cocaine, had become a popular drink.

Public concerns about addiction and dangerous patent medicines, and an active campaign for drug laws waged by Dr. Harvey Wiley, a chemist in the U.S. Department of Agriculture, led Congress to pass the first national drug regulation act in 1906. The Pure Food and Drug Act required that medicines containing certain drugs, such as opium, must say so on their labels. The Harrison Narcotic Act of 1914 went much further and cut off completely the supply of legal opiates to addicts. Since then, ever-stricter drug laws have been passed by Congress and by state legislatures.

Drug abuse in America again came to the forefront of public discourse during the 1960s, when heroin addiction started growing rapidly in inner-city neighborhoods. Also, by the end of the decade, drug experimentation had spread to the middle-class, affluent baby boomers who were then attending college. Indeed, certain types of drugs began to be celebrated by some of the leaders of the counterculture. Heroin was still taboo, but other drugs, notably marijuana and LSD (a psychedelic drug), were regarded as harmless and even spiritually transforming. At music festivals like Woodstock in 1969, marijuana and LSD were used openly and associated with love, peace, and heightened sensitivity. Much of this enthusiasm cooled over the next 20 years as baby boomers entered the workforce full-time and began their careers. But even among the careerists, certain types of drugs enjoyed high status. Cocaine, noted for its highly stimulating effects, became the drug of choice for many hard-driving young lawyers, television writers, and Wall Street bond traders.

The high price of cocaine put it out of reach for many people, but in the early 1980s, cheap substitutes began to appear on the streets and to overtake poor urban communities. Crack cocaine, a potent, highly addictive, smok-able form of cocaine, came into widespread use. By the end of the 1980s, the drug known as "ice," or as it is called on the West Coast, "L.A. glass," a smok-able form of amphetamine, had hit the streets. These stimulants tend to produce very violent, disorderly behavior. Moreover, the street gangs who sell them are frequently at war with one another and are well armed. Not only gang members but also many innocent people have become victims of contract killings, street battles, and drive-by shootings.

This new drug epidemic prompted President George Bush to declare a "war on drugs," and in 1989 he asked Congress to appropriate $10.6 billion for the fight. Although most Americans support such measures against illegal drugs, some say that in the years since Bush made his declaration, the drug situation has not showed any signs of improvement. Some believe that legalization would be the best way to fight the drug problem.

The drug decriminalization issue is especially interesting to sociologists because it raises basic questions about what should be socially sanctioned or approved, what is illegal or legal, and what is immoral or moral. An aspect of the basic value system of America is under review. The process of value change may be taking place in front of our eyes. As part of this debate, Ethan A. Nadelmann argues that the present policy does not work and that it is counterproductive. Legalization, he contends, would stop much of the disease, violence, and crime associated with illegal drugs. Although Nadelmann concedes that it may increase the use of lower-potency drugs, he believes that legalization would reduce the use of the worst drugs. Eric A. Voth maintains that legalization would be madness because he asserts that the current drug policies in effect are working.

Ethan A. Nadelmann

 **YES**

Commonsense Drug Policy

First, Reduce Harm

In 1988 Congress passed a resolution proclaiming its goal of "a drug-free America by 1995." U.S. drug policy has failed persistently over the decades because it has preferred such rhetoric to reality, and moralism to pragmatism. Politicians confess their youthful indiscretions, then call for tougher drug laws. Drug control officials make assertions with no basis in fact or science. Police officers, generals, politicians, and guardians of public morals qualify as drug czars—but not, to date, a single doctor or public health figure. Independent commissions are appointed to evaluate drug policies, only to see their recommendations ignored as politically risky. And drug policies are designed, implemented, and enforced with virtually no input from the millions of Americans they affect most: drug users. Drug abuse is a serious problem, both for individual citizens and society at large, but the "war on drugs" has made matters worse, not better.

Drug warriors often point to the 1980s as a time in which the drug war really worked. Illicit drug use by teenagers peaked around 1980, then fell more than 50 percent over the next 12 years. During the 1996 presidential campaign, Republican challenger Bob Dole made much of the recent rise in teenagers' use of illicit drugs, contrasting it with the sharp drop during the Reagan and Bush administrations. President Clinton's response was tepid, in part because he accepted the notion that teen drug use is the principal measure of drug policy's success or failure; at best, he could point out that the level was still barely half what it had been in 1980.

In 1980, however, no one had ever heard of the cheap, smokable form of cocaine called crack, or drug-related HIV infection or AIDS. By the 1990s, both had reached epidemic proportions in American cities, largely driven by prohibitionist economics and morals indifferent to the human consequences of the drug war. In 1980, the federal budget for drug control was about $1 billion, and state and local budgets were perhaps two or three times that. By 1997, the federal drug control budget had ballooned to $16 billion, two-thirds of it for law enforcement agencies, and state and local funding to at least that. On any day in 1980, approximately 50,000 people were behind bars for violating a drug law. By 1997, the number had increased eightfold, to about 400,000.

From Ethan A. Nadelmann, "Commonsense Drug Policy," *Foreign Affairs,* vol. 77, no. 1 (January/February 1998). Copyright © 1998 by The Council on Foreign Relations, Inc. Reprinted by permission of *Foreign Affairs*. Notes omitted.

These are the results of a drug policy overreliant on criminal justice "solutions," ideologically wedded to abstinence-only treatment, and insulated from cost-benefit analysis.

Imagine instead a policy that starts by acknowledging that drugs are here to stay, and that we have no choice but to learn how to live with them so that they cause the least possible harm. Imagine a policy that focuses on reducing not illicit drug use per se but the crime and misery caused by both drug abuse and prohibitionist policies. And imagine a drug policy based not on the fear, prejudice, and ignorance that drive America's current approach but rather on common sense, science, public health concerns, and human rights. Such a policy is possible in the United States, especially if Americans are willing to learn from the experiences of other countries where such policies are emerging.

Attitudes Abroad

Americans are not averse to looking abroad for solutions to the nation's drug problems. Unfortunately, they have been looking in the wrong places: Asia and Latin America, where much of the world's heroin and cocaine originates. Decades of U.S. efforts to keep drugs from being produced abroad and exported to American markets have failed. Illicit drug production is bigger business than ever before. The opium poppy, source of morphine and heroin, and *cannabis sativa*, from which marijuana and hashish are prepared, grow readily around the world; the coca plant, from whose leaves cocaine is extracted, can be cultivated far from its native environment in the Andes. Crop substitution programs designed to persuade Third World peasants to grow legal crops cannot compete with the profits that drug prohibition makes inevitable. Crop eradication campaigns occasionally reduce production in one country, but new suppliers pop up elsewhere. International law enforcement efforts can disrupt drug trafficking organizations and routes, but they rarely have much impact on U.S. drug markets. . . .

While looking to Latin America and Asia for supply-reduction solutions to America's drug problems is futile, the harm-reduction approaches spreading throughout Europe and Australia and even into corners of North America show promise. These approaches start by acknowledging that supply-reduction initiatives are inherently limited, that criminal justice responses can be costly and counterproductive, and that single-minded pursuit of a "drug-free society" is dangerously quixotic. Demand-reduction efforts to prevent drug abuse among children and adults are important, but so are harm-reduction efforts to lessen the damage to those unable or unwilling to stop using drugs immediately, and to those around them.

Most proponents of harm reduction do not favor legalization. They recognize that prohibition has failed to curtail drug abuse, that it is responsible for much of the crime, corruption, disease, and death associated with drugs, and that its costs mount every year. But they also see legalization as politically unwise and as risking increased drug use. The challenge is thus making drug prohibition work better, but with a focus on reducing the negative consequences of both drug use and prohibitionist policies. . . .

Harm-reduction innovations include efforts to stem the spread of HIV by making sterile syringes readily available and collecting used syringes; allowing doctors to prescribe oral methadone for heroin addiction treatment, as well as heroin and other drugs for addicts who would otherwise buy them on the black market; establishing "safe injection rooms" so addicts do not congregate in public places or dangerous "shooting galleries"; employing drug analysis units at the large dance parties called raves to test the quality and potency of MDMA, known as Ecstasy, and other drugs that patrons buy and consume there; decriminalizing (but not legalizing) possession and retail sale of cannabis and, in some cases, possession of small amounts of "hard" drugs; and integrating harm-reduction policies and principles into community policing strategies. Some of these measures are under way or under consideration in parts of the United States, but rarely to the extent found in growing numbers of foreign countries.

Stopping HIV With Sterile Syringes

The spread of HIV, the virus that causes AIDS, among people who inject drugs illegally was what prompted governments in Europe and Australia to experiment with harm-reduction policies. During the early 1980s public health officials realized that infected users were spreading HIV by sharing needles. Having already experienced a hepatitis epidemic attributed to the same mode of transmission, the Dutch were the first to tell drug users about the risks of needle sharing and to make sterile syringes available and collect dirty needles through pharmacies, needle exchange and methadone programs, and public health services. Governments elsewhere in Europe and in Australia soon followed suit. The few countries in which a prescription was necessary to obtain a syringe dropped the requirement. Local authorities in Germany, Switzerland, and other European countries authorized needle exchange machines to ensure 24-hour access. In some European cities, addicts can exchange used syringes for clean ones at local police stations without fear of prosecution or harassment. Prisons are instituting similar policies to help discourage the spread of HIV among inmates, recognizing that illegal drug injecting cannot be eliminated even behind bars.

These initiatives were not adopted without controversy. Conservative politicians argued that needle exchange programs condoned illicit and immoral behavior and that government policies should focus on punishing drug users or making them drug-free. But by the late 1980s, the consensus in most of Western Europe, Oceania, and Canada was that while drug abuse was a serious problem, AIDS was worse. Slowing the spread of a fatal disease for which no cure exists was the greater moral imperative. There was also a fiscal imperative. Needle exchange programs' costs are minuscule compared with those of treating people who would otherwise become infected with HIV.

Only in the United States has this logic not prevailed, even though AIDS was the leading killer of Americans ages 25 to 44 for most of the 1990s and is now No. 2. The Centers for Disease Control (CDC) estimates that half of new HIV infections in the country stem from injection drug use. Yet both the White

House and Congress block allocation of AIDS or drug-abuse prevention funds for needle exchange, and virtually all state governments retain drug paraphernalia laws, pharmacy regulations, and other restrictions on access to sterile syringes. During the 1980s, AIDS activists engaging in civil disobedience set up more syringe exchange programs than state and local governments. There are now more than 100 such programs in 28 states, Washington, D.C., and Puerto Rico, but they reach only an estimated 10 percent of injection drug users.

Governments at all levels in the United States refuse to fund needle exchange for political reasons, even though dozens of scientific studies, domestic and foreign, have found that needle exchange and other distribution programs reduce needle sharing, bring hard-to-reach drug users into contact with health care systems, and inform addicts about treatment programs, yet do not increase illegal drug use. In 1991 the National AIDS Commission appointed by President Bush called the lack of federal support for such programs "bewildering and tragic." In 1993 a CDC-sponsored review of research on needle exchange recommended federal funding, but top officials in the Clinton administration suppressed a favorable evaluation of the report within the Department of Health and Human Services. In July 1996 President Clinton's Advisory Council on HIV/AIDS criticized the administration for its failure to heed the National Academy of Sciences' recommendation that it authorize the use of federal money to support needle exchange programs. An independent panel convened by the National Institute[s] of Health reached the same conclusion in February 1997. Last summer, the American Medical Association, the American Bar Association, and even the politicized U.S. Conference of Mayors endorsed the concept of needle exchange. In the fall, an endorsement followed from the World Bank.

To date, America's failure in this regard is conservatively estimated to have resulted in the infection of up to 10,000 people with HIV. Mounting scientific evidence and the stark reality of the continuing AIDS crisis have convinced the public, if not politicians, that needle exchange saves lives; polls consistently find that a majority of Americans support needle exchange, with approval highest among those most familiar with the notion. Prejudice and political cowardice are poor excuses for allowing more citizens to suffer from and die of AIDS, especially when effective interventions are cheap, safe, and easy.

Methadone and Other Alternatives

The United States pioneered the use of the synthetic opiate methadone to treat heroin addiction in the 1960s and 1970s, but now lags behind much of Europe and Australia in making methadone accessible and effective. Methadone is the best available treatment in terms of reducing illicit heroin use and associated crime, disease, and death. In the early 1990s the National Academy of Sciences' Institute of Medicine stated that of all forms of drug treatment, "methadone maintenance has been the most rigorously studied modality and has yielded the most incontrovertibly positive results. . . . Consumption of all illicit drugs, especially heroin, declines. Crime is reduced, fewer individuals become HIV positive, and individual functioning is improved." However, the institute went on to declare, "Current policy . . . puts too much emphasis on protecting society from methadone, and not enough on protecting society from the epidemics of addiction, violence, and infectious diseases that methadone can help reduce."

Methadone is to street heroin what nicotine skin patches and chewing gum are to cigarettes—with the added benefit of legality. Taken orally, methadone has little of injected heroin's effect on mood or cognition. It can be consumed for decades with few if any negative health consequences, and its purity and concentration, unlike street heroin's, are assured. Like other opiates, it can create physical dependence if taken regularly, but the "addiction" is more like a diabetic's "addiction" to insulin than a heroin addict's to product brought on the street. Methadone patients can and do drive safely, hold good jobs, and care for their children. When prescribed adequate doses, they can be indistinguishable from people who have never used heroin or methadone.

Popular misconceptions and prejudice, however, have all but prevented any expansion of methadone treatment in the United States. The 115,000 Americans receiving methadone today represent only a small increase over the number 20 years ago. For every ten heroin addicts, there are only one or two methadone treatment slots. Methadone is the most tightly controlled drug in the pharmacopoeia, subject to unique federal and state restrictions. Doctors cannot prescribe it for addiction treatment outside designated programs. Regulations dictate not only security, documentation, and staffing requirements but maximum doses, admission criteria, time spent in the program, and a host of other specifics, none of which has much to do with quality of treatment. Moreover, the regulations do not prevent poor treatment; many clinics provide insufficient doses, prematurely detoxify clients, expel clients for offensive behavior, and engage in other practices that would be regarded as unethical in any other field of medicine. Attempts to open new clinics tend to be blocked by residents who don't want addicts in their neighborhood. . . .

The Swiss government began a nationwide trial in 1994 to determine whether prescribing heroin, morphine, or injectable methadone could reduce crime, disease, and other drug-related ills. Some 1,000 volunteers—only heroin addicts with at least two unsuccessful experiences in methadone or other conventional treatment programs were considered—took part in the experiment. The trial quickly determined that virtually all participants preferred heroin, and doctors subsequently prescribed it for them. Last July the government reported the results so far: criminal offenses and the number of criminal offenders dropped 60 percent, the percentage of income from illegal and semi-legal activities fell from 69 to 10 percent, illegal heroin *and* cocaine use declined dramatically (although use of alcohol, cannabis, and tranquilizers like Valium remained fairly constant), stable employment increased from 14 to 32 percent, physical health improved enormously, and most participants greatly reduced their contact with the drug scene. There were no deaths from overdoses, and no prescribed drugs were diverted to the black market. More than half those who dropped out of the study switched to another form of drug treatment, including 83 who began abstinence therapy. A cost-benefit analysis of the program found a net economic benefit of $30 per patient per day, mostly because of reduced criminal justice and health care costs.

The Swiss study has undermined several myths about heroin and its habitual users. The results to date demonstrate that, given relatively unlimited availability, heroin users will voluntarily stabilize or reduce their dosage and some will even choose abstinence; that long-addicted users can lead relatively normal, stable lives if provided legal access to their drug of choice; and that ordinary citizens will support such initiatives. In recent referendums in Zurich, Basel, and Zug, substantial majorities voted to continue funding local arms of the experiment. And last September, a nationwide referendum to end the government's heroin maintenance and other harm-reduction initiatives was rejected by 71 percent of Swiss voters, including majorities in all 26 cantons. . . .

Reefer Sanity

Cannabis, in the form of marijuana and hashish, is by far the most popular illicit drug in the United States. More than a quarter of Americans admit to having tried it. Marijuana's popularity peaked in 1980, dropped steadily until the early 1990s, and is now on the rise again. Although it is not entirely safe, especially when consumed by children, smoked heavily, or used when driving, it is clearly among the least dangerous psychoactive drugs in common use. In 1988 the administrative law judge for the Drug Enforcement Administration, Francis Young, reviewed the evidence and concluded that "marihuana, in its natural form, is one of the safest therapeutically active substances known to man."

As with needle exchange and methadone treatment, American politicians have ignored or spurned the findings of government commissions and scientific organizations concerning marijuana policy. In 1972 the National Commission on Marihuana and Drug Abuse—created by President Nixon and chaired by a former Republican governor, Raymond Shafer—recommended that possession of up to one ounce of marijuana be decriminalized. Nixon rejected the recommendation. In 1982 a panel appointed by the National Academy of Sciences reached the same conclusions as the Shafer Commission.

Between 1973 and 1978, with attitudes changing, 11 states approved decriminalization statutes that reclassified marijuana possession as a misdemeanor, petty offense, or civil violation punishable by no more than a $100 fine. Consumption trends in those states and in states that retained stricter sanctions were indistinguishable. A 1988 scholarly evaluation of the Moscone Act, California's 1976 decriminalization law, estimated that the state had saved half a billion dollars in arrest costs since the law's passage. Nonetheless, public opinion began to shift in 1978. No other states decriminalized marijuana, and some eventually recriminalized it.

Between 1973 and 1989, annual arrests on marijuana charges by state and local police ranged between 360,000 and 460,000. The annual total fell to 283,700 in 1991, but has since more than doubled. In 1996, 641,642 people were arrested for marijuana, 85 percent of them for possession, not sale, of the drug. Prompted by concern over rising marijuana use among adolescents and fears of being labeled soft on drugs, the Clinton administration launched its own anti-marijuana campaign in 1995. But the administration's claims to have identified new risks of marijuana consumption—including a purported link between marijuana and violent behavior—have not withstood scrutiny. Neither Congress nor the White House seems likely to put the issue of marijuana policy before a truly independent advisory commission, given the consistency with which such commissions have reached politically unacceptable conclusions. . . .

Will It Work?

Both at home and abroad, the U.S. government has attempted to block resolutions supporting harm reduction, suppress scientific studies that reached politically inconvenient conclusions, and silence critics of official drug policy. In May 1994, the State Department forced the last-minute cancellation of a World Bank conference on drug trafficking to which critics of U.S. drug policy had been invited. That December the U.S. delegation to an international meeting of the U.N. Drug Control Program refused to sign any statement incorporating the phrase "harm reduction." In early 1995 the State Department successfully pressured the World Health Organization to scuttle the release of a report it had commissioned from a panel that included many of the world's leading experts on cocaine because it included the scientifically incontrovertible observations that traditional use of coca leaf in the Andes causes little harm to users and that most consumers of cocaine use the drug in moderation with few detrimental effects. Hundreds of congressional hearings have addressed multitudinous aspects of the drug problem, but few have inquired into the European harm-reduction policies described above. When former Secretary of State George Shultz, then–Surgeon General M. Joycelyn Elders, and Baltimore Mayor Kurt Schmoke pointed to the failure of current policies and called for new approaches, they were mocked, fired, and ignored, respectively—and thereafter mischaracterized as advocating the outright legalization of drugs.

In Europe, in contrast, informed, public debate about drug policy is increasingly common in government, even at the EU level. In June 1995 the European Parliament issued a report acknowledging that "there will always be a demand for drugs in our societies . . . the policies followed so far have not been able to prevent the illegal drug trade from flourishing." The EU called for serious consideration of the Frankfurt Resolution, a statement of harm-reduction principles supported by a transnational coalition of 31 cities and regions. In October 1996 Emma Bonino, the European commissioner for consumer policy, advocated decriminalizing soft drugs and initiating a broad prescription program for hard drugs. Greece's minister for European affairs, George Papandreou, seconded her. Last February the monarch of Liechtenstein, Prince Hans Adam, spoke out in favor of controlled drug legalization. Even Raymond Kendall, secretary general of Interpol, was quoted in the August 20, 1994, *Guardian* as saying, "The prosecution of thousands of otherwise law-abiding citizens every year is both hypocritical and an affront to individual, civil and human rights. . . . Drug use should no longer be a criminal offense. I am totally against legalization, but in favor of decriminalization for the user." . . .

The lessons from Europe and Australia are compelling. Drug control policies should focus on reducing drug-related crime, disease, and death, not the number of casual drug users. Stopping the spread of HIV by and among drug users by making sterile syringes and methadone readily available must be the first priority. American politicians need to explore, not ignore or automatically condemn, promising policy options such as cannabis decriminalization, heroin prescription, and the integration of harm-reduction principles into community policing strategies. Central governments must back, or at least not hinder, the efforts of municipal officials and citizens to devise pragmatic approaches to local drug problems. Like citizens in Europe, the American public has supported such innovations when they are adequately explained and allowed to prove themselves. As the evidence comes in, what works is increasingly apparent. All that remains is mustering the political courage.

America's Longest "War"

Bashing our drug policy is a popular activity. The advocates of legalization and decriminalization repeatedly contend that restrictive drug policy is failing, in the hope that this becomes a self-fulfilling prophecy. An objective look at the history of drug policy in the United States, especially in comparison to other countries, demonstrates that, indeed, our policies are working. What we also see is the clear presence of a well-organized and well-financed drug culture lobby that seeks to tear down restrictive drug policy and replace it with permissive policies that could seriously jeopardize our country's viability.

To understand our current situation, we must examine the last 25 years. The 1970s were a time of great social turmoil for the United States, and drug use was finding its way into the fabric of society. Policymakers were uncertain how to deal with drugs. As permissive advisers dominated the discussion, drug use climbed. The National Household Survey and the Monitoring the Future Survey both confirm that drug use peaked in the late 1970s. Twenty-five million Americans were current users of drugs in 1979, 37 percent of high school seniors had used marijuana in the prior 30 days, and 10.7 percent of them used marijuana daily. During the same time frame, 13 states embraced the permissive social attitude and legalized or decriminalized marijuana.

In the late 1970s, policymakers, parents, and law enforcement began to realize that our drug situation was leading to Armageddon. As never before, a coordinated war on drugs was set in motion that demanded a no-use message. This was largely driven by parents who were sick of their children falling prey to drugs. The "Just Say No" movement was the centerpiece of antidrug activities during the subsequent years. A solid national antidrug message was coupled with rigorous law enforcement. The results were striking. As perception of the harmfulness of drugs increased, their use dropped drastically. By 1992, marijuana use by high school students in the prior 30 days had dropped to 11.9 percent and daily use to 1.9 percent.

Breakdown in the 1990s

Unfortunately, several major events derailed our policy successes in the early 1990s, resulting in an approximate doubling of drug use since that time. From a national vantage point, a sense of complacency set in. Satisfied that

From Eric A. Voth, "America's Longest 'War,' " *The World & I* (February 2000). Copyright © 2000 by The Washington Times Corporation. Reprinted by permission of *The World & I*, a publication of The Washington Times Corporation.

the drug war was won, we lost national leadership. Federal funding for antidrug programs became mired in bureaucracy and difficult for small prevention organizations to obtain. A new generation of drug specialists entered the scene. Lacking experience of the ravages of the 1970s, they were willing to accept softening of policy. The Internet exploded as an open forum for the dissemination of inaccurate, deceptive, and manipulative information supporting permissive policy, even discussions of how to obtain and use drugs. The greatest audience has been young people, who are exposed to a plethora of drug-permissive information without filter or validation.

The entertainment media have provided a steady diet of alcohol and drug use for young people to witness. A recent study commissioned by the White House Office of National Drug Control Policy found that alcohol appeared in more than 93 percent of movies and illicit drugs in 22 percent, of which 51 percent depicted marijuana use. Concurrently, the news media have begun to demonstrate bias toward softening of drug policy, having the net effect of changing public opinion.

The single most dramatic influence, however, came in the transformation of the drug culture from a disorganized group of legalization advocates to a well-funded and well-organized machine. With funding from several large donors, drug-culture advocates were able to initiate large-scale attacks on the media and policymakers. The most prominent funder is the billionaire George Soros, who has spent millions toward the initiation of organizations such as the Drug Policy Foundation, Lindesmith Center, medical-marijuana-advocacy and needle-handout groups, to name a few projects.

A slick strategic shift toward compartmentalizing and dissecting restrictive drug policy has resulted in what is termed the "harm reduction" movement. After all, who would oppose the idea of reducing the harm to society caused by drug use? The philosophy of the harm reduction movement is well summarized by Ethan Nadelman of the Lindesmith Center (also funded by Soros), who is considered the godfather of the legalization movement:

> Let's start by dropping the "zero tolerance" rhetoric and policies and the illusory goal of drug-free societies. Accept that drug use is here to stay and that we have no choice but to learn to live with drugs so that they cause the least possible harm. Recognize that many, perhaps most, "drug problems" in the Americas are the results not of drug use per se but of our prohibitionist policies. . . .

The harm reduction movement has attacked the individual components of restrictive drug policy and created strategies to weaken it. Some of these strategies include giving heroin to addicts; handing out needles to addicts; encouraging use of crack cocaine instead of intravenous drugs; reducing drug-related criminal penalties; teaching "responsible" drug use to adolescents instead of working toward prevention of use; the medical marijuana movement; and the expansion of the industrial hemp movement.

Softening Drug Policies

The move toward soft drug policy has created some strange bedfellows. On one hand, supporters of liberal policy such as Gov. Gary Johnson of New Mexico have always taken the misguided view that individuals should have a right to use whatever they want in order to feel good. They often point to their own "survival" of drug use as justification for loosening laws and letting others experiment. Interestingly, the governor's public safety secretary quit as a result of being undermined by Johnson's destructive stand on legalization. Libertarian conservatives such as Milton Friedman and William Buckley have attacked drug policy as an infringement of civil liberties and have incorrectly considered drug use to be a victimless event. Societal problems such as homelessness, domestic abuse, numerous health problems, crimes under the influence, poor job performance, decreased productivity, and declining educational levels have strong connections to drug use and cost our society financially and spiritually.

The notion that decriminalizing or legalizing drugs will drive the criminal element out of the market is flawed and reflects a total lack of understanding of drug use and addiction. Drug use creates its own market, and often the only thing limiting the amount of drugs that an addict uses is the amount of money available. Further, if drugs were legalized, what would the legal scenario be? Would anyone be allowed to sell drugs? Would they be sold by the government? If so, what strengths would be available? If there were any limitations on strength or availability, a black market would immediately develop. Most rational people can easily recognize this slippery slope.

Consistently, drug-culture advocates assert that policy has failed and is extremely costly. This is a calculated strategy to demoralize the population and turn public sentiment against restrictive policy. The real question is, has restrictive policy failed? First we should consider the issues of cost. An effective way to determine cost-effectiveness is to compare the costs to society of legal versus illegal drugs. Estimates from 1990 suggest that the costs of illegal drugs were $70 billion, as compared to that of alcohol alone at $99 billion and tobacco at $72 billion. Estimates from 1992 put the costs of alcohol dependence at $148 billion and all illegal drugs (including the criminal justice system costs) at $98 billion.

Referring to the National Household Survey data from 1998, there were 13.6 million current users of illicit drugs compared to 113 million users of alcohol and 60 million tobacco smokers. There is one difference: legal status of the drugs. The Monitoring the Future Survey of high school seniors suggests that in 1995, some 52.5 percent of seniors had been drunk within the previous year as compared to 34.7 percent who had used marijuana. *Yet,* alcohol is illegal for teenagers. The only difference is, again, the legal status of the two substances.

Results of Legalization

Permissive drug policy has been tried both in the United States and abroad. In 1985, during the period in which Alaska legalized marijuana, the use of marijuana and cocaine among adolescents was more than twice as high as in other parts of the country. Baltimore has long been heralded as a centerpiece for harm reduction drug policy. Interestingly, the rate of heroin use found among arrestees in Baltimore was higher than in any other city in the United States. Thirty-seven percent of male and 48 percent of female arrestees were positive, compared with 6–23 percent for Washington, D.C., Philadelphia, and Manhattan.

Since liberalizing its marijuana-enforcement policies, the Netherlands has found that marijuana use among 11- to 18-year-olds has increased 142 percent from 1990 to 1995. Crime has risen steadily to the point that aggravated theft and breaking and entering occur three to four times more than in the United States. Along with the staggering increases in marijuana use, the Netherlands has become one of the major suppliers of the drug Ecstacy. Australia is flirting with substantial softening of drug policy. That is already taking a toll. Drug use there among 16- to 29-year-olds is 52 percent as compared with 9 percent in Sweden, a country with a restrictive drug policy. In Vancouver in 1988, HIV prevalence among IV drug addicts was only 1–2 percent. In 1997 it was 23 percent, after wide adoption of harm reduction policies. Vancouver has the largest needle exchange in North America.

Clearly, the last few years have witnessed some very positive changes in policy and our antidrug efforts. A steady national voice opposing drug use is again being heard. Efforts are being made to increase cooperation between the treatment and law enforcement communities to allow greater access to treatment. The primary prevention movement is strong and gaining greater footholds. The increases in drug use witnessed in the early 1990s have slowed.

On the other hand, the drug culture has been successful at some efforts to soften drug policy. Medical marijuana initiatives have successfully passed in several states. These were gross examples of abuse of the ballot initiative process. Large amounts of money purchased slick media campaigns and seduced the public into supporting medical marijuana under the guise of compassion. Industrial hemp initiatives are popping up all over the country in an attempt to hurt anti-marijuana law enforcement and soften public opinion. Needle handouts are being touted as successes, while the evidence is clearly demonstrating failures and increases in HIV, hepatitis B, and hepatitis C. Internationally, our Canadian neighbors are moving down a very destructive road toward drug legalization and harm reduction. The Swiss are experimenting with the lives of addicts by implementing heroin handouts and selective drug legalization. In this international atmosphere, children's attitudes about the harmfulness of drugs teeter in the balance.

Future drug policy must continue to emphasize and fund primary prevention, with the goal of no use of illegal drugs and no illegal use of legal drugs. Treatment availability must be seriously enhanced, but treatment must not be a revolving door. It must be carefully designed and outcomes based. The Rand Drug Policy Research Center concluded that the costs of cocaine use could be reduced by $33.9 billion through the layering of treatment for heavy users on top of our current enforcement efforts.

Drug screening is an extremely effective means for identifying drug use. It should be widely extended into business and industry, other social arenas, and schools. Screening must be coupled with a rehabilitative approach, however, and not simply punishment. The self-serving strategies of the drug culture must be exposed. The public needs to become aware of how drug-culture advocates are manipulating public opinion in the same fashion that the tobacco industry has for so many years.

A compassionate but restrictive drug policy that partners prevention, rehabilitation, and law enforcement will continue to show the greatest chance for success. Drug policy must focus on harm prevention through clear primary prevention messages, and it must focus upon harm elimination through treatment availability and rigorous law enforcement.

POSTSCRIPT

Should Drug Use Be Decriminalized?

The analogy often cited by proponents of drug legalization is the ill-fated attempt to ban the sale of liquor in the United States, which lasted from 1919 to 1933. Prohibition has been called "an experiment noble in purpose," but it was an experiment that greatly contributed to the rise of organized crime. The repeal of Prohibition brought about an increase in liquor consumption and alcoholism, but it also deprived organized crime of an important source of income. Would drug decriminalization similarly strike a blow at the drug dealers? Possibly, and such a prospect is obviously appealing. But would drug decriminalization also exacerbate some of the ills associated with drugs? Would there be more violence, more severe addiction, and more crack babies born to addicted mothers?

There are a variety of publications and theories pertaining to drug use and society. For a comprehensive overview of the history, effects, and prevention of drug use, see Mike Gray, *Drug Crazy: How We Got Into This Mess and How We Can Get Out* (Random House, 1998). Terry Williams describes the goings-on in a crackhouse in *Crackhouse: Notes From the End of the Zone* (Addison-Wesley, 1992). Works that examine the connection of drugs with predatory crime include Charles Bowden, *Down by the River: Drugs, Money, Murder, and Family* (Simon & Schuster, 2002); Philip Bean, *Drugs and Crime* (Willan, 2002); and Pierre Kipp, *Political Economy of Illegal Drugs* (Routledge, 2004). Three works that advocate or debate legalizing drugs are Douglas N. Husak, *Legalize This!: The Case for Decriminalizing Drugs* (Verso, 2002) Jacob Sullum, *Saying Yes: In Defense of Drug Use* (J.P. Tarcher, 2003), and *The Drug Legalization Debate,* edited by James A. Inciardi (Sage, 1999). For a relatively balanced yet innovative set of drug policies, see Elliott Carrie, *Reckoning: Drugs, the Cities, and the American Future* (Hill & Wang, 1993). William O. Walker III, ed., *Drug Control Policy* (Pennsylvania State University Press, 1992) critically evaluates drug policies from historical and comparative perspectives. On the legalization debate, see Eric Goode, *Between Politics and Reason: The Drug Legalization Debate* (St. Martin's Press, 1997). For criticism of the current drug policies, see Dan Baum, *Smoke and Mirrors: The War on Drugs and the Politics of Failure* (Little, Brown, 1996) and Leif Rosenberger, *America's Drug War Debacle* (Avebury, 1996).

ISSUE 18

Does the Threat of Terrorism Warrant Curtailment of Civil Liberties?

YES: Robert H. Bork, from "Liberty and Terrorism: Avoiding a Police State," *Current* (December 2003)

NO: Barbara Dority, "Your Every Move," *The Humanist* (January/February 2004)

ISSUE SUMMARY

YES: Robert H. Bork, senior fellow at the American Enterprise Institute, recognizes that the values of security and civil rights must be balanced while we war against terrorism, but he is concerned that some commentators would hamstring security forces in order to protect nonessential civil rights. For example, to not use ethnic profiling of Muslim or Arab persons would reduce the effectiveness of security forces, while holding suspected terrorists without filing charges or allowing them council would increase their effectiveness.

NO: Barbara Dority, president of Humanists of Washington, describes some specific provisions of the Patriot Act to show how dangerous they could be to the rights of all dissidents. She argues that provisions of the act could easily be abused.

America was very optimistic at the end of the twentieth century. The cold war had ended, and the 1990s brought the longest economic boom in American history. The only danger on the horizon was the Y2K problem, and that vanished like the mist. September 11, 2001, changed everything. Now Americans live in fear of terrorism, and this fear led the government to launch two wars—the first against the Taliban and Al Qaeda in Afghanistan and the second against Saddam Hussein's regime in Iraq. The United States has also aggressively pursued international terrorists throughout the world and pushed many countries to aid in the capture of known terrorists. All of these efforts have been quite successful in specific strategic objectives but not in reducing our fear of terrorism. The number of terrorists dedicated to mass terrorist events in America have even increased in the past three years, because hatred of America has increased greatly.

The German sociologist and political leader Ralph Dahrendorf, who was a child when Hitler came to power in his country, said that fear is antithetical to democracy. In fearful times the public wants the government to do whatever it must to solve the crisis, whether the crisis is economic failure; social disorder; or danger from criminals, terrorists, or foreign powers. Some civil rights are often the first things sacrificed. During the economic crisis of the 1930s Germany turned to Hitler, and Italy turned to Mussolini. Democracy was sacrificed for the hope of a more prosperous economy.

Fortunately, during the Great Depression the United States turned to President Franklin D. Roosevelt, not to a dictator. But in other dangerous times our history has proven to be less democratic. In the 1860s President Abraham Lincoln suspended habeas corpus and detained hundreds of suspected confederate sympathizers. The chief justice of the Supreme Court ruled Lincoln's suspension of habeas corpus as unconstitutional, but Lincoln ignored the ruling. There were widespread violations of civil liberties during World War I and again during World War II, including the shameful internment of Japanese-American citizens in concentration camps. Civil liberties were diminished again during the McCarthy era in the 1950s, a time when a witch-hunt atmosphere occurred due to anticommunist hysteria. American history caused civil rights advocates to become quite concerned when Attorney General John Ashcroft said after September 11th, "We should strengthen our laws to increase the ability of the Department of Justice and its component agencies to identify, prevent, and punish terrorism." Of course he is right, but the question is whether the government will go too far in policing us and whether the newly authorized powers will be badly abused. Senator Joseph Biden, Jr. remarked that "if we alter our basic freedom, our civil liberties, change the way we function as a democratic society, then we will have lost the war before it has begun in earnest." As of this writing the Patriot Act has been passed in an attempt to give the government the power it needs to better protect citizens from terrorism. Does this act go too far? Will its results be shameful?

One of the great aspects of America is our freedom to debate issues such as this one. This gives us the hope that through passionate and/or reasoned dialogue we will work toward the right balance between the values of security and civil rights. The articles that have been selected to debate this issue are both passionate and well-reasoned. Robert H. Bork discusses many of the provisions of the Patriot Act and explains how useful they are in the war against terrorism. He also argues that the Act contains safeguards such as judicial approval that should adequately protect against abuse. Barbara Dority also discusses specific provisions of the Patriot Act but for the purpose of pointing out how excessive and open to abuse they are. In her view, this act is a "brazen attack" on our civil liberties.

Liberty and Terrorism: Avoiding a Police State

When a nation faces deadly attacks on its citizens at home and abroad, it is only reasonable to expect that its leaders will take appropriate measures to increase security. And, since security inevitably means restrictions, it is likewise only reasonable to expect a public debate over the question of how much individual liberty should be sacrificed for how much individual and national safety.

That, however, is not the way our national debate has shaped up. From the public outcry over the Bush administration's measures to combat terrorism, one might suppose that America is well on the way to becoming a police state. A full-page newspaper ad by the American Civil Liberties Union (ACLU), for instance, informs us that the Patriot Act, the administration's major security initiative, goes "far beyond fighting terrorism" and has "allowed government agents to violate our civil liberties—tapping deep into the private lives of innocent Americans." According to Laura W. Murphy, director of the ACLU's Washington office, Attorney General John Ashcroft has "clearly abused his power," "systematically erod[ing] free-speech rights, privacy rights, and due-process rights." From the libertarian Left, Anthony Lewis in the *New York Times Magazine* has charged President Bush with undermining safeguards for the accused in a way that Lewis "did not believe was possible in our country," while from the libertarian Right, William Safire has protested the administration's effort to realize "the supersnoop's dream" of spying on all Americans.

The charge that our civil liberties are being systematically dismantled must be taken seriously. America has, in the past, overreacted to perceived security threats; the Palmer raids after World War I and the internment of Japanese-Americans during World War II are the most notorious examples. Are we once again jeopardizing the liberties of all Americans while also inflicting particular harm on Muslims in our midst? . . .

Security and Ethnic Profiling

According to Ibrahim Hooper, a spokesman for the Council on American-Islamic Relations, American Muslims have already lost many of their civil rights. "All Muslims are now suspects," Hooper has protested bitterly. The most salient outward sign of this is said to be the ethnic profiling that now occurs routinely in this country, particularly at airports but elsewhere as well— a form of discrimination widely considered to be self-evidently evil.

For most of us, airport security checks are the only first-hand experience we have with counter-measures to terrorism, and their intrusiveness and often seeming pointlessness have, not surprisingly, led many people to question such measures in general. But minor vexations are not the same as an assault on fundamental liberties. As for ethnic profiling, that is another matter, and a serious one. It is serious, however, not because it is rampant but because it does not exist.

That profiling is wicked *per se* is an idea that seems to have originated in connection with police work, when black civil-rights spokesmen began to allege that officers were relying on race as the sole criterion for suspecting someone of criminal activity. Profiling, in other words, equaled racism by definition. Yet, as Heather Mac Donald has demonstrated in *Are Cops Racist?*, the idea rests on a false assumption—namely, that crime rates are constant across every racial and ethnic component of our society. Thus, if blacks, who make up 11 percent of the population, are subject to 20 percent of all police stops on a particular highway, racial bias must be at fault.

But the truth is that (to stick to this particular example) blacks do speed more than whites, a fact that in itself justifies a heightened awareness of skin color as one of several criteria in police work. Of course, there is no excuse for blatant racism; but, as Mac Donald meticulously documents in case after case around the country, there is by and large no evidence that police have relied excessively on ethnic or racial profiling in conducting their normal investigations.

The War on Terror

The stigma attached to profiling where it hardly exists has perversely carried over to an area where it should exist but does not: the war against terrorism. This war, let us remember, pre-dates 9/11. According to Mac Donald, when a commission on aviation security headed by then-Vice President Al Gore was considering a system that would take into account a passenger's national origin and ethnicity—by far the best predictors of terrorism—both the Arab lobby and civil libertarians exploded in indignation. The commission duly capitulated—which is why the final Computer-Assisted Passenger Prescreening System (CAPPS) specified that such criteria as national origin, religion, ethnicity, and even gender were not to be taken into consideration.

This emasculated system did manage, even so, to pinpoint two of the September 11 terrorists on the day of their gruesome flight, but prevented any action beyond searching their luggage. As Mac Donald points out, had the system been allowed to utilize all relevant criteria, followed up by personal searches, the massacres might well have been averted.

Ironically, it is the very randomness of the new security checks that has generated so much skepticism about their efficacy. Old ladies, children, Catholic priests—all have been subject to searches of San Quentin-like thoroughness despite being beyond rational suspicion. According to the authorities, this randomness is itself a virtue, preventing would-be terrorists from easily predicting who or what will draw attention. But it is far more probable that frisking unlikely persons has nothing to do with security and everything to do with political correctness. Frightening as the prospect of terrorism may be, it pales, in the minds of many officials, in comparison with the prospect of being charged with racism.

Ethnic Profiling

Registration, Tracking, and Detention of Visitors

Ethnic Profiling, it is charged, is also responsible for the unjustified harassment and occasional detention of Arab and Muslim visitors to the United States. This is said to be an egregious violation not only of the rights of such persons but of America's traditional hospitality toward foreign visitors.

An irony here is that the procedures being deplored are hardly new, although they are being imposed with greater rigor. The current system has its roots in the 1950's in the first of a series of statutes ordering the Immigration and Naturalization Service (INS) to require aliens from countries listed as state sponsors of terrorism, as well as from countries with a history of breeding terrorists, to register and be fingerprinted, to state where they will be while in the U.S., and to notify the INS when they change address or leave the country.

Historically, however, the INS has been absurdly lax about fulfilling its mandate. When a visitor with illegal status—someone, for example, thought to have overstayed a student visa or committed a crime—is apprehended, the usual practice of immigration judges has been to release him upon the posting of a bond, unless he is designated a "person of interest." In the latter case, he is held for deportation or criminal prosecution and given a handbook detailing his rights, which include access to an attorney. It is a matter of dispute whether the proceedings before an immigration judge can be closed, as authorities prefer, or whether they must be open; the Supreme Court has so far declined to review the practice.

The procedures are now being adhered to more strictly, and this is what has given rise to accusations of ethnic or religious profiling. But such charges are as beside the point as in the case of domestic police work, if not more so. There is indeed a correlation between detention and ethnicity or religion, but that is because most of the countries identified as state sponsors or breeders of terrorism are, in fact, populated by Muslims and Arabs.

Stricter enforcement has also led to backlogs, as the Justice Department has proved unable to deal expeditiously with the hundreds of illegal immigrants rounded up in the aftermath of September 11. A report by the department's inspector general, released in early June, found "significant problems" with the processing of these cases. There is no question that, in an ideal world, many of them would have been handled with greater dispatch, but it is also hardly surprising that problems that have long plagued our criminal justice system should reappear in the context of the fight against terrorism. In any case, the department has already taken steps to ameliorate matters. The only way for the problems to vanish would be for the authorities to cease doing their proper job; we have tried that route, and lived to regret it.

Discovery, Detention, and Prosecution of Suspected Terrorists

According to civil libertarians, the constitutional safeguards that normally protect individuals suspected of criminal activity have been destroyed in the case of persons suspected of links with terrorism. This accusation reflects an ignorance both of the Constitution and of long-established limits on the criminal-justice system.

History

Prior to 1978, and dating back at least to World War II, attorneys general of the United States routinely authorized warrantless FBI surveillance, wire taps, and break-ins for national-security purposes. Such actions were taken pursuant to authority delegated by the President as commander-in-chief of the armed forces and as the officer principally responsible for the conduct of foreign affairs. The practice was justified because obtaining a warrant in each disparate case resulted in inconsistent standards and also posed unacceptable risks. (In one notorious instance, a judge had read aloud in his courtroom from highly classified material submitted to him by the government; even under more conscientious judges, clerks, secretaries, and others were becoming privy to secret materials.)

Attorneys general were never entirely comfortable with these warrantless searches, whose legality had never been confirmed by the Supreme Court. The solution in 1978 was the enactment of the Foreign Intelligence Surveillance Act (FISA). Henceforth, sitting district court judges would conduct secret hearings to approve or disapprove government applications for surveillance.

A further complication arose in the 1980's, however, when, by consensus of the Department of Justice and the FISA court, it was decided that the act authorized the gathering of foreign intelligence only for its own sake ("primary purpose"), and not for the possible criminal prosecution of any foreign agent. The effect was to erect a "wall" between the gathering of intelligence and the enforcement of criminal laws. But last year, the Foreign Intelligence Surveillance Court of Review held that the act did not, in fact, preclude or limit the government's use of that information in such prosecutions. In the opinion of the court, arresting and prosecuting terrorist agents or spies might well be the best way to inhibit their activities, as the threat of prosecution might persuade an agent to cooperate with the government, or enable the government to "turn" him.

When the wall came down, Justice Department prosecutors were able to learn what FBI intelligence officials already knew. This contributed to the arrest of Sami al-Arian, a professor at the University of South Florida, on charges that he raised funds for Palestinian Islamic Jihad and its suicide bombers. Once the evidence could be put at the disposition of prosecutors, al-Arian's longstanding claim that he was being persecuted by the authorities as an innocent victim of anti-Muslim prejudice was shattered.

Treatment of Captured Terrorists

According, by depriving certain captured individuals of access to lawyers, and by holding them without filing charges, the government is violating the Geneva Convention's protections of lawful combatants or prisoners of war. This is nonsense.

Lawful Combatants

Four criteria must be met to qualify a person as a lawful combatant. He must be under the command of a person responsible for his subordinates; wear a fixed distinctive emblem recognizable at a distance; carry arms openly; and conduct operations in accordance with the laws and customs of war. The men the United States has captured and detained so far do not meet these criteria.

The government's policy is as follows: if a captured unlawful enemy combatant is believed to have further information about terrorism, he can be held without access to legal counsel and without charges being filed. Once the government is satisfied that it has all the relevant information it can obtain, the captive can be held until the end of hostilities, or be released, or be brought up on charges before a criminal court. . . .

The Terrorist Information Awareness Program

Among Menaces to American liberty, this has been widely held to be the most sinister of all. Here is William Safire:

Every purchase you make with a credit card, every magazine subscription you buy and medical prescription you fill, every website you visit and e-mail you send or receive, every academic grade you receive, every bank deposit you make, every trip you book and every event you attend—all these transactions and communications will go into what the Defense Department describes as "a virtual, centralized grand database."

To this computerized dossier on your private life from commercial sources, add every piece of information that government has about you—passport application, driver's license and bridge toll records, judicial and divorce records, complaints from nosy neighbors to the F.B.I., your lifetime paper trail plus the latest hidden camera surveillance—and you have the supersnoop's dream.

Information Awareness

What is the reality? The Terrorist Information Awareness program (TIA) is still only in a developmental stage; we do not know whether it can even be made to work. If it can, it might turn out to be one of the most valuable weapons in America's war with terrorists.

In brief, the program would seek to identify patterns of conduct that indicate terrorist activity. This entails separating small sets of transactions from a vast universe of similar transactions. Since terrorists use the same avenues of communication, commerce, and transportation that everybody else uses, the objective is to build a prototype of an intelligence system whose purpose would be to find terrorists' signals in a "sea of noise." Taking advantage of the integrative power of computer technology, the system would allow the government to develop hypotheses about possible terrorist activity, basing itself entirely on data that are *already legally available*.

But we may never find out whether the program's objective can be achieved, since TIA has been effectively gutted in advance. Impressed, no doubt, by the ideological breadth of the opposition to TIA, Congress was led to adopt a vague prohibition, sponsored by Democratic Senator Ron Wyden, draining TIA of much of its value. The amendment specifies that the program's technology may be used for military operations outside the U.S. and for "lawful foreign intelligence activities conducted wholly against non-United States persons." By inference, TIA may therefore *not* be used to gather information about U.S. citizens or resident aliens—despite the clear fact that significant number of persons in these categories have ties to terrorist groups. . . .

Possible Safeguards

Are there techniques that could be devised to prevent TIA from becoming the playground of Safire's hypothetical supersnoop without disabling it altogether? In domestic criminal investigations, courts require warrants for electronic surveillances. As we have seen, the Foreign Intelligence Surveillance Act also requires judicial approval of surveillances for intelligence and counterintelligence purposes. While there would be no need for a warrant-like requirement in initiating a computer search, other safeguards can be imagined for TIA. Among them, according to Taylor, might be "software designs and legal rules that would block human agents from learning the identities of people whose transactions are being 'data-mined' by TIA computers unless the agents can obtain judicial warrants by showing something analogous to the 'probable cause' that the law requires to justify a wiretap." . . .

The benefits of the TIA program are palpable, and potentially invaluable; the hazards are either hyped or imaginary. There is nothing to prevent Congress from replacing the Wyden amendment with oversight provisions, or from requiring reasonable safeguards that would preserve the program's efficacy.

What Remains to Be Done

The fact that opponents of the Bush administration's efforts to protect American security have resorted to often shameless misrepresentation and outright scare-mongering does not mean those efforts are invulnerable to criticism. They are indeed vulnerable—for not going far enough.

In addition to the lack of properly targeted security procedures at airports, and the failure to resist the gutting of TIA, a truly gaping deficiency in our arrangements is the openness of our northern and southern borders to illegal entrants. In the south, reportedly, as many as 1,000 illegal aliens *a day* enter through Arizona's Organ Pipe National Monument park. . . .

There is, in short, plenty of work to go around. The war we are in, like no other we have ever faced, may last for decades rather than years. The enemy blends into our population and those of other nations around the world, attacks without warning, and consists of men who are quite willing to die in order to kill us and destroy our civilization. Never before has it been possible to imagine one suicidal individual, inspired by the promise of paradise and armed with a nuclear device, able to murder tens or even hundreds of thousands of Americans in a single attack. Those facts justify what the administration has already done, and urgently require more. . . .

NO

Barbara Dority

Your Every Move

On November 11, 2003, former President Jimmy Carter condemned U.S. leaders' attacks on American civil liberties, particularly the Uniting and Strengthening America by Providing Appropriate Tools Required to Intercept and Obstruct Terrorism Act (USA PATRIOT Act). Speaking at a gathering of Human Rights Defenders on the Front Lines of Freedom at the Carter Center in Washington, D.C., Carter said that post-9/11 policies "work against the spirit of human rights" and are "very serious mistakes." Egyptian human rights activist and sociology professor Saad Eddin Ibrahim added, "Every dictator is using what the United States has done under the Patriot Act to justify human rights abuses in the past, as well as a license to continue human rights abuses."

Since its passage in October 2001, the Patriot Act has decimated many basic American civil liberties. The law gives broad new powers to domestic law enforcement and international intelligence agencies. Perhaps worse still, it eliminates the system of checks and balances that gave courts the responsibility of ensuring that these powers weren't abused. The Electronic Frontier Foundation (EFF), an electronic privacy watchdog group, believes that the opportunities for abuse of these broad new powers are immense.

A particularly egregious part of the Patriot Act gives the government access to "any tangible things." This section grants the Federal Bureau of Investigation (FBI) the authority to request an order "requiring the production of any tangible things (including books, records, papers, documents, and other items)" relevant to an investigation of terrorism or clandestine intelligence activities. Although the section is entitled "Access to Certain Business Records," the scope of its authority is far broader and applies to any records pertaining to an individual. This section, which overrides state library confidentiality laws, permits the FBI to compel production of business records, medical records, educational records, and library records without showing probable cause.

Many aspects of the Patriot Act unfairly target immigrants. The attorney general has the ability to "certify" that the government has "reasonable grounds to believe that an alien is a terrorist or is engaged in other activity that endangers the national security of the United States." Once that certification is made and someone is labeled a potential threat, the government

From *The Humanist,* January/February 2004, pp. 14–19. Copyright © 2004 by American Humanist Association. Reprinted with permission.

may detain him or her indefinitely—based on secret evidence it isn't required to share with anyone.

Currently over thirteen thousand Arab and Muslim immigrants are being held in deportation proceedings. Not one of them has been charged with terrorism. Most are being deported for routine immigration violations that normally could be rectified in hearings before immigration judges. Families are being separated and lives ruined because of selective enforcement of immigration laws that have been on the books for many years and are now being used to intimidate and deport law-abiding Arab and Muslim Americans. Fear and confusion are pervasive in the Arab-American community today. Many people are too afraid to step forward when they are harassed on the job or fired, when they are denied housing because of their last name, or when a family member is picked up by immigration authorities and detained in another state on evidence that remains undisclosed to both detainees and lawyers alike. According to Karen Rignal's article "Beyond Patriotic" on Alternet.org, some of these people have been detained for as long as eight months, mistreated, and confined twenty-three hours a day. Some Arab immigrants have opted to return to the Middle East because they no longer feel welcome in the United States.

Nearly seven hundred men are being held at "Camp X-Ray" in Guantanamo Bay, Cuba. But it isn't just "foreigners" who are being deemed dangerous and un-American. For example, there is Tom Treece, a teacher who taught a class on "public issues" at a Vermont high school. A uniformed police officer entered Treece's classroom in the middle of the night because a student art project on the wall showed a picture of Bush with duct ape over his mouth and the words, "Put your duct tape to good use. Shut your mouth." Residents refused to pass the school budget if Treece wasn't fired, resulting in his removal.

The American Civil Liberties Union (ACLU) went to court to help a fifteen year-old who faced suspension from school when he refused to take off a T-shirt with the words "International Terrorist" written beneath a picture of Bush. And there was the college student from North Carolina who was visited at home by secret service agents who told her, "Ma'am, we've gotten a report that you have anti-American material." She refused to let them in but eventually showed them what she thought they were after, an anti-death-penalty poster showing Bush and a group of lynched bodies over the epithet "We hang on your every word." The agents then asked her if she had any "pro-Taliban stuff."

Then there's art dealer Doug Stuber, who ran the 2000 North Carolina presidential campaign for Green Party candidate Ralph Nader. Stuber was told he couldn't board a plane to Prague, Czech Republic, because no Greens were allowed to fly that day. He was questioned by police, photographed by two secret service agents, and asked about his family and what the Greens were up to. Stuber reports that he was shown a Justice Department document suggesting that Greens were likely terrorists.

Michael Franti, lead singer of the progressive hip hop band Spearhead, reports that the mother of one of his colleagues, who has a sibling in the

Persian Gulf, was visited by "two plain-clothes men from the military" in March 2003. They came in and said, "You have a child who's in the Gulf and you have a child who's in this band Spearhead who's part of the resistance." They had pictures of the band at peace rallies, their flight records for several months, their banking records, and the names of backstage staff.

A report by the ACLU called "Freedom Under Fire" states, "There is a pall over our country. The response to dissent by many government officials so clearly violates the letter and the spirit of the supreme law of the land that they threaten the very underpinnings of democracy itself."

In the face of these cases and many more, Justice Department spokespeople have repeatedly claimed that the Patriot Act doesn't apply to Americans. But this is false. First of all, under the Patriot Act the four tools of surveillance—wiretaps, search warrants, pen/trap orders, and subpoenas—are increased. Second, their counterparts under the Foreign Intelligence Surveillance Act (FISA), which allows spying in the United States by foreign intelligence agencies, are concurrently expanded. New definitions of terrorism also increase the amount of government surveillance permitted. And three expansions of previous terms increase the scope of spying allowed. The Patriot Act provides a FISA detour around limitations on federal domestic surveillance and a domestic detour around FISA limitations. The attorney general can nullify domestic surveillance limits on the Central Intelligence Agency, for example, by obtaining a FISA wiretap where probable cause cannot be shown but the person is a suspected foreign government agent. All this information can be shared with the FBI and vice versa.

In sum, the Patriot Act allows U.S. foreign intelligence agencies to more easily spy on U.S. citizens and FISA now provides for increased information sharing between domestic law enforcement and foreign intelligence officials. This partially repeals the protections implemented in the 1970s after the revelation that the FBI and CIA were conducting investigations on thousands of U.S. citizens during and after the McCarthy era. The Patriot Act allows sharing wiretap results and grand jury information when that constitutes "foreign intelligence information."

In response to other criticisms, Justice Department spokespeople have also claimed that the Patriot Act applies only to "terrorists and spies" and that the FBI can't obtain a person's records without probable cause. As one might expect, all of this is false as well.

The Patriot Act specifically gives the government and the FBI authority to monitor people not engaged in criminal activity or espionage and to do so in complete secrecy. It also imposes a gag order that prohibits an organization that has been forced to turn over records from disclosing the fact of the search to its clients, customers, or anyone else.

Furthermore, in other statements, federal officials contradict themselves by saying that the government is using its expanded authority under the far-reaching law to investigate suspected blackmailers, drug traffickers, money launderers, pornographers, and white-collar criminals. Dan Dodson, speaking to the Associated Press this past September on behalf of the National Association of Criminal Defense Attorneys, reported, "Within six months of passing the Patriot Act, the Justice Department was conducting seminars on how to stretch the new wiretapping provisions to extend them beyond terror cases.

A guidebook used in a 2002 Justice Department employee seminar on financial crimes says: "We all know that the USA Patriot Act provided weapons for the war on terrorism. But do you know how it affects the war on crime as well?" . . .

Publicly, of course, Attorney General John Ashcroft continues to speak almost exclusively of how Patriot Act powers are helping fight terrorism. In his nationwide tour this past fall to bolster support for the act (which has engendered growing discontent), Ashcroft lauded its "success" stories. However, his department also officially labels many cases as terrorism which aren't. A January 2003 study by the General Accounting Office concluded that, of those convictions classified as "international terrorism," fully 75 percent actually dealt with more common nonterrorist crimes. . . .

Perhaps the most frightening thing about the Patriot Act—even putting aside these other impending restrictions on civil liberties—is how similar the act is to legislation enacted in the eighteenth century. The Alien and Sedition Acts are notorious in history for their abuse of basic civil liberties. For example, in 1798, the Alien Friends Act made it lawful for the president of the United States "to order all such aliens, as he shall judge dangerous to the peace and safety of the United States, or shall have reasonable grounds to suspect are concerned in any treasonable or secret machinations against the government thereof, to depart out of the territory of the United States." For years Americans have pointed to legislation like this as a travesty never to be repeated. Yet now it is back!

It seems unimaginable that any presidential administration would impose such brazen attacks as these on the civil liberties of a supposedly free people. Apparently, many Americans were initially so traumatized by 9/11 that they were ready to surrender their most treasured liberties. But pockets of resistance are developing and organizations forming. Three states and more than two hundred cities, counties, and towns around the country have passed resolutions opposing the Patriot Act. Many others are in progress. The language of these resolutions includes statements affirming a commitment to the rights guaranteed in the Constitution and directives to local law enforcement not to cooperate with federal agents involved in investigations deemed unconstitutional. A bill has also been introduced in the House to exclude bookstore and library records from the materials that could be subpoenaed by law enforcement without prior notification of the targeted person.

Some leading organizations, such as the ACLU and EFF, continue to keep the pressure on and are always worthy of support. American citizens who treasure their heritage of freedom should find at least one group to join and support—keeping in mind that the government may one day know the organizations they have checked out.

POSTSCRIPT

Does the Threat of Terrorism Warrant Curtailment of Civil Liberties?

Since September 11th, books and articles on terrorism have increased greatly. Some recent notable general works on terrorism include Clifford E. Simonsen and Jeremy R. Spindlove, *Terrorism Today: The Past, the Players, the Future*, 2d ed. (Prentice Hall, 2004); Cindy C. Combs, *Terrorism in the Twenty-First Century*, 3rd ed. (Prentice Hall, 2003); and Pamala Griset and Sue Mahan, *Terrorism in Perspective* (Sage Publications, 2003); and Gus Martin, *Understanding Terrorism: Challenges, Perspectives, and Issues* (Sage Publications, 2003).

Terrorism with weapons of mass destruction has been labeled "the new terrorism," and an extensive literature on it has rapidly formed, including Walter Laqueur, *No End to War: Terrorism in the Twenty-First Century* (Continuum, 2003); Nadine Gurr and Benjamin Cole, *The New Face of Terrorism: Threats From Weapons of Mass Destruction* (St. Martin's Press, 2000); and Paul Gilbert, *New Terror, New Wars* (Georgetown University Press, 2003). Another threatening aspect of terrorism is the terrorists' willingness to commit suicide. To explore this issue, see Christopher Reuter, *My Life as a Weapon: A Modern History of Suicide Bombing* (Princeton University Press, 2004).

The critical issue is how the United States deals with the terrorist threat. Richard A. Clark provides an insider's revelation of the U.S. response in *Against All Enemies: Inside America's War on Terror* (Free Press, 2004). See also Michael Ignatieff, *The Lesser Evil: Political Ethics in an Age of Terror* (Princeton University Press, 2004); *The Politics of Terror: The U.S. Response to 9/11*, edited by William Crotty (Northwestern University Press, 2004); Lawrence Freedman, ed., *Superterrorism: Policy Responses* (Blackwell Publishers, 2002); Dilip K. Das and Peter C. Kratcoski, eds., *Meeting the Challenges of Global Terrorism: Prevention, Control, and Recovery* (Lexington, 2003); Hayim Granot and Jay Levinson, *Terror Bombing: The New Urban Threat: Practical Approaches for Response Agencies and Security* (Dekel, 2002); and Amy Sterling Casil, *Coping With Terrorism* (Rosen, 2004). Works that discuss the issue of balancing the need for greater police powers and the desire for strong civil rights include *National Security: Opposing Viewpoints*, edited by Helen Cothern (Greenhaven Press, 2004); *American National Security and Civil Liberties in an Age of Terrorism*, edited by David B. Cohen and John W. Wells (Palgrave Macmillan, 2004); and Raneta Lawson Mack and Michael J. Kelly, *Equal Justice in the Balance: America's Legal Responses to the Emerging Terrorist Threat* (University of Michigan Press, 2004). Two works that criticize the U.S. legal response are *Lost Liberties: Ashcroft and the Assault on Personal Freedom*, edited by Cynthia Brown (New

Press, 2003) and Jeffrey Rosen *The Naked Crowd: Reclaiming Security and Freedom in an Anxious Age* (Random House, 2004). Another side of the story is provided by Alan M. Dershowitz in *Why Terrorism Works* (Yale University Press, 2002).

On the Internet . . .

United Nations Environment Program (UNEP)

The United Nations Environment Program (UNEP) Web site offers links to environmental topics of critical concern to sociologists. The site will direct you to useful databases and global resource information.

http://www.unep.ch

Worldwatch Institute Home Page

The Worldwatch Institute is dedicated to fostering the evolution of an environmentally sustainable society in which human needs are met without threatening the health of the natural environment. This site provides access to World Watch Magazine and State of the World 2000.

http://www.worldwatch.org

WWW Virtual Library: Demography and Population Studies

The WWW Virtual Library provides a definitive guide to demography and population studies. A multitude of important links to information about global poverty and hunger can be found at this site.

http://demography.anu.edu.au/VirtualLibrary/

William Davidson Institute

The William Davidson Institute at the University of Michigan Business School is dedicated to the understanding and promotion of economic transition. Consult this site for discussions of topics related to the changing global economy and the effects of globalization on society.

http://www.wdi.bus.umich.edu

World Future Society

The World Future Society is an educational and scientific organization for those interested in how social and technological developments are shaping the future.

http://www.wfs.org

PART 6

The Future: Population/ Environment/Society

T he leading issues for the beginning of the twenty-first century include global warming, environmental decline, and globalization. The state of the environment and the effects of globalization produce strong arguments concerning what can be harmful or beneficial. Technology has increased enormously in the last 100 years, as have worldwide population growth, consumption, and new forms of pollution that threaten to undermine the world's fragile ecological support system. Although all nations have a stake in the health of the planet, many believe that none are doing enough to protect its health. Will technology itself be the key to controlling or accommodating the increase of population and consumption, along with the resulting increase in waste production? Perhaps so, but new policies will also be needed. Technology is driving the process of globalization, which can be seen as both good and bad. Those who support globalization theory state that globalization increases competition, production, wealth, and the peaceful integration of nations. However, not everyone agrees. This section explores what is occurring in our environment and in our current global economy.

- Is Mankind Dangerously Harming the Environment?

- Is Globalization Good for Mankind?

ISSUE 19

Is Mankind Dangerously Harming the Environment?

YES: Lester R. Brown, from *Rescuing a Planet under Stress and a Civilization in Trouble* (W.W. Norton, 2003)

NO: Bjorn Lomborg, from "The Truth About the Environment," *The Economist* (August 4, 2001)

ISSUE SUMMARY

YES: Lester R. Brown, founder of the Worldwatch Institute and now president of the Earth Policy Institute, reviews the stress humans have inflicted on the environment in depleting its natural capital and adversely affecting its ecosystems. The result may soon be economic hardship unless we change our course soon.

NO: Bjorn Lomborg, a statistician at the University of Aarhus, Denmark, presents evidence that population growth is slowing down, natural resources are not running out, species are disappearing very slowly, the environment is improving in some ways, and assertions about environmental decline are exaggerated.

Much of the literature on socioeconomic development in the 1960s was premised on the assumption of inevitable material progress for all. It largely ignored the impacts of development on the environment and presumed that the availability of raw materials would not be a problem. The belief was that all societies would get richer because all societies were investing in new equipment and technologies that would increase productivity and wealth. Theorists recognized that some poor countries were having trouble developing, but they blamed those problems on the deficiencies of the values and attitudes of those countries and on inefficient organizations.

In the late 1960s and early 1970s an intellectual revolution occurred. Environmentalists had criticized the growth paradigm throughout the 1960s, but they were not taken very seriously at first. By the end of the 1960s, however, marine scientist Rachel Carson's book *Silent Spring* (Alfred A. Knopf, 1962) had worked its way into the public's consciousness. Carson's book traces the noticeable loss of birds to the use of pesticides. Her book made the middle and upper classes in the United States realize that pollution affects complex ecological systems in ways that put even the wealthy at risk.

In 1968 Paul Ehrlich, a professor of population studies, published *The Population Bomb* (Ballantine Books), which states that overpopulation is the major problem facing mankind. This means that population has to be controlled or the human race might cause the collapse of the global ecosystems and the deaths of many humans. Ehrlich explained why he thought the devastation of the world was imminent:

> Because the human population of the planet is about five times too large, and we're managing to support all these people—at today's level of misery— only by spending our capital, burning our fossil fuels, dispersing our mineral resources and turning our fresh water into salt water. We have not only overpopulated but overstretched our environment. We are poisoning the ecological systems of the earth—systems upon which we are ultimately dependent for all of our food, for all of our oxygen and for all of our waste disposal.

In 1973 *The Limits to Growth* (Universe) by Donella H. Meadows et al. was published. It presents a dynamic systems computer model for world economic, demographic, and environmental trends. When the computer model projected trends into the future, it predicted that the world would experience ecological collapse and population die-off unless population growth and economic activity were greatly reduced. This study was both attacked and defended, and the debate about the health of the world has been heated ever since.

Let us examine the population growth rates for the past, present, and future. At about A.D. 1, the world had about one-quarter billion people. It took about 1,650 years to double this number to one-half billion and 200 years to double the world population again to 1 billion by 1850. The next doubling took only about 80 years, and the last doubling took about 45 years (from 2 billion in 1930 to about 4 billion in 1975). The world population may double again to 8 billion sometime between 2015 and 2025. At the same time that population is growing people are trying to get richer, which means consuming more, polluting more, and using more resources. Are all these trends threatening the carrying capacity of the planet and jeopardizing the prospects for future generations?

In the following selections, Lester R. Brown warns that human activity is damaging the environment and depleting its resources with potentially devastating results. Some nations have instituted policies, which have improved a few indicators of the health of the environment, but have not addressed some increasingly acute problems that threaten the prosperity and well-being of many societies. Bjorn Lomborg counters that the evidence supports optimism—not environmental pessimism. He maintains that resources are becoming more abundant, food per capita is increasing, the extinction of species is at a very slow rate, and environmental problems are transient and will get better.

Lester R. Brown

YES

Rescuing a Planet under Stress and a Civilization in Trouble

A Planet under Stress

As world population has doubled and as the global economy has expanded sevenfold over the last half-century, our claims on the earth have become excessive. We are asking more of the earth than it can give on an ongoing basis, creating a bubble economy.

We are cutting trees faster than they can regenerate, overgrazing rangelands and converting them into deserts, overpumping aquifers, and draining rivers dry. On our cropland, soil erosion exceeds new soil formation, slowly depriving the soil of its inherent fertility. We are taking fish from the ocean faster than they can reproduce.

We are releasing carbon dioxide (CO_2) into the atmosphere faster than nature can absorb it, creating a green-house effect. As atmospheric CO_2 levels rise, so does the earth's temperature. Habitat destruction and climate change are destroying plant and animal species far faster than new species can evolve, launching the first mass extinction since the one that eradicated the dinosaurs 65 million years ago.

Throughout history, humans have lived on the earth's sustainable yield—the interest from its natural endowment. But now we are consuming the endowment itself. In ecology, as in economics, we can consume principal along with interest in the short run, but in the long run it leads to bankruptcy.

In 2002, a team of scientists led by Mathis Wackernagel, an analyst at Redefining Progress, concluded that humanity's collective demands first surpassed the earth's regenerative capacity around 1980. Their study, published by the U.S. National Academy of Sciences, estimated that our demands in 1999 exceeded that capacity by 20 percent. We are satisfying our excessive demands by consuming the earth's natural assets, in effect creating a global bubble economy.

Bubble economies are not new. American investors got an up-close view of this when the bubble in high-tech stocks burst in 2000 and the NASDAQ, an indicator of the value of these stocks, declined by some 75 percent. Japan had a similar experience in 1989 when the real estate bubble burst, depreciating stock and real estate assets by 60 percent. The bad-debt fallout and other effects of this collapse have left the once-dynamic Japanese economy dead in the water ever since.

The bursting of these two bubbles affected primarily people living in the United States and Japan, but the global bubble economy that is based on the overconsumption of the earth's natural capital assets will affect the entire world. When the food bubble economy, inflated by the overpumping of aquifers, bursts, it will raise food prices worldwide. The challenge for our generation is to deflate the economic bubble before it bursts. . . .

In February 2003, U.N. demographers made an announcement that was in some ways more shocking than the September 11th attack: the worldwide rise in life expectancy has been dramatically reversed for a large segment of humanity—the 700 million people living in sub-Saharan Africa. The HIV epidemic has reduced life expectancy among this region's people from 62 to 47 years. The epidemic may soon claim more lives than all the wars of the twentieth century. If this teaches us anything, it is the high cost of neglecting newly emerging threats.

The HIV epidemic is not the only emerging mega-threat. Numerous countries are feeding their growing populations by overpumping their aquifers—a measure that virtually guarantees a future drop in food production when the aquifers are depleted. In effect, these countries are creating a food bubble economy—one where food production is artificially inflated by the unsustainable use of groundwater.

Another mega-threat—climate change—is not getting the attention it deserves from most governments, particularly that of the United States, the country responsible for one fourth of all carbon emissions. Washington wants to wait until all the evidence on climate change is in, by which time it will be too late to prevent a wholesale warming of the planet. Just as governments in Africa watched HIV infection rates rise and did little about it, the United States is watching atmospheric CO_2 levels rise and doing little to check the increase.

Other mega-threats being neglected include eroding soils and expanding deserts, which are threatening the livelihood and food supply of hundreds of millions of the world's people. These issues do not even appear on the radar screen of many national governments.

Thus far, most of the environmental damage has been local: the death of the Aral Sea, the burning rainforests of Indonesia, the collapse of the Canadian cod fishery, the melting of the glaciers that supply Andean cities with water, the dust bowl forming in northwestern China, and the depletion of the U.S. Great Plains aquifer. But as these local environmental events expand and multiply, they will progressively weaken the global economy, bringing closer the day when the economic bubble will burst.

Ecological Bills Coming Due

Humanity's demands on the earth have multiplied over the last half-century as our numbers have increased and our incomes have risen. World population grew from 2.5 billion in 1950 to 6.1 billion in 2000. The growth during those

50 years exceeded that during the 4 million years since we emerged as a distinct species.

Incomes have risen even faster than population. Income per person worldwide nearly tripled from 1950 to 2000. Growth in population and the rise in incomes together expanded global economic output from just under $7 trillion (in 2001 dollars) of goods and services in 1950 to $46 trillion in 2000, a gain of nearly sevenfold.

Population growth and rising incomes together have tripled world grain demand over the last half-century, pushing it from 640 million tons in 1950 to 1,855 million tons in 2000. To satisfy this swelling demand, farmers have plowed land that was highly erodible—land that was too dry or too steeply sloping to sustain cultivation. Each year billions of tons of topsoil are being blown away in dust storms or washed away in rainstorms, leaving farmers to try to feed some 70 million additional people, but with less topsoil than the year before.

Demand for water also tripled as agricultural, industrial, and residential uses climbed, outstripping the sustainable supply in many countries. As a result, water tables are falling and wells are going dry. Rivers are also being drained dry, to the detriment of wildlife and ecosystems.

Fossil fuel use quadrupled, setting in motion a rise in carbon emissions that is overwhelming nature's capacity to fix carbon dioxide. As a result of this carbon-fixing deficit, atmospheric CO_2 concentrations climbed from 316 parts per million (ppm) in 1959, when official measurement began, to 369 ppm in 2000.

The sector of the economy that seems likely to unravel first is food. Eroding soils, deteriorating rangelands, collapsing fisheries, falling water tables, and rising temperatures are converging to make it more difficult to expand food production fast enough to keep up with demand. In 2002, the world grain harvest of 1,807 million tons fell short of world grain consumption by 100 million tons, or 5 percent. This shortfall, the largest on record, marked the third consecutive year of grain deficits, dropping stocks to the lowest level in a generation.

Now the question is, Can the world's farmers bounce back and expand production enough to fill the 100-million-ton shortfall, provide for the more than 70 million people added each year, and rebuild stocks to a more secure level? In the past, farmers responded to short supplies and higher grain prices by planting more land and using more irrigation water and fertilizer. Now it is doubtful that farmers can fill this gap without further depleting aquifers and jeopardizing future harvests.

In 1996, at the World Food Summit in Rome, hosted by the U.N. Food and Agriculture Organization (FAO), 185 countries plus the European Community agreed to reduce hunger by half by 2015. Using 1990–92 as a base, governments set the goal of cutting the number of people who were hungry— 860 million—by roughly 20 million per year. It was an exciting and worthy goal, one that later became one of the U.N. Millennium Development Goals.

But in its late 2002 review of food security, the United Nations issued a discouraging report: "This year we must report that progress has virtually ground to a halt. Our latest estimates, based on data from the years 1998–2000, put the number of undernourished people in the world at 840 million . . . a decrease of barely 2.5 million per year over the eight years since 1990–92."

Since 1998–2000, world grain production per person has fallen 5 percent, suggesting that the ranks of the hungry are now expanding. As noted earlier, life expectancy is plummeting in sub-Saharan Africa. If the number of hungry people worldwide is also increasing, then two key social indicators are showing widespread deterioration in the human condition.

Farmers Facing Two New Challenges

As we exceed the earth's natural capacities, we create new problems. For example, farmers are now facing two new challenges: rising temperatures and falling water tables. Farmers currently on the land may face higher temperatures than any generation since agriculture began 11,000 years ago. They are also the first to face widespread aquifer depletion and the resulting loss of irrigation water.

The global average temperature has risen in each of the last three decades. The 16 warmest years since record-keeping began in 1880 have all occurred since 1980. With the three warmest years on record—1998, 2001, and 2002—coming in the last five years, crops are facing heat stresses that are without precedent.

Higher temperatures reduce crop yields through their effect on photosynthesis, moisture balance, and fertilization. As the temperature rises above 34 degrees Celsius (94 degrees Fahrenheit), photosynthesis slows, dropping to zero for many crops when it reaches 37 degrees Celsius (100 degrees Fahrenheit). When temperatures in the U.S. Corn Belt are 37 degrees or higher, corn plants suffer from thermal shock and dehydration. They are in effect on sick leave. Each such day shrinks the harvest.

In addition to decreasing photosynthesis and dehydrating plants, high temperatures also impede the fertilization needed for seed formation. Researchers at the International Rice Research Institute in the Philippines and at the U.S. Department of Agriculture have together developed a rule of thumb that each 1-degree-Celsius rise in temperature above the optimum during the growing season reduces grain yields by 10 percent.

These recent research findings indicate that if the temperature rises to the lower end of the range projected by the Intergovernmental Panel on Climate Change, grain harvests in tropical regions could be reduced by an average of 5 percent by 2020 and 11 percent by 2050. At the upper end of the range, harvests could drop 11 percent by 2020 and 46 percent by 2050. Avoiding these declines will be difficult unless scientists can develop crop strains that are not vulnerable to thermal stress.

The second challenge facing farmers, falling water tables, is also recent. With traditional animal- or human-powered water-lifting devices it was almost impossible historically to deplete aquifers. With the worldwide spread of powerful diesel and electric pumps during the last half-century, however, overpumping has become commonplace.

As the world demand for water has climbed, water tables have fallen in scores of countries, including China, India, and the United States, which together produce nearly half of the world's grain. Water tables are falling throughout the northern half of China. As the water table falls, springs and rivers go dry, lakes disappear, and wells dry up. Northern China is literally drying out. Water tables under the North China Plain, which accounts for a fourth or more of China's grain harvest, are falling at an accelerating rate.

In India, water tables are also falling. As India's farmers try to feed an additional 16 million people each year, nearly the population equivalent of another Australia, they are pumping more and more water. This is dropping water tables in states that together contain a majority of India's 1 billion people.

In the United States, the third major grain producer, water tables are falling under the southern Great Plains and in California, the country's fruit and vegetable basket. As California's population expands from 26 million to a projected 40 million by 2030, expanding urban water demands will siphon water from agriculture.

Scores of other countries are also overpumping their aquifers, setting the stage for dramatic future cutbacks in water supplies. The more populous among these are Pakistan, Iran, and Mexico. Overpumping creates an illusion of food security that is dangerously deceptive because it enables farmers to support a growing population with a practice that virtually ensures a future drop in food production.

The water demand growth curve over the last half-century looks like the population growth curve, except that it climbs more steeply. While world population growth was doubling, the use of water was tripling. Once the growing demand for water rises above the sustainable yield of an aquifer, the gap between the two widens further each year. As this happens, the water table starts to fall. The first year after the sustainable yield is surpassed, the water table falls very little, with the drop often being scarcely perceptible. Each year thereafter, however, the annual drop is larger than the year before.

In addition to falling exponentially, water tables are also falling simultaneously in many countries. This means that cutbacks in grain harvests will occur in many countries at more or less the same time. And they will occur at a time when the world's population is growing by more than 70 million a year.

These, then, are the two new challenges facing the world's farmers: rising temperatures and falling water tables. Either one by itself could make it difficult to keep up with the growth in demand. The two together provide an early test of whether our modern civilization can cope with the forces that threaten to undermine it. . . .

NO

Bjorn Lomborg

The Truth About the Environment

Ecology and economics should push in the same direction. After all, the "eco" part of each word derives from the greek word for "home", and the protagonists of both claim to have humanity's welfare as their goal. Yet environmentalists and economists are often at loggerheads. For economists, the world seems to be getting better. For many environmentalists, it seems to be getting worse.

These environmentalists, led by such veterans as Paul Ehrlich of Stanford University, and Lester Brown of the Worldwatch Institute, have developed a sort of "litany" of four big environmental fears:

- Natural resources are running out.
- The population is ever growing, leaving less and less to eat.
- Species are becoming extinct in vast numbers: forests are disappearing and fish stocks are collapsing.
- The planet's air and water are becoming ever more polluted.

Human activity is thus defiling the earth, and humanity may end up killing itself in the process.

The trouble is, the evidence does not back up this litany. First, energy and other natural resources have become more abundant, not less so since the Club of Rome published "The Limits to Growth" in 1972. Second, more food is now produced per head of the world's population than at any time in history. Fewer people are starving. Third, although species are indeed becoming extinct, only about 0.7% of them are expected to disappear in the next 50 years, not 25–50%, as has so often been predicted. And finally, most forms of environmental pollution either appear to have been exaggerated, or are transient—associated with the early phrases of industrialisation and therefore best cured not by restricting economic growth, but by accelerating it. One form of pollution—the release of greenhouse gases that causes global warming—does appear to be a long-term phenomenon, but its total impact is unlikely to pose a devastating problem for the future of humanity. A bigger problem may well turn out to be an inappropriate response to it.

Can Things Only Get Better?

Take these four points one by one. First, the exhaustion of natural resources. The early environmental movement worried that the mineral resources on which modern industry depends would run out. Clearly, there must be some limit to the amount of fossil fuels and metal ores that can be extracted from the earth: the planet, after all, has a finite mass. But that limit is far greater than many environmentalists would have people believe.

Reserves of natural resources have to be located, a process that costs money. That, not natural scarcity, is the main limit on their availability. However, known reserves of all fossil fuels, and of most commercially important metals, are now larger than they were when "the Limits to Growth" was published. In the case of oil, for example, reserves that could be extracted at reasonably competitive prices would keep the world economy running for about 150 years at present consumption rates. Add to that the fact that the price of solar energy has fallen by half in every decade for the past 30 years, and appears likely to continue to do so into the future, and energy shortages do not look like a serious threat either to the economy or to the environment.

The development for non-fuel resources has been similar. Cement, aluminum, iron, copper, gold, nitrogen and zinc account for more than 75% of global expenditure on raw materials. Despite an increase in consumption of these materials of between two- and ten-fold over the past 50 years, the number of years of available reserves has actually grown. Moreover, the increasing abundance is reflected in an ever-decreasing price: *The Economist*'s index of prices of industrial raw materials has dropped some 80% in inflation-adjusted terms since 1845.

Next, the population explosion is also turning out to be a bugaboo. In 1968, Dr Ehrlich predicted in his best selling book, "The Population Bomb", that "the battle to feed humanity is over. In the course of the 1970s the world will experience starvation of tragic proportions—hundreds of millions of people will starve to death."

That did not happen. Instead, according to the United Nations, agricultural production in the developing world has increased by 52% per person since 1961. The daily food intake in poor countries has increased from 1,932 calories, barely enough for survival, in 1961 to 2,650 calories in 1998, and is expected to rise to 3,020 by 2030. Likewise, the proportion of people in developing countries who are starving has dropped from 45% in 1949 to 18% today, and is expected to decline even further to 12% in 2010 and just 6% in 2030. Food, in other words, is becoming not scarcer but ever more abundant. This is reflected in its price. Since 1800 food prices have decreased by more than 90%, and in 2000, according to the World Bank, prices were lower than ever before.

Modern Malthus

Dr Ehrlich's prediction echoes that made 170 years earlier by Thomas Malthus. Malthus claimed that, if unchecked, human population would expand exponentially, while food production could increase only linearly, by

Figure 1

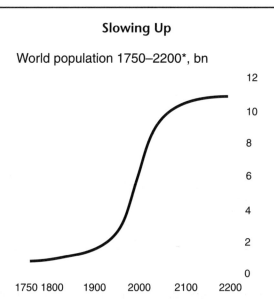

Slowing Up

World population 1750–2200*, bn

*UN medium-variant forecast from 2000
Source: UNPD

bringing new land into cultivation. He was wrong. Population growth has turned out to have an internal check: as people grow richer and healthier, they have smaller families. Indeed, the growth rate of the human population reached its peak, of more than 2% a year, in the early 1960s. The rate of increase has been declining ever since. It is now 1.26%, and is expected to fall to 0.46% in 2050. The United Nations estimates that most of the world's population growth will be over by 2100, with the population stabilising at just below 11 billion (see Figure 1).

Malthus also failed to take account of developments in agricultural technology. These have squeezed more and more food out of each hectare of land. It is this application of human ingenuity that has boosted food production, not merely in line with, but ahead of, population growth. It has also, incidentally, reduced the need to take new land into cultivation, thus reducing the pressure on biodiversity.

Third, that threat of biodiversity loss is real, but exaggerated. Most early estimates used simple island models that linked a loss in habitat with a loss of biodiversity. A rule-of-thumb indicated that loss of 90% of forest meant a 50% loss of species. As rainforests seemed to be cut at alarming rates, estimates of annual species loss of 20,000–100,000 abounded. Many people expected the number of species to fall by half globally within a generation or two.

However, the data simply does not bear out these predictions. In the eastern United States, forests were reduced over two centuries to fragments totalling just 1–2% of their original area, yet this resulted in the extinction of

Figure 2

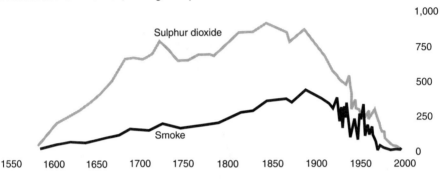

Cleaning Up

Concentrations in London, micrograms per cubic metre

Source: B. Lomborg

only one forest bird. In Puerto Rico, the primary forest area has been reduced over the past 400 years by 99%, yet "only" seven of 60 species of bird has become extinct. All but 12% of the Brazilian Atlantic rainforest was cleared in the 19th century, leaving only scattered fragments. According to the rule-of-thumb, half of all its species should have become extinct. Yet, when the World Conservation Union and the Brazilian Society of Zoology analysed all 291 known Atlantic forest animals, none could be declared extinct. Species, therefore, seem more resilient than expected. And tropical forests are not lost at annual rates of 2.4%, as many environmentalists have claimed: the latest UN figures indicate a loss of less than 0.5%.

Fourth, pollution is also exaggerated. Many analyses show that air pollution diminishes when a society becomes rich enough to be able to afford to be concerned about the environment. For London, the city for which the best data are available, air pollution peaked around 1890 (see Figure 2). Today, the air is cleaner than it has been since 1585. There is good reason to believe that this general picture holds true for all developed countries. And, although air pollution is increasing in many developing countries, they are merely replicating the development of the industrialised countries. When they grow sufficiently rich they, too, will start to reduce their air pollution.

All this contradicts the litany. Yet opinion polls suggest that many people, in the rich world, at least, nurture the belief that environmental standards are declining. Four factors cause this disjunction between perception and reality.

Always Look on the Dark Side of Life

One is the lopsidedness built into scientific research. Scientific funding goes mainly to areas with many problems. That may be wise policy, but it will also create an impression that many more potential problems exist than is the case.

Secondly, environmental groups need to be noticed by the mass media. They also need to keep the money rolling in. Understandably, perhaps, they sometimes exaggerate. In 1997, for example, the Worldwide Fund for Nature issued a press release entitled, "Two-thirds of the world's forests lost forever". The truth turns out to be nearer 20%.

Though these groups are run overwhelmingly by selfless folk, they nevertheless share many of the characteristics of other lobby groups. That would matter less if people applied the same degree of scepticism to environmental lobbying as they do to lobby groups in other fields. A trade organisation arguing for, say, weaker pollution controls is instantly seen as self-interested. Yet a green organisation opposing such a weakening is seen as altruistic, even if a dispassionate view of the controls in question might suggest they are doing more harm than good.

A third source of confusion is the attitude of the media. People are clearly more curious about bad news than good. Newspapers and broadcasters are there to provide what the public wants. That, however, can lead to significant distortions of perception. An example was America's encounter with El Niño in 1997 and 1998. This climatic phenomenon was accused of wrecking tourism, causing allergies, melting the ski-slopes and causing 22 deaths by dumping snow in Ohio.

A more balanced view comes from a recent article in the *Bulletin of the American Meteorological Society*. This tries to count up both the problems and the benefits of the 1997–98 Niño. The damage it did was estimated at $4 billion. However, the benefits amounted to some $19 billion. These came from higher winter temperatures (which saved an estimated 850 lives, reduced heating costs and diminished spring floods caused by meltwaters, and from the well-documented connection between past Niños and fewer Atlantic hurricanes. In 1998, America experienced no big Atlantic hurricanes and thus avoided huge losses. These benefits were not reported as widely as the losses.

The fourth factor is poor individual perception. People worry that the endless rise in the amount of stuff everyone throws away will cause the world to run out of places to dispose of waste. Yet, even if America's trash output continues to rise as it has done in the past, and even if the American population doubles by 2100, all the rubbish America produces through the entire 21st century will still take up only the area of a square, each of whose sides measures 28 km (18 miles). That is just one-12,000th of the area of the entire United States.

Ignorance matters only when it leads to faulty judgments. But fear of largely imaginary environmental problems can divert political energy from dealing with real ones. The table, showing the cost in the United States of various measures to save a year of a person's life, illustrates the danger. Some environmental policies, such as reducing lead in petrol and sulphur-dioxide emissions from fuel oil, are very cost-effective. But many of these are already in place. Most environmental measures are less cost-effective than interventions aimed at improving safety (such as installing air-bags in cars) and those involving medical screening and vaccination. Some are absurdly expensive.

Table 1

The Price of a Life

Cost of saving one year of one person's life – 1993$

Passing laws to make seat-belt use mandatory	69
Sickle-cell anaemia screening for black new-borns	240
Mammography for women aged 50	810
Pneumonia vaccination for people aged over 65	2,000
Giving advice on stopping smoking to people who smoke more than one packet a day	9,800
Putting men aged 30 on a low-cholesterol diet	19,000
Regular leisure-time physical activity, such as jogging for men aged 35	38,000
Making pedestrians and cyclists more visible	73,000
Installing air-bags (rather than manual lap belts) in cars	120,000
Installing arsenic emission-control at glass-manufacturing plants	51,000,000
Setting radiation emission standards for nuclear-power plants	180,000,000
Installing benzene emission control at rubber-tyre manufacturing plants	20,000,000,000

Source: T. Tengs et al, *Risk Analysis*, June 1995

Yet a false perception of risk may be about to lead to errors more expensive even than controlling the emission of benzene at tyre plants. Carbon-dioxide emissions are causing the planet to warm. The best estimates are that the temperature will rise by some 2°-3°C in this century, causing considerable problems, almost exclusively in the developing world, at a total cost of $5,000 billion. Getting rid of global warming would thus seem to be a good idea. The question is whether the cure will actually be more costly than ailment.

Despite the intuition that something drastic needs to be done about such a costly problem, economic analyses clearly show that it will be far more expensive to cut carbon-dioxide emissions radically than to pay the costs of adaptation to the increased temperatures. The effect of the Kyoto Protocol on the climate would be minuscule, even if it were implemented in full. A model by Tom Wigley, one of the main authors of the reports of the UN Climate Change Panel, shows how an expected temperature increase of 2.1°C in 2100 would be diminished by the treaty to an increase of 1.9°C instead. Or, to put it another way, the temperature increase that the planet would have experienced in 2094 would be postponed to 2100.

So the Kyoto agreement does not prevent global warming, but merely buys the world six years. Yet, the cost of Kyoto, for the United States alone, will be higher than the cost of solving the world's single most pressing health problems: providing universal access to clean drinking water and sanitation. Such measures would avoid 2m deaths every year, and prevent half a billion people from becoming seriously ill.

And that is the best case. If the treaty were implemented inefficiently, the cost of Kyoto could approach $1 trillion, or more than five times the cost of worldwide water and sanitation coverage. For comparison, the total global-aid budget today is about $50 billion a year.

To replace the litany with facts is crucial if people want to make the best possible decisions for the future. Of course, rational environmental management and environmental investment are good ideas—but the costs and benefits of such investments should be compared to those of similar investments in all the other important areas of human endeavour. It may be costly to be overly optimistic—but more costly still to be too pessimistic.

POSTSCRIPT

Is Mankind Dangerously Harming the Environment?

Though a number of works (see below) support Lomborg's argument, his evidence has come under heavy attack (see Richard C. Bell, "How Did *The Skeptical Environmentalist* Pull the Wool Over the Eyes of So Many Editors?" *WorldWatch* [March–April 2002] and *Scientific American* [January 2002]). The issue of the state of the environment and prospects for the future have been hotly debated for over 30 years with little chance of ending soon. Two key issues are the potential impacts of global warming and the net effects of future agricultural technologies, which will be used to feed growing populations with richer diets. On the former, see Douglas Long, *Global Warming* (Facts on File, 2004); Robert Hunter, *Thermageddon: Countdown to 2030* (Arcade Pub., 2003); and the journal *The Ecologist* (March 2002). Ronald Bailey and others debunk the global warming "scare" in his edited book, *Global Warming and Other Eco-Myths: How the Environmental Movement Uses False Science to Scare Us to Death* (Prima, 2002). On agricultural technologies, see Vaclav Smil, *Feeding the World: A Challenge for the Twenty-First Century* (MIT Press, 2000).

Paul R. Ehrlich and Anne H. Ehrlich wrote *Betrayal of Science and Reason: How Anti-Environmental Rhetoric Threatens Our Future* (Island Press, 1996) to refute statements by those who do not agree with the messages of the concerned environmentalists. Julian Lincoln Simon counters with *Hoodwinking the Nation* (Transaction, 1999). For a debate on this issue see Norman Myers and Julian L. Simon, *Scarcity or Abundance? A Debate on the Environment* (W. W. Norton, 1994).

Publications that are optimistic about the availability of resources and the health of the environment include Ronald Bailey, ed., *The True State of the Planet* (Free Press, 1995) and Gregg Easterbrook, *A Moment on the Earth: The Coming Age of Environmental Optimism* (Viking, 1995). Publications by some who believe that population growth and human interventions in the environment have dangerous consequences for the future of mankind include Joseph Wayne Smith, Graham Lyons, and Gary Sauer-Thompson, *Healing a Wounded World* (Praeger, 1997); Douglas E. Booth, *The Environmental Consequences of Growth* (Routledge, 1998); and Kirill Kondratyev et al. *Stability of Life on Earth: Principal Subject of Scientific Research in the 21st Century* (Springer 2004); and James Gustive Speth, *Red Sky at Morning: America and the Crisis of the Global Environment* (Yale University Press, 2004).

Several works relate environmental problems to very severe political, social, and economic problems, including Michael Renner, *Fighting for Survival* (W. W. Norton, 1996); Michael N. Dobkowski and Isidor Wallimann, eds., *The Coming Age of Scarcity: Preventing Mass Death and Genocide in the Twenty-First*

Century (Syracuse University Press, 1998); and one with a long timeframe, Sing C. Chew, *World Ecological Degradation: Accumulation, Urbanization, and Deforestation, 3000BC–AD2000* (Roman and Littlefield, 2001). An important series of publications on environmental problems is by the Worldwatch Institute, including two annuals: *State of the World* and *Vital Signs*.

ISSUE 20

Is Globalization Good for Mankind?

YES: Murray Weidenbaum, from "Globalization Is Not a Dirty Word: Dispelling the Myth About the Global Economy," *Vital Speeches of the Day* (March 1, 2001)

NO: Herman E. Daly, from "Globalization and Its Discontents," *Philosophy & Public Policy Quarterly* (Spring/Summer 2001)

ISSUE SUMMARY

YES: Murray Weidenbaum, chairman of the Weidenbaum Center at Washington University in St. Louis, argues that economic globalization benefits all countries that participate in world markets. Globalization produces more jobs than it eliminates, he contends, both for the world and for the United States.

NO: Herman E. Daly, professor at the School of Public Affairs at the University of Maryland, does not object to international trade and relations, but he does object to globalization that erases national boundaries and hurts workers and the environment.

A really big issue of today is globalization, which stands for worldwide processes, activities, and institutions. It involves world markets, world finance, world communications, world media, world religions, world popular culture, world rights movements, world drug trade, etc. The focus of most commentators is on the world economy, which many believe promises strong growth in world wealth. Critics focus on the world economy's negative impacts on workers' wages, environmental protections and regulations, and national and local cultures. Many say that it is easy for Americans to feel positive toward globalization because America and its businesses, media, and culture are at the center of the globalized world, which ensures that America gains more than its proportional share of the benefits. But the real debate is whether or not globalization benefits all mankind. When the whole world is considered, there may be far more minuses to be weighed against the pluses. It is hard to settle this debate because so many different dimensions that are incomparable must be included in the calculation of the cost-benefit ratio.

The concept of globalization forces us to think about many complicated issues at the same time. There are technological, economic, political, cultural, and ethical aspects of globalization. Technological developments make possible the communication, transportation, coordination, and organization that make economic globalization possible. Political factors have made this a relatively free global economy. Restrictions on trade and production have been greatly reduced, and competition has greatly increased. The results have been increased production and wealth and celebration in financial circles. But competition creates losers as well as winners, so peoples throughout the world are protesting and resisting economic globalization. Many are also resisting cultural globalization because their own cultures are threatened. They feel that the global culture is materialistic, sexualized, secular, and egocentric—and they may be right. But many also consider the strengths of the global culture, such as championing human rights, democracy, and justice.

In the selections that follow, Murray Weidenbaum reports on the benefits of the global economy by arguing against what he calls "dangerous myths" that are used to critique economic globalization. He asserts that globalization produces more jobs than it replaces. Herman E. Daly opposes globalization and favors the alternative of internationalization. Both involve the increasing importance of relations among nations, but globalization erases national boundaries while internationalization does not. The negative effects of globalization, he states, are standards-lowering competition, an increased tolerance of mergers and monopoly power, intense national specialization, and the excessive monopolization of knowledge as "intellectual property."

Murray Weidenbaum

 **YES**

Globalization Is Not a Dirty Word

Delivered to the Economic Club of Detroit, Detroit, Michigan, January 22, 2001

Today I want to deal with a perplexing conundrum facing the United States: this is a time when the American business system is producing unparalleled levels of prosperity, yet private enterprise is under increasing attack. The critics are an unusual alliance of unions, environmentalists, and human rights groups and they are focusing on the overseas activities of business. In many circles, globalization has become a dirty word.

How can we respond in a constructive way? In my interaction with these interest groups, I find that very often their views arise from basic mis-understandings of the real world of competitive enterprise. I have identified ten myths about the global economy—dangerous myths—which need to be dispelled. Here they are:

1. Globalization costs jobs.
2. The United States is an island of free trade in a world of protectionism.
3. Americans are hurt by imports.
4. U.S. companies are running away, especially to low-cost areas overseas.
5. American companies doing business overseas take advantage of local people, especially in poor countries. They also pollute their environments.
6. The trade deficit is hurting our economy and we should eliminate it.
7. It's not fair to run such large trade deficits with China or Japan.
8. Sanctions work. So do export controls.
9. Trade agreements should be used to raise environmental and labor standards around the world.
10. America's manufacturing base is eroding in the face of unfair global competition.

That's an impressive array of frequently heard charges and they are polluting our political environment. Worse yet, these widely held myths fly in the face of the facts. I'd like to take up each of them and knock them down.

1. Globalization Costs Jobs

This is a time when the American job miracle is the envy of the rest of the world, so it is hard to take that charge seriously. Yet some people do fall for it. The facts are clear: U.S. employment is at a record high and unemployment is at a 30 year low. Moreover, the United States created more than 20 million new jobs between 1993 and 2000, far more than Western Europe and Japan combined. Contrary to a widely held view, most of those new jobs pay well, often better than the average for existing jobs.

Of course, in the best of times, some people lose their jobs or their businesses fail, and that happens today. However, most researchers who have studied this question conclude that, in the typical case, technological progress, not international trade, is the main reason for making old jobs obsolete. Of course, at the same time far more new jobs are created to take their place.

2. The United States Is an Island of Free Trade in a World of Protectionism

Do other nations erect trade barriers? Of course they do—although the trend has been to cut back these obstacles to commerce. But our hands are not as clean as we like to think. There is no shortage of restrictions on importers trying to ship their products into this country. These exceptions to free trade come in all shapes, sizes, and varieties. They are imposed by federal, state, and local governments. U.S. import barriers include the following and more:

Buy-American laws give preference in government procurement to domestic producers. Many states and localities show similar favoritism. Here in Michigan, preference is given to in-state printing firms; the Jones Act prohibits foreign ships from engaging in waterborne commerce between U.S. ports;

many statutes limit the import of specific agricultural and manufactured products, ranging from sugar to pillowcases;

we impose selective high tariffs on specific items, notably textiles; and many state and local regulatory barriers, such as building codes, are aimed at protecting domestic producers.

It's strange that consumer groups and consumer activists are mute on this subject. After all, it is the American consumer who has to pay higher prices as a result of all of this special interest legislation. But these barriers to trade ultimately are disappointing. Nations open to trade grow faster than those that are closed.

3. Americans Are Hurt by Imports

The myth that imports are bad will be quickly recognized by students of economics as the mercantilist approach discredited by Adam Smith over two centuries ago. The fact is that we benefit from imports in many ways. Consumers get access to a wider array of goods and services. Domestic companies obtain lower cost components and thus are more competitive. We get access to vital metals and minerals that are just not found in the United States. Also, imports prod our own producers to improve productivity and invest in developing new technology.

I'll present a painful example. By the way, I have never bought a foreign car. But we all know how the quality of our domestic autos has improved because of foreign competition. More recently, we had a striking example of the broader benefits to imports. In 1997–98 the expanded flow of lower-cost products from Asia kept inflation low here at a time when otherwise the Fed could have been raising interest rates to fight inflation. The result would have been a weaker economy. Moreover, in a full employment economy, imports enable the American people to enjoy a higher living standard than would be possible if sales were limited to domestic production.

In our interconnected economy, the fact is that the jobs "lost" from imports are quickly replaced by jobs elsewhere in the economy—either in export industries or in companies selling domestically. The facts are fascinating: the sharp run-up in U.S. imports in recent years paralleled the rapid growth in total U.S. employment. Both trends, of course, reflected the underlying health of our business economy.

The special importance of imports was recently highlighted by the director of the Washington State Council on International Trade: "The people who benefit most critically are families at the lower end of the wage scale who have school-age children and those elderly who must live frugally." She goes on to conclude: "It is a cruel deception that an open system of the free trade is not good for working people."

4. U.S. Companies Are Running Away Especially to Low Cost Areas Overseas

Right off the bat, the critics have the direction wrong. The flow of money to buy and operate factories and other businesses is overwhelmingly into the United States. We haven't had a net outflow of investment since the 1960s. That's the flip side of our trade deficit. Financing large trade deficits means that far more investment capital comes into this country than is leaving.

But let us examine the overseas investments by American companies. The largest proportion goes not to poor countries, but to the most developed nations, those with high labor costs and also high environmental standards. The primary motive is to gain access to markets. That's not too surprising when we consider that the people in the most industrially advanced nations are the best customers for sophisticated American products. By the way, only one-third of the exports by the foreign branches of U.S. companies goes to the United States. About 70 percent goes to other markets, primarily to the industrialized nations.

Turning to American investments in Mexico, China, and other developing countries, the result often is to enhance U.S. domestic competitiveness and job opportunities. This is so because many of these overseas factories provide low-cost components and material to U.S.-based producers who are thus able to improve their international competitiveness.

In some cases, notably the pharmaceutical industry, the overseas investments are made in countries with more enlightened regulatory regimes, such as the Netherlands. "More enlightened" is not a euphemism for lower standards. The Dutch maintain a strong but more modern regulatory system than we do.

5. American Companies Doing Business Overseas Take Advantage of Local People and Pollute Their Environments

There are always exceptions. But by and large, American-owned and managed factories in foreign countries are top-of-the-line in terms of both better working conditions and higher environmental standards than locally-owned firms. This is why so many developing countries compete enthusiastically for the overseas location of U.S. business activities—and why so many local workers seek jobs at the American factories. After all, American companies manufacturing overseas frequently follow the same high operating standards that they do here at home.

I serve on a panel of Americans who investigate the conditions in some factories in China. I wish the critics could see for themselves the differences between the factories that produce for an American company under its worldwide standards and those that are not subject to our truly enlightened sense of social responsibility.

I'll give you a very personal example of the second category of facilities. While making an inspection tour, I tore my pants on an unguarded piece of equipment in one of those poorly-lit factories. An inch closer and that protruding part would have dug into my thigh. I also had to leave the factory floor every hour or so to breathe some fresh air. When I said that, in contrast, the American-owned factories were top-of-the-line, that wasn't poetry.

Yes, foreign investment is essential to the economic development of poor countries. By definition, they lack the capability to finance growth. The critics do those poor countries no favor when they try to discourage American firms from investing there. The critics forget that, during much of the nineteenth century, European investors financed many of our canals, railroads, steel mills, and other essentials for becoming an industrialized nation. It is sad to think where the United States would be today if Europe in the nineteenth century had had an array of powerful interest groups that were so suspicious of economic progress.

6. The Trade Deficit Is Hurting Our Economy and We Should Eliminate It

Yes, the U.S. trade deficit is at a record high. But it is part of a "virtuous circle" in our economy. The trade deficit mainly reflects the widespread prosperity in the United States, which is substantially greater than in most of the countries we trade with. After all, a strong economy, such as ours operating so close to full employment and full capacity, depends on a substantial amount of imports to satisfy our demands for goods and services. Our exports are lower primarily because the demand for imports by other nations is much weaker.

The acid test is that our trade deficit quickly declines in the years when our economy slows down and that deficit rises again when the economy perks up. Serious studies show that, if the United States had deliberately tried to curb the trade deficit in the 1990s, the result would have been a weak economy with high inflation and fewer jobs. The trade deficit is a byproduct of economic performance. It should not become a goal of economic policy.

There is a constructive way of reducing the trade deficit. To most economists, the persistence of our trade imbalance (and especially of the related and more comprehensive current account deficit) is due to the fact that we do not generate enough domestic saving to finance domestic investment. The gap between such saving and investment is equal to the current account deficit.

Nobel laureate Milton Friedman summed up this point very clearly: "The remarkable performance of the United States economy in the past few years would have been impossible without the inflow of foreign capital, which is a mirror image of large balance of payments deficits."

The positive solution is clear: increase the amount that Americans save. Easier said than done, of course. The shift from budget deficits (dissaving) to budget surpluses (government saving) helps. A further shift to a tax system that does not hit saving as hard as ours does would also help. The United States taxes saving more heavily than any other advanced industrialized nation. Replacing the income tax with a consumption tax, even a progressive one, would surely be in order—but that deserves to be the subject of another talk.

7. It's Not Fair to Run Such Large Trade Deficits With China or Japan

Putting the scary rhetoric aside, there really is no good reason for any two countries to have balanced trade between them. We don't have to search for sinister causes for our trade deficits with China or Japan. Bilateral trade imbalances exist for many benign reasons, such as differences in per capita incomes and in the relative size of the two economies. One of the best kept secrets of international trade is that the average Japanese buys more U.S. goods than the average American buys Japanese goods. Yes, Japan's per capita imports from the United States are larger than our per capita imports from Japan ($539 versus $432 in 1996). We have a large trade deficit with them because we have more "capita" (population).

8. Sanctions Work, So Do Export Controls

It is ironic that so many people who worry about the trade deficit simultaneously support sanctions and export controls. There is practically no evidence that unilateral sanctions are effective in getting other nations to change their policies or actions. Those restrictions on trade do, however, have an impact: they backfire. U.S. business, labor, and agriculture are harmed. We lost an overseas market for what is merely a symbolic gesture. Sanctions often are evaded. Shipping goods through third countries can disguise the ultimate recipient in the nation on which the sanctions are imposed. On balance, these sanctions reduced American exports in 1995 by an estimated $15–20 billion.

As for export controls, where American producers do not have a monopoly on a particular technology—which is frequent—producers in other nations can deliver the same technology or product without the handicap imposed on U.S. companies. A recent report at the Center for the Study of American Business showed that many business executives believe that sanctions and export controls are major obstacles to the expansion of U.S. foreign trade.

9. Trade Agreements Should Be Used to Raise Environmental and Labor Standards Around the World

At first blush, this sounds like such a nice and high-minded way of doing good. But, as a practical matter, it is counterproductive to try to impose such costly social regulations on developing countries as a requirement for doing business with them. The acid test is that most developing nations oppose these trade restrictions. They see them for what they really are—a disguised form of protectionism designed to keep their relatively low-priced goods out of the markets of the more advanced, developed nations. All that feeds the developing nations' sense of cynicism toward us.

In the case of labor standards, there is an existing organization, the International Labor Organization [ILO], which has been set up to deal specifically with these matters. Of all the international organizations, the ILO is unique in having equal representation from business, labor, and government. The United States and most other nations *are* members. The ILO is where issues of labor standards should be handled. To be taken more seriously, the United States should support the ILO more vigorously than it has.

As for environmental matters, we saw at the unsuccessful meetings on climate change at the Hague [recently] how difficult it is to get broad international agreement on environmental issues even in sympathetic meetings of an international environmental agency. To attempt to tie such controversial environmental matters to trade agreements arouses my suspicions about the intent of the sponsors. It is hard to avoid jumping to the conclusion that the basic motivation is to prevent progress on the trade front.

I still recall the signs carried by one of the protesters in Seattle, "Food is for people, not for export." Frankly, it's hard to deal with such an irrational position. After all, if the United States did not export a major part of its abundant farm output, millions of people overseas would be starving or malnourished. Also, thousands of our farmers would go broke.

The most effective way to help developing countries improve their working conditions and environmental protection is to trade with and invest in them. As for the charge that companies invest in poor, developing nations in order to minimize their environmental costs, studies of the issue show that environmental factors are not important influences in business location decisions. As I pointed out earlier, most U.S. overseas direct investment goes to developed nations with high labor costs and also high environmental standards.

10. America's Manufacturing Base Is Eroding in the Face of Unfair Global Competition

Unfortunately, some of our fellow citizens seem to feel that the only fair form of foreign competition is the kind that does not succeed in landing any of their goods on our shores. But to get to the heart of the issue, there is no factual basis for the charge that our manufacturing base is eroding—or even stagnant. The official statistics are reporting record highs in output year after year. Total industrial production in the United States today is 45 percent higher than in 1992—that's not in dollars, but in terms of real output.

Of course, not all industries or companies go up—or down—in unison. Some specific industries, especially low-tech, have had to cut back. But simultaneously, other industries, mainly high-tech, have been expanding rapidly. Such changes are natural and to be expected in an open, dynamic economy. By the way, the United States regularly runs a trade surplus in high-tech products.

It's important to understand the process at work here. Technological progress generates improved industrial productivity. In the United States, that means to some degree fewer blue-collar jobs and more while-collar jobs. That is hardly a recent development. The shift from physical labor to knowledge workers has been the trend since the beginning of the 20th century. On balance, as I noted earlier, total U.S. employment is at an all-time high.

If you have any doubt about the importance of rising productivity to our society, just consider where we would be if over the past century agriculture had not enjoyed rising productivity (that is, more output per worker/hour). Most of us would still be farmers.

It is vital that we correct the erroneous views of the anti-globalists. Contrary-to their claims, our open economy has raised living standards and helped to contain inflation. International commerce is more important to our economy today than at any time in the past. By dollar value and volume, the United States is the world's largest trading nation. We are the largest importer, exporter, foreign investor, and host to foreign investment. Trying to stop the global economy is futile and contrary to America's self-interest.

Nevertheless, we must recognize that globalization, like any other major change, generates costs as well as benefits. It is essential to address these consequences. Otherwise, we will not be able to maintain a national consensus that responds to the challenges of the world marketplace by focusing on opening markets instead of closing them. The challenge to all of us is to urge courses of action that help those who are hurt without doing far more harm to the much larger number who benefit from the international marketplace.

We need to focus more attention on those who don't share the benefits of the rapid pace of economic change. Both private and public efforts should be increased to provide more effective adjustment assistance to those who lose their jobs. The focus of adjustment policy should not be on providing relief from economic change, but on positive approaches that help more of our people participate in economic prosperity.

As you may know, I recently chaired a bipartisan commission established by Congress to deal with the trade deficit. Our commission included leaders of business and labor, former senior government officials, and academics. We could not agree on all the issues that we dealt with. But we were unanimous in concluding that the most fundamental part of an effective long-run trade adjustment policy is to do a much better job of educating and training. More Americans should be given the opportunity to become productive and highwage members of the nation's workforce.

No, I'm not building up to a plea to donate to the college of your choice, although that's a pretty good idea.

Even though I teach at major research universities—and strongly believe in their vital mission—let me make a plea for greater attention to our junior colleges. They are an overlooked part of the educational system. Junior colleges have a key role to play. Many of these community oriented institutions of learning are now organized to specially meet the needs of displaced workers, including those who need to brush up on their basic language and math skills. In some cases, these community colleges help people launch new businesses, especially in areas where traditional manufacturing is declining. A better trained and more productive workforce is the key to our long-term international competitiveness. That is the most effective way of resisting the calls for economic isolationism.

Let me leave you with a final thought. The most powerful benefit of the global economy is not economic at all, even though it involves important economic and business activities. By enabling more people to use modern technology to communicate across traditional national boundaries, the international marketplace makes possible more than an accelerated flow of data. The worldwide marketplace encourages a far greater exchange of the most powerful of all factors of production—new ideas. That process enriches and empowers the individual in ways never before possible.

As an educator, I take this as a challenge to educate the anti-globalists to the great harm that would result from a turn to economic isolationism. For the twenty-first century, the global flow of information is the endless frontier.

Herman E. Daly  **NO**

Globalization and Its Discontents

Every day, newspaper articles and television reports insist that those who oppose globalization must be isolationists or—even worse—xenophobes. This judgment is nonsense. The relevant alternative to globalization is internationalization, which is neither isolationist nor xenophobic. Yet it is impossible to recognize the cogency of this alternative if one does not properly distinguish these two terms.

"Internalization" refers to the increasing importance of relations among nations. Although the basic unit of community and policy remains the nation, increasingly trade, treaties, alliances, protocols, and other formal agreements and communications are necessary elements for nations to thrive. "Globalization" refers to global economic integration of many formerly national economies into one global economy. Economic integration is made possible by free trade—especially by free capital mobility—and by easy or uncontrolled migration. In contrast to internationalization, which simply recognizes that nations increasingly rely on understandings among one another, globalization is the effective erasure of national boundaries for economic purposes. National boundaries become totally porous with respect to goods and capital, and ever more porous with respect to people, who are simply viewed as cheap labor—or in some cases as cheap human capital.

In short, globalization is the economic integration of the globe. But exactly what is "integration"? The word derives from *integer*, meaning one, complete, or whole. Integration means much more than "interdependence"—it is the act of combining separate although related units into a single whole. Since there can be only one whole, only one unity with reference to which parts are integrated, it follows that global economic integration logically implies national economic *dis*integration—parts are torn out of their national context (dis-integrated), in order to be re-integrated into the new whole, the globalized economy.

As the saying goes, to make an omelet you have to break some eggs. The disintegration of the national egg is necessary to integrate the global omelet. But this obvious logic, as well as the cost of disintegration, is frequently met with denial. This article argues that globalization is neither inevitable nor to be embraced, much less celebrated. Acceptance of globalization entails several serious consequences, namely, standards-lowering

From Herman E. Daly, "Globalization and Its Discontents," *Philosophy & Public Policy Quarterly*, vol. 21, no. 2/3 (Spring/Summer 2001). Copyright © 2001 by The Institute for Philosophy & Public Policy. Reprinted by permission.

competition, an increased tolerance of mergers and monopoly power, intense national specialization, and the excessive monopolization of knowledge as "intellectual property." This article discusses these likely consequences, and concludes by advocating the adoption of internationalization, and not globalization.

The Inevitability of Globalization?

Some accept the inevitability of globalization and encourage others in the faith. With admirable clarity, honesty, and brevity, Renato Ruggiero, former director-general of the World Trade Organization, insists that "We are no longer writing the rules of interaction among separate national economies. We are writing the constitution of a single global economy." His sentiments clearly affirm globalization and reject internationalization as above defined. Further, those who hold Ruggiero's view also subvert the charter of the Bretton Woods institutions. Named after a New Hampshire resort where representatives of forty-four nations met in 1944 to design the world's post–World War II economic order, the institutions conceived at the Bretton Woods International Monetary Conference include the World Bank and the International Monetary Fund. The World Trade Organization evolved later, but functions as a third sister to the World Bank and the International Monetary Fund. The nations at the conference considered proposals by the U.S., U.K., and Canadian governments, and developed the "Bretton Woods system," which established a stable international environment through such policies as fixed exchange rates, currency convertibility, and provision for orderly exchange rate adjustments. The Bretton Woods Institutions were designed to facilitate *internationalization, not globalization,* a point ignored by director-general Ruggiero.

The World Bank, along with its sister institutions, seems to have lost sight of its mission. After the disruption of its meetings in Washington, D.C. in April 2000, the World Bank sponsored an Internet discussion on globalization. The closest the World Bank came to offering a definition of the subject under discussion was the following: "The most common core sense of economic globalization . . . surely refers to the observation that in recent years a quickly rising share of economic activity in the world seems to be taking place between people who live in different countries (rather than in the same country)." This ambiguous description was not improved upon by Mr. Wolfensohn, president of the World Bank, who told the audience at a subsequent Aspen Institute Conference that "Globalization is a practical methodology for empowering the poor to improve their lives." That is neither a definition nor a description—it is a wish. Further, this wish also flies in the face of the real consequences of global economic integration. One could only sympathize with demonstrators protesting Mr. Wolfensohn's speech some fifty yards from the Aspen conference facility. The reaction of the Aspen elite was to accept as truth the title of Mr. Wolfensohn's speech, "Making Globalization Work for the Poor," and then ask in grieved tones, "How could anyone demonstrate against *that?*"

Serious consequences flow from the World Banks' lack of precision in defining globalization but lauding it nonetheless. For one thing, the so-called definition of globalization conflates the concept with that of internalization. As a result, one cannot reasonably address a crucial question: Should these increasing transactions between people living in different countries take place *across national boundaries* that are economically significant, or *within an integrated world* in which national boundaries are economically meaningless?

The ambiguous understanding of globalization deprives citizens of the opportunity to decide whether they are willing to abandon national monetary and fiscal policy, as well as the minimum wage. One also fails to carefully consider whether economic integration entails political and cultural integration. In short, will political communities and cultural traditions wither away, subsumed under some monolithic economic imperative? Although one might suspect economic integration would lead to political integration, it is hard to decide which would be worse—an economically integrated world *with,* or *without,* political integration. Everyone recognizes the desirability of community for the world as a whole—but one can conceive of two very different models of world community: (1) a federated community of real national communities (internationalization), versus (2) a cosmopolitan direct membership in a single abstract global community (globalization). However, at present our confused conversations about globalization deprive us of the opportunity to reflect deeply on these very different possibilities.

This article has suggested that at present organizations such as the International Monetary Fund and the World Bank (and, by extension, the World Trade Organization) no longer serve the interests of their member nations as defined in their charters. Yet if one asks whose interests are served, we are told they service the interests of the integrated "global economy." If one tries to glimpse a concrete reality behind that grand abstraction, however, one can find no individual workers, peasants, or small businessmen represented, but only giant fictitious individuals, the transnational corporations. In globalization, power is drained away from national communities and local enterprises, and aggregates in transnational corporations.

The Consequences of Globalization

Globalization—the erasure of national boundaries for economic purposes—risks serious consequences. Briefly, they include, first of all, standards-lowering competition to externalize social and environmental costs with the goal of achievement of a competitive advantage. This results, in effect, in a race to the bottom so far as efficiency in cost accounting and equity in income distribution are concerned. Globalization also risks increased tolerance of mergers and monopoly power in domestic markets in order that corporations become big enough to compete internationally. Third, globalization risks more intense national specialization according to the dictates of competitive advantage. Such specialization reduces the range of choice of ways to earn a livelihood, and increases dependence on other countries. Finally, worldwide enforcement of a muddled and self-serving doctrine of "trade-related intellectual property rights" is a direct contradiction of the Jeffersonian dictum that "knowledge is the common property of mankind."

Each of these risks of globalization deserves closer scrutiny.

1. Standards-lowering competition   Globalization undercuts the ability of nations to internalize environmental and social costs into prices. Instead, economic integration under free market conditions promotes standards-lowering competition—a race to the bottom, in short. The country that does the poorest job of internalizing all social and environmental costs of production into its prices gets a competitive advantage in international trade. The external social and environmental costs are left to be borne by the population at large. Further, more of world production shifts to countries that do the poorest job of counting costs—a sure recipe for reducing the efficiency of global production. As uncounted, externalized costs increase, the positive correlation between gross domestic product (GDP) growth and welfare disappears, or even becomes negative. We enter a world foreseen by the nineteenth-century social critic John Ruskin, who observed that "that which seems to be wealth is in verity but a gilded index of far-reaching ruin."

Another dimension of the race to the bottom is that globalization fosters increasing inequality in the distribution of income in high-wage countries, such as the U.S. Historically, in the U.S. there has been an implicit social contract established to ameliorate industrial strife between labor and capital. As a consequence, the distribution of income between labor and capital has been considered more equal and just in the U.S. compared to the world as a whole. However, global integration of markets necessarily abrogates that social contract. U.S. wages would fall drastically because labor is relatively more abundant globally than nationally. Further, returns to capital in the U.S. would increase because capital is relatively more scarce globally than nationally. Although one could make the theoretical argument that wages would be *bid up* in the rest of the world, the increase would be so small as to be insignificant. Making such an argument from the relative numbers would be analogous to insisting that, theoretically, when I jump off a ladder gravity not only pulls me to the earth, but also moves the earth towards me. This technical point offers cold comfort to anyone seeking a softer landing.

2. Increased tolerance of mergers and monopoly power   Fostering global competitive advantage is used as an excuse for tolerance of corporate mergers and monopoly in national markets. Chicago School economist and Nobel laureate Ronald Coase, in his classic article on the theory of the firm, suggests that corporate entities are "islands of central planning in a sea of market relationships." The islands of central planning become larger and larger relative to the remaining sea of market relationships as a result of merger. More and more resources are allocated by within-firm central planning, and less by between-firm market relationships. Corporations are the victor, and the market principle is the loser, as governments lose the strength to regulate corporate capital and maintain competitive markets in the public interest. Of the hundred largest economic organizations, fifty-two are corporations and forty-eight are nations. The distribution of income within these centrally-planned corporations has become much more concentrated. The ratio of the salary of the Chief Executive Officer to the average employee has passed 400 (as one would expect, since chief central planners set their own salaries).

3. Intense national specialization   Free trade and free capital mobility increase pressures for specialization in order to gain or maintain a competitive advantage. As a consequence, globalization demands that workers accept an ever-narrowing range of ways to earn a livelihood. In Uruguay, for example, everyone would have to be either a shepherd or a cowboy to conform to the dictates of competitive advantage in the global market. Everything else should be imported in exchange for beef, mutton, wool, and leather. Any Uruguayan who wants to play in a symphony orchestra or be an airline pilot should emigrate.

Of course, most people derive as much satisfaction from how they earn their income as from how they spend it. Narrowing that range of choice is a welfare loss uncounted by trade theorists. Globalization assumes either that emigration and immigration are costless, or that narrowing the range of occupational choice within a nation is costless. Both assumptions are false.

While trade theorists ignore the range of choice in *earning* one's income, they at the same time exaggerate the welfare effects of range of choice in *spending* that income. For example, the U.S. imports Danish butter cookies and Denmark imports U.S. butter cookies. Although the gains from trading such similar commodities cannot be great, trade theorists insist that the welfare of cookie connoisseurs is increased by expanding the range of consumer choice to the limit.

Perhaps, but one wonders whether those gains might be realized more cheaply by simply trading recipes? Although one would think so, *recipes*— trade-related intellectual property rights—are the one thing that free traders really want to protect.

4. Intellectual property rights   Of all things, knowledge is that which should be most freely shared, since in sharing, knowledge is multiplied rather than divided. Yet trade theorists have rejected Thomas Jefferson's dictum that "Knowledge is the common property of mankind" and instead have accepted a muddled doctrine of "trade-related intellectual property rights." This notion of rights grants private corporations monopoly ownership of the very basis of life itself—patents to seeds (including the patent-protecting, life-denying terminator gene) and to knowledge of basic genetic structures.

The argument offered to support this grab is that, without the economic incentive of monopoly ownership, little new knowledge and innovation will be forthcoming. Yet, so far as I know, James Watson and Francis Crick, co-discoverers of the structure of DNA, do not share in the patent royalties reaped by their successors. Nor of course did Gregor Mendel get any royalties—but then he was a monk motivated by mere curiosity about how Creation works!

Once knowledge exists, its proper price is the marginal opportunity cost of sharing it, which is close to zero, since nothing is lost by sharing knowledge. Of course, one does lose the *monopoly* on that knowledge, but then economists have traditionally argued that monopoly is inefficient as well as unjust because it creates an artificial scarcity of the monopolized item.

Certainly, the cost of production of new knowledge is not zero, even though the cost of sharing it is. This allows biotech corporations to claim that they deserve a fifteen- or twenty-year monopoly for the expenses incurred in research and development. Although corporations deserve to profit from their efforts, they are not entitled to monopolize on Watson and Crick's contribution—without which they could do nothing—or on the contributions of Gregor Mendel and all the great scientists of the past who made fundamental discoveries. As early twentieth-century economist Joseph Schumpeter emphasized, being the first with an innovation already gives one the advantage of novelty, a natural temporary monopoly, which in his view was the major source of profit in a competitive economy.

As the great Swiss economist, Jean Sismondi, argued over two centuries ago, not all new knowledge is of benefit to humankind. We need a sieve to select beneficial knowledge. Perhaps the worse selective principle is hope for private monetary gain. A much better selective motive for knowledge is a search in hopes of benefit to our fellows. This is not to say that we should abolish all intellectual property rights—that would create more problems than it would solve. But we should certainly begin restricting the domain and length of patent monopolies rather than increasing them so rapidly and recklessly. We should also become much more willing to share knowledge. Shared knowledge increases the productivity of all labor, capital, and resources. Further, international development aid should consist far more of freely-shared knowledge, and far less of foreign investment and interest-bearing loans.

Let me close with my favorite quote from John Maynard Keynes, one of the founders of the recently subverted Bretton Woods Institutions:

> I sympathize therefore, with those who would minimize, rather than those who would maximize, economic entanglement between nations. Ideas, knowledge, art, hospitality, travel—these are the things which should of their nature be international. But let goods be homespun whenever it is reasonably and conveniently possible; and, above all, let finance be primarily national.

POSTSCRIPT

Is Globalization Good for Mankind?

Weidenbaum's argument in favor of economic globalization emphasizes the economic benefits it produces. He maintains that even groups that expect to be economically hurt by globalization will benefit from it. Daly, however, believes that the economy is inexorably connected to culture and politics. He therefore asks, "Will political communities and cultural traditions wither away, subsumed under some monolithic economic imperative?" Economic integration will spawn greater political integration and cultural integration, he concludes, theorizing that in globalization, power is drained away from national communities and local enterprises and aggregates in transnational corporations.

There has been an explosion of books on globalization recently. A best-seller is Thomas Friedman's *The Lexus and the Olive Tree* (Farrar, Straus, Giroux, 2000), which tells the story of the new global economy and many of its ramifications. Friedman sees the United States as the nation that is best able to capitalize on that global economy, so it has the brightest future. Other works that explore the role of America in globalization include Jim Garrison, *America as Empire: Global Leader or Rogue Power?* (Berret-Koehler Publishers, 2004); *Global America?: The Cultural Consequences of Globalization,* edited by Ulrich Beck et al. (Liverpool University Press, 2003); and Will Hutton, *World We're in: A Declaration of Interdependence: Why America Should Join the World* (W.W. Norton, 2003). Works that applaud globalization include Barry Asmas, *The Best Is Yet to Come* (AmeriPress, 2001); Diane Coyle, *Paradoxes of Prosperity: Why the New Capitalism Benefits All* (Texere, 2001); John Micklethwait and Adrian Wooldridge, *Future Perfect: The Challenge and Hidden Promise of Globalization* (Crown Business, 2000); and Jacques Bandot, ed., *Building a World Community: Globalization and the Common Good* (University of Washington Press, 2001).

Attacks on globalization are prolific and include Robert Went, *Globalization: Neoliberal Challenge, Radical Responses* (Pluto Press, 2000); William K. Tabb, *The Amoral Elephant: Globalization and the Struggle for Social Justice in the Twenty-First Century* (Monthly Review Press, 2001); Walden Bello, *Future in Balance: Essays on Globalization and Resistance* (Food First Books, 2001); Vic George and Paul Wilding, *Globalization and Human Welfare* (Palgrave, 2002); Gary Teeple, *Globalization and the Decline of Social Reform* (Humanity Books, 2000); Noreena Hertz, *The Silent Takeover: Global Capitalism and the Death of Democracy* (Free Press, 2002); Alan Tomelson, *Race to the Bottom: Why a Worldwide Worker Surplus and Uncontrolled Free Trade Are Sinking American Living Standards* (Westview, 2000); and *Civilizing Globalization: A Survival Guide,* edited by Richard Sandbrook (SUNY Press, 2003).

For relatively balanced discussions of globalization see Arthur P. J. Mol, *Globalization and Environmental Reform: The Ecological Modernization of the Global Economy* (MIT Press, 2001), which points to the environmental degradation that results from globalization but also actions that retard degradation and improve environmental quality; Richard Langhome, *The Coming of Globalization: Its Evolution and Contemporary Consequences* (St. Martin's Press, 2001); Barbara Harris-White, ed., *Globalization and Insecurity: Political, Economic, and Physical Challenges* (Palgrave, 2002); Dani Rodnik, *Has Globalization Gone Too Far?* (Institute for International Economics, 1997); *Global Transformations Reader: An Introduction to the Globalization debate,* edited by David Held et al. (Policy Press, 2003); Tony Schirato and Jennifer Webb, *Understanding Globalization* (Sage, 2003); and *Globalization and Antiglobalization: Dynamics of Change in the New World,* edited by Henry Veltmeyer (Ashgate, 2004). For interesting discussions of the cultural aspects of globalization see Paul Kennedy and Catherine J. Danks, eds., *Globalization and National Identities: Crisis or Opportunity* (Palgrave, 2001); Tyler Cowen, *Creative Destruction: How Globalization Is Changing the World's Cultures* (Princeton University Press, 2002); Alison Brysk, ed., *Globalization and Human Rights* (University of California Press, 2002); and Elisabeth Madimbee-Boyi, ed., *Beyond Dichotomies: Histories, Identities, Cultures, and the Challenge of Globalization* (SUNY, 2002).

ISSUE 21

Are the Negative Consequences of Divorce on Children Substantial?

YES: James Q. Wilson, from *The Marriage Problem: How Our Culture Has Weakened Families* (HarperCollins, 2002)

NO: E. Mavis Hetherington and John Kelly, from *For Better or For Worse: Divorce Reconsidered* (W.W. Norton, 2002)

ISSUE SUMMARY

YES: Professor of management and public policy James Q. Wilson summarizes the research on the impacts of divorce, which shows that divorce has significant and long-term negative impacts on children.

NO: Developmental psychologist E. Mavis Hetherington and writer John Kelly present the results from over 30 years of research, which show that "The vast majority of young people from these families are reasonably well adjusted and are coping reasonably well in relationships with their families, friends, and intimate partners."

Currently, first marriages have a 45 percent chance of ending in divorce, and second marriages have a 60 percent chance. Clearly family life has dramatically changed in the past half-century. In 1950, divorce was shameful and difficult to attain legally. Now divorce is easy to attain, socially acceptable, and quite common. Some even say that the United States has developed a divorce culture. It is also clear that there is no going back to the time when divorce was very difficult to obtain, since most people want to be able to escape from a bad marriage. But what are the consequences of this change? More specifically, what are the impacts of divorce on the children? Divorce may solve some problems for the parents, but for the children it mainly creates problems. Everyone agrees that the children suffer, but the question is how injurious are the impacts, and how long do the negative impacts last?

The issue of the consequences of divorce on children should be examined in the larger context of the importance of marriage for society, the parents, and the children. Sociologists have known for a long time that strong families are important for strong societies and well-adjusted and productive people. Strong families help present and future generations to function better in school, in the workplace, in communities, and in other social institutions. Weak families, whether dual or single, are associated with many kinds of social costs, including the costs of more crime, interpersonal problems, and the need for more health care. Another common finding is that marriage benefits spouses. Married people have many advantages over unmarried people, including better physical and psychological health, greater happiness, more money, and many other benefits. The definitive study of this comparison by Linda J. Waite and Maggie Ghalligher puts its major finding in the title, *The Case for Marriage: Why Married People Are Happier, Healthier and Better Off Financially* (Doubleday, 2000).

Strong families also provide many benefits for children, which help them to be better adjusted and better functioning in school and later careers. In contrast, divorce worsens their functioning and increases their personal problems. As a result, children become more involved in crime, drugs, dropping out of school, poor school performance, and later in life have worse work records, more unemployment, and less successful marriages. Why is this so? Consider the experience of many children of divorce. Many are surprised by the divorce, and few are prepared for what follows. They commonly are fearful and angry. Many somehow feel responsible for the divorce. They learn from divorce that relations that they should be able to count on may be unreliable. This experience colors their subsequent relationships. Many are forced to move and leave familiar schools and close friends. They have to manage two parents in two homes and often problematic relations with the noncustodial parent. Neither parent is likely to spend as much time with them as before. As the divorced parents go on with their lives, the children must deal with their parents dating, their parents' lovers (perhaps live-in), stepfathers and stepmothers, half-brothers and sisters, and stepbrothers and stepsisters. The new stepparent may not want to be close to them and may not want them to be close to their biological parent. Some of the new arrangements work out very well, but the research shows that these are in the minority. The research also shows that they have more trouble than average forming intimate relationships as teenagers and adults.

Despite the above problems, some divorce researchers defend divorce. It enables a spouse to exit a bad marriage. Though the children of divorce are worse off on average than the children of intact families, it is not clear that this is due to the divorce or the conflict before the divorce. Researchers, therefore, differ on whether a divorce is worse for the children than a bad marriage. Obviously some divorces are good for the children, especially when the children are being abused. But how bad do marriages have to be to be worse than divorce? In the following debate, James Q. Wilson emphasizes how much divorce harms the children, and E. Mavis Hetherington and John Kelly emphasize how well most children adapt to changes resulting from divorce.

James Q. Wilson  **YES**

The Marriage Problem: How Our Culture Has Weakened Families

. . . the central question is how great a risk divorce poses for children. You might think that by now scholars would have come to some agreement on a matter of considerable national importance, but in fact there are two schools of thought. The first is that whatever harms befall children, it is not the result of the divorce but of the conflict between the parents before they divorced. The second view is that divorce harms children independently of predivorce conflict and the harm lasts a long time. The implication of the first view is that divorce is not the chief cause of any psychological harm and in fact may constitute a cure for it; the implication of the second is that society ought to do whatever it can to cut back on the rate of divorce. Of course, many scholars think that both forces are at work and they quarrel only over the emphasis that should be given to each. Let me guide you through a few of the leading studies and then suggest that the second view is gaining the upper hand.

The first view initially rested on the confident predictions by counselors and therapists that divorce was a way of solving marital problems and even liberating the child from parental tension. In fact, a divorce may make children more tolerant of others with an accompanying increase in cooperation and respect. And even if the child is hurt by the divorce, the hurt will last only briefly, especially if the financial loss to the mother and child can be set right. This claim about the advantages of divorce meant that its advocates, in Barbara Dafoe Whitehead's words, had "shifted the weight of expert opinion from protecting the interests of children to defending the rights and prerogatives of parents to pursue their own satisfactions."

The most influential writings about divorce asserted that it was marital conflict, not divorce itself, that hurt the child; divorce added little lasting burden to this problem. Frank Furstenberg and Andrew Cherlin, two distinguished students of family life, argued in 1991 that long-term studies of children showed that their problems mostly arose from marital discord. A minority of them might be hurt by divorce, but it was only a minority; children differ greatly, and most adjust reasonably well to parental breakup. And when the mother remarried and the children acquired a stepfather, most seemed to do quite well.

Cherlin repeated this view the following year. Some studies, he said, showed that divorce can be beneficial in the long run for some children because it takes them out of a conflict-ridden family. At the same time, he noted, it can impose serious psychological distress on other children, but fortunately this tended to last only a short time. In part this happens because most divorced parents remarry.

This is a remarkable argument, for it suggests one or both of two implausible views. One is that children can be raised as well by a mother as by a mother and father. Since the great majority of children live with the divorced mother rather than with the father, lacking a father does not make much of a difference. And they indeed lack a father: "The vast majority of children [of divorced parents] will have little or no contact with their fathers." David Popenoe notes that more than half of all adolescent children living with separated or divorced mothers had not seen their fathers in over a year; only one-seventh saw them as often as once a week.

The weight of scientific evidence seems clearly to support the view that fathers matter. We have already seen that children in mother-only families are worse off, even after controlling for income, than are those in two-parent ones. Matters may be better among the most affluent single moms, but most mothers will suffer a significant loss in income after they divorce and at a minimum expose their children to frequent relocations. One study found that the standard of living of a divorced woman fell by 27 percent whereas that of a divorced man increased by 10 percent. Glendon has argued that the United States appears unique among Western Countries in failing to assure either public or private responsibility for "the economic casualties of divorce." We have, she suggests, "no-fault, no-responsibility divorce. School-age children who have a father do better than those without one in cognitive development, academic achievement, and impulse control. Of course, an inattentive father at home can produce some of the same effects, but father absence, owing to a divorce, almost guarantees inattention.

Of course, many divorced women remarry, taking their children with them. If that happens, we come to the second argument: step fathers will do as well as biological ones in raising children. If the first argument is true, then marriage itself is a questionable venture, since fathers are not really necessary beyond providing sperm and money. If the second argument is true, then all of the stories we have heard about wicked stepfathers must be no more than fiction designed to frighten but not teach its readers. Those who deny that divorce is very harmful may be right, but they have a steep hurdle to overcome.

Earlier in this book we noted that the rate at which children are abused or killed is vastly higher when they live with stepfathers rather than their biological ones. (Nine out of ten stepchildren live with a stepfather and their biological mother.) To repeat: preschool children living with a stepfather were forty times more likely than those living with their biological parents to become the victims of child abuse and seventy to one hundred times more likely to be murdered by the stepparent. Though there are many caring and devoted stepfathers, on average they create a much greater risk not only for abuse but for inattention and emotional distance. They do not watch, monitor, and control their children as much as do parents who are genetically connected to their offspring. In their careful study of stepfamilies, Sarah McLanahan and Gary Sandefur show that, even after controlling for family income, children with a stepparent are more likely than those living with both biological parents to drop out of high school; female children are more likely to become teen moms and male children more likely to be idle.

Some scholars had reached a view different from that of Cherlin and Furstenberg. In a long follow-up of divorced children, Judith S. Wallerstein and various coauthors found that divorce is a long-lasting and wrenching experience for many of them. Almost half entered adulthood as "worried, underachieving self-deprecating, and sometimes angry young men and women." Boys had a tougher time than girls and that adolescence was a worse time for divorce than childhood. But these findings were dismissed by their critics on the grounds that Wallerstein had found the families they studied from among the ranks of people who had sought marriage counseling, suggesting that they represented, not the universe of all divorced families, but those that had particular psychological problems. The authors, by contrast, had claimed that their families were middle-class people who had not sought psychological help (other than marital advice). Though they were initially praised, the Wallerstein books were soon criticized by journalists writing on behalf of a culture that had come to see divorce as a rational way to dissolve the marriage contract. And, in fact, it is hard to know just how representative were the families that Wallerstein studied. We know they were middle-class people from around San Francisco, but the authors seem to have taken volunteers that (except for having weeded out children in psychological distress) may or may not have been typical of families undergoing a divorce.

The disagreement between Cherlin and his colleagues with Wallerstein and hers was overstated by many observers. The former found some children who were hurt by divorce, the latter found some who were helped by divorce. It was a question of numbers. What proportion suffered long-term problems? The former said that "a substantial portion" of boys' problems preceded the divorce and that perhaps only 6 to 9 percent of their postdivorce problems were caused by the divorce itself. The latter said that about 30 percent of both boys and girls had serious postdivorce problems. Though the differences might strike you as modest, they carried a lot of weight. If only 6 to 9 percent of the children had lasting problems, divorce seemed like a good bet for many people, but if 30 percent or more were made worse, the odds had shifted dramatically against you.

The most recent data tend to lean more in the direction of Wallerstein. In 1997, when some scholars compared teenagers living in intact, divorced, and about-to-be-divorced families, they found that divorce was much more important than marital discord in explaining difficulties in adolescent adjustment. Earlier views that children are already unhappy in families that later divorced, the authors wrote, must be modified. Another study published at about the same time came to much the same conclusion. This group discovered that adolescents in divorced families are much more likely to become delinquent, engage in early sex, and suffer from depression than those living in intact families, even after taking into account the quality of the parents' marriage. But the most important study was done by Cherlin himself. In 1998 he and his colleagues published a new study of divorce in Great Britain in which they measured its long-term effects on the mental health of children. Some of the adverse effects were, as they had suggested some years earlier, the result of marital discord or other things not involving divorce. But now they added that divorce itself is harmful. Their earlier views "should be modified," a commendable and wholly scholarly attitude toward how one expresses new and unexpected findings. Not so commendable was much of the national press that gave great publicity to his earlier view that marital conflict was much more important than divorce and next to no coverage to his later view that divorce itself is a large problem.

Cherlin's new findings were reinforced by a study done by Paul R. Amato and Alan Booth. They interviewed more than two thousand married people several times between 1980 and 1992 and their children in 1992 and 1995. They looked at how happy or discordant the marriages were and studied the couples who later got divorced, and they related all of this to how well the children fared. Their findings make it clear that both discord and divorce make a difference. Not only does a lousy marriage produce unhappy children, so does a divorce. Both forces operate: "Low parental marital quality lowers offspring well-being, and parental divorce lowers it even further." But what is most worrisome about these results is that most divorces do not result from conflict-ridden marriages. Only about one-third of all divorced couples reported any prior abuse, frequent arguments, or serious quarrels. But they got divorced anyway. As the authors put it, "People are leaving marriages at lower thresholds of unhappiness now than in the past." For the children of these marriages, the divorce alone was the chief source of harm.

This conclusion ought to be unsettling to those who see divorce in purely legal terms. Max Rheinstein argued that none of the harms to marriage are produced by divorce because an unhappy family will find one way or another, such as separations, formal or informal, to cope with that distress. Divorce, he argued, was merely a legal device, a decree of a court, that gives public recognition to an established social fact. I think he was mistaken. While it is true that a divorce decree is a legal formality, its significance does not end with the document. The decree sets aside a lifetime commitment on the basis of which two people have managed their emotions, attachments, income, property, and children. When people believe that commitment, they behave differently than when they doubt it. As we have seen, married couples share income and wealth more readily than do cohabiting ones because they assume that their relationship is permanent. Suppose divorce is very difficult. That provides a constraint on your freedom of action so that you will take a different view of your spouse's faults than you will if the law makes divorce very easy. That constraint will, at the margin, lead many people to stick it out by coping with their spouses and helping their children. Marriage is a commitment that alters how people evaluate each other.

If you think divorce is difficult and wrong, you stick together for "the sake of the children." If you think divorce is easy and acceptable, you break apart for the sake of yourselves. There is some evidence that supports this view. "There is no such thing as a nice divorce," a character in a Hollywood movie once said, and by and large he is right. The divorce may occur for very good reasons—perhaps infidelity or abuse—but the wrangling over the children is still likely to be intense. When two scholars studied forty-four elementary schoolchildren who had lived with contentious parents, each parent tried to mobilize the child against the former spouse after the divorce. Three children were in their mothers' cars when the raging women rammed their ex-husbands' cars, with an injury to at least one child. One was in her mother's car when the ex-husband threw a piece of furniture that broke the windshield. And even when there was no violence, the children were often mobilized in a tug-of-war between two angry parents, with angry speeches, denials of visiting rights, and hiding (or even kidnapping) a child to keep him or her away from the former spouse.

Obviously, some married couples should get a divorce, even if a child feels hurt. And just as obviously, some children, distressed by long periods of parental conflict, will feel better after the divorce occurs. But just as obviously, many children will be hurt by a divorce, with the hurt lasting for many years. Some intact families hurt children through discord, some divorced families hurt children by separating, and some families do both. The problem is to find, somehow, the optimum number of divorces. It surely will be greater than zero and probably lower than what it is today. The optimum number, one that nobody can calculate, would look like this: It would be high enough to permit the correction of a serious mistake but low enough so as not to encourage couples to think that they have made only a weak commitment. A weak commitment destroys the idea of marriage by leading people to think that tough but manageable problems need not be addressed. . . .

A New Story About Divorce

Neighbors, friends, even some of the women in Liddy Pennybaker's* book group knew about James's infidelities, so when word spread that Liddy had asked for a divorce, everyone thought they knew why.

James frequently went to social events alone, and just as frequently left with an attractive female on his arm. But to Liddy, James's affairs were more in the nature of a last straw than anything else. By the time receipts from out-of-town hotels began appearing in the Pennybakers' American Express bills, Liddy was already halfway out of the marriage. She resented James not spending more time with the children. She had grown tired of his scowls when she ate anything with more than a hundred calories in it. She was sick of his aloofness and condescension when she had friends from her church group to the house. She hated James's social climbing and phony laugh when he was around powerful people. . . .

Every divorce is a unique tragedy because every divorce brings an end to a unique civilization—one built on thousands of shared experiences, memories, hopes, and dreams. That wonderful Two-for-the-Road summer in Europe, the first day in the new house, the heart-stopping trip to the emergency room—only the people who shared those moments know what it means to lose them forever. So divorce takes a uniquely personal toll on the divorced. But the experience of divorce also has many commonalities. The end of a marriage always, or almost always, produces heartache, fear, self-doubt, confusion, and of course many anxious questions.

What happens to me and my children now? What should I expect, fear, hope for? What kinds of challenges and pitfalls do I face? And how do I go about building a better life?

Like other books on divorce, *For Better or For Worse* offers answers to these questions. But the answers you will find here are different. *For Better or For Worse* has a new story to tell about divorce, and it is an important story because it is based on the most comprehensive examination of divorce ever conducted: an in-depth examination of nearly 1,400 families and over 2,500 children, many followed for more than three decades. When I finished my research, the adults I had met as young men and women were now in middle age and most had been remarried for a decade or more, and the children I had met as pre-

---

*All names and recognizable details have been changed to protect the privacy of the participants.

schoolers were now teachers, accountants, computer scientists, and engineers; many were married; a few had already gone through a divorce of their own.

The unparalleled scope of my research has produced new and surprising findings about divorce and its immediate aftermath, findings that will make us better able to anticipate the consequences of marital failure for ourselves, our children, and for future partners and marriages. . . .

On one level, *For Better or For Worse* is a portrait of the new ways Americans have learned to live and love and parent in a divorce-prone society. On another level, the book serves as a primer on what might be called the post-nuclear family experience. . . .

At the center of the primer is a new and, I think, more balanced view of divorce and its consequences. After forty years of research, I harbor no doubts about the ability of divorce to devastate. It can and does ruin lives. I've seen it happen more times than I like to think about. But that said, I also think much current writing on divorce—both popular and academic—has exaggerated its negative effects and ignored its sometimes considerable positive effects. Divorce has undoubtedly rescued many adults and children from the horror of domestic abuse, but it is not just a preventative measure. I have seen divorce provide many women and girls, in particular, with a remarkable opportunity for life-transforming personal growth, as we shall see later.

The reason our current view of marital failure is so unremittingly negative is that it is based on studies that have only examined people for a year or two after their divorce, and a year or two is not enough time to distinguish between short- and long-term effects. Additionally, many divorce studies do not employ a comparison group of married couples, and thus are unable to distinguish between problems common to all families and problems unique to divorced families.

Once you remove these distortions by doing what I did, examining men, women, and children for over twenty years and including a comparison group of non-divorced married couples, many of our current beliefs about marital failure turn out to be myths. . . .

Myth: Children Always Lose Out After a Divorce

This is another article of faith in popular wisdom and it contains an undeniable truth. In the short run, divorce usually is brutally painful to a child. But its negative long-term effects have been exaggerated to the point where we now have created a self-fulfilling prophecy. At the end of my study, a fair number of my adult children of divorce described themselves as permanently "scarred." But objective assessments of these "victims" told a different story. Twenty-five percent of youths from divorced families in comparison to 10 percent from non-divorced families did have serious social, emotional, or psychological problems. But most of the young men and women from my divorced families looked a lot like their contemporaries from non-divorced homes. Although they looked back on their parents' breakup as a painful experience, most were successfully going about the chief tasks of young adulthood: establishing careers, creating intimate relationships, building meaningful lives for themselves.

Most unexpectedly—since it has seldom been reported before—a minority of my young adults emerged from divorce and postnuclear family life enhanced. Uncommonly resilient, mature, responsible, and focused, these children of divorce blossomed, not despite the things that had happened to them during divorce and after, but, like Enhanced adults, because of them. . . .

Children at Two Years Past Divorce

For adults, divorce brings *a* world to an end; for young children, whose lives are focused in the family, it seems to bring *the* world to an end. Yet the adjustment patterns of adults and children are remarkably similar: a decline in function in the first year and a notable improvement in the second. Still, at two years, many youngsters remained anxious and whiny, and clingy and oppositional, while others had school and social problems. And children, like their parents, showed wide variation in how they coped with divorce. Some sailed through a turbulent divorce and emerged relatively unscathed; others showed permanent emotional or behavioral problems; and still others appeared to be adjusting well initially, but delayed problems emerged in adolescence or young adulthood.

As with adults, how well children coped with divorce depended on the stresses they encountered and the personal and social resources they had to deal with in their changing life. For some children, who had moved from conflictual, hostile, or abusive homes into a more harmonious family situation with a capable, involved parent, divorce was in the long run advantageous. By two years after divorce, these children were happier and better behaved than they had been before the breakup. For others, who had come from homes in which they felt secure and where marital conflict was concealed or muted, the breakup was unexpected, incomprehensible, frightening, and these children had greater losses to deal with. For all young children, divorce led to changes in their life that were difficult to cope with, and how well they coped to a large extent depended on the behavior of the custodial parent. An involved, competent custodial parent was the most effective buffer a young child could have against postdivorce stress; an irritable, punitive, uncaring, or disengaged parent put the child at great risk for developing problems. . . .

Six years after the divorce, Bethany Pennybaker's anger, anxiety, and resentment were gone. She had emerged as an unusually mature and responsible child, who was accomplished both academically and socially. And much to her parents' delight, she was showing an interest and talent in the arts—in writing poetry and drawing—that drew them together. "With Bethany, there are never any problems," James said to me one day.

With Adam, in contrast, there often were problems. At six, Adam had been diagnosed as hyperactive and having an attention deficit disorder. Although his hyperactivity had abated by age ten, his problems lingered in the form of a severe reading disability. "It breaks my heart to see him struggle so," Liddy said. "Adam's so bright and he's hurting so much and nothing we do seems to help with his reading. He's being absolutely turned off school by his dyslexia."

The Pennybaker children illustrate some of our important findings about how children cope with their parents' marital breakup that were emerging six years after divorce. As with adults, how well children were doing depended on risk and protective factors, and as we found with Adam Pennybaker, these factors could shift over time. It was the current stresses and resources, rather than the ones that had surrounded the divorce, that were now most important. These factors were so individual that as in the Pennybaker case, we often saw siblings from the same family take very different paths out of divorce. In addition, by the six-year follow-up, a dramatic change had occurred. The cloud of anxiety and depression that hung over children in the first year usually had diminished or evaporated. Some boys and girls remained deeply troubled, but three quarters of the children from divorced families were now functioning well within the normal range. Like their parents, children were showing diverse patterns of adjustment and had taken varied routes to get there.

By six years after divorce, we were gaining a clearer understanding of how social relationships within and outside the family, as well as individual characteristics of the child, could undermine or promote the child's well-being. When the children were ten, the behavior of the custodial parent was still the most significant influence on their adjustment. But other relationships with siblings, peers, teachers, and mentors were becoming increasingly important. And to a large extent this was influenced by the attributes and behavior of the child. Was the child easygoing or hard to get along with, pretty or plain, shy or outgoing, and did the child have particular skills in academics, social relations, or athletics that might make him feel better about himself and be well regarded by others? . . .

Children Coping in the First Six Years

Almost all children are distressed by their parents' divorce; initially, they become confused, anxious, apprehensive, and angry. In the home, they often are both clingy and whiny, and demanding, disobedient, and irritable; at school and with peers, they often become distractable, withdrawn, and aggressive. The cycle of coercive exchanges found in homes with divorced mothers and young sons can lead to prolonged problems in a boy's adjustment. Although fantasies of parental reconciliation may continue, both boys and girls show considerable behavioral improvement at two years after a divorce.

By six years later, children show diverse patterns of coping with their parents' divorce and their new life in a single-parent household. Although twice as many children in divorced and remarried families as those in non-divorced families are anxious, antisocial, and lack self-control, the vast majority are functioning within the normal range of adjustment; they have some problems, but none that are overwhelming. Some of our children—especially girls—developed into remarkably competent, responsible, resilient youngsters.

Coping with the challenges of divorce and life in a single-parent family seems actually to enhance the ability of some children to deal with future stresses. But children can't cope alone; there needs to be a supportive adult in their lives to help buffer them from adversity, and that adult is most often a loving, responsive, firm, authoritative, custodial parent.

Children who move from a conflictual to a more harmonious situation with an authoritative parent usually show better adjustment by two years than they had exhibited before divorce. But children who move into a more stressful, contentious situation, with an inept parent, show an increase in distress, resentment, and problem behaviors.

Points to Remember

- Divorce does not inevitably produce permanent scars. Parents can buffer a child against many of the stresses associated with both divorce and life in a single-parent home.
- You don't have to be a perfect parent to be a good buffer. Naturally self-correcting, children can adjust to divorce with a moderate amount of support.
- Parental love is not enough; firm but responsive discipline is also important to a child of divorce. It teaches the child self-control and how to control his or her emotions.
- Just as it is important to prepare children for the divorce before it happens, it is important to talk to them about the changes that are happening after. Get your children to discuss their concerns and fears so you can help them deal with their anxieties. Make your children understand that you will always be there for them.
- Be consistent. It's hard to overstate the importance of a predictable environment after divorce. With so many things changing in children's lives, they need to know there are some things that can be relied on.
- Remember, your child is a child. Don't confide in her or lean on her for support she is incapable of giving. Solve your own problems; the child has enough problems of her own.
- It is difficult for a non-residential parent to protect a child from the consequences of a hostile, rejecting, or neglecting residential parent. Non-residential parents just aren't around enough to buffer the child in the day-to-day hassles of family living.
- Girls are more likely to benefit from contact with a non-custodial mother, boys with a non-custodial father.
- Preadolescent boys have more difficulty adjusting to life in a family where the mother is the single parent; preadolescent girls have more difficulty adjusting to life in the stepfamily.
- Think about cooperative co-parenting; it is a major protective factor for children, and by working together, parents lighten the burden for each other.
- Rivalry and lack of support are common among siblings in divorced and remarried families. When a protective sibling relationship does develop, it is more likely to occur among sisters.
- A completely stress-free environment is not necessarily the best one. Solving moderately stressful problems in a supportive environment prepares a child for dealing with future challenges. However, the support of a caring adult is critical.

- Girls are more likely than boys to be strengthened by coping with the stresses of divorce.
- Although children from divorced and remarried families are more likely than those in non-divorced families to have problems, the vast majority are adjusting reasonably well six years after divorce.

Mostly Happy: Children of Divorce as Young Adults

In the 1970s, a fierce debate broke out about the future of children like David and Leah. Critics of the divorce revolution believed that as the generation of children from divorced families matured, American society would descend into disorder and chaos. The collapse of the two-parent family, the traditional engine of socialization, critics argued, would lead to a *Clockwork Orange* generation of unstable, reckless, indulgent young adults, who would overrun the nation's prisons, substance abuse centers, and divorce courts.

"Nonsense," declared supporters of the divorce revolution, who saw divorce as a kind of cleansing agent. At last, the dark gloomy oppressive Victorian house that was the nuclear family would get a long-overdue spring cleaning, one that would produce a new and more egalitarian, tolerant, and fulfilled generation of men and women.

While I found evidence to support both views, the big headline in my data is that *80 percent of children from divorced homes eventually are able to adapt to their new life and become reasonably well adjusted*. A subgroup of girls even become exceptionally competent as a result of dealing with the challenges of divorce, enjoy a normal development, and grow into truly outstanding young adults. The 20 percent who continue to bear the scars of divorce fall into a troubled group, who display impulsive, irresponsible, antisocial behavior or are depressed. At the end of the VLS, troubled youths were having difficulty at work, in romantic relationships, and in gaining a toehold in adult life. They had the highest academic dropout rate and the highest divorce rate in the study, and were more likely to be faring poorly economically. In addition, being troubled and a girl made a young woman more likely to have left home early and to have experienced at least one out-of-wedlock pregnancy, birth, or abortion.

However, coming from a non-divorced family did not always protect against growing into a troubled young adult. Ten percent of youths in non-divorced families, compared to 20 percent in divorced and remarried families, were troubled. Most of our troubled young men and women came from families where conflict was frequent and authoritative parenting rare. In adulthood, as was found in childhood and adolescence, those who had moved from a highly contentious intact home situation to a more harmonious divorced family situation, with a caring, competent parent, benefited from the divorce and had fewer problems. But the legacy of the stresses and inept parenting associated with divorce and remarriage, and especially with living in a complex stepfamily, are still seen in the psychological, emotional, and social problems in 20 percent of young people from these families.

A piece of good news about our youths was that their antisocial behavior declined as they matured. Much of the adolescent exploration, experimentation, and sense of invulnerability had abated. Although excessive use of alcohol remained a problem for one quarter, drug abuse and lawbreaking had declined in all of our groups; but the decrease had been most marked in those who married.

What about the other 80 percent of young people from divorced and remarried families?

While most were not exactly the New Man or New Woman that the divorce revolution's supporters had predicted, they were behaving the way young adults were supposed to behave. They were choosing careers, developing permanent relationships, ably going about the central tasks of young adulthood, and establishing a grown-up life.

They ranged from those who were remarkably well adjusted to Good Enoughs and competent-at-a-costs, who were having a few problems but coping reasonably well to very well.

Finally, it should be a reassuring finding for divorced and remarried parents, and their children, that for every young man or woman who emerged from postnuclear family life with problems, four others were functioning reasonably or exceptionally well.

I think our findings ultimately contain two bottom-line messages about the long-term effects of divorce on children. The first is about parents, especially mothers. If someone creates a Nobel Prize for Unsung Hero, my nominee will be the divorced mother. Even when the world was collapsing round them, many divorced mothers found the courage and resiliency to do what had to be done. Such maternal tenacity and courage paid off. Despite all the emotional and financial pressures imposed by marital failure, most of our divorced women managed to provide the support, sensitivity, and engagement their children needed for normal development. And while divorce creates developmental risks, except in cases of extraordinary stress, children can be protected by vigorous, involved, competent parenting.

The second bottom line is about flexibility and diversity. Divorce is not a form of developmental predestination. Children, like adults, take many different routes out of divorce; some lead to unhappiness, others to a rewarding and fulfilling life. And since over the course of life, new experiences are being encountered and new relationships formed, protective and risk factors alter, and the door to positive change always remains open. . . .

Twenty Years Later

The adverse effects of divorce and remarriage are still echoing in some divorced families and their offspring twenty years after divorce, but they are in the minority. The vast majority of young people from these families are reasonably well adjusted and are coping reasonably well in relationships with their families, friends, and intimate partners. Most are moving toward establishing careers, economic independence, and satisfying social and intimate relationships. Some are caring spouses and parents. Although the divorce may resonate more in the memories of these children, most parents and children see the divorce as having been for the best, and have moved forward with their lives.

Points to Remember

- Parent, child, and sibling relationships that have been close in childhood seldom deteriorate in adulthood.
- Even if absence doesn't make the heart grow fonder, conflict usually diminishes once the protagonists are apart and contact becomes optional. Disengagement often replaces conflict in stepparent-stepchild and sibling relationships in divorced and remarried families in young adulthood.
- Biologically related siblings, whether in divorced, non-divorced, or remarried families, tend to have both more attached and more rivalrous relationships than those found in stepsiblings.
- Men remain reluctant to do their fair share. In most first- and second-generation VLS homes, the burden of household labor continued to fall predominantly on female shoulders. After a demanding eight- or ten-hour day at the office, many of our women would come home to cope with unmade beds, unwashed laundry, unfed children, and the morning's unwashed breakfast dishes in the sink.
- A family history of divorce does leave children of divorce relationship- and marriage-challenged. Children of divorce are often reluctant to commit wholeheartedly to a marriage, have fewer relationship skills, and in some cases show a genetic predisposition to destabilizing behaviors like antisocial behavior, impulsivity, and depression.
- Gender affects a person's divorce risk more than the kind of family the person was brought up in. In divorced, remarried, and non-divorced families alike, male belligerence, withdrawal, and lack of affection often produce thoughts of divorce in a woman; female contempt, nagging, or reciprocated aggression, thoughts of divorce in a man.
- Although marital instability is higher in offspring from divorced families, marriage to a stable, supportive spouse from a non-divorced family eliminates the intergenerational transmission of divorce. A caring, mature spouse can teach their partner from a divorced family skills they never learned at home.
- Young adults from complex stepfamilies continue to have more adjustment and family problems than young adults in other kinds of stepfamilies.
- For most youths, the legacy of divorce is largely overcome. Twenty years after divorce, most men and women who had grown up in divorced families and stepfamilies are functioning reasonably well. Only a minority still exhibited emotional and social problems, and had difficulties with intimate relationships and achievement. . . .

POSTSCRIPT

Are the Negative Consequences of Divorce on Children Substantial?

James Q. Wilson is to be commended for avoiding the ad hominem argument that often enters this debate that says that those who minimize the negative consequences of divorce on children are guided more by a liberal antitraditional ideology than by good research. Though his book derives from his passion to strengthen marriage, nevertheless, Wilson's commitment to truth causes him to acknowledge that some divorces are good for the children. This acknowledgment changes the debate from whether divorce is good or bad to where to set the line between good and bad divorces. Wilson's main point is that researchers are increasingly seeing divorce in negative terms. E. Mavis Hetherington and John Kelly emphasize how adaptive children are and how sometimes overcoming adversities develops their character.

Wilson's footnotes and references were not included in this reprint but the following are the references for some of the studies cited by him: Barbara Dafoe Whitehead, *The Divorce Culture* (Alfred A. Knopf, 1997); Frank F. Furstenberg, Jr., and Andrew J. Cherlin, *Divided Families: What Happens to Children When Parents Part* (Harvard University Press, 1991); P. Lindsey Chase-Landale, Andrew J. Cherlin, and Kathleen E. Kiernan, "The Long-Term Effects of Parental Divorce on the Mental Health of Young Adults," *Child Development* (vol. 66, 1995, pp. 1614–34); David Popenoe, *Life without Father* (Free Press, 1996); Richard R. Peterson, "A Re-evaluation of the Economic Consequences of Divorce," *American Sociological Review* (vol. 61, 1996, pp. 528–38); Karla B. Hackstaff, *Marriage in the Culture of Divorce* (Temple University Press, 1999); Sara McLanahan and Gary Sandefur, *Growing Up with a Single Parent* (Harvard University Press, 1994); Judith S. Wallerstein and Sandra Blakeslee, *Second Chances: Men, Women, and Children a Decade After Divorce* (Ticknor & Fields, 1989); Judith S. Wallerstein, Julia Lewis, and Sandra Blakeslee, *The Unexpected Legacy of Divorce* (Hyperion, 2000); Ronald L. Simons, et al., *Understanding the Differences between Divorced and Intact Families* (Sage, 1996); Andrew Cherlin, P. Lindsay Chase-Lansdale, and Christine McRae, "Effects of Parental Divorce on Mental Health Throughout the Life Course," *American Sociological Review* (vol. 63, 1998, pp. 157-64); and Paul R. Amoto and Alan Booth, *A Generation at Risk: Growing Up in an Era of Family Upheaval* (Harvard University Press, 1997).

Recent works that focus on the effects of divorce on children include John H. Harvey and Mark A. Fine, *Children of Divorce: Stories of Loss and Growth* (Lawrence Eribaum, 2004); Ian Butler, et al., *Divorcing Children: Children's Experience of Their Parents' Divorce* (Jessica Kingsley, 2003); Alva Chin, ed., *Split: Stories from a Generation Raised on Divorce* (Contemporary Books, 2002); Carol Smart, Bren Neale, and Amanda Wade, *The Changing Experience of Childhood: Families and Divorce* (Blackwell, 2001); and Robert E. Emery, *Marriage, Divorce, and Children's Adjustment* (Sage, 1999). Two more general treatments of divorce are Lita Linzer Schwartz and Florence W. Kaslow, *Painful Partings: Divorce and Its Aftermath* (J. Wiley, 1997) and Ross A. Thompson and Paul R. Amato, ed., *The Postdivorce Family: Children, Parenting, and Society* (Sage, 1999). Two books that give advice to divorcing parents are Hanna McDonough and Cristina Bartha, *Putting Children First: A Guide for Parents Breaking Up* (University of Toronto Press, 1999) and E. Mavis Hetherington, *Coping with Divorce, Single Parenting, and Remarriage* (Lawrence Erlbaum, 1999). Three works that offer suggestions for reducing divorce are Alan J. Hawkins, Lyn D. Wardle, and David Orgon Coolidge, eds., *Revitalizing the Institution of Marriage for the Twenty-First Century: An Agenda for Strengthening Marriage* (Praeger, 2002); William J. Bennett, *The Broken Hearth: Reversing the Moral Collapse of the American Family* (Doubleday, 2001); and David Popenoe, Jean Bethke Elshtain, and David Blankenhorn, eds., *Promises to Keep: Decline and Renewal of Marriage in America* (Rowman & Littlefield, 1996). William Jeynes focuses on the effects of divorce on school performance in *Divorce, Family Structure, and the Academic Success of Children* (Haworth Press, 2002).

ISSUE 22

Should the United States Legitimize Its Actions of World Leadership?

YES: Joseph S. Nye, Jr., from "The Decline of America's Soft Power: Why Washington Should Worry," *Foreign Affairs* (May/June 2004)

NO: Charles Krauthammer, from "The Unipolar Moment Revisited," *The National Interest* (Winter 2002/2003)

ISSUE SUMMARY

YES: Dean of Harvard's John F. Kennedy School of Government, Joseph S. Nye, argues that American unilateralism is increasing worldwide anti-American sentiment and reducing what we can achieve abroad. America needs allies and needs to attract, not repel, them. For example, our war on Islamic terrorists requires much help from Islamic moderates.

NO: Journalist and TV pundit Charles Krauthammer argues that the United States is the world's single superpower that should use its power to extend "the peace by advancing democracy and preserving the peace by acting as balancer of last resort." He is adamant that the United States should pursue its interests with little heed to world opinion. It should act unilaterally when necessary.

George Bush said in his second inaugural, "It is the policy of the United States to seek and support the growth of democratic movements and institutions in every nation and culture, with the ultimate goal of ending tyranny in our world." To the world he said, "When you stand for your liberty, we will stand with you." People throughout the world wondered what he meant by "seek and support." Did he mean more Iraq-type military interventions to depose dictators, or did he mean that the United States would just encourage, without military support, democratic movements in nondemocratic countries? An unfortunate example of the latter was America's encouragement of the Shiites to resist Saddam Hussein in the 1990s, but the United States gave them no military support. When they did resist, Saddam crushed them. One thing is clear: The United States is the leading world power with all other countries far behind in military might. What is not clear is what the United

States will do with this power. In other words, what kind of world leadership was Bush declaring, and what kind of world would the implementation of the Bush doctrine bring about?

Until the leveling of the Berlin Wall, the world was bipolar. Since then, the world has become more unipolar but is still multipolar. The United States is by far the dominant world power, but many countries act quite independent of it, so the world is not fully unipolar. In this situation, what role should the United States play in the world? To what extent should it force its will on other countries, assuming its will is benevolent? Should it seek global hegemony? A hegemon is the single pole in a unipolar world. The Roman Empire was an example, at least for the part of the world that was interrelated. There has been no hegemon power since. Is the Roman Empire a model for the United States today? And what is to be gained by such a domineering role in the world?

Obviously there are costs for being a world hegemon and even of being the world leader. If the United States seeks world dominance, it would require an expensive military and vast expenditures to reward countries for supporting our causes. Even so, the United States would likely be more hated than appreciated. Nevertheless, some argue that strong U.S. leadership would benefit both the world and the United States. This view assumes that the main objective of United States leadership would be to advance democracy, free enterprise, and other American values, which would benefit all countries and make the world safer for the United States. As Bush said in his inaugural, "the best hope for peace in our world is the expansion of freedom in all the world." Others argue that strong United States leadership would overextend the United States and could lead to its moral decline if it must follow self interested, realist strategies. Furthermore, strong United States leadership might not be beneficial to the rest of the world. The United States has supported dictators, oppressive regimes, and other evils when this serves our interests, so it is not clear that United States hegemony would be benevolent.

With the tragedy of 9/11 the United States assumed the mantle of world leadership and dedicated itself to a war on terrorism. It led a coalition of forces against the Taliban and Al Qaeda in Afghanistan and another one to oust Saddam Hussein in Iraq. Now Bush is subsuming America's war on terrorism under his campaign to advance freedom and democracy throughout the world.

What is most unique about the Bush administration's foreign policy compared to previous administrations is its unilateralism. Bush has not signed treaties on land mines, nuclear proliferation, global warming, and other issues and has attacked Iraq against the wishes of most of the world. This has strained relations with most of our allies. In the selections that follow, this type of United States leadership is advocated by Charles Krauthammer and opposed by Joseph S. Nye.

Joseph S. Nye, Jr.

 **YES**

The Decline of America's Soft Power: Why Washington Should Worry

Anti-Americanism has increased in recent years, and the United States' soft power—its ability to attract others by the legitimacy of U.S. policies and the values that underlie them—is in decline as a result. According to Gallup International polls, pluralities in 29 countries say that Washington's policies have had a negative effect on their view of the United States. A Eurobarometer poll found that a majority of Europeans believes that Washington has hindered efforts to fight global poverty, protect the environment, and maintain peace. Such attitudes undercut soft power, reducing the ability of the United States to achieve its goals without resorting to coercion or payment.

Skeptics of soft power (Secretary of Defense Donald Rumsfeld professes not even to understand the term) claim that popularity is ephemeral and should not guide foreign policy. The United States, they assert, is strong enough to do as it wishes with or without the world's approval and should simply accept that others will envy and resent it. The world's only superpower does not need permanent allies; the issues should determine the coalitions, not vice-versa, according to Rumsfeld.

But the recent decline in U.S. attractiveness should not be so lightly dismissed. It is true that the United States has recovered from unpopular policies in the past (such as those regarding the Vietnam War), but that was often during the Cold War, when other countries still feared the Soviet Union as the greater evil. It is also true that the United States' sheer size and association with disruptive modernity make some resentment unavoidable today. But wise policies can reduce the antagonisms that these realities engender. Indeed, that is what Washington achieved after World War II: it used soft-power resources to draw others into a system of alliances and institutions that has lasted for 60 years. The Cold War was won with a strategy of containment that used soft power along with hard power.

The United States cannot confront the new threat of terrorism without the cooperation of other countries. Of course, other governments will often cooperate out of self-interest. But the extent of their cooperation often depends on the attractiveness of the United States.

From *Foreign Affairs*, Vol. 83, No. 3, May/June 2004, pp. 16–20. Copyright © 2004 by Foreign Affairs. Reprinted by permission.

Soft power, therefore, is not just a matter of ephemeral popularity; it is a means of obtaining outcomes the United States wants. When Washington discounts the importance of its attractiveness abroad, it pays a steep price. When the United States becomes so unpopular that being pro-American is a kiss of death in other countries' domestic politics, foreign political leaders are unlikely to make helpful concessions (witness the defiance of Chile, Mexico, and Turkey in March 2003). And when U.S. policies lose their legitimacy in the eyes of others, distrust grows, reducing U.S. leverage in international affairs.

Some hard-line skeptics might counter that, whatever its merits, soft power has little importance in the current war against terrorism; after all, Osama bin Laden and his followers are repelled, not attracted, by American culture and values. But this claim ignores the real metric of success in the current war, articulated in Rumsfeld's now-famous memo that was leaked in February 2003: "Are we capturing, killing or deterring and dissuading more terrorists every day than the madrassas and the radical clerics are recruiting, training and deploying against us?"

The current struggle against Islamist terrorism is not a clash of civilizations; it is a contest closely tied to the civil war raging within Islamic civilization between moderates and extremists. The United States and its allies will win only if they adopt policies that appeal to those moderates and use public diplomacy effectively to communicate that appeal. Yet the world's only superpower, and the leader in the information revolution, spends as little on public diplomacy as does France or the United Kingdom—and is all too often outgunned in the propaganda war by fundamentalists hiding in caves.

Lost Savings

With the end of the Cold War, soft power seemed expendable, and Americans became more interested in saving money than in investing in soft power. Between 1989 and 1999, the budget of the United States Information Agency (USIA) decreased ten percent; resources for its mission in Indonesia, the world's largest Muslim nation, were cut in half. By the time it was taken over by the State Department at the end of the decade, USIA had only 6,715 employees (compared to 12,000 at its peak in the mid-1960s). During the Cold War, radio broadcasts funded by Washington reached half the Soviet population and 70 to 80 percent of the population in Eastern Europe every week; on the eve of the September 11 attacks, a mere two percent of Arabs listened to the Voice of America (VOA). The annual number of academic and cultural exchanges, meanwhile, dropped from 45,000 in 1995 to 29,000 in 2001. Soft power had become so identified with fighting the Cold War that few Americans noticed that, with the advent of the information revolution, soft power was becoming more important, not less.

It took the September 11 attacks to remind the United States of this fact. But although Washington has rediscovered the need for public diplomacy, it has failed to master the complexities of wielding soft power in an information age. Some people in government now concede that the abolition of USIA was a mistake, but there is no consensus on whether to recreate it or to reorganize its mistake, but there is no consensus on whether to recreate it or to reorganize its functions, which were dispersed within the State Department after the Clinton administration gave in to the demands of Senator Jesse Helms (R-N.C.). The board that oversees the VOA , along with a number of specialized radio stations, has taken some useful steps—such as the establishment of Radio Sawa to broadcast in Arabic, Radio Farda to broadcast in Farsi, and the Arabic-language TV station Al Hurra. The White House has created its own Office of Global Communications. But much more is needed, especially in the Middle East.

Autocratic regimes in the Middle East have eradicated their liberal opposition, and radical Islamists are in most cases the only dissenters left. They feed on anger toward corrupt regimes, opposition to U.S. policies, and popular fears of modernization. Liberal democracy, as they portray it, is full of corruption, sex, and violence—an impression reinforced by American movies and television and often exacerbated by the extreme statements of some especially virulent Christian preachers in the United States.

Nonetheless, the situation is not hopeless. Although modernization and American values can be disruptive, they also bring education, jobs, better health care, and a range of new opportunities. Indeed, polls show that much of the Middle East craves the benefits of trade, globalization, and improved communications. American technology is widely admired, and American culture is often more attractive than U.S. policies. Given such widespread (albeit ambivalent) moderate views, there is still a chance of isolating the extremists.

Democracy, however, cannot be imposed by force. The outcome in Iraq will be of crucial importance, but success will also depend on policies that open regional economies, reduce bureaucratic controls, speed economic growth, improve educational systems, and encourage the types of gradual political changes currently taking place in small countries such as Bahrain, Oman, Kuwait, and Morocco. The development of intellectuals, social groups, and, eventually, countries that show that liberal democracy is not inconsistent with Muslim culture will have a beneficial effect like that of Japan and South Korea, which showed that democracy could coexist with indigenous Asian values. But this demonstration effect will take time—and the skillful deployment of soft-power resources by the United States in concert with other democracies, nongovernmental organizations, and the United Nations.

First Responders

In the wake of September 11, Americans were transfixed by the question "Why do they hate us?" But many in the Middle East do not hate the United States. As polls consistently show, many fear, misunderstand, and oppose U.S. policies, but they nonetheless admire certain American values and aspects of American culture. The world's leader in communications, however, has been inept at recognizing and exploiting such opportunities.

In 2003, a bipartisan advisory group on public diplomacy for the Arab and Muslim world found that the United States was spending only $150 million on public diplomacy in majority-Muslim countries, including $25 million on outreach programs. In the advisory group's words, "to say that recommended appointing a new White House director of public diplomacy, building libraries and information centers, translating more Western books into Arabic, increasing the number of scholarships and visiting fellowships, and training more Arabic speakers and public relations specialists.

The development of effective public diplomacy must include strategies for the short, medium, and long terms. In the short term, the United States will have to become more agile in responding to and explaining current events. New broadcasting units such as Radio Sawa, which intersperses news with popular music, is a step in the right direction, but Americans must also learn to work more effectively with Arab media outlets such as Al Jazeera.

In the medium term, U.S. policymakers will have to develop a few key strategic themes in order to better explain U.S. policies and "brand" the United States as a democratic nation. The charge that U.S. policies are indifferent to the destruction of Muslim lives, for example, can be countered by pointing to U.S. interventions in Bosnia and Kosovo that saved Muslim lives, and to assistance to Muslim countries for fostering development and combating AIDS. As Assistant Secretary of State for Near Eastern Affairs William Burns has pointed out, democratic change must be embedded in "a wider positive agenda for the region, alongside rebuilding Iraq, achieving the president's two-state vision for Israelis and Palestinians, and modernizing Arab economies."

Most important will be a long-term strategy, built around cultural and educational exchanges, to develop a richer, more open civil society in Middle Eastern countries. To this end, the most effective spokespeople are not Americans but indigenous surrogates who understand American virtues and faults. Corporations, foundations, universities, and other nongovernmental organizations—as well as governments—can all help promote the development of open civil society. Corporations can offer technology to modernize educational systems. Universities can establish more exchange programs for students and faculty. Foundations can support institutions of American studies and programs to enhance the professionalism of journalists. Governments can support the teaching of English and finance student exchanges.

In short, there are many strands to an effective long-term strategy for creating soft-power resources and the conditions for democracy. Of course, even the best advertising cannot sell an unpopular product: a communications strategy will not work if it cuts against the grain of policy. Public diplomacy will not be effective unless the style and substance of U.S. policies are consistent with a broader democratic message.

Ante Up

The United States' most striking failure is the low priority and paucity of resources it has devoted to producing soft power. The combined cost of the State Department's public diplomacy programs and U.S. international broadcasting is just over a billion dollars, about four percent of the nation's international affairs budget. That total is about three percent of what the United States spends on intelligence and a quarter of one percent of its military bud-

States spends on intelligence and a quarter of one percent of its military budget. If Washington devoted just one percent of its military spending to public diplomacy—in the words of Newton Minow, former head of the Federal Communications Commission, "one dollar to launch ideas for every 100 dollars we invest to launch bombs"—it would mean almost quadrupling the current budget.

It is also important to establish more policy coherence among the various dimensions of public diplomacy, and to relate them to other issues. The Association of International Educators reports that, despite a declining share of the market for international students, "the U.S. government seems to lack overall strategic sense of why exchange is important. ... In this strategic vacuum, it is difficult to counter the day-to-day obstacles that students encounter in trying to come here." There is, for example, little coordination of exchange policies and visa policies. As the educator Victor Johnson noted, "while greater vigilance is certainly needed, this broad net is catching all kinds of people who are no danger whatsoever." By needlessly discouraging people from coming to the United States, such policies undercut American soft power.

Public diplomacy needs greater support from the White House. A recent Council on Foreign Relations task force recommended the creation of a "White House Public Diplomacy Coordinating Structure," led by a presidential designee, and a nonprofit "Corporation for Public Diplomacy" to help mobilize the private sector. And ultimately, a successful strategy must focus not only on broadcasting American messages, but also on two-way communication that engages all sectors of society, not just the government.

It Goes Both Ways

Above all, Americans will have to become more aware of cultural differences; an effective approach requires less parochialism and more sensitivity to perceptions abroad.

The first step, then, is changing attitudes at home. Americans need a better understanding of how U.S. policies appear to others. Coverage of the rest of the world by the U.S. media has declined dramatically since the end of the Cold War. Training in foreign languages has lagged. Fewer scholars are taking up Fulbright visiting lectureships. Historian Richard Pells notes "how distant we are from a time when American historians—driven by a curiosity about the world beyond both the academy and the United States—were able to communicate with the public about the issues, national and international, that continue to affect us all."

Wielding soft power is far less unilateral than employing hard power—a fact that the United States has yet to recognize. To communicate effectively, Americans must first learn to listen.

NO

Charles Krauthammer

The Unipolar Moment Revisited

In late 1990, shortly before the collapse of the Soviet Union, it was clear that the world we had known for half a century was disappearing. The question was what would succeed it. I suggested then that we had already entered the "unipolar moment." The gap in power between the leading nation and all the others was so unprecedented as to yield an international structure unique to modern history: unipolarity.

At the time, this thesis was generally seen as either wild optimism or simple American arrogance. The conventional wisdom was that with the demise of the Soviet empire the bipolarity of the second half of the 20th century would yield to multipolarity. The declinist school, led by Paul Kennedy, held that America, suffering from "imperial overstretch", was already in relative decline. The Asian enthusiasm, popularized by (among others) James Fallows, saw the second coming of the Rising Sun. The conventional wisdom was best captured by Senator Paul Tsongas: "The Cold War is over; Japan won."

They were wrong, and no one has put it more forcefully than Paul Kennedy himself in a classic recantation published earlier this year. "Nothing has ever existed like this disparity of power; nothing", he said of America's position today. "Charlemagne's empire was merely western European in its reach. The Roman empire stretched farther afield, but there was another great empire in Persia, and a larger one in China. There is, therefore, no comparison."[1] . . . As Stephen Brooks and William Wohlforth argue in a recent review of the subject, those denying unipolarity can do so only by applying a ridiculous standard: that America be able to achieve all its goals everywhere all by itself. This is a standard not for unipolarity but for divinity. Among mortals, and in the context of the last half millennium of history, the current structure of the international system is clear: "If today's American primacy does not constitute unipolarity, then nothing ever will."[2] . . .

I suggested that a third feature of this new unipolar world would be an increase rather than a decrease in the threat of war, and that it would come from a new source: weapons of mass destruction wielded by rogue states. This would constitute a revolution in international relations, given that in the past it was great powers who presented the principal threats to world peace.

From *The National Interest*, Winter 2002/2003. Copyright © 2002 by Charles Krauthammer. Reprinted by permission of the author.

Where are we twelve years later? The two defining features of the new post-Cold War world remain: unipolarity and rogue states with weapons of mass destruction. Indeed, these characteristics have grown even more pronounced. Contrary to expectation, the United States has not regressed to the mean; rather, its dominance has dramatically increased. And during our holiday from history in the 1990s, the rogue state/WMD problem grew more acute. Indeed, we are now on the eve of history's first war over weapons of mass destruction.

Unipolarity After September 11, 2001

There is little need to rehearse the acceleration of unipolarity in the 1990s. Japan, whose claim to power rested exclusively on economics, went into economic decline. Germany stagnated. The Soviet Union ceased to exist, contracting into a smaller, radically weakened Russia. The European Union turned inward toward the great project of integration and built a strong social infrastructure at the expense of military capacity. Only China grew in strength, but coming from so far behind it will be decades before it can challenge American primacy—and that assumes that its current growth continues unabated.

The result is the dominance of a single power unlike anything ever seen. Even at its height Britain could always be seriously challenged by the next greatest powers. Britain had a smaller army than the land powers of Europe and its navy was equaled by the next two navies combined. Today, American military spending exceeds that of the next *twenty* countries combined. Its navy, air force and space power are unrivaled. Its technology is irresistible. It is dominant by every measure: military, economic, technological, diplomatic, cultural, even linguistic, with a myriad of countries trying to fend off the inexorable march of Internet-fueled MTV English. . . .

The American hegemon has no great power enemies, an historical oddity of the first order. Yet it does face a serious threat to its dominance, indeed to its essential security. It comes from a source even more historically odd: an archipelago of rogue states (some connected with transnational terrorists) wielding weapons of mass destruction. . . .

What does this conjunction of unique circumstances—unipolarity and the proliferation of terrible weapons—mean for American foreign policy? That the first and most urgent task is protection from these weapons. The catalyst for this realization was again September 11. Throughout the 1990s, it had been assumed that WMD posed no emergency because traditional concepts of deterrence would hold. September 11 revealed the possibility of future WMD-armed enemies both undeterrable and potentially undetectable. The 9/11 suicide bombers were undeterrable; the author of the subsequent anthrax attacks has proven undetectable. The possible alliance of rogue states with such undeterrables and undetectables—and the possible transfer to them of weapons of mass destruction—presents a new strategic situation that demands a new strategic doctrine.

The Crisis of Unipolarity

Accordingly, not one but a host of new doctrines have come tumbling out since September 11. First came the with-us-or-against-us ultimatum to any state aiding, abetting or harboring terrorists. Then, pre-emptive attack on any enemy state developing weapons of mass destruction. And now, regime change in any such state.

The boldness of these policies—or, as much of the world contends, their arrogance—is breathtaking. The American anti-terrorism ultimatum, it is said, is high-handed and permits the arbitrary application of American power everywhere. Pre-emption is said to violate traditional doctrines of just war. And regime change, as Henry Kissinger has argued, threatens 350 years of post-Westphalian international practice. Taken together, they amount to an unprecedented assertion of American freedom of action and a definitive statement of a new American unilateralism.

To be sure, these are not the first instances of American unilateralism. Before September 11, the Bush Administration had acted unilaterally, but on more minor matters, such as the Kyoto Protocol and the Biological Weapons Convention, and with less bluntness, as in its protracted negotiations with Russia over the ABM treaty. The "axis of evil" speech of January 29, however, took unilateralism to a new level. Latent resentments about American willfulness are latent no more. American dominance, which had been tolerated if not welcomed, is now producing such irritation and hostility in once friendly quarters, such as Europe, that some suggest we have arrived at the end of the opposition-free grace period that America had enjoyed during the unipolar moment.[3]

In short, post-9/11 U.S. unilateralism has produced the first crisis of unipolarity. It revolves around the central question of the unipolar age: Who will define the hegemon's ends?

The issue is not one of style but of purpose. Secretary of Defense Donald Rumsfeld gave the classic formulation of unilateralism when he said (regarding the Afghan war and the war on terrorism, but the principle is universal), "the mission determines the coalition." We take our friends where we find them, but only in order to help us in accomplishing the mission. The mission comes first, and we decide it.

Contrast this with the classic case study of multilateralism at work: the U.S. decision in February 1991 to conclude the Gulf War. As the Iraqi army was fleeing, the first Bush Administration had to decide its final goal: the liberation of Kuwait or regime change in Iraq. It stopped at Kuwait. Why? Because, as Brent Scowcroft has explained, going further would have fractured the coalition, gone against our promises to allies and violated the UN resolutions under which we were acting. "Had we added occupation of Iraq and removal of Saddam Hussein to those objectives", wrote Scowcroft in the *Washington Post* on October 16, 2001, ". . . our Arab allies, refusing to countenance an invasion of an Arab colleague, would have deserted us." The coalition defined the mission.

Who should define American ends today? This is a question of agency but it leads directly to a fundamental question of policy. If the coalition—whether NATO,

NATO, the wider Western alliance, *ad hoc* outfits such as the Gulf War alliance, the UN, or the "international community"—defines America's mission, we have one vision of America's role in the world. If, on the other hand, the mission defines the coalition, we have an entirely different vision. . . .

Realism and the New Unilateralism

The basic division between the two major foreign policy schools in America centers on the question of what is, and what should be, the fundamental basis of international relations: paper or power. Liberal internationalism envisions a world order that, like domestic society, is governed by laws and not men. Realists see this vision as hopelessly utopian. The history of paper treaties—from the prewar Kellogg-Briand Pact and Munich to the post-Cold War Oslo accords and the 1994 Agreed Framework with North Korea—is a history of naiveté and cynicism, a combination both toxic and volatile that invariably ends badly. Trade agreements with Canada are one thing. Pieces of parchment to which existential enemies affix a signature are quite another. They are worse than worthless because they give a false sense of security and breed complacency. For the realist, the ultimate determinant of the most basic elements of international life—security, stability and peace—is power.

Which is why a realist would hardly forfeit the current unipolarity for the vain promise of goo-goo one-worldism. Nor, however, should a realist want to forfeit unipolarity for the familiarity of traditional multipolarity. Multipolarity is inherently fluid and unpredictable. Europe practiced multipolarity for centuries and found it so unstable and bloody, culminating in 1914 in the catastrophic collapse of delicately balanced alliance systems, that Europe sought its permanent abolition in political and economic union. Having abjured multipolarity for the region, it is odd in the extreme to then prefer multipolarity for the world.

Less can be said about the destiny of unipolarity. It is too new. Yet we do have the history of the last decade, our only modern experience with unipolarity and it was a decade of unusual stability among all major powers. It would be foolish to project from just a ten-year experience, but that experience does call into question the basis for the claims that unipolarity is intrinsically unstable or impossible to sustain in a mass democracy.

I would argue that unipolarity, managed benignly, is far more likely to keep the peace. Benignity is, of course, in the eye of the beholder. But the American claim to benignity is not mere self-congratulation. We have a track record. Consider one of history's rare controlled experiments. In the 1940s, lines were drawn through three peoples—Germans, Koreans and Chinese—one side closely bound to the United States, the other to its adversary. It turned into a controlled experiment because both states in the divided lands shared a common culture. Fifty years later the results are in. Does anyone doubt the superiority, both moral and material, of West Germany vs. East Germany, South Korea vs. North Korea and Taiwan vs. China.[4]

Benignity is also manifest in the way others welcome our power. It is the reason, for example, that the Pacific Rim countries are loath to see our tary presence diminished: They know that the United States is not an imperial power with a desire to rule other countries—which is why they so readily accept it as a balancer. It is the reason, too, why Europe, so seized with complaints about American high-handedness, nonetheless reacts with alarm to the occasional suggestion that America might withdraw its military presence. America came, but it did not come to rule. Unlike other hegemons and would-be hegemons, it does not entertain a grand vision of a new world. No Thousand Year Reich. No New Soviet Man. It has no great desire to remake human nature, to conquer for the extraction of natural resources, or to rule for the simple pleasure of dominion. Indeed, America is the first hegemonic power in history to be obsessed with "exit strategies." It could not wait to get out of Haiti and Somalia; it would get out of Kosovo and Bosnia today if it could. Its principal aim is to maintain the stability and relative tranquility of the current international system by enforcing, maintaining and extending the current peace.

The form of realism that I am arguing for—call it the new unilateralism—is clear in its determination to self-consciously and confidently deploy American power in pursuit of those global ends. Note: global ends. There is a form of unilateralism that is devoted only to narrow American self-interest and it has a name, too: It is called isolationism. Critics of the new unilateralism often confuse it with isolationism because both are prepared to unashamedly exercise American power. But isolationists oppose America acting as a unipolar power not because they disagree with the unilateral means, but because they deem the ends far too broad. Isolationists would abandon the larger world and use American power exclusively for the narrowest of American interests: manning Fortress America by defending the American homeland and putting up barriers to trade and immigration.

The new unilateralism defines American interests far beyond narrow self-defense. In particular, it identifies two other major interests, both global: extending the peace by advancing democracy and preserving the peace by acting as balancer of last resort. Britain was the balancer in Europe, joining the weaker coalition against the stronger to create equilibrium. America's unique global power allows it to be the balancer in every region. We balanced Iraq by supporting its weaker neighbors in the Gulf War. We balance China by supporting the ring of smaller states at its periphery (from South Korea to Taiwan, even to Vietnam). Our role in the Balkans was essentially to create a microbalance: to support the weaker Bosnian Muslims against their more dominant neighbors, and subsequently to support the weaker Albanian Kosovars against the Serbs. . . .

⋅◈⋅

A third critique comes from what might be called pragmatic realists, who see the new unilateralism I have outlined as hubristic, and whose objections are practical. They are prepared to engage in a pragmatic multilateralism. They value great power concert. They seek Security Council support not because it confers any moral authority, but because it spreads risk. In their view, a single hegemon risks far more violent resentment than would a power that consistently acts as *primus inter pares*, sharing rule-making functions with others.[5]

I have my doubts. The United States made an extraordinary effort in the Gulf War to get UN support, share decision-making, assemble a coalition and, as we have seen, deny itself the fruits of victory in order to honor coalition goals. Did that diminish the anti-American feeling in the region? Did it garner support for subsequent Iraq policy dictated by the original acquiescence to the coalition?

The attacks of September 11 were planned during the Clinton Administration, an administration that made a fetish of consultation and did its utmost to subordinate American hegemony and smother unipolarity. The resentments were hardly assuaged. Why? Because the extremist rage against the United States is engendered by the very structure of the international system, not by the details of our management of it.

Pragmatic realists also value international support in the interest of sharing burdens, on the theory that sharing decision-making enlists others in our own hegemonic enterprise and makes things less costly. If you are too vigorous in asserting yourself in the short-term, they argue, you are likely to injure yourself in the long-term when you encounter problems that require the full cooperation of other partners, such as counter-terrorism. As Brooks and Wohlforth put it, "Straining relationships now will lead only to a more challenging policy environment later on."[6]

If the concern about the new unilateralism is that American assertiveness be judiciously rationed, and that one needs to think long-term, it is hard to disagree. One does not go it alone or dictate terms on every issue. On some issues such as membership in and support of the WTO, where the long-term benefit both to the American national interest and global interests is demonstrable, one willingly constricts sovereignty. Trade agreements are easy calls, however, free trade being perhaps the only mathematically provable political good. Others require great skepticism. The Kyoto Protocol, for example, would have harmed the American economy while doing nothing for the global environment. (Increased emissions from China, India and Third World countries exempt from its provisions would have more than made up for American cuts.) Kyoto failed on its merits, but was nonetheless pushed because the rest of the world supported it. The same case was made for the chemical and biological weapons treaties—sure, they are useless or worse, but why not give in there in order to build good will for future needs? But appeasing multilateralism does not assuage it; appeasement merely legitimizes it. Repeated acquiescence to provisions that America deems injurious reinforces the notion that legitimacy derives from international consensus, thus undermining America's future freedom of action—and thus contradicting the pragmatic realists' own goals.

America must be guided by its independent judgment, both about its own interest and about the global interest. Especially on matters of national security, war-making and the deployment of power, America should neither defer nor contract out decision-making, particularly when the concessions involve permanent structural constrictions such as those imposed by an national Criminal Court. Prudence, yes. No need to act the superpower in East Timor or Bosnia. But there is a need to do so in Afghanistan and in Iraq. No need to act the superpower on steel tariffs. But there is a need to do so on missile defense. . . .

The new unilateralism argues explicitly and unashamedly for maintaining unipolarity, for sustaining America's unrivaled dominance for the foreseeable future. It could be a long future, assuming we successfully manage the single greatest threat, namely, weapons of mass destruction in the hands of rogue states. This in itself will require the aggressive and confident application of unipolar power rather than falling back, as we did in the 1990s, on paralyzing multilateralism. The future of the unipolar era hinges on whether America is governed by those who wish to retain, augment and use unipolarity to advance not just American but global ends, or whether America is governed by those who wish to give it up—either by allowing unipolarity to decay as they retreat to Fortress America, or by passing on the burden by gradually transferring power to multilateral institutions as heirs to American hegemony. The challenge to unipolarity is not from the outside but from the inside. The choice is ours. To impiously paraphrase Benjamin Franklin: History has given you an empire, if you will keep it.

Notes

1. Kennedy, "The Eagle has Landed", *Financial Times*, February 2, 2002.
2. Brooks and Wohlforth, "American Primacy in Perspective", *Foreign Affairs* (July/August 2002).
3. A Sky News poll finds that even the British public considers George W. Bush a greater threat to world peace than Saddam Hussein. The poll was conducted September 2–6, 2002.
4. This is not to claim, by any means, a perfect record of benignity. America has often made and continues to make alliances with unpleasant authoritarian regimes. As I argued recently in *Time* ("Dictatorships and Double Standards", September 23, 2002), such alliances are nonetheless justified so long as they are instrumental (meant to defeat the larger evil) and temporary (expire with the emergency). When Hitler was defeated, we stopped coddling Stalin. Forty years later, as the Soviet threat receded, the United States was instrumental in easing Pinochet out of power and overthrowing Marcos. We withdrew our support for these dictators once the two conditions that justified such alliances had disappeared: The global threat of Soviet communism had receded, and truly democratic domestic alternatives to these dictators had emerged.
5. This basic view is well-represented in *The National Interest's* Fall 2002 symposium, "September 11th One Year On: Power, Purpose and Strategy in U.S. Foreign Policy."
6. Brooks and Wohlforth, "American Primacy in Perspective."

POSTSCRIPT

Should the United States Legitimize Its Actions of World Leadership?

The debate on American world leadership raises a number of issues. First, how powerful is the United States relative to the rest of the world? Krauthammer makes a good case for the uniqueness of American supremacy. The ratio of American power relative to the power of the next and subsequent powers is greater than any country has had for many centuries. Another issue is the relative importance of military power to the soft power that Nye writes about. Nye argues that military power without soft power is greatly limited in what it can do. Another issue is, what foreign policies are the American people willing to support? The administration may want to follow a strong interventionist policy on the advice of realist experts but may run into extensive public opposition. Finally, how do power theories take into account terrorism and the probability that terrorists will someday use weapons of mass destruction? The danger of foreign terrorists can justify the threatened country taking preemptive actions and aggressively warring against the terrorists and the states that support them. On the other hand, successful wars on terrorism requires extensive diplomacy to gain needed allies in the war.

There have been an explosion of books recently on American leadership. The majority are critical of American unilateralism and the elements of empire. Niall Ferguson argues that the price of the American empire is way too much in *Colossus: The Price of America's Empire* (Penguin Press, 2004). Chalmers A. Johnson's critique of American empire in *The Sorrows of Empire: Militarism, Secrecy, and the End of the Republic* (Metropolitan Books, 2004) emphasizes the adverse impacts of the required growth in secrecy and the military for democratic processes. In a similar vein, Benjamin R. Barber argues in *Fear's Empire: War, Terrorism, and Democracy* (W.W. Norton, 2003) that maintaining an empire moves America away from its democratic and other ideals. Other critics include T. D. Allman, *Rogue State: America at War with the World* (Nations Books); Zbigniew Brzezinski, *The Choice: Global Domination or Global Leadership* (Basic Books, 2004); Jim Garrison, *America as Empire: Global Leader or Rogue Power?* (Berret-Koehler); Stanley Hoffman, *Gulliver Unbound: America's Imperial Temptation and the War in Iraq* (Rowman & Littlefield, 2004); John B. Judis, *The Folly of Empire: What George Bush Could Learn from Theodore Roosevelt and Woodrow Wilson* (Scribner, 2004); Robert J. Lifton, *Superpower Syndrome: America's Apocalyptic Confrontation with the World* (Nations Books, 2003); George Liska, *Twilight of a Hegemony: The Late Career of Imperial America* (University Press of America, 2003); John Newhouse, *Imperial America: The Bush Assault on the World Order* (Knopf, 2003); Clyde V. Prestowitz, *Rogue Nation: American Unilateralism and the Failure of*

Good Intentions (Basic Books, 2003); George Soros, *The Bubble of American Supremacy: Correcting the Misuse of American Power* (Public Affairs, 2004); and Emmanuel Todd, *After the Empire: The Breakdown of the American Order* (Columbia University Press, 2003). Some critiques of unilateralism include an element of Bush-bashing in their reports. They include Roger Burbach and Jim Tarbell, *Imperial Overstretch: George W. Bush and the Hubris of Empire* (Zed Books, 2004); Robert C. Byrd, *Losing America: Confronting a Reckless and Arrogant Presidency* (W.W. Norton, 2004); Craig R. Eisendrath and Melvin A. Goodman, *Bush League Diplomacy: How the Neoconservatives Are Putting the World at Risk* (Prometheus Books, 2004); Michael Mann, *Incoherent Empire* (Verso, 2003); and Mark Crispin Miller, *Cruel and Unusual: Bush/Cheney's New World Order* (W.W. Norton, 2004).

The main work justifying unilateralism is Charles Krauthammer's *Democratic Realism: An American Foreign Policy for a Unipolar World* (AEI Press, 2004). Other supporters include Robert J. Art, *A Grand Strategy for America* (Cornell University Press, 2003); James J. Hentz, ed., *The Obligation of Empire: United States' Grand Strategy for a New Century* (University Press of Kentucky, 2004); Lawrence J. Korb, *A New National Security Strategy in an Age of Terrorists* (Council of Foreign Relations, 2003); and Walter Russell Mead, *Power, Terror, Peace, and War: America's Grand Strategy in a World at Risk* (Knopf, 2004). For an account of the development of the Bush doctrine, see Robert Woodward, *Plan of Attack* (Simon & Schuster, 2004). For an analysis of the terrorism that provoked the Bush doctrine, see Richard Crockatt, *America Embattled: September 11, Anti-Americanism, and the Global Order* (Routledge, 2003) and George Friedman, *America's Secret War: Inside the Hidden Worldwide Struggle between America and Its Enemies* (Doubleday, 2004). For multiple views on U.S. world leadership, see John Ikenberry, ed., *America Unrivaled: The Future of the Balance of Power* (Cornell University Press, 2002) and Robert J. Lieber, ed., *Eagle Rules? Foreign Policy and American Primacy in the Twenty-First Century* (Prentice Hall, 2002). For the international perspective, see David M. Malone and Yuen Foong Khong, eds., *Unilateralism and U.S. Foreign Policy: International Perspectives* (Lynne Rienner, 2003).

Contributors to This Volume

EDITOR

KURT FINSTERBUSCH is a professor of sociology at the University of Maryland at College Park. He received a B.A. in history from Princeton University in 1957, a B.D. from Grace Theological Seminary in 1960, and a Ph.D. in sociology from Columbia University in 1969. He is the author of *Understanding Social Impacts* (Sage Publications, 1980), and he is the coauthor, with Annabelle Bender Motz, of *Social Research for Policy Decisions* (Wadsworth, 1980) and, with Jerald Hage, of *Organizational Change as a Development Strategy* (Lynne Rienner, 1987). He is the editor of *Annual Editions: Sociology* (McGraw-Hill/Dushkin); *Annual Editions: Social Problems* (McGraw-Hill/Dushkin); and *Sources: Notable Selections in Sociology*, 3rd ed. (McGraw-Hill/Dushkin, 1999).

STAFF

Larry Loeppke	Managing Editor
Jill Peter	Senior Developmental Editor
Nichole Altman	Developmental Editor
Beth Kundert	Production Manager
Jane Mohr	Project Manager
Tara McDermott	Design Coordinator
Bonnie Coakley	Editorial Assistant

AUTHORS

ANN ROSEGRANT ALVAREZ, PhD, is co-chair of the Graduate Concentration in Community Practice and Social Action at the Wayne State University School of Social Work in Detroit, Michigan. Her research and teaching interests include community practice, multi-cultural community organizing, feminist practice, international social work, social work history and policy issues.

DAVID A. ANDERSON is a Blazer Associate Professor of Economics. He teaches many courses including law and economics, as well as the economics of crime. He is the author of *Environmental Economics* (Southwestern, 2004).

JEFFREY M. BERRY is John Richard Skuse Professor of Political Science at Tufts University. He is the author of *The New Liberalism: The Rising Power of Citizen Groups* (Brookings Institution Press, 2000) and *The Interest Group Society,* 3rd ed. (Addison-Wesley, 2001).

CLINT BOLICK is vice president of the Institute for Justice, has litigated many crucial school choice decisions. His book Voucher Wars: Waging the Legal Battle Over School Choice has just been published by the Cato Institute.

ROBERT H. BORK is a senior fellow at the American Enterprise Institute. He has been a partner at a major law firm, taught constitutional law as the Alexander M. Bickel Professor of Public Law at the Yale law school, and served as Solicitor General and as Attorney General of the United States. He is the author of the bestselling *Slouching Toward Gomorrah: Modern Liberalism and American Decline* (HarperCollins Publishers).

LESTER R. BROWN was the founder and president of the Worldwatch Institute, a non-profit organization dedicated to the analysis of the global environment. He served as advisor to Secretary of Agriculture Orville Freeman and served as administrator of the International Agricultural Service in that department. In 1969, he helped James Grant establish the Overseas Development Council. He is the author and coauthor of numerous books.

PATRICK BUCHANAN was a presidential candidate in 2000. Currently, he is a political analyst, television commentator, and the author of *The Death of the West* (Thomas Dunne Books, 2000), which focuses on the issue of immigration.

STEPHANIE COONTZ teaches history and family studies at the Evergreen State College in Olympia, Washington. She is the author of *The Way We Never Were: American Families and the Nostalgia Trap* (Basic Books, 1992) and *The Way We Really Are: Coming to Terms With America's Changing Families* (Basic Books, 1997). She is coeditor of *American Families: A Multicultural Reader* (Routledge, 1998).

CURTIS CRAWFORD is the editor and co-author of the website `www.DebatingRacialPreferences.org`.

MARY CRAWFORD is a professor of psychology at the University of Connecticut. She is the author, with Rhoda Unger, of *Talking Difference: On Gender and Lan-*

guage (Sage Publications, 1995) and *Women and Gender: A Feminist Psychology,* 3rd ed. (McGraw-Hill, 2000).

HERMAN E. DALY is a professor in the School of Public Affairs at the University of Maryland and the author of a classic on the subject of environmental economics, *Steady-State Economics: The Economics of Biophysical Equilibrium and Moral Growth* (W. H. Freeman, 1977). Recently he authored *Beyond Growth: The Economics of Sustainable Development* (Beacon Press, 1996) and *Ecological Economics and the Ecology of Economics: Essays in Criticism* (Edward Elgar, 1999).

CHRISTOPHER C. DeMUTH is president of the American Enterprise Institute for Public Policy. He is also editor, with William Kristol, of *The Neoconservative Imagination: Essays in Honor of Irving Kristol* (American Enterprise Institute for Public Policy Research, 1995) and coauthor of *The Reagan Doctrine and Beyond* (American Enterprise Institute for Public Policy Research, 1988).

G. WILLIAM DOMHOFF has been teaching psychology and sociology at the University of California, Santa Cruz, since 1965. His books on political sociology include *Who Rules America?* (Prentice-Hall, 1967); *The Power Elite and the State: How Policy Is Made in America* (Aldine de Gruyter, 1990); and *Diversity in the Power Elite* (Yale University Press, 1998).

BARBARA DORITY is president of Humanists of Washington, executive director of the Washington Coalition Against Censorship, and cochair of the Northwest Feminist Anti-Censorhip Task Force.

SUSAN FALUDI is a Pulitzer Prize–winning journalist who writes for magazines such as *The Nation* and the *New Yorker.* She is the author of *Backlash: The Undeclared War Against American Women* (Random House, 1995) and *Stiffed: The Betrayal of the American Man* (William Morrow & Company, 1999).

JOHN BELLAMY FOSTER is an editor of *Monthly Review.* He is author of *The Vulnerable Planet,* and co-editor of *Hungry for Profit: The Agribusiness Threat to Farmers, Food, and the Environment,* all published by Monthly Review Press.

JEFF GRABMEIER is managing editor of research news at Ohio State University in Columbus, Ohio.

SHARON HAYES is the author of *Flat Broke with Children* and is a professor of Sociology and women's studies at the University of Virginia.

RICHARD T. HULL is professor emeritus of philosophy at the State University of New York at Buffalo. He is editor of *Ethical Issues in the New Reproductive Technologies* (Wadsworth, 1990).

CHRISTOPHER JENCKS is a professor of social policy at the Kennedy School at Harvard University and the author of many books on poverty and inequality, including *Rethinking Social Policy: Race, Poverty, and the Underclass* (Harvard University Press, 1992).

ROBERT KUTTNER is a founder and co-editor of *The American Prospect*, a longtime contributor to *The Atlantic*, and the author of *Everything For Sale: The Virtues and Limits of Markets* (Alfred A. Knopf, 1997).

LAMBDA LEGAL DEFENSE and **EDUCATION FUND** is a national organization committed to achieving full recognition of the civil rights of lesbians, gay ment, bisexuals, the transgendered, and people with HIV or AIDS through impact litigation, education, and public policy work.

BJORN LOMBORG is a statistician at the University of Aarhus and the author of the controversial book *The Skeptical Environmentalist: Measuring the Real State of the World* (Cambridge University Press, 2001).

BRUNO V. MANNO is a former assistant secretary of education and currently is senior program associate with the Annie E. Casey Foundation. He is the author, with Chester E. Finn, Jr. and Gregg Vanourek, of *Charter Schools in Action: Renewing Public Education* (Princeton University Press, 2000).

ROBERT W. McCHESNEY is the author of eight books on media and politics, professor of communication at the University of Illinois at Urbana-Champaign, and host of the weekly talk show, Media Matters, on WILL-AM radio. McChesney also writes widely for both academic and non-academic publications. He gives talks frequently on issues related to media and politics in the United States and world today.

WILLIAM McGOWAN has reported for *Newsweek International* and the BBC and has written for the *New York Times*, the *Washington Post, Columbia* Journalism Review and other national publications. A regular contributor to the *Wall Street Journal*, he is currently a senior fellow at the *Manhattan Institute*. He is also the author of *Only Man Is Vile: The Tragedy of Sri Lanka* (Farrar, Straus & Giroux).

CHARLES MURRAY is Bradley Fellow at the American Enterprise Institute. He is the author of *Losing Ground: American Social Policy, 1950–1980,* 10th ed. (Basic Books, 1994) and *The Underclass Revisited* (AEI Press, 1999). He is coauthor, with Richard J. Herrnstein, of *The Bell Curve* (Free Press, 1994).

ETHAN A. NADELMANN is director of the Lindesmith Center of the Drug Policy Foundation, a New York drug policy research institute, and professor of politics and public affairs in the Woodrow Wilson School of Public and International Affairs at Princeton University. He is the author of *Cops Across Borders: The Internationalization of U.S. Criminal Law Enforcement* (Pennsylvania State University Press, 1993).

DAVID POPENOE is a professor of sociology at Rutgers–The State University in New Brunswick, New Jersey. He is the author of *Disturbing the Nest* (Aldine de Gruyter, 1988) and *Life Without Father: Compelling New Evidence That Fatherhood and Marriage are Indispensable for the Good of Children and Society* (Martin Kessler Books, 1996). He is editor, with Jean Bethke Elshtain and David Blankenhorn, of *Promises to Keep: Decline and Renewal of Marriage in America* (Rowman & Littlefield Publishers, 1996).

JEFFREY REIMAN is the William Fraser McDowell Professor of Philosophy at American University in Washington, D.C. He is the author of *Justice and Modern Moral Philosophy* (Yale University Press, 1992) and *The Rich Get Richer and the Poor Get Prison: Ideology, Class, and Criminal Justice,* 6th ed. (Allyn and

Bacon, 2001). He is also editor, with Paul Leighton, of *Criminal Justice Ethics* (Prentice Hall, 2001).

SAM SCHULMAN is a New York writer whose work appears in New York Press, the Spectator (London), and elsewhere. He was formerly publisher of Wigwag and a professor of English at Boston University.

BARRY SCHWARTZ is the Dorwin Cartwright Professor of Social Theory and Social Action and professor of psychology at Swarthmore College. He is the author of *The Costs of Living: How Market Freedom Erodes the Best Things in Life* (W. W. Norton, 1994).

MARGARET SOMERVILLE holds professorships in both the Faculty of Law and the Faculty of Medicine at McGill University, Montreal. She is Samuel Gale Professor of Law (as such, she is the first woman in Canada to hold a named Chair in Law) and the Founding Director of the McGill Centre for Medicine, Ethics and Law. She plays an active role in the world-wide development of bioethics and the study of the wider legal and ethical aspects of medicine and science.

JOHN STOSSEL works for the ABC news magazine *20/20*, has received 19 Emmy Awards and has been honored five times for excellence in consumer reporting by the National Press Club.

GREGG VANOUREK is vice president of KIZ, heads its Charter School Division, and is the author, with Chester E. Finn, Jr. and Gregg Vanourek, of *Charter Schools in Action: Renewing Public Education* (Princeton University Press, 2000).

ERIC A. VOTH is a physician and chairman of the International Drug Strategy Institute.

BEN WATTENBERG is a senior fellow at the American Enterprise Institute and is the author of *The First Universal Nation: Leading Indicators and Ideas About the Surge of America in the 1990s* (Free Press, 1991). He is coauthor, with Theodore Caplow and Louis Hicks, of *The First Measured Century: An Illustrated Guide to Trends in America, 1900–2000* (AEI Press, 2001).

MURRAY WEIDENBAUM is the chairman of the Weidenbaum Center at Washington University in St. Louis. He is also the author of *Business and Government in the Global Marketplace,* 6th ed. (Prentice Hall, 1999) and *Looking for Common Ground on U.S. Trade Policy* (Center for Strategic and International Studies, 2001).

DAVID WHITMAN is a senior writer for *U.S. News & World Report* and the author of *The Optimism Gap: The I'm Ok—They're Not Syndrome and the Myth of American Decline* (Walker & Company, 1998). *Judgment: Does the Abuse Excuse Threaten Our Legal System?* (Basic Books, 1997); and *The Decline of Marriage* (HarperCollins, 2002).

PHILIP YANCEY serves as editor-at-large for *Christianity Today* magazine. He has authored numerous books, including *The Jesus I Never Knew* (Zondervan Publishing House, 1995) and *What's so Amazing About Grace?* (Zondervan Publishing House, 1997).

MATTHEW YGLESIAS is a fellow for *The American Prospect*. His column, Broadside, appears weekly.

Index